py
in
b

Bryan Faussett:
Antiquary Extraordinary

David Wright

Archaeopress

Archaeopress

Gordon House
276 Banbury Road
Oxford OX2 7ED
www.archaeopress.com

Archaeological Lives

ISBN 978 1 78491 084 6
ISBN 978 1 78491 085 3 (e-Pdf)

© Archaeopress and D Wright 2015

www.drdavidwright.co.uk

Cover illustration: Jewelled brooches from the Faussett collection: Plate II of *Inventorium Sepulchrale* engraved by Frederick William Fairholt. One of the most exquisite illustrations in any English book.
(Courtesy of The Society of Antiquaries, London).

Printed in England by Hollywell Press Ltd, Oxford

This book is available direct from Archaeopress or from our website
www.archaeopress.com

Bryan Faussett painted in 1758 by Thomas Hudson. The appellation of 'the handsome commoner' is easy to see. (*Courtesy of National Museums Liverpool (World Museum)*)

Contents

List of Figures

Abbreviations employed in the text

Arch. Cant.	*Archaeologia Cantiana*
BAA	British Archaeological Association
CCA/L	Canterbury Cathedral Archives/Library
FRS	Fellow of the Royal Society
FSA	Fellow of the Society of Antiquaries
Inv. Sep.	*Inventorium Sepulchrale*
KHLC	Kent History and Library Centre
MS(S)	Manuscript(s)
TNA	The National Archives

Foreword

Work on this book started seven years ago and brought the usual predictably unpredictable journey through archives and libraries and meetings with all kinds of people, some tangential, some highly germane to my task. In 2007 I visited the tercentenary exhibition at Burlington House in celebration of the founding of the Society of Antiquaries, and there saw in a glass case a selection of Bryan Faussett's beautiful Anglo-Saxon gold brooches and other artefacts. I needed to look no further for the subject of a biography. However, if you look in the *Oxford Dictionary of National Biography* you will find a rather short entry about him, so short in fact that I immediately wondered whether I would find enough to write about, but, as Cicero said, the beginnings of all things are small. Undaunted, I made a start and enjoyed that pleasurable journey of one setting out to gather whatever he can find from any quarter, no matter where it might lead in this case to sitting in a draughty barn at Harty on the Isle of Sheppey balancing several of Bryan Faussett's household account books on a rickety table whilst I made notes.

It is my pleasure to record thanks to the following: firstly to Seamus Cullen for his discernment and encouragement in my putting pen to paper. Mr Ashley Cooke made me welcome at the Liverpool World Museum and put his entire corpus of files, knowledge and Faussett artefacts at my disposal. Equally valuable were the continued assistance and hospitality of the library staff of the Society of Antiquaries during my examination of the Faussett manuscripts and a great deal of reading and other investigations. Colleagues at the Canterbury and Maidstone archives extended to me their usual courteous and unstinting help, and Mr Duncan Harrington FSA, Mr Christopher Miller, Mr John Owen FSA, and Mr Michael Rhodes also supplied useful information.

Especial thanks go to Mr David Godfrey-Faussett, Mr Richard Godfrey-Faussett and Mr Tom Godfrey-Faussett, each of whom was invaluable in setting before me portions of the family archives. As far as I know, I am the first to have been accorded this privilege, and the results are amply evidenced throughout the book. All quotations and extracts not specifically acknowledged in the text are taken from this archive.

Finally, I gratefully acknowledge an award by the Allen Grove Local History Fund of the Kent Archaeological Society and a grant from the Canterbury Archaeological Society towards the costs of research and publication.

Introduction

For the biographer a life of Bryan Faussett as a Kentish clergyman would be moderately interesting; as a genealogist and heraldist more so; as an antiquary and pioneering archaeologist almost compelling; but when all three are combined his cup fairly runs over. To this might be added the personal excitement of the writer knowing all the churches that Faussett visited, the lanes and tracks he must have walked, and the parish where he lived. And yet more: to handle some of the artefacts that he excavated, and to turn the pages of his daily account books and sumptuous genealogical manuscripts truly brings the quarry alive – and almost literally, for there are today legion descendants to perpetuate their industrious ancestor's memory.

We are lucky indeed that Charles Roach Smith put into print Faussett's six archaeological notebooks as the *Inventorium Sepulchrale*; no longer did they lie hidden along with the collections of coins, jewels and so many other artefacts in the study at Heppington, but were published for the world to begin to learn something of an extraordinary life and its dedication to investigating the (if only he had known) Anglo-Saxon centuries of English history. The *Inventorium* breathes Faussett as he describes the losses and the disappointments, the excitements and the triumphs of excavating over 770 barrows dotted about the landscape of east Kent; his narrative takes us with him over nearly two decades as he plans his sites, assembles his workforces, personally oversees excavations, and returns home to describe and catalogue the day's findings and the graves from which they were taken.

And amid all this antiquarian panoply let not be forgotten his domestic and very human affairs. Ample correspondence and household accounts survive to make flesh and blood of the Georgian parson in all his varying moods: his concern for his family and children, his frustration as an ill-paid curate, his escapist jaunts to London, his vanity over his ancestors, his gout-ridden enforced stays at home, his unparson-like predilection for litigation, and his perfunctory interest in clerical duties.

Faussett often described his graves as lying under or within tumuli, sometimes under or within mounds or barrows. For the sake of consistency I have adopted 'barrow' throughout, although the three are more or less archaeologically interchangeable. In citing his and others' correspondence I have generally employed modern punctuation, silently expanded such abbreviations as 'yr' and 'wch', and modernised misleading spelling in order not to exasperate the reader – Faussett, a highly educated man, sometimes wrote erratically, even in the form of his own surname. He is not always consistent either in describing certain commonly occurring artefacts such as the *umbo* or shield-boss, and *fibula* or brooch, and here I italicise when preferring the Latin nomenclature.

My text has benefited in part from the watchful eyes of Dr Georgina Muskett of the World Museum in Liverpool, particularly in regard to those parts of the text concerned with artefacts in her care. The much greater task of checking the entire narrative for infelicities and inconsistencies was undertaken by Peter Ewart; but for the complexities of Anglo-Saxon archaeology, burial customs and related matters I am hugely indebted to Dr Andrew Richardson of the Canterbury Archaeological Trust for allowing me to profit from his doctoral thesis (coincidentally dedicated to the memory of Bryan Faussett) and for agreeing to act as a wise and well-informed cicerone on my journey through such a fascinating world. Whatever other errors may remain are mine alone.

David Wright, autumn 2014

Bryan Faussett – A Chronology

1720 October 30	born at Heppington House, Nackington
1720s (late)	sees Heppington House demolished
1730 June	watches Cromwell Mortimer excavating
1733	rebuilding of Heppington House starts
1738 October	goes up to University College, Oxford
1742	receives Bachelor's Degree
1744 June	made Fellow of University College, Oxford
1745	receives Master's Degree
1746 April 28	made Fellow of All Souls, Oxford
1746 May 25	made Deacon at Christ Church, Oxford
1747 June 14	priested at Christ Church, Oxford, by Thomas Secker
1747 November 9	presented to the living of Alberbury, Shropshire
1748 November 15	marries Elizabeth Curtois at Magdalen College
1749 November 18	birth of first son, Henry Godfrey, at Alberbury
1750 September 19	death of father, Bryan Faussett senior
1750 November	leaves Alberbury and returns to Heppington
1750-56	Curate of Kingston
1750s	sells outlying estates for £2850
1753 April 11	birth of second son, Bryan, at Kingston
1754 March 2	birth of third son, Charles, at Bishopsbourne
1756 February 11	birth of only daughter, Elizabeth, at Bishopsbourne
1756-61	Curate of Petham and Waltham
1756-60	visits churches to record monumental inscriptions
1757-1759	excavates at Tremworth Down, Crundale
1758	portrait painted by Thomas Hudson
1759-63	excavates at Gilton Town, Ash
1761 May 23	death of mother, Elizabeth Faussett (formerly Godfrey)
1763 March	elected Fellow of the Society of Antiquaries
1764-73	excavates at Chartham Down, Chartham
1765 May 8	inducted as Rector of Monks Horton
1765-72	Curate of Lower Hardres
1767-75	Curate of Nackington
1767-1773	excavates at Kingston Down, Kingston
1760s	sells outlying estates for £6220
1769 July	draws up his will
c.1769	garden pavilion at Heppington constructed
1770s	sells outlying estates for £4870

1771 July	excavates at Bishopsbourne Down, Bishopsbourne
1772 July-August	excavates at Barfriston Down, Barfriston
1772 October	excavates at Iffin Wood
1772-73	excavates at Sibertswold Down, Sibertswold
1773 May-August	excavates at Adisham Down, Bekesbourne
1776 February 10	dies at Heppington and is buried at Nackington
1776 February 27	will proved by his widow
1787 January 22	death of widow, Elizabeth Faussett formerly Curtois
1793	James Douglas publishes *Nenia Britannica*
1841	Charles Roach Smith twice visits Heppington
1844	British Archaeological Association Congress at Canterbury
1853	Faussett collections rejected by the British Museum
1854	Joseph Mayer purchases the collections for £700
1856	publication of *Inventorium Sepulchrale*

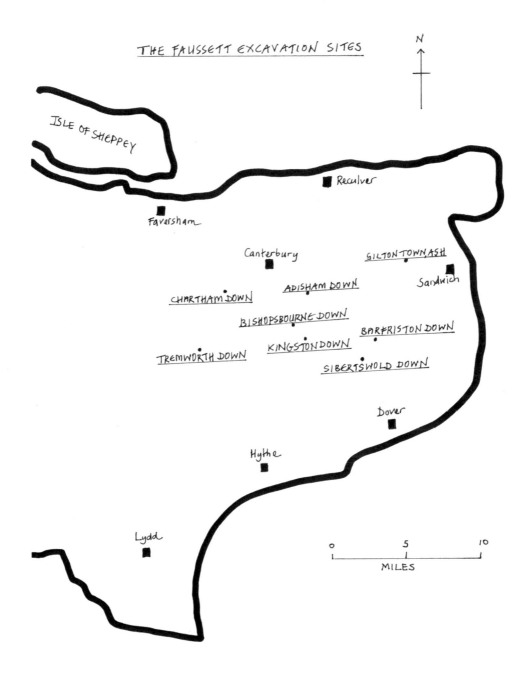

Figure 1. The Faussett Excavation Sites.

Chapter 1
Godfreys and Faussetts

Of the Faussett ancestry, both maternal and paternal, we are tolerably well informed. They were armigerous (although in the case of the Faussetts, not initially), and consequently, enough has survived in parchment and paper, and on marble, stone and glass, to afford the following narrative from early times down to the uniting of the two families in 1719, and beyond.

As might well befit a Georgian clergyman, the ancestors of Bryan Faussett were not insubstantial, but nor were they particularly grand, and they were not titled. Bryan the antiquary was the first to go to university and the first to enter the church, the latter, of course, usually a natural corollary of the former in the 18th century. Successful trade and the gradual acquisition of lands meant that by the time Bryan senior, the heir to the family estates, was born in 1691 he could look forward to an inheritance of relative comfort, a guaranteed income from rents, a good marriage and the occasional legacy, all of which would be sufficient to enable him to rebuild the family mansion on a fairly grand scale.

Bryan Faussett's mother was descended from the Godfrey family, originally of Romney and Lydd at the edge of Romney Marsh, but widely spread around east Kent and elsewhere by the early 18th century. It was to their memory that the Faussetts changed their surname to the double-barrelled Godfrey-Faussett in the 1870s. A full pedigree of a family which was prolific at an early period (producing sets of 18 and 20 children in the mid-1600s), the consequent myriad descendants, and the further complications of common and repetitive Christian names, means that the following account must necessarily be selective.

Today the remote parishes on Romney Marsh are little changed from previous centuries, the only true visible intrusions being Dungeness power station at the very tip of the most distinctive point of the county's coastline, and the endless lines of pylons snaking their way across the quintessentially flat landscape. Remote

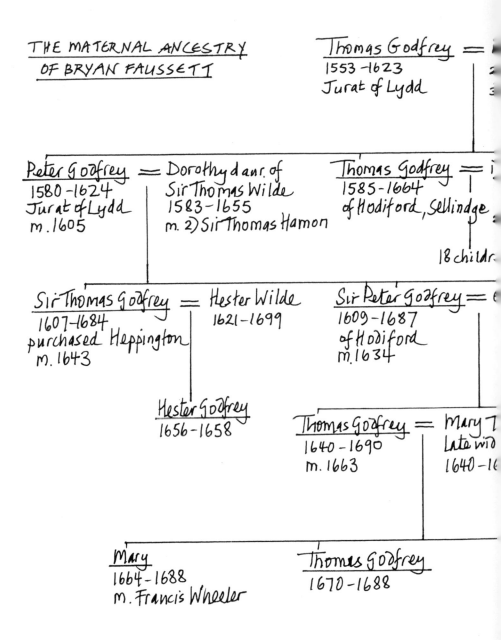

THE MATERNAL ANCESTRY
OF BRYAN FAUSSETT

Thomas Godfrey =
1553 -1623
Jurat of Lydd

Peter Godfrey = Dorothy daur. of
1580 -1624   Sir Thomas Wilde
Jurat of Lydd   1583 - 1655
m. 1605   m. 2) Sir Thomas Hamon

Thomas Godfrey = i
1585 - 1664
of Hodiford, Sellindge

18 childr.

Sir Thomas Godfrey = Hester Wilde
1607 - 1684   1621 - 1699
purchased Heppington
m. 1643

Sir Peter Godfrey =
1609 - 1687
of Hodiford
m. 1634

Hester Godfrey
1656 - 1658

Thomas Godfrey = Mary T
1640 - 1690   Late wid
m. 1663   1640 - 16

Mary
1664 - 1688
m. Francis Wheeler

Thomas Godfrey
1670 - 1688

Figure 2. The maternal ancestry of Bryan Faussett.

) 1578 Mary Partriche d. 1580
) 1582 Elizabeth Pix d. 1589
) 1590 Elizabeth Allard, 1556-1635

) Margaret	Richard Godfrey = Mary Moyle	5 others
Lambard	1592-1641, M.P.	1598-1652
1585-1611	of More Court,	
) Sarah Isles	Ivychurch	

en

20 children

Elizabeth	Ann	5 others
Heyman	1613-1679	
	m. Sir Richard Hardres	

oke,
ow of Sir Robert Moyle
598

Robert Godfrey
1643-

Henry Godfrey = Catherine Pittis
1674-1718   1670-1726
inherited Heppington
m. 1699

| Mary = Bryan Faussett, | Catherine |
| 1699-1761   senior | 1701-1702 |

indeed it must have been 600 years ago when the Godfreys were chiefly resident in Old Romney and Lydd. Scattered early references include an inquisition *post mortem* for a John Fitz Godfrey in 1246 in the Romney Marsh area, and a 14th-century roll listing Godfreys at Burmarsh, Eastbridge, Eastwell in Newchurch, Horton, Snave and Blackmanstone. In 1313 the Kent Feet of Fines record James and Lucy Godfrey selling 67 acres in Midley and Old Romney, and in 1314 James Godefroy of Winchelsea and his wife Lucia holding lands in Old Romney.

In the 1400s there is the complication of the surname Fermor being used, seemingly indiscriminately, as an alias for Godfrey, evidenced by half a dozen testators, all of Lydd, between 1463 and 1527, including one John Godfrey *alias* Fermor who left £5 towards the repair of All Saints' church in 1484. A Thomas Godfrey, tenant to the manor of Old Langport, died at Lydd in 1430, and his kinsman William 'Godfey *alias* Fermor' of Westbrooke in Lydd, so styled in his will of 1455, named one executor as John Godfrey, with a subsequent reference to John 'Godfrey *alias* Fermor'. It is interesting to observe that the interchange of names is frequent in probate records, but never occurs in the Lydd parish registers where the name Godfrey is alone used, and also that there were Fermors at Brookland in the 1400s who never used the name Godfrey. (Such is the enduring power of family names, however, that 'Fermor' was still being given to male Faussett descendants in the later 1800s.)

The principal branch kept the Godfrey name and moved in the reign of Henry V from Old Romney to Lydd, where they had possessed lands from the time of the earliest family references, and had intermittently been buried in Lydd church. Three generations followed from the Thomas Godfrey who died in 1430, two of which were cited by Bryan Faussett himself, but could not be substantiated by the investigations of later descendants, even though the reference works are all in agreement.

The family is now of the opinion that the earliest proven ancestor is Thomas Godfrey (the third of the just-mentioned three generations, and described as the son of Peter and grandson of Thomas), whose will[1] of 1542 describes him as 'the elder' of Allhallowne in Lydd. His son Peter was executor, to whom he left his principal tenements with 40 acres in Lydd and Old Romney. Peter Godfrey, a jurat of Lydd, was born around 1515 and 'of age' when he took on his father's executorship in 1542. He married Joan Epps of Ashford at Old Romney in 1540, and died 10 March 1566. It was he who first acquired More Court in Ivychurch in the reign of Edward VI, which would descend to his grandson Richard Godfrey of Wye.

Their son Thomas Godfrey was born at Lydd in 1553. He was a farmer at New Romney, and later elected as a jurat for Lydd. He died in early 1623, having reached a venerable 70, and was buried in the chancel of All Saints, Lydd, the ancestor of countless future descendants by his three sons, conveniently summarised as the Godfreys of Heppington in Nackington, the Godfreys of Hoddiford in Sellindge

---

[1] KHLC: PRC32/19/14

Figure 3. Thomas Godfrey (1553-1623). He is worthily commemorated in Lydd church.
(Godfrey-Faussett family archives.)

Figure 4. Elizabeth Godfrey née Allard (1556-1635) third wife of Thomas.
(Godfrey-Faussett family archives.)

Figure 5. Dorothy Godfrey (1583-1655), daughter of Sir Thomas Wilde of Canterbury and 3 x great-grandmother of Bryan.
(Godfrey-Faussett family archives.)

Figure 6. Sir Thomas Godfrey (1640-1690) of Boughton Aluph, great-grandfather of Bryan. By his marriage he brought the Moyle and Toke families into the pedigree.
(Godfrey-Faussett family archives.)

and the Godfreys of More Court in Ivychurch. He died at his son Richard's house in New Romney and was taken back for burial at Lydd. His will[2] provided for the poor of many marsh parishes, and left gold and plate to members of his large family.

His fulsome mural monument with bust on the chancel north wall at Lydd is worthy of repeating:

> To the memory of Thomas Godfrey, Esq, born at New Romney in ye year of Our Lord God 1553, son and heir of Peter Godfrey of Lydd, gent, where he and his ancestors have continued in good esteem and reputation for above 200 years, as appears by their funeral monuments yet extant in ye said church, and by their several wills and testaments proved in ye Registers Office at Canterbury and London. He was Captain of ye horse for above 40 years together before his death; notwithstanding which he himself was charged with and did find at every muster 5 Light Horse and 20 Foot. He was a frank housekeeper, hospitable to strangers and charitable to ye needy. He lived beloved and died lamented of all, especially by ye poor, in three score and eleventh year of his age, being in ye year of Our Lord God 1623. The said Thomas Godfrey hereby interred left issue by his several three wives three sons and one daughter, viz. Peter, Thomas, Richard and Mary, all which he lived to see well disposed of in marriage into several worthy families, and to be parents of many hopeful children, to his great comfort. To whom in return for pious gratitude and duty his 2nd son Thomas and Sarah his wife have placed these memorials.

We may look briefly at his surviving four children, all born at Lydd, in reverse order of seniority. Mary (1602-1638) was the youngest, married Sir John Honywood of Elmsted, and left seven children. The third son, Richard Godfrey (1592-1641), was MP for New Romney *temp*. Charles I, receiving a cup from the Corporation for his services. He married Mary the daughter of John Moyle of Buckwell in Boughton Aluph, producing twenty children, some of whom later lived at More Court, Ivychurch and at Wye, and others moving to London.

We are singularly well informed about the second son, Thomas Godfrey (1585-1664) as he kept a domestic chronicle[3] from around 1608 until 1655, recording voluminous autobiographical details, regularly punctuated by the births of his eighteen children. He went to St John's College, Cambridge, and thereafter enjoyed a full and colourful life, which took in a keenness for erecting church monuments (including his own in the chancel at Sellindge), and being a JP, master of chancery, arms-bearer at the funeral of James II, freeman of Winchelsea, and traveller. He acquired and lived for 47 years at Hodiford in Sellindge, enjoying a fine library and becoming, typically for a man of this time,

> a great lover of learning and all ingenuity which he showed in ye generous education of his children. He served his generation eminently and faithfully in several capacities, and with Christian courage he overcame many infirmities of this life.

---

[2] KHLC: PRC32/46/281
[3] British Library, MS Lansdowne 235; Nichols, *The Topographer and Genealogist*, II: 450-467

By his first wife Margaret Lambard he had sons Lambard and Thomas born at Winchelsea, the elder of whom in his father's will[4] received the second best flock bed and the study full of books. His second marriage of 52 years to Sarah Isles produced 16 children and innumerable descents, of whom the eldest son Peter inherited Hodiford, and the fifth, the Westminster magistrate and coal-merchant Sir Edmund Berry Godfrey, who was famously found murdered at Primrose Hill in 1678. (There is a highly unusual genealogical memorial to these 18 children in the east walk of the cloisters of Westminster Abbey.) Other children of Thomas produced descents at Norton near Faversham and at Woodford in Essex, the latter impinging upon Bryan the antiquary's life in the 1770s (on which see below).

The eldest son and direct ancestor, Peter Godfrey (1580-1624), died possessed of extensive lands in Kent and Sussex, a handful of houses including a great one and four others in Lydd, and was a bailiff of that town in 1615 and 1623. He married Dorothy, the daughter of Sir Thomas Wilde of St Martin's Canterbury, who as a widow would remarry to Sir Thomas Hamon and, like some of the later Faussetts, remove herself to west Kent, where she died at North Cray in 1655. Unremarkably, she was carried back to Upper Hardres to be buried alongside her second husband.

The eight children of Sir Peter and Dorothy Godfrey form the next generation of the pedigree. The first son, Sir Thomas Godfrey (1607-1684) was long-lived but died without issue. He was knighted at Whitehall in 1641 and, crucially for the Faussetts, purchased Heppington from the Hale family in 1640. He was one of the leaders of the Kent Insurrection favouring Charles I, and raised a troop of horse which was defeated by General Fairfax in 1648. Some indication of the size of Heppington may be gained from the 1664 Hearth Tax returns, in which he appears with the eminently respectable total of 16 hearths. In 1643 he married his cousin Hester Wilde, who survived him and all her in-laws to die 14 years later as a childless widow in 1699.

Her fulsome will[5] affords many interesting insights: she was to be buried alongside her husband at Nackington, with no escutcheons to be made or provided, no rooms to be hanged in black or mourning, and to be buried privately in the evening in the presence only of neighbours from the parish of Lower Hardres. Her assets were less interesting: money to the poor, jewels, a coachman, footman and servants, together with lands on Romney Marsh and elsewhere descended to her by the death of Lady Frasier. Dame Hester had no close relatives, so who was to inherit Heppington?

Her husband's next brother, Sir Peter Godfrey (1609-1687) of Hodiford, Sellindge, was knighted on the same day as his elder brother. He was married at North Cray in 1634 to Elizabeth, the daughter of Sir Peter Heyman of Somerfield in Sellindge. Their eldest child, Sir Thomas Godfrey (1640-1690), died three years after his father and before his aunt Hester. He had married Mary, the daughter and coheiress of Nicholas Toke of Godinton and the widow of Sir Robert Moyle

---

[4] KHLC: PRC17/72/49
[5] KHLC: 17/79/271

THE PATERNAL ANCESTRY
OF BRYAN FAUSSETT

Henry Faussei
c.1590-1653
grazier of St Saviour, So;

John Faussett   =
1612-1672
of Dartford

Henry Faussett   =   Catherine
c.1635-1679   d.1705
brewer, m.1664

William Faussett = Mary, daur of   Sarah   Mary   N
1670-1711   John Bryan   d.1670   d.1670   16
m.1690   m.(2)
                 Robert Echlin

Bryan Faussett = Mary Godfrey   Peregrine   William   Sarah
1691-1750   1699-1761   d 1693   1694-   d.169
landed proprtr   1701
of Rochester and
Heppington

Bryan Faussett   13 others
1720-1776

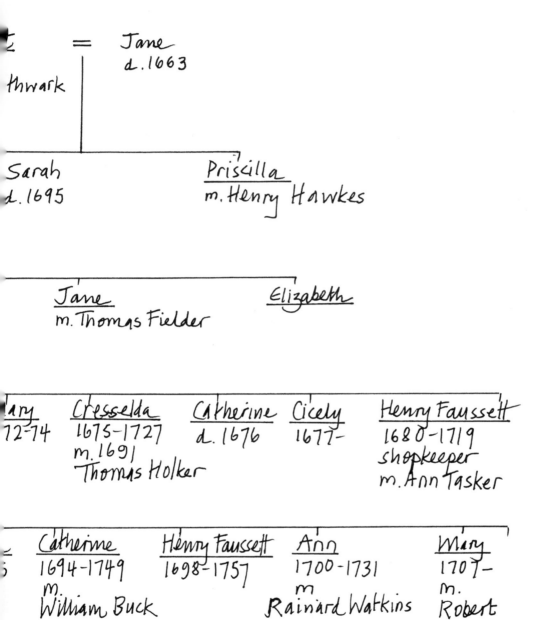

≥ = Jane
⌐thwark │ d.1663

Sarah   Priscilla
d.1695   m. Henry Hawkes

Jane   Elizabeth
m. Thomas Fielder

⌐ary   Cresselda   Catherine   Cicely   Henry Faussett
72-74   1675-1727   d. 1676   1677-   1680-1719
          m.1691   shopkeeper
          Thomas Holker   m. Ann Tasker

⌐   Catherine   Henry Faussett   Ann   Mary
5   1694-1749   1698-1757   1700-1731   1707-
          m.   m   m.
          William Buck   Rainard Watkins Robert
                                                           Lucas

Figure 7. The paternal ancestry of Bryan Faussett.

of Buckwell in Boughton Aluph. Their first son, another Thomas, died as a youth of 18, and so his younger brother, Major Henry Godfrey (1674-1718) became the owner of Heppington, enjoying it for 19 years before dying young at 44. His wife, Catherine, the daughter of Thomas Pittis, Rector of St Botolph, Bishopsgate, on the eastern edge of the City of London, survived him just eight years. Their only surviving daughter and heir, Mary Godfrey (1699-1761) would marry Bryan Faussett senior, and so become the mother of the antiquary. The marriage of Bryan Faussett and Mary Godfrey at Nackington on 4 October 1719 saw the union of two ancient families, and the Heppington estates move from one to the other.

Family portraits have survived, but further evidence of good looks is available in print, for we are informed that Mary Godfrey, the mother of the antiquary, was something of a beauty and did not escape local attention. A Mr Gent's little volume of 1718, 'most respectfully and humbly inscrib'd to all the aforesaid bright young LADIES in and near the aforesaid City', praises her in regular (and exclamatory) verses thus:

> Thus GODFRY shines, appearing next in Play,
> And adds a Lustre to the Glorious Day !
> Thousands of Darts, a thousand sev'ral Ways
> She throws on all who dare profanely gaze !
> Strange Power of Beauty ! that by looking on,
> Each rash Admirers sure to be undone !
> Oh, Nymph ! Then cease to shine thus radiant Bright !
> Contract the Beams of such amazing Light !
> We dye if we refrain; and if we look, 'tis Night !
> For still like Heav'n her glories all do shine,
> And, show She's form'd above, by Hands Divine !

The earliest Faussetts were not Kentish, but originated from not too far away over the county boundary in Southwark. In common with countless other families, there was a gradual drifting away from the capital to the outer suburbs and, with the progress of time, outwards to one of the English shire counties. The earliest proven paternal ancestor of the antiquary is one Henry Forsett (the 'Faussett' spelling was not to be regularised until a century or more later) of St Saviour, Southwark, that area today immediately south of the River Thames around the present Southwark Cathedral. In the reigns of James I and Charles I he was a grazier and butcher in the fields of that parish now long changed out of all recognition from its rural origins. He died in 1653, during those two decades so tiresome to genealogy when the exigencies of civil war meant that the keeping of parish registers was largely abandoned.

Henry's will,[6] proved shortly after his death, left a customary bequest of £5 to the poor of his parish, and then proceeded to leave land at the cornmarket in Plumstead to his wife Jane, and then to his son-in-law Henry Hawkes, adding details of further

---

[6] TNA: PROB11/228

lands at Bermondsey and elsewhere in Surrey, and a house in Little Eastcheap in St Andrew Hubbard parish, ultimately to be sold by Bryan the antiquary in 1758. His widow survived him by a decade, dying in the same parish in 1664, when her grandson Henry Hawkes proved her will[7] under the name of Fassett.

Their only son John was baptised in 1612 at St Saviour Southwark, after which nothing is known of his marriage to a Sarah, or his death (perhaps around 1672). His father left him one third of the personal property, and his mother £10. They had three children, all infants in their grandfather's will. His widow moved down to Dartford where she was buried in 1695.

John's sister Priscilla (for whom, again, no dates are known) married Henry Hawkes, a substantial tallowchandler, also of St Saviour's, Southwark. He died young in 1658, leaving a will[8] to be proved by his widow. He bequeathed lands and tenements in Essex and Hertfordshire to his sons Henry and William, and mentioned his mother-in-law Mrs Jane 'Fassett', directing that she could dwell in his house for as long as she wanted. Daughters named Jane and Priscilla completed his family of four children. Henry's probable father, another Henry Hawkes, and also a tallowchandler of St Saviour, died in 1700, again devising lands[9] in Essex and Hertfordshire as well as at the old cornmarket in Plumstead, these latter doubtless the same ones as Henry Forsett devised in 1653.

Henry Faussett, perhaps the eldest child and another only son, was a minor in 1652, and so perhaps born around 1635. He was a salter of St Saviour, having clearly been born there before the departure of the family to Kent, firstly to Plumstead where his grandfather had bequeathed him lands, and then to the substantial Thames Estuary town of Dartford, where the Faussetts would enjoy a long residence. He is described as a brewer in 1675 when mentioned in a case of debt,[10] which business his widow would ultimately inherit and continue. Hasted notes that the family had resided at the entrance of the town from London, that is, the west end, and that the seat passed (as we shall see) to the Bucks who in turn sold it to John Tasker of the same town. At the time of Hasted's writing the building was occupied as a boarding school for young ladies.

The Dartford parish registers sometimes compliment Henry with the epithet of 'Captain' when recording the baptisms of his sequence of eight children. Few precise episodes in his life are known, although in 1676 a minor chancery case[11] records him in a dispute with one Isaac Peake over costs of £114 for the transporting to Aylesford of large quantities of timber he had purchased at Brenchley, Yalding and Mereworth. Henry died intestate at Dartford in 1679, having lost much money and in considerable debt. An inheritance of 40s. from his grandmother, the mortgaging

[7] TNA: PROB11/314
[8] TNA: PROB11/285
[9] TNA: PROB11/458
[10] TNA: C10/480/74
[11] TNA: C5/479/68

of the Plumstead estate in 1668 for £350, and the receipt of £300 for indentures in 1675 seem not to have contributed materially to his fortunes or alleviated his debts.

His probable marriage is that to Catherine Wilkin at St Giles Camberwell in 1664. She survived him by nearly a generation until 1705, by which time the usual run of infant mortality meant that there were but three surviving children to inherit from what would prove to be a complicated estate, and one complicated further by the will having been executed 23 years previously in 1682, thus allowing a long intervening period of loss and decline. Henry's sister Jane married Thomas Fielder of Dartford, a maltman with a surname common in that town and its environs, and from her Faussett grandfather inherited a dozen apostle spoons. They had children Thomas and Sarah Fielder. Of Henry's other sister Elizabeth, nothing is known.

After Henry's death in 1679, his widow Catherine, clearly a woman of some acumen and determination, set up a brewing business in Dartford. She long struggled to recover the family fortunes, seemingly lost during her marriage, and appeared in numerous chancery proceedings, chasing the recovery of debts of varying sizes. In 1692 she was claiming[12] £150 due to her from Edward Hall, a victualler of Purfleet in Essex, who had predeceased her, and whose widow Elizabeth had now become liable. Two years later she was suing[13] Richard Fitchett, a victualler of Bexley, for having supplied him with quarts of beer and ale for carrying on his trade, again to the value of £150. This case was complicated by Richard Collett, a gentleman of Dartford, who appeared and fraudulently persuaded Fitchett to pass the debt over to him. (One wonders here, in looking at this substantial list of lawsuits, whether Bryan Faussett himself inherited some element of his litigious tendencies from his like-minded great-grandmother.)

Her son William proved her will[14] in February 1705. In it she continued the executorship of her late husband 'to make good my own estate to his and my children what was intended to them by my said husband with an overplus'. Her three younger children were to have had £1000 each from their father, and her eldest all his lands after she was deceased, 'but a great portion of Henry's estate consists in debts and is lost and never likely to be recovered. Debts paid, very little remains overplus'. However, she had valiantly attempted to rectify matters and had managed to raise some estate and clear the debts with a view to advancing her children. The son and heir William was now to have his inheritance of his father's lands plus the debts and personal estate yet recovered, together with the residue of his mother's undisposed estate, but with the uncomfortable caveat that he would have to settle all unpaid remaining debts incurred by both parents.

Poor William – at the time of writing he was only 12! But he did also receive copyhold lands in Middlesex, his mother's personal inheritance, if he would pay his grandmother Sarah Faussett £1500 by quarterly instalments for the rest of her life

[12] TNA: C9/281/77
[13] TNA: C9/447/122
[14] TNA: PROB11/486

(fortunately, perhaps, she was by now long dead). His brother Henry would receive his moiety of lands 'in Kent lying of the nature of gavelkind, as I am informed', and would further have £1500 at 21 in lieu of whatever he could claim from his father's or mother's estates, but on condition that he gave his brother a satisfactory account of his right and title to the same, failing which a mere £5 would be his lot. Additionally there was for him a small annuity until he was apprenticed or entered Oxbridge (alas for the future shopkeeper!) The two daughters would enjoy £1200 each when 21 or married, but only £500 if married without the approval of the executors. This careful and foresighted mother allowed a maximum of £20 apiece for the funerals of any child dying before they had inherited, but £50 for her own. All the poor widows of Dartford were to share 40s.

William Faussett, the eldest of the eight children of Henry and Catherine, and grandfather to the antiquary, was baptised at Dartford on 7 March 1670 and was buried there in 1711. His infant elder sister Sarah died the same year. Six further sisters followed, four dying as infants, one, Cicely, surviving at least infancy to be left 12 silver spoons by her mother, and the last, Cresselda, marrying Thomas Holker Esquire of Gravesend at Farningham in 1691. Her mother left her damask, plate and 'my silver candlesticks and their sockets'. She died in 1726 and her will[15] bequeathed property at West Street, Gravesend and at Hartley to her sons Thomas and Lawrence Holker, the latter sometime of Browne Place, Bexley. The second son and youngest of the eight was Henry, a shopkeeper of Dartford, who died young in 1719 mentioning in his will[16] three surviving children out of an original six. His widow Ann survived him eight years until 1727, by which time just one child remained, the eldest, Catherine, who the following year was married at Sutton-at-Hone to Samuel Thoyts, an insurance broker (and later a cornfactor of Goodmans Fields) originally from Whitechapel, but then of Dartford. By the terms of his mother's will Henry was left her 'great silver salt' – something perhaps not quite in keeping with a shopkeeper's establishment.

In August 1690, two months before William's highly advantageous marriage to Mary the daughter of John Bryan, a rich brewer of Rochester, a tripartite indenture was drawn up between the Bryans, William and his widowed mother, and John Crompe, a gentleman of St Margaret, Rochester. Therein it was agreed that John Bryan would give his future son-in-law £1000 as a marriage portion over and beyond such lands, tenements and hereditaments as he had already settled on William by previous indentures. Mother and son therefore agreed that they would convey sundry lands as a jointure for Mary Bryan, but problems lay in William not being quite 21, and that everything hinged on the wedding actually taking place. It was therefore agreed that the Faussetts, at their sole cost and charge, and within three months of William reaching his majority, would settle on John Bryan and John Crompe a group of their lands comprising various woods and groves totalling 122

[15] TNA: PROB11/613
[16] TNA: PROB11/569

acres all lying in Prittlewell parish in Essex, together with a toft where a tenement stood before the great Fire of 1666 in St Andrew Hubbard parish, and New Marsh ground at Plumstead. William Faussett would pay interest of ½% on the £1000 until he conveyed the agreed lands to his new wife, this jointure to continue for her life 'for a yearly value of £100 over and beyond all reprisals'.

In 1706 a further indenture was drawn up between William and Mary Faussett, and her father John Bryan, with the express aim of increasing Mary's jointure. John Bryan would now devise to William, and afterwards to his widow and her heirs, a valuable group of Dartford properties comprising a capital messuage or mansion and appurtenances, three paper-mills with their engines, islands, streams and instruments, a cherry orchard of five acres, a further two acres near the paper-mill, Iron Mill Brooks (now called Paper Mill Brooks) of 12 acres, and a brewhouse called the Sign of the George.

The intended marriage of William Faussett and Mary Bryan was duly solemnised on 28 October 1690 at St Michael Cornhill in the City of London. At the baptisms of their sons and daughters the father was variously described as a gentleman or 'Captain'. Sometime of Plumstead, and later of Dartford, he had inherited lands at Chatham and Prittlewell, and is recorded as the first Receiver General for Kent in 1709. A family story relates that he was robbed of government money while travelling over the Kent Downs, an incident which broke his heart and led to his early death. The second part of this is certainly true, for he made his will[17] in September 1711, two months before his death at the early age of 41, leaving five out of an original eight children, all infants. His two sons Bryan and Henry were to have the benefit of that part of the real estate which he had settled on his wife before marriage. Other unsettled lands in the City of London, Essex, Kent and elsewhere went in trust to his wife, who was charged with the guardianship and education of the surviving children 'that they be dutifull and obedient to her in all things and ready and willing on all occasions to be governed and advised by her, but more especially in the disposall of themselves in marriage to her liking'.

One might expect the occasional moderately unusual forename in a family of some wealth, and Bryan, which would fit that description, first appears in 1691, but for a more prosaic reason: the Faussett pedigree, like hundreds of others, then showed a keen desire to perpetuate a woman's maiden name. This, together with that of Henry, would appear regularly in each of numerous succeeding generations.

Bryan Faussett, the above-mentioned heir, and father of the antiquary, was born 13 October and baptised 6 November 1691 at St Nicholas, Rochester, the parish church lying almost in the shadow of the cathedral.

Before looking at him in more detail, it may be best to tabulate his siblings, who were born at either Rochester or Dartford, whence the Faussetts had not quite finally departed.

---

[17] TNA: PROB11/524

Peregrine Faussett was born at Rochester 7 April 1693 and buried aged one week. The unusual forename would never recur in the family.

William Faussett was born at Rochester on 25 September 1694. The baptismal entry is possibly wrong in saying 'Bryan', as there is a burial for an infant William at Dartford in 1701 (with no corresponding baptism). The first Bryan by now was nearly three, and beyond the first critical two years of life, so the insurance of a similarly-named sibling was perhaps unnecessary.

Sarah Faussett was buried at Dartford as an infant in 1695.

Catherine Faussett was born at Rochester on 14 May 1696 and died at Dartford in 1749. On her would fall the many problems of winding up her mother's estate. An administration was granted[18] to her daughter Elizabeth, her estate having not been fully wound up by her husband Samuel Buck who died a widower and a debtor in the King's Bench prison in 1752. Four of their children died young, leaving two sisters who survived into early old age, but died as spinsters to extinguish this branch of the family.

Henry Faussett was born 24 March 1698 at Dartford, and may have died in 1757. He married but had no issue. As the only other son, and with his brother Bryan already succeeded to his estates, he inherited well from his mother, receiving the family brewery and the Blackamoor's Head public house, both at East Gate, Rochester, along with four tenements in Crow Lane. The poll books record him as a freeholder of Rochester (abode London) in the 1730s, when he was at Seething Lane near the Tower. Towards the end of his life, in 1755, he was in St James' Clerkenwell, and had relinquished the brewing trade to become a weighing-porter.

Ann Faussett was born 10 September 1700 and was living at St Dunstan in the West when she married Reinard Watkins, gentleman of Gray's Inn, around March 1727. She died young in 1731 leaving no issue.

Mary Faussett was born 5 April 1707 and married Robert Lucas of the Inner Temple and Monmouthshire, Esquire. There were two sons, one a clergyman, and 'the other rich'. One was named William, with issue, the other childless.

Bryan Faussett senior was twenty when his father died in 1711. What career or prospects did he look forward to? His inheritance was far from settled, and Heppington estate eight years away. He had no degree, thus precluding the usual respectable careers of a son and heir, but had, on 29 May 1705 at the age of thirteen, been apprenticed for the customary period of seven years to John Bryan, gentleman, a Rochester brewer, and father of his future wife. The apprenticeship ran its full course to 1712, after which Bryan worked with the older man in the Rochester brewery until the latter's death in 1715. The brewing business kept Bryan gainfully employed for a further seven years or so, for in a chancery case of 1720 he declared that 'in 1718 I kept, held, used and occupied a public brewhouse in Eastgate Street,

---

18 TNA: PROB6/128

Rochester, and carried on a considerable trade there',[19] while pursuing a debt with Bridget Fordham of the Five Bells Inn for supplies of 'mild beer and butt or starting beer'.

All this would come to an end with the definitive move of the Faussetts from west to east Kent. This occurred with the marriage of Bryan Faussett and Mary Godfrey at the village church of Nackington just south of Canterbury on 4 October 1719. In this parish lay the manorial house of Heppington, hitherto the home of the Godfreys, and now to be that of the Faussetts for another century and a half. Bryan's world had suddenly changed from that of a bachelor in business at Rochester, from where he took out a licence to marry, to that of newly-married householder and father-to-be in pleasant east Kent countryside. Ahead of him lay the responsibilities of 14 children, the upkeep of his house, and the overseeing of many and disparate nearby and distant estates. His mother, approaching 50, remained at Dartford, her endless endeavours to bring back financial stability now more or less completed.

Four months after the wedding, another small family problem arose, as Bryan's bride, the Godfrey heiress, had still not reached her majority. An indenture of 17 January 1720 recognised that she was seized in demesne as of fee of all the capital messuage or mansion house called Heppington, plus its lands, in all 175 acres, lying in Nackington, Lower Hardres and Petham, but there were other lands inherited on the death of her mother which she could not yet settle. The latter were now disposed of freehold, a sum having being paid by the purchaser to bar the estate tail and so secure future free descent without impediment.

Just a few months into married life, his new account books were already recording crucial income. In October 1721 he received from his mother three bank notes for £250 and a promissory note for £88. In January 1723 a further £700 came from his mother, promised by her to him at his marriage 'to lay down goods at Heppington … but was not done till now, so the interest was for £600 three years odd months, £100 the Principall, £600 which made it £700'. The careful eye for recording both small and large amounts of money, so soon apparent, would before long be inherited by his eldest son, and so too would financial problems. Not for the first time, in April 1723 he paid 5s. for him and his wife to be bled – a standard, if somewhat expensive precaution, but with inoculation hardly yet known, an easily obtained prophylactic. The following month the midwife was paid two guineas to deliver his first daughter Mary, soon after which he lent his sister Mary £1 10s. to stand godmother to 'Molly'. His wife was well dressed, or at least had her hands decently covered, when he bought her a dozen gloves for £1 4s. 0d. Soon after the death of his mother, his expenses in London and elsewhere in laying out mourning cost him £12 2s. 6d.

A few months after William Faussett's death in 1711, his widow Mary was involved in what would be only the beginning of years of litigation over more than one matter. She was complaining[20] that Reuben Jeffery, a butcher, and his wife Ann had

---

[19] TNA: C11/2638/27
[20] TNA: C9/470/51

sold to her late husband assorted property, namely barns, stables, a slaughterhouse and a forge in Dartford High St, the Angell public house in Spittle St, and further lands at Hooke Green, Wilmington. The Jefferys had assured William Faussett that the said lands were free of encumbrances and would be mortgaged to him for £300, and this indeed was done, but Mary's grievance lay in the fact that the Jefferys were still in occupation. In the next year, 1712, she was chasing[21] a debt of £400 owed to her late husband by Edward Trimmer, a London corn factor, where William was again described as 'Captain'.

Within three years of her husband's death Mary had remarried to Robert Echlin, a widower and Lieutenant-General of His Majesty's Forces of St James' Westminster. Hardly settled into a second marriage, Mary Echlin lost her father John Bryan at Rochester in 1715, who in his lengthy will[22] mentioned, *inter alia*, his grandson Bryan Faussett (the father of the future antiquary) and a married daughter whose own son, John Bryan Osterland, bore a middle name soon to be familiar within the family. Mary Echlin's second husband died just before her, in 1723, and by his will[23] left her his money, securities and estate in Suffolk. Here now lay the seeds of protracted future expense in the law courts, for Mary's father John Bryan had left a fortune of £40,000 mostly in trust to her and her children, exclusive of her second husband; after the death of Robert Echlin she was nominated sole executrix of her father's estate; and thus at her own death she was seized of portions of the estates of both her father and of her two husbands. All this came to a head when Mary nominated as sole executrix her daughter Catherine, the wife of Samuel Buck, a seemingly rapacious individual who saw a fortune waiting to be distributed, but a circumstance which did not obviate his later incarceration in the King's Bench prison.

The will of Mary Echlin, formerly Faussett, was duly proved in December 1724[24] and shared among her five surviving children. Her first husband had already made provision for them, and thus she was at pains to ensure that they should have no claim on the estates of either her late father or her late second husband. The son and heir Bryan would inherit £500 and the estates at Purfleet in the parishes of West Thurrock and Aveley, Essex, other lands at Eltham, late his father's, and the mortgage of a house and lands at Staplehurst in the weald of Kent, late her father's. Her other son Henry was to receive all interests, rights and title in property at East Gate, Rochester, together with a house called The Sign of the Blackmoor's Head, also in East Gate, further houses held on lease from the church and bishop of Rochester and the Warden of Rochester Bridge, and four tenements in Crow Lane in the same city [the 1734 poll book lists Henry Fosset, freeholder of Rochester, residing in London]. This substantial legacy was augmented by £500 and a right, title and share in the Rochester waterworks. The three daughters would enjoy, other than sharing their mother's clothes, £4000 each.

---

[21] TNA: C9/217/43
[22] TNA: PROB11/546
[23] TNA: PROB11/590
[24] TNA: came to him as the eldest son and heir PROB11/600

In February 1725/6 Bryan Faussett senior signed a release[25] confirming that he had received from his sister Catherine Buck, the sole executrix of his late mother's will, his bequest of £500, whereupon he confirmed that he had no further claims upon the estates of either his late grandfather or of either parent. His inheritance now came to him as the eldest son and heir:

> Purfleet Mill, Essex (and its estate map), purchased by his grandfather Henry Faussett in 1673;
> lands in Eltham and Chislehurst and a house called *The Five Bells* in Eltham purchased by his grandfather in 1671;
> assorted messuages, cottages, mills, gardens, meadows, pastures and appurtenances at Rochester, Dartford, Eltham and Crayford;
> similar lands and property at Aveley and West Thurrock, Essex;
> a messuage and toft in St Andrew Hubbard parish in the City, the house of which had been destroyed in the Great Fire;
> letters patent of Edward VI concerning three messuages and appurtenances called Baldox Chantry in St Andrew Undershaft parish;
> messuages and lands at Staplehurst, Marden and Hawkhurst.

Appended to these schedules is what is perhaps the only surviving autograph letter of Bryan Faussett senior, written at Heppington in November 17[20?] as a 'dutiful son' to his mother Mrs Echlin at her lodgings at the King's Arms and Civet, next to a perfumer's in Temple Bar. He entreats his mother to settle a debt of £58 for woodland bought in the preceding year from Mrs Catherine Bovey of Queen St, Westminster. The general tenor strongly suggests that the owner of Heppington is already enmeshed in financial worries – something which would become only too apparent in the next generation:

> … you will certainly not think it strange that I am so straitened when you know as well as I do that I have received nothing considerable from either Staplehurst, Day, Gibbons, Hall, nor any of the estate, nor can either dispose of hops or corn unless I almost give them away, and then trust for the money. Indeed at present I had almost been as well without any estate at all, for what I receive on the one part only goes to defray the charges on the other.[26]

Bryan senior's household accounts are as fascinating and intimate as his son's would be. In early 1726 he paid Hatch the goldsmith, £5 7s. 6d. for mourning rings distributed at his mother-in-law Catherine Godfrey's funeral. Other household items included £3 8s. for a card table, £1 7s. for a parrot plus a guinea for its cage, 5s. for Havana snuff and 10s. for a pound of tea. Expenses laid out by his wife over two years for butchers' bills and sundry other things came to a rather alarming £331, but we should perhaps remember that there were a dozen mouths to feed in those

[25] KHLC: U36/T1273
[26] *ibid.*

early years of family life. In 1729 the servants' wages for one whole year comprised 'Rachael' and Mary the cook who received £4 each, Mary the children's maid £3, Margaret the dairy maid £3, George the hogboy £1 5s., Peter the footboy £2 5s., and Sam the gardener £12, this last-mentioned perhaps overpaid, considering the extent of the grounds.

Bryan kept voluminous records of his lands and rents, starting from the very beginning of his married life. He had inherited many things and no doubt wished to keep on top of so much bookkeeping, being hardly yet fully cognisant of everything he now owned. He took firstly details of the size of his own home estate.

Heppington mansion house with the manor and its lands of orchards, closes and fields: 101 acres;
Stockfield Land near Canterbury: 52 acres;
Woodlands at Swadling and Iffin Down: 28 acres;
Fox's house with land hired with it: 5 acres;
Further hopground and ploughland adjoining Stockfield, worth £120 annually if let: 200 acres

Between 1719 and the mid-1720s annual rents were collected as follows:

A small cottage in Lower Hardres let to the parishioners: 40s.;
A small cottage and orchard near Heppington: £5;
32 acres at Stockfield: £11 10s.;
Mrs Catherine Godfrey's jointure on Romney Marsh, and mine after her death: £100;
Land called Summers in Lower Hardres directly against the Three Horses: £3 10s;
Purfleet Mills, Purfleet, Essex, with house and lands: £105;
A house called Ye Lighter (later Ye Hoy) at Purfleet: £22;
The King's Arms at Eltham: £10;
Two houses, one with a bakehouse, &c. at Eltham: £22;
102 acres at Brookland in Walland Marsh ('Elderton's Innings') with the running of a horse every year: £130;
Fullers, Iden and Wallerland farms at Staplehurst: £125;
A house at Eastcheap: £50;
Cookham Hill Farm, St Margaret Rochester: £50;
Four fields and a farm at Northfleet: £40;
Prittlewell and Leigh in Essex: £40;
Marshland at Plumstead Levels: £20

The above may not be an absolutely full picture, but does suggest an annual income from property rents of some £700 or more. In addition, Bryan senior sold the old barn and cottages at Eltham to a Mrs Drake for £180 in April 1728.

The accounts end in 1749, the year before his death, after which follow separate accounts kept by his widow for each child, charging their expenses against their father's estate. Curiously there is no mention of anything for the eldest daughter's marriage, and nor are there any sums for the funerals of the four children who had predeceased their father. In 1753 Mary paid £84 for a new coach and pair of

Figure 8. The ledger-stone of Bryan Faussett senior in the sanctuary at St Mary,
Nackington. His proud and complex coat of arms is there for all to see.
(Copyright Neil Anthony.)

harness; later she would record giving five guineas to 'a very unworthy creature', and
a guinea towards the losses incurred by fire at Chartham.

Bryan Faussett senior died on 19 September 1750. He was not young at 58,
and as a tidy and orderly man, one might have supposed he would have left a
will, but none was proved. The fulsome details of his probate inventory are listed
elsewhere. This substantial task would necessarily have preceded the winding up and
distribution of the estate which at his death comprised assets totalling £4,017 7s.
10d¾. Administration fees reduced this by £385 2s. 4d., leaving a little over £1,210
for his widow and some £242 each to the ten surviving children, all of which was
distributed (down to the nearest farthing) on 27 December 1751.

His widow died 23 May 1761 and her will[27] was proved by her son Bryan as sole
executor. She was to be privately buried in the same grave 'as my dear and honoured
father in the chancel at Nackington with an inscription for me under that for my
dearest father on his gravestone'. United in death indeed. Most, but not all, of her

[27] KHLC: PRC17/96/251

children received £10 each, with the residue of 'living stock, husbandry tackle, corn, household goods, linen, china, plate, money &c.' as the supplementary inheritance of her eldest son and heir Bryan, now in the prime of life aged 40, and busy as a landowner and clergyman, father of three young children, and zealous antiquary.

Chapter 2
A World of Antiquarianism

As a schoolboy of ten Faussett saw Cromwell Mortimer lift with a spade gold brooches and other treasures from the ground on Chartham Down within three miles of Heppington. What effect was impressed upon his juvenile mind and what seeds were sown for his future lifelong passion? Who could tell what other wondrous objects might lie hidden a few feet deep within a short walk of his home? The exciting, colourful and slightly mysterious world of Georgian antiquarianism would soon now beckon – a world where British historical chronology was imperfectly understood, where Roman and Anglo-Saxon still coalesced, and where artefacts revealed by the turning of the plough had not long ceased to be considered the handiwork of giants rather than of men.

Who were the earliest antiquaries? Little has perhaps been said about them as human beings. Not all were bookworms sitting in their libraries or grubbing about in ivy-clad ruins (Dr Johnson summed it up by saying 'a mere antiquarian is a rugged thing'), but one thing does unite them all to a man – they were amateurs. None made a living out of writing a county history, or even from the wider study of antiquities. Most of them had to be self-financing, and so the history of antiquarianism, as this book will show, is peppered with the gentry and the clergy, many of whom were both at the same time. The writing of a county history more often than not brought little recompense, and was often superseded by the wish to illuminate and glorify the writer's own class and friends, and to instruct and edify them.

But self-advantage and educational fervour, however attractive, were not the wellspring of all this frenetic activity. Rather, it was an emotional need. What began as a passion in early youth (as with Faussett) became so often a lifelong obsession (again, as with Faussett), sometimes supported by financial independence and sometimes not. We may adduce Hasted to prove the point: largely because of the heavy expenditure he incurred in his *History of Kent* he spent seven years in the King's Bench Prison, completing his last volume (and also the whole 12 volumes of the improved second edition) while incarcerated, and still somehow managed to get them published. His *magnum opus*, a life's consuming passion, took precedence over living abroad and the exploration of other counties – all fell before the relentless march towards the triumphant completion of writing about Kent. Sir Richard Colt Hoare, unimpeded by the irritation of insufficient funds, but dogged by ill-health, steadfastly continued with his *Modern Wiltshire*, and yet it remained incomplete at his death.

Historical works fall into three categories; description, analysis, and narrative. Description attempts to reveal a manifestation of the past; analysis, likewise static, places the thing described in a wider context of situations and tries to establish causes and motives; while narrative tells a story, irrespective of time span. Antiquaries and chroniclers wrote works which were for the most part, it cannot be denied, the lower forms of description and analysis, as opposed to the higher form of meaningful and analytical description of the past. The basic procedures and purposes were not at fault; it was the quality of mind brought to the task, and the degree to which perceptive questions were asked and penetrating answers given.

Antiquarianism's hallmark, therefore, is a devotion to detail for it own sake: the antiquary wants to know, not to understand, and he is not bothered by what knowledge is being acquired: one fact is well-nigh as good as any other to him, their accumulation his *modus operandi*. His true and comfortable home is parish history, local archaeology and local genealogy; that is, areas where many facts can be accumulated without strain on reason or synthesis. This is not to deprecate, for we should be immensely the poorer without the fruits of the researches of those centuries, but it must be seen for what it is – antiquarian work has value of a kind because the facts collected can in the proper light contribute to the answering of real, difficult and intellectually challenging questions, but the man who has little to say cannot disguise the fact by putting his notes down in a sort of connected sequence.

So let not antiquarianism pretend to be history, for then doubts will arise. A work is not complete when the finding-out part of it is over. The antiquary believes in accuracy and thinks that the work of others is soon overturned by finding a handful of factual inaccuracies. Accuracy is indeed the beginning of the work, but not its sole purpose. We should not deny the chronicle its rightful place in the scheme of things, but nor should we forget that it is the narrative expression of antiquarian fact-collecting, a setting down of events one after another, without discrimination or obvious purpose except that of merely recording.

Faussett, of course, well fits this categorisation. His education and mental acumen are in no doubt, but his research and investigations, both archaeological and genealogical, were local in the extreme, in part circumscribed by his physical location at the near edge of a maritime county. He asked many questions, some perceptive, but mostly unanswerable in the then present state of knowledge of his recondite interests. The value of his work, above all things, lies in the method and the comprehensiveness of his recording. By the time he was middle-aged, organised site-excavation was about a century old and, like other sciences, continually evolving from crude origins: diligent as he was compared with the Jacobeans, we inevitably see him today as old-fashioned in the light of extraordinary modern scientific techniques.

And today? Whatever imperfections we find in the noble catalogue of early antiquarian writing, and however much we judge them by the standards of our own time, they did not write in vain. Few are now read for pleasure or in their entirety, but they are still constantly consulted and will continue to be. Every succeeding generation of researchers did and will acknowledge an immense debt to those diligent, and persevering, selfless amateurs who turned to the subject of pre-Roman Britain and its peoples, endlessly committing the 'unrepeatable experiment' by the opening of barrows to see what of instruction or illumination lay hidden within.

Humans have always speculated about their past, and most cultures have their own foundation myths to explain why society is how it is. The Greek poet Hesiod (*c*.800 BC) envisaged the human past as divided into five stages from gold to iron, each consonant with man's progressive fall from happiness to misery. Most cultures, too, have been fascinated by the societies that preceded them. Nabonidus, the last native king of Babylon in the 500s BC, took a keen interest in antiquities and housed his finds, which included a two-thousand-year-old temple foundation stone, in a kind of early museum.

Italy in the 14th century saw the birth of humanism, inspired by the glories of Greece and Rome, whose rediscovery and celebration would soon consume so many curious minds. The glories of classical literature and the superabundance of physical remains in art, architecture, inscriptions and coins were enticing flames that would now be fanned for centuries. The men so purposefully involved in such things saw themselves as proud heirs of the ancients who had sought their own past with equal curiosity; by the end of the 15th century, the Italian humanists would recognize the antiquary as a fellow researcher and a respected *primus inter pares*.

By the later 16th century students of the ancient past came to be known, individually or corporately, as antiquaries. It was they who pursued the earliest tentative investigations into Britain's prehistoric past and in so doing trod the first steps on a long, hesitant and unconsciously pursued path to what would become in the mid-19th century the recognizable discipline of prehistoric archaeology. They would have numbered true scholars alongside lackadaisical dabblers, eccentrics, pedants, legal historians, genealogists and rabid collectors, not all, by any means, interested in the remains of Roman and pre-Roman antiquity, and united only by personal collections of the most diverse and miscellaneous natures. From the Mediterranean in the south some turned their gaze towards more northern lands and the study of the local relics of their own remote past, frequently displaying their curios and ancient artefacts along with haphazard collections of minerals and natural history specimens in cabinets of curiosities – the precursors of modern museums.

Were the first antiquaries mediaeval annalists or Renaissance and humanist scholars? The antiquary was interested in providing a system of collections or sources relating to certain subjects and institutions, and determining their historical origins and continuity, and to do so he compiled and organised his documents and ancient objects accordingly. The historian, on the other hand, was concerned with the explanation and interpretation of facts and events, and so presented his story in a flowing chronological narrative, ever concerned with causality. Francis Bacon distinguished between 'civil' and 'natural' history, the former comprising ecclesiastical, civil (i.e. political) history and the history of learning. Antiquities, an aspect of civil history, were 'remnants' of the past, and included coins, monuments and traditions, or 'memorials'; that is, textual sources.

The antiquarian emphasis on documentation came with the work of Roger Dodsworth and William Dugdale, who were indefatigable in collecting material for their *Monasticon Anglicanum* of 1655. From the Tudors to the Georgians, the narrative historian saw the antiquary's work as an irrelevant and uncritical amassing of material, whose diligence found facts but who also kept myth alive by an accompanying credulity. But to separate these two types of historical scholar was scarcely possible, for each needed the other's techniques and both skills were often combined in the one man. Antiquaries of the 17th century actually contributed more than historians to the knowledge of history, and the difficulty in distinguishing between the two is clearly evidenced in such men as William Camden and Sir Robert Cotton who were zealous as much in the one field as in the other.

The history of England was a subject shrouded in mystery before the reign of Elizabeth, and one much influenced by pagan or Christian beliefs and ancestral myths. The story of the coming of Joseph of Arimathea with the Holy Grail to spread the Christian gospel enjoyed a currency rather longer than objective enquiry would have preferred, and the Anglo-Saxon view that the monuments of their time had been built by giants was a truth not quickly dislodged. But how, indeed, was anyone to recognise a Roman coin or a Saxon sword? The Bible implied with unshakeable conviction that human activity was but a few millennia old, different periods were with difficulty distinguished, and material remains were in large part objects of mystery. Few people travelled far on a rudimentary system of roads which maps ignored, or in a countryside whose buildings were for the most part undescribed and unrecorded.

In the Middle Ages not many men had tried to date King Arthur, for few would have demanded proof of his existence. Renaissance classical scholars looked back to a far distant and exactly dated Greek and Roman past, when men whose existence could be proven were greater than the men of their own time, as thinkers, writers, builders and sculptors. To recover their books and buildings and statues was no mere work of piety, for it was only by their study and imitation that men could hope to equal and excel them – an essentially Italian view, for with luck and by dint of hard work anyone resident not too far from the city of Rome might hope to recover the Roman past from literally under his feet.

The question of whence man had originated was answered by two works of radically opposing natures. The first attempt to discover the history of the English was made by Bede in his *Ecclesiastical History of the English People*, where in a clear and compelling narrative, squarely based on painstaking chronology, he described the conversion to Christianity of the Anglo-Saxon world of the sixth to eighth centuries – a perfect model of written history. Geoffrey of Monmouth's *History of the Kings of Britain* treated of the Anglo-Saxon world just after the Norman invasion and attemped to fill in Bede's annoying gaps. Nobody, including Geoffrey, knew the answers to such imponderables, but this was no barrier to some historical flights of fancy, opening with the wandering survivors of the Trojan war arriving into Albion as refugees, at which point Brutus and his companions became the Britons, and closing with the legendary King Arthur and Merlin resisting their doughty foes. But for centuries, *faute de mieux*, Geoffrey's tales were believed, and indeed approved by a Tudor dynasty descended from his kings, until Renaissance scholarship again preferred the erudition and sagacity of Bede for the clearer light that it threw.

How old was man? Nobody knew, and would have no inkling until Faussett's time and beyond, when, for the first time, Anglo-Saxon remains would be identified as such. The earliest mention of what are probably Anglo-Saxon graves is that by the 13th-century chronicler Roger of Wendover in his *Flores Historiarum* where he describes the excavation by monks of St Albans in 1178 of ten human skeletons at Redbourne, Hertfordshire, believing some of them to be the bones of St Amphibalus, the cleric sheltered by St Alban. Sir Thomas Browne's *Hydriotaphia*, or *Urne Buriall* of 1658 was a pioneering English excavation report which displayed for the first time splendid engravings of the Anglo Saxon pots he had taken from the cemetery at Walsingham in Norfolk, and described as the 'Sad sepulchral pitchers … fetched from the passed world'. One of those 40 or 50 urns, reported to have contained burnt bones, survived in the 'closet of rarities' at Lambeth known as Tradescant's Ark, which in 1682 formed the basis of Elias Ashmole's bequest to the University of Oxford.

Archbishop Ussher's dating of the world to 4004 BC (a fact quoted in the margins of the King James Bible for over 200 years) displayed seemingly irrefutable belief in the infallible Word of God, but did not perhaps offer such an insurmountable barrier as some have claimed. Nevertheless, at the beginning of the Victorian era most well-read people would have reckoned the age of the world at a few millennia at the most, and believed that all that could be known of the remote past must perforce be derived from the surviving pages of the earliest historians, and especially those of the ancient Near East, Egypt, and Greece. There was no awareness that any kind of coherent history of the periods before the development of writing was possible at all. The Danish scholar Rasmus Nyerup, writing in the generation after Faussett, saw everything of the ancient and heathen world wrapped in a thick fog and belonging to a space of time which was immeasurable. It was older than Christendom, certainly, but whether by a couple of years or centuries, or even by a millennium or more, was anyone's guess.

Today, of course, we can penetrate that fog of the remote past not simply by virtue of new discoveries, but because we have learnt to ask some of the right questions and have developed some of the right methods for answering them – we have a new awareness that the methods of archaeology can give us information about the past, and even the prehistoric past before the invention of writing. Archaeology has proceeded from a history of ideas, of theory and of ways at looking at the past to developing research methods, employing those ideas and investigating those questions: thus now we have a history of actual discoveries on which to build.

The date of creation made no difference to the study of Roman and Saxon antiquities in Britain, and the biblical chronology, although not long, did allow two millennia from the flood and the Noachian family down to the Roman invasions of 55 BC and AD 43. This was latitude enough for those excavating until the age of the Enlightenment, and a critical issue only when the demands of stratigraphy came into play in the early 19th century and thereby demanded a longer timescale. Even James Douglas, when writing on the longer chronology of the earth, did not address the question of a greater length for human antiquity, but only whether people might have existed in Europe in antediluvian times.

Sometimes of course men found or saw things but had no way to comprehend their age, nature or purpose. Stone tools were not discovered until the late 1600s; they were not unknown, but simply not understood as being of human origin. The Dane Ole Worm (d.1655) formed a famous museum in Copenhagen which included examples of perforated stone axes categorised by him as *ceraunia* or thunder-stones, to be explained by their dropping from the sky in the fashion of meteorites, whereas others described (and published) them as sharks' teeth. But mystery and superstition notwithstanding, William Dugdale's 1656 history of Warwickshire included a carefully drawn engraving of a polished stone axe without any comment other than its physical description, thereby displaying the power of simple observation over received wisdom.

Conservatism and emotional ties with the past were ever close to the antiquary's heart. Architects competing for the commission to rebuild Canterbury cathedral after the disastrous fire of 1174 were, as the monk Gervase informs us and the building itself shows us, required to preserve as much as possible of the original fabric of Conrad's 'glorious choir'. The extent to which William of Sens and his successor William the Englishman actually stuck to the intention of the brief need not now concern us; the important point is that this was typical mediaeval conservatism, rather than conservationism, born of sentiment rather than any historical concern about monuments of the recent past.

Two centuries later the Middle Ages showed little awareness of the styles of the past, for fashion was not in any way dominated by historicism. And so it is all the more remarkable that when Henry Yevele was confronted in 1375 by the task of completing the 13th-century nave of Westminster Abbey, he decided on a course unparalleled outside England in electing not to insist on something in his own style or the style of the day, but rather to show reverence for the 13th century by continuing with a minimum of change in the design – uniformity reigned supreme at the cost of being seen as old-fashioned. As a coronation church of supreme architectural significance, Yevele's archaeological awareness bowed squarely to the past, and anticipated the 'dimension of historic time' which the Renaissance was to give to Western culture in the fifteenth century.

The pursuit of antiquarian knowledge, like so many other types of learning, spread from Italy to other parts of Europe in the 1400s and 1500s. In England this development coincided with a reluctant debate about the veracity of the traditional account of the history of Britain – the *Brut* which Geoffrey of Monmouth had compiled so comprehensively four centuries earlier. To the unease of scholars, its discordance with similar histories now being written in Italy and France was only too apparent. The growing consciousness of Tudor England as a prominent identity in the world stimulated the desire to discover afresh the remains of England's past, in both documents and artefacts.

The study of English local history begins in the 15th century. In his *Warwick Roll* of 1477 John Rous, even at that early date, was able to represent correctly the armour of the members of that house. A small circle of courtly humanists might doubt the very existence of King Arthur, but they had little influence on the Tudor world, which for political reasons was more inclined to glorify Celtic legend. Even the introduction of printing in the 1450s seemed to perpetuate the Middle Ages rather than encourage new genres – Chaucer, for example, was reprinted six times before 1550.

The fifth-century *Notitia Dignitatum*, Ptolemy's *Geographia* of 1475 and the *Antonine Itinerary* (first translated in 1512), were the first framework for English antiquarian study. Lists of names they might have been, but lists were all that historians had on which to build, and with the painful dearth of references to Roman Britain, such texts were pure gold, assuming a greater importance for Britain than for other lands. In the later 1400s and the 1500s English scholars were often heralds based at the recently established College of Arms, whose job was to establish and elucidate the national heritage. It would not do for the study of antiquity in England to be a romantic view of ancient things freshly dug up, because the binding forces of continuity and familiarity made an historic view of things seen habitually extremely difficult. No – study must lie in the slow and piecemeal understanding of buildings and monuments which had been familiar for generations, such study not the preserve of men ensconced in a comfortable academy, but rather that of solitary and determined individuals who would literally tread the ground they were so interested in.

The Renaissance saw the gentle fanning of a wind of change: an increasing interest in and availability of ancient manuscripts, the teaching of Greek, and foundations of schools and universities would help to move antiquarianism away from a mediaeval attitude to the past which had shown scant systematic interest in dating or the study of material remains; and so too would the need to establish a more viable lineage for the English crown and the desire to find documentary precedent for important aspects of political and religious power. The principle of establishing the priority of something, whether it were law, the ownership of land, or kingship, required a framework or chronology to be convincing – and the need to provide such a framework or chronology was one motive for early antiquarian work, along with which came the need to map the country so that events that appeared within earlier sources could be located.

The Reformation saw an end of continuity and the smashing of the familiar. The cataclysm of the dissolution of some 850 monasteries and abbeys between 1535 and 1539 was on a scale never to be repeated in English history, but, ironically, the surviving ruins then unintentionally became historical monuments, no longer fulfilling their original functions. In a twist of irony, the perpetrator, Henry VIII, was the patron of John Leland's *New Year's Gift to King Henry the VIII* of 1546, which ended with its author proudly signing 'Joannes Leylandus Antiquarius scripsit'. Leland had risen to be Keeper of the King's Libraries in 1530; three years later, Henry, ever the Renaissance prince and scholar, gave him authority to search the libraries of the surviving monasteries and colleges for manuscripts of ancient authors, a passion augmented by extensive travelling for the same purpose of compiling his *Itinerary*, although he was yet more passionate for documentary and topographical studies, allowing himself neither aesthetic reactions nor artistic criticism. The geographer in him was entirely satisfied by seeing a late mediaeval county and committing to writing its topography, economics and local history, although, alas, his compendious notes gave precious little detail about towns and villages, and almost no mention of genuine antiquities – the Saxon world was beyond Leland's purview, let alone the Roman origins beneath it. True research, based on close knowledge of classical texts and comprehension of Old English, the minimum requirement for unlocking England's past, was as yet unheard of.

Leland's loss of sanity in 1550 delayed the development of English antiquarianism for a generation and more; yet the climate of public opinion for the subject was now becoming more favourable. Under Mary Tudor there grew a new clemency towards the Catholic past; antiquarianism came to be equated with recusancy as interest in mediaeval buildings as historical monuments was fostered by the Catholic revival. At her death there was an injection of patriotic enthusiasm for the history and identity of the country, culminating in an Elizabethan proclamation of 1560 forbidding the defacing of ancient monuments set up in churches and other public places 'for memory and not for superstition', and positively encouraging the repairing of such monuments as far as was convenient and practicable. Losses had to be investigated and the smashed remains re-erected by the offenders. The edict was but little followed, yet still significant, as the clauses forbidding the destruction of armorial glass suggested an interest in both those commemorated as well their descendants still living.

As the reign of Elizabeth proceeded, the intellectual climate made antiquarian studies increasingly possible, yet there were still serious limits to what antiquarians could achieve. Access to texts was limited, for there were few large repositories of such sources available outside of London, and although many of the more famous antiquaries of the 16th and 17th centuries had lived in Oxford, London or abroad in such centres as Paris, they were often writing at a distance from their primary sources and so remained highly dependent on each other for mutual support. Thus it was at this time that extended networks of communication by way of friendship, visits, exchanges of drafts and letters became established.

Early modern society now set great store by the primacy of the text, and the more venerable the better, for the Greek and Roman writers represented the legitimacy of the classical world. Despite the increase in the numbers of new translations coming into circulation there was a relatively small amount of primary material to draw on, and all too often its scope and value was reduced by an original purpose or location. It was a simple and undeniable fact that few classical texts referred to Britain, and where they did, the references were all too brief and hard to substantiate.

Around this time, when John Stow was researching London under the patronage of Archbishop Parker, he soon got into difficulties as being 'an Admirer of Antiquity in Religion as well as in History'. His justly famous *Survey of London* is antiquarianism of the highest order, clearly demonstrating what he has actually seen for himself, yet his view is still essentially a documentary one, transcribing inscriptions as documents, but with no care for architectural description.

Lambarde's *A Perambulation of Kent* of 1576 was the first topographical survey for a very long time, and an excellent example of the approach which antiquaries were to take in describing English places; indeed it was taken as a model for humanist county surveys for years to come. The pioneering author expressed a fervent desire that books should be written about all the counties, his own work thus the beginning of a nation-wide description.

A decade later when Camden wrote his *Britannia* he himself described the work as a perambulation, but its form and purpose were far clearer than that of Leland, and it was he who first reached Leland's missed goal. His noble apologia set a standard to study the truth and not dishonour a nation or an individual. His *raison d'être* was a yearning 'to know much' – cartography was immaterial, unadulterated history paramount. Behind the modern English counties he discerned the original tribes as recorded by the Roman historians; dispensing with a tourist's eye he enriched his text with transcriptions of Romano-British inscriptions and recorded far more visible antiquities than Leland, the solitary eccentric, ever did, even briefly mentioning the Anglo-Saxons whose language he had studied. Now in his prime, and with more leisure at his disposal since becoming Clarenceux Herald in 1597, he was at the heart of a circle of intelligentsia which relished exchanging ideas, and one which included Sir Robert Cotton, his quondam Westminster pupil.

From the 16th century, antiquaries became acutely aware of the importance of national archives and libraries for politics as well as for scholarship. Various attempts were made to petition for the foundation of libraries and learned societies, granted with much difficulty and suspicion, if at all, because of the political and polemic use scholars might make of their knowledge of state papers and legal documents. The Cottonian library was feared as a centre of political resistance to the royal prerogative and was closed in 1629.

From the end of the Tudors down to Faussett's time there was no concept of unknown or extinct peoples, or of periods of unwritten time, and, consequently, no concept of human prehistory; all human time was history because of the Biblical account, pre-human time short indeed because without humanity the earth had no purpose. And still, crucially, nobody had yet considered actually digging to find artefacts to promote investigation – archaeology was still to see the light of day.

The first English antiquarian society, a predominantly protestant and patriotic gathering, was probably established in about 1572 through the munificence of Archbishop Matthew Parker. The members, all scholarly, none clerical, were mostly graduates, lawyers, courtiers and knights interested in historical fact rather than literature, and then only English sources. Naturally, heraldry and genealogy were of consuming interest, for the history of the nobility and gentry was central to national and local history, and, happily, many antiquaries were also heralds. This led to accusations of parochialism and insularity, but their avowed purpose was to establish a cultural longevity for their country, taking Parliament back to the Romans and Christianity back to Joseph of Arimathea. Papers were read and discussions held on such predictable and innocuous subjects as the nobility and gentry, the antiquity of arms, property, counties and their buildings, the privileges of cities, funeral customs, and the venerableness of the Christian religion. The fortunes of the society wavered upwards and downwards, and the quality of papers read at it was all too often unspeakably dismal.

Meetings were held for nearly 20 years at the home of Sir Robert Cotton (who had started acquiring his tremendous library as a mere teenager), and then application made to Queen Elizabeth in 1589 for incorporation and for a building to house a library. Their noble intentions were to establish an academy for the study of antiquity and history under the auspices of a president, two librarians and a number of fellows, with a body of statutes and a library to be called 'The Library of Queen Elizabeth'. The members were to take the oath of supremacy and another oath to preserve the intended library of books, charters, muniments and other manuscripts. The signatories were Sir Robert Cotton, Sir John Dodderidge and Sir James Lee. Nothing came of this petition, for incorporation, perhaps frustrated by the Queen's death in 1603, was probably extinguished by the following year with James I now on the throne.

The last recorded date of members' admissions is 1607, by which time many were then dead or had retired to the country, and so the informal society would soon suspend its meetings, and not survive an abortive attempt to revive them in 1614. Many of its members had been legal antiquaries who tried to concentrate on law and heraldry more than on politics, but its greatest names were politically motivated scholars and antiquaries to whom, allegedly, James I 'took a little Mislike'. The list of the earliest fellows' names makes for a grand roll-call: Sir John Dethicke (1555); Archbishop Parker (1572); Sir Robert Cotton, Sir John Dodderidge, Sir James Lee and Archbishop Whitgift (1589); and Sergeant Fleetwood, Arthur Agard, Lancelot Andrews and Robert Beale (1590).

Unlike France, England had no official learned or literary body, outside the universities, and several schemes were afoot to remedy it in the early 1600s. Sir John Dodderidge submitted a petition to the Queen with Sir Robert Cotton and Sir James Lee for the establishment of an academy, but it never saw the light of day. In 1617 Edmund Mary Bolton sought the support of the Duke of Buckingham, the rising favourite, to establish an academy at Windsor Castle which would go beyond the usual goal of setting up a finishing school for gentry and nobility, and be dedicated to the study of history, antiquities, heraldry and literature in general. It would be more than a revived Society of Antiquaries – rather an elaborate tripartite structure chartered and endowed by the crown with £200 annually.

Bolton had looked back to the Elizabethan Society as a possible model for what he called his 'Academ Roial', which, as it turned out, would include few antiquaries or heralds and not enough Catholics, but rather Knights of the Garter, the Lord Chancellor and the two university chancellors, select members of the aristocracy, and leading gentlemen of prominent families of independent means and scholarly interests. County historians and authors with a strong sense of loyalty to the Church of England were now the next generation of antiquaries, and upon them all would fall great privileges and the rôle of cultural police (the Tudor *arbitri elegantiae*), licensing non-theological books and reviewing translations of learned works.

The names selected for the original membership of 84 included some of the leading poets and scholars, Bolton's friends prominent among them, including Sir Henry Spelman, Sir John Selden, Sir Kenelm Digby, Sir Edward Coke, Endymion Porter, Sir Henry Wotton, Sir Robert Cotton, Ben Jonson and Michael Drayton. The scheme seems to have enjoyed Buckingham's support until 1624, but to have died with James I in 1625, the then new monarch, and magnificent art connoisseur, Charles I, being more interested in collecting antiquities and paintings than fostering literary scholarship. The dead rather than the living offered Charles a more secure and less troubling relationship.

The court of James I had looked less favourably on antiquarian study as it was unlikely to glorify the House of Stuart or praise the King's characteristic view of religion; such men would now only recall the achievements of the Plantagenets and Tudors and the former glories of a Catholic church. London was now not a milieu for that kind of learning mainly practised by country gentlemen and cathedral clergy; and moreover, as England succumbed to the onward march of Renaissance discovery, it was inevitable that scholarly interest should turn from that of its own country to the distinctly more tangible glories of ancient Greece and Rome. Such connoisseurs as Thomas Howard, Earl of Arundel, and the young Prince of Wales filled their corridors with marble statuary, and ran classical gold and silver coins and antique gems through their fingers as a poor man might as many halfpennies.

James I commissioned Inigo Jones to survey Stonehenge in 1620, and thereby reflected an awakening interest in prehistoric and Roman monuments as well as mediaeval remains. The rather startling conclusion of Jones that the stone circle was of Roman origin shows how primitive archaeology was in the early 1600s, but the profuse topographical and historical studies of the Stuart period, often enhanced by fine engravings, provide a unique record of the threatened and fast-disappearing past.

A decade later, Jones's addition of a fashionable classical portico at the west end of old St Paul's highlighted one way (along with neglect and natural disasters) in which threats to ancient buildings were increasingly present. War is no respecter of culture, and the Commonwealth brought also a deliberate programme of destruction, underwritten by the House of Commons which in 1641 ordered commissions around the realm whereby churches and chapels were systematically ransacked for the defacing, demolition and taking away of all superstitious and idolatrous images and pictures. Such iconoclasm ritually exorcized Catholicism and, as at the Dissolution, fuelled the fires of antiquarianism.

County histories were a popular subject for writing and research. Although their physical shapes were arbitrary, the products of historical accidents, they were generally at least a thousand years old, and their divisions the basis of English local government. These divisions might be cumbrous and artificial, but English counties had their own followings, especially among members of the families traditionally associated with their past governance, and this was a major part of their attraction to students of history. Excepting Yorkshire, Lincolnshire, and perhaps also Devon, each was of a manageable size for one individual to investigate fully: the topographer could familiarise himself with the lie of the land, the genealogist or herald with the noble families and their relationships, the gentry and the yeoman stock, the economic historian with the commercial, industrial and agricultural life of the area.

Today, of course, no such undertaking by one person is remotely possible – the accumulation of source material in such large quantities means that a team effort is the inescapable desideratum. But their authors were members of a scholarly profession which has no corresponding counterpart today, the nearest approach now being the use of the adjective 'antiquarian' in relation to old or rare books. That the profession was obsolescent casts light on our understanding of the needs of a past society and its differences from our own. Antiquarianism at that time was a sophisticated, even arcane, field of learning, and one which ploughed a relatively narrow furrow: county families, heraldry, genealogy and the descent of estates its mainstay, the overview of the whole of their topic of no relevance. The origins of institutions, laws, names, families and estates were sought from manuscripts, seals, coins, monuments, epitaphs and the representations of arms in stained glass and on tombs; the countryside and its historical features, for the most part, remained a closed book.

Many had studied or were practising law, or were gentlemen rabidly interested in their own pedigree, and therefore able to offer a pertinent service to a restricted clientele: those who owned land. They were frequently called upon in support of litigation, and their services were especially in demand after the dissolution of the monasteries, when a far-reaching redistribution of property forced landowners to seek evidence of title to lands held on the basis of ancestry.

The Elizabethan tradition was continued in, for example, William Burton's *Description of Leicestershire* of 1622 which had more to say about the Middle Ages than classical times, and John Weever's *Funeral Monuments* of 1631 which was inspired 'in part by the destructions of his own and former times'. The latter wrote with much sympathy for the period of his subject and a natural dislike for the destructiveness of the reformers of any age. William Somner published his *Antiquities of Canterbury* in 1640 just before the London city churches were devastated by Cromwell. Replete with genealogy and heraldry, it soon became an indispensable work of reference and a monument to Laudian antiquarianism. But not even the horrors of the civil war could change men's tastes and interests, and even the royal soldiers on their enforced marches across the countryside made time to record antiquarian observations. Stormy times did not preclude the gradual unravelling of the past as a communal activity.

Even at this early date antiquaries attracted scorn and derision – yes, they were members of the English world of learning, but also figures of fun; but moreover, ridicule implied recognition within society and its subject sufficiently well-known for the joke to be understood, on a par with other social classes such as the church and the law. John Earle, the future Bishop of Salisbury, published in 1628 his *Micro-cosmographie or a Piece of the World discovered in Essayes and Characters*. His barbed satires were based on the classical model of the Greek philosopher Theophrastus, and included 78 character sketches of which the Antiquary was the ninth:

> He is a man strangely thrifty of Time past, and an enemy indeed to his Maw, whence he fetches out many things when they are now all rotten and stinking. Hee is one that hath that unnatural disease to bee enamour'd of old age and wrinckles, and loves all things (as Dutchmen doe Cheese) the better for being mouldy and worme-eaten … A great admirer is he of the rust of old Monuments … Hee will goe you forty miles to see a Saints Well or a ruin'd Abbey … His estate consists much in shekels, and Roman Coynes … Beggars cozen him with musty things they have rak'd from dunghills … His chamber is commonly hung with strange Beasts skins, and is a kinde of Charnel-house of bones extraordinary … His grave do's not frighten him, for he ha's bene us'd to Sepulchers, and he likes Death the better, because it gathers him to his Fathers.

Ah, what truth in jest! Witty but compassionate, Earle epitomised the educated layman's view of antiquarianism as an incurable and hopeless affliction, a view that would stick for two centuries, and in no small measure because so many of its practitioners were indeed just like that.

By the outbreak of the Civil War in 1642, and even before, there were tensions at many levels of society: between institutions of government, between classes of citizens, between adherents of differing religious practices. Iconoclasm was rife, social change rapid, all ending in a world turned upside down in which the most threatened were the nobility and gentry, those traditional holders of political and social power and of wealth and influence, the very men who were writing and describing histories of places in which the dominant concern became the documentation of title and heritage. Thus Dugdale's study of his native Warwickshire read like a genealogical treatise, desperate to record monuments in marble, stone and glass that faced such an uncertain future.

Those who considered themselves, or were considered by others, as antiquaries, were in varying degrees really historians using exclusively documentary sources for their study of the past. Dugdale's *Antiquities of Warwickshire* of 1656 was a county history which would become a well-known type, whereas his *Monasticon* contained no architectural history, the concept of which was as yet unknown. Historian and antiquarian fields were quite separate and had been since the time of Leland and Camden, a fact underlain by the Elizabethan society that had called itself one of antiquaries. Renaissance historians, working with the legacy of classical antiquity, would have thanked no one to go out into muddy fields and collapsing ruins to pursue their enquiries.

By now the writing of county surveys and genealogy had begun to wane, and slowly gave way to a greater range of material produced by antiquarian scholars. With the benefit of the accumulations of books and manuscripts begun by John Leland and keenly continued by Matthew Parker and others, editions of ancient documents, surveys and investigations of pre-Conquest inhabitants and institutions, derived chiefly from the study of such documents, were now being printed.

The business of collecting, classifying and interpreting the remains of the past was not the same as that of the historian, who although also concerned with the past, had different goals in dealing with it. The Middle Ages had produced chroniclers whose narratives merely related reigns and annual events as they happened, with no interest in cause and effect. The writing of real history demanded analysis of the past, such analysis to be shown in a narrative informed by comprehension of the motives and results of those whose lives it treated. It would be didactic and offer an extension into the past where lessons could be learnt from human experience – meat indeed for those who sought to lead, for history was made by the heads of nations, of churches, of armies, and of monasteries. Future generals and princes would find moral instruction in the study of the moral significance of past events.

Small wonder, then, that antiquarian scholarship had been considered by some for rather too long as inferior. As far back as 1574 Thomas Blundeville had remarked in his treatise on history-writing that 'I cannot tell whyther I may deride, or rather pittie the great follie of those which having consumed all theyr lyfe in histories, doe know nothing in the ende, but the discents, genealoges, and petygrees, of noble men, and when such a King or Emperour raigned, & such lyke stuffe.' History could no longer be presented in lists, tables and bald transcripts of documents.

By Camden's time what was needed were new approaches to the records and the publication of accurate original records; society looked for a reassessment of institutional origins and privileges, and here the antiquary and historian coalesced in the genealogist and herald who could affirm the standing of families, both present and future, in the social hierarchy. The College of Arms, now well into its second century, slipped effortlessly into an enhanced role as official guardian and authenticator of pedigrees and arms – from now on heraldry and antiquarianism would become almost synonymous, and men like Camden and Dugdale both wrote and rose high in the heraldic hierarchy.

In 1638 William Dugdale, Sir Christopher Hatton, Sir Thomas Shirley and Sir Edward Dering signed an agreement to work together at the a meeting of the antiquarian association formed by the last-mentioned, which Dering called *Antiquitas Rediviva*; all were gentlemen in the prime of life, comfortable on their own estates and experienced in the then current forms of research. A dozen and more points tabulated the aims of the society: mutual help; inventories of notes and books; common consent over inviting others and the lending of items; and the gathering of all possible material relating to each man's home county. The heraldic work was apportioned: Hatton was to collect and register rolls of arms and books of arms; Shirley would collect and register patents and copies of new grants of arms; to Dering fell the gathering and comparing of a full and complete book of arms; and Dugdale oversaw the collecting and copying of all armorial seals (noting the dimensions) and deeds.

The exigencies of civil war made travel difficult in the extreme, but Dugdale, as a member of the College of Heralds, was more fortunate in that he had the gifts and opportunity for original work, and with the benefit of royal warrants was able to journey around the country and gain admission to garrisons in order to make direct observations of antiquities. Enthusiastic and meticulous, he was nevertheless a lesser scholar than Roger Dodsworth, with whom he had collaborated on the latter's *Monasticon Anglicanum*, taking over after Dodsworth's death not as proof-corrector but rather as editor of the entire work to which he added his name. But the work had little appeal in Puritan England, and especially to its intended recipients, the country gentlemen, who were less than keen to have the histories of their former monastic estates made public.

But *Antiquitas Rediviva* was doomed not to survive even though other learned men continued to convene less formal meetings. The incipient Royal Society saw the light of day in the early 1640s when men of science felt that, 'We are coldly drawne into discourses of Antiquities, who have scarce time before us to comprehend new things, or make out learned novelties'.

There are sporadic references to revivals of antiquarian meetings mentioned by, among others, Ashmole and Ducarel, but whether formal or not cannot be declared with certainty. Yet most certainly there were enough suitably-minded individuals for such proceedings to have taken place; Gough in his 1770 edition of *Archaeologia* itemised a starry cast: Roger Dodsworth, Sir William Dugdale, William Somner, Sir Henry Spelman, John Selden, Archbishop Ussher, Elias Ashmole, Anthony Wood and Abraham Wheeloc. After the restoration of the monarchy in 1660, historical students could breathe more easily again, and the foundations of many types of British archaeology were now soon to be laid through the tireless exertions of squires, lawyers, doctors and the leisured clergy who beavered away at unlocking the problems and splendours of England's past. The Fire of London of 1666 was a cogent reminder that even monuments known to all were not imperishable.

The immense effort of recovery in England after the Civil War was not entirely in learning's favour, for the present was so absorbing that there was less time for the past; antiquarian nostalgia succumbed to the problem of re-establishing both tradition and prosperity. Nevertheless, the period from the Restoration to the advent of the house of Hanover saw an unprecedented and prolific spate of mediaeval research, and a spate which did not exclude Anglo-Saxon studies or Anglo-Norman history. Editions of mediaeval texts were many, and clerical scholars did not stint on cataloguing and describing ecclesiastical antiquities. Stonehenge became again the subject of much enquiry and even controversy, some claiming Danish, some Roman, and others Phoenician, origins for the portentous circle of stones. John Aubrey was the first to ascribe it to the Druids, but never published his argument. In 1663 Dr Charleton presented to the Royal Society its first antiquarian contribution – a plan of the Avebury stones, and thus displayed the scientific spirit at work in the archaeological field. The essays of the time of the Elizabethan college were now left behind in favour of investigations far closer to contemporary fieldwork, as men were more concerned with objects, not documents, and tried to interpret them in what we can recognise as a modern spirit.

Notwithstanding such progress, the earlier methods of enquiry had not quite entirely been left behind, for a county history such as Robert Thoroton's *Antiquities of Nottinghamshire* of 1677 carried on the Elizabethan tradition remarkably unchanged, and demonstrated that the impetus towards writing county histories was far from extinguished. John Aubrey gathered together in his native Wiltshire a coterie of country gentlemen to collect material for such a work but was frustrated by their inertia. Ploughing a lonely furrow, he followed the limitations of his time when describing a church by looking at its monuments rather than the architecture unless it was a building of particular richness. Ultimately wearied by the size of his task, he carried on undaunted by general ignorance of, and scorn for, his labour.

After the Civil War, the importance of the great collections as well as the need to take care of them was fully recognized. Antiquaries were admitted to the collections of the Cottonian Library, which had by then come to the state, to the King's Library, to the Harleian collections and to the stores of the Inner Temple and the College of Arms. Catalogues of the Cottonian and Bodleian Libraries were published, and bibliographical descriptions of private collections and book-sales were circulated in manuscript. Men like Humfrey Wanley drew attention to questions of ownership and provenance in their descriptions of various collections. With the Restoration and rise of the scientific Royal Society, the need for a new Society of Antiquaries began to be felt.

The old school still naturally viewed antiquarian pursuits as trivial in comparison with the historians working in the grand manner. Sir William Temple argued in 1695 that history should not concern itself with matters that 'neither argue the Virtues or Vices of Princes nor Serve for Example or Instruction to Posterity, which are the great ends of History and ought to be the chief Care of all historians.' Alas, this excluded charters and chronicles, antiquaries and genealogists, and even more definitely Roman pots and coins and inscriptions, all irrelevant trivia, and as useless to the cause as were ancient Britons with their stone tools and crude monuments which offered nothing as an example of instruction to posterity. Polite learning had no use for material culture – the advent of archaeology and prehistory would arrive with such luminaries as Bacon, Gresham and the Virtuosi of the Royal Society, who were initially scorned but ultimately carried the intellectual day with their empirical approach to phenomena, natural or man-made, and objective observation and interpretation, epitomised by classification and ordering, that is, taxonomy. It was in such a climate that a part of established antiquarianism could now break away and move tentatively towards a new discipline, which the late 19th century would rename archaeology.

Chapter 3
Birth, Education and Marriage

The birth of a first child is always an occasion for much rejoicing, and so it must have been when Bryan and Mary Faussett's first child and eldest son, to be named after his father, was born 30 October 1720 at Heppington and baptised in Nackington parish church, a short walk across the fields, three days later. Little can they have known what lay in store for their heir – the first Faussett to go to university, the first to be ordained, the first antiquary, and one to be remembered after his death for a short but frenetic antiquarian career which would make him locally important and, with the efforts of others long after his death, worthy of future national remembrance.

We know from his father's account books that there was a predilection for exotic animals in the family, a fact which almost led to Faussett's early demise. Shortly after his marriage a family friend gave Bryan senior a young monkey, but a year later when the infant Bryan had arrived, it was fully grown and characteristically mischievous. As the baby lay in his nursery cradle he was snatched away by simian arms and thrown on the fire. Hearing his screams the truant nurse rushed in and grabbed him, the baby apparently none the worse for such an ordeal. The monkey escaped through a dormer onto the roof, to be given another chance by its master. But the very next day 'Jacko' was seen on the roof with the baby in his arms again; a verbal rebuke with the shaking of fists ensued before it skulked back down into the nursery. The footman was summoned, poker in hand, his fondness for the son and heir overcoming any hesitation about using such a bludgeon, with which the monkey received a fatal blow to its skull, and upon which the infant Bryan slid down to the floor unharmed. (In the 1850s the animal's remains were discovered under an old walnut tree near the house, and positively identified by its skull displaying the marks of the footman's unswerving blow.) Thus ends a colourful story long preserved in the family, and recalled by Godfrey Godfrey-Faussett in 1886 when describing a visit to Cairo.

As early as June 1730, when not even ten, he watched the young Cromwell Mortimer digging on Swadling Down at Chartham, a half-mile or so south of the parish church, an experience which clearly early kindled what would be an increasing passion for antiquarianism (his future 'hobby horse'), although at this age he was in no way a child prodigy. The location was above the 200-foot contour along one of the innumerable slopes and summits of the rolling chalk landscape which contained so many Anglo-Saxon cemeteries, and had been briefly investigated in an earlier period by Heneage Finch, Earl of Winchilsea, FSA (1657-1726). The excavation, admittedly brief and unsatisfactory, was under the auspices of Sir Charles Fagg of nearby Mystole House, a well-known country squire of the time, who had encouraged the meeting after some workmen had accidentally unearthed a virtually complete skeleton in a grave cut into the chalk bedrock whilst engaged in widening the road in the previous year. Sir Charles then became curious to examine the 100-odd barrows (Faussett, in 1773, said 'about eighty') which stood close together in the vicinity along the top of the hill, called by the locals the 'Danes' Banks', and Dr Cromwell Mortimer was called in to excavate.

Mortimer (*c.*1693-1752) had started life in Westminster as 'an impertinent, assuming empiric physician' who had introduced the novel practices (to the disgust of his fellows) of offering free medicines at consultations, and the treatment of certain types of patients at an annual fixed fee. He became an FSA in 1734 and in the last few years of his life, as one of the first council members, worked for the incorporation of the society, as well as being the second secretary of the Royal Society.

He compiled a dull, laboured and densely written four-page account of the proceedings at Chartham. The copy manuscript[1] is enhanced by six watercolour plates of the finds and a good, coloured sketch-map of the site, measured and drawn by Jared Hill, a member of the Canterbury-based family of surveyors, who subdivided the 100 or so barrows into 'great' (of which half-a-dozen, 33 feet in diameter), 'middle' (about fifty, 23 feet) and 'little' (the balance, 13 feet).

Mortimer opened about 26 barrows but described the contents of only six of varying sizes, which he labelled as graves A-F; of the remainder he recorded merely that all contained a single skeleton lying east-west. His account is notable only for its excellent technical descriptions, especially of the jewelled gold brooches, one of which is the earliest known detailed account of a minor piece of antiquity excavated in Britain. Notable, alas, for other reasons were his comments that the graves were those of soldiers killed in battle between Caesar and the ancient Britons – comments that both James Douglas and Faussett would savage later on.

A fine coloured drawing of the Chartham antiquities was made much later by Faussett's son and added to the blank pages at the end of his father's excavation journal. The grave-goods included urns, glass vessels, shield-bosses, brooches, pendants, keys, buckles, pins, beads, spear-heads, knives and a pair of shears, along

---

[1] British Library MS Addl 45,663

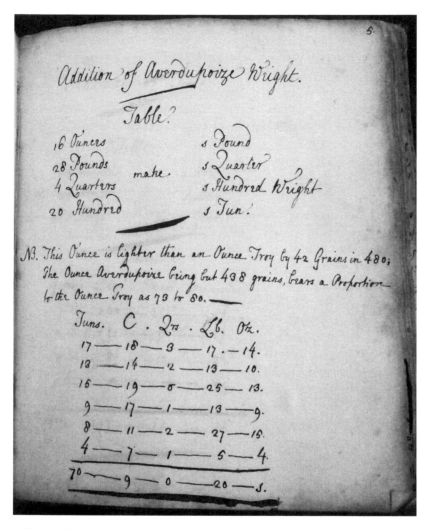

Figure 9. Early mathematical exercises in Faussett's own hand – the sign of a keen and ordered mind.
(Reproduced by kind permission of Mr Christopher Miller.)

with a moderately rich and varied range of Anglo-Saxon jewellery comprising a composite disc-brooch, gold and amethyst drop-pendants, and amethyst beads, the likes of which Faussett was destined later to see in far greater numbers and immeasurably finer quality.

Faussett received a grammar school education according to the old country fashion, probably at Ashford where he sent his own sons. By virtue of his descent from the Heyman family of Sellindge who had intermarried with the Godfreys, he was entitled to an exhibition at the King's School, Canterbury, but there is no positive record of his attendance there. However, he did later join the King's School Feast Society in 1750, the majority of whose members were former scholars but which also included local notables, gentry and clergy (such as John Lewis and Edward Hasted). He was a regular attender, frequently signed the minutes, missed very few years between admittance and 1770, and was one of the three stewards in 1752. The society's annual meeting was in September, advertised in the local newspapers, and billed as the 'Anniversary Meeting of the Gentlemen educated at the King's School'; a note added that 'the company of any Gentleman who is willing to encourage the Charity (tho' not educated at the School) will be very welcome.' The normal proceedings included a sermon in the cathedral, usually given by a former pupil, a dinner with speeches, and the business part which involved collecting money to fund exhibitions for boys at university. Faussett was clearly a conscientious member, although as he never preached, it seems probable that he was not a former pupil.

He went up to University College, Oxford, in October 1738 with ten guineas in his pocket, a gift from his doting father, and entered the college as a member on 8 December. As an undergraduate, Faussett's academic ability gave no cause for especial comment; indeed he received rather more attention for his appellation of 'the handsome commoner', an opinion with which Hudson's portrait of him does not disagree. He graduated as a commoner in 1742, presumably having studied not only divinity but also classics and philosophy, this course the natural precursor to the present *Literae Humaniores* degree. We cannot tell how much work this actually involved, as the form of the examination was then quite different in being wholly oral and somewhat lax and corrupt in its administration and conduct, so that a graduand might do as little or as much as he chose.

A notebook of around this time has a dozen pages in Faussett's distinctively legible handwriting showing mathematical exercises and tables, the addition of weights and sums of money, and the calculation of time and calendrical dates – all signs of a keen mind and the future necessities of a scientific career. Added in later on are recipes for assorted kinds of minor medical complaints, an inoculation diet, and, more presciently, a poultice for the gout, Faussett's lifelong bugbear to come.

The automatic MA was conferred in 1745, shortly after which followed an episode which would gently shake his young gentleman's roots and threaten his keenly sought fellowship of All Souls' College (he had already become a fellow of University College in June 1744). This signal honour had suddenly been called into question for a somewhat mundane, if colourful, reason.

In 1743 Faussett was attempting to win a much-coveted fellowship of All Souls, based on 'founder's blood', that is, his maternal relationship to Henry Chichele, Archbishop of Canterbury who had founded All Souls in 1438. Faussett persuaded the authorities of his sufficiently direct kinship to that (inevitably unmarried) prelate by producing a pedigree chart stretching back to Sir Robert Chichele, Lord Mayor of London and brother of the archbishop. The document subsequently passed to Edward Hasted, the great Kentish historian for his work on that county's families, who inscribed it 'Pedigree of Godfrey & Faussett in the late Rev. Bryan Faussett's own handwriting'. The old-style drop-circle ('*pied de gru*') chart is embellished with coloured shields and entitled:

A True and exact copy of the consanguinity of Bryan Faussett to Henry Chicheley, Lord Archbishop of Canterbury and Founder of All Souls College in Oxford, as taken out by the Heralds in the City of London 22 July 1743, and afterwards delivered to the Warden and Fellows of the said College.[2]

From Robert Chichele the descent is to Sir Thomas Kemp of Olantigh near Wye, John Toke of Godinton who died in 1656 aged 80 and was buried at Great Chart near Ashford, and then several further Toke generations down to Nicholas Toke of Godinton whose daughter Mary married Thomas Godfrey of Buckwell in Boughton Aluph. Their son was Henry Godfrey of Heppington, he and his wife Catherine Pittis being the maternal grandparents of the antiquary. Faussett's parents had been involved in this enterprise, and understandably, as his mother was the direct Chichele descendant, and had attended an attorney in Canterbury to supply the appropriate genealogical details and swear a declaration as to their veracity. The pedigree was duly registered at the College of Arms that same year, and another one of 1746, mainly concerned with the Toke ancestry, shows Bryan junior as an elected fellow of All Souls.

The path to a fellowship, however, would be far from direct. An allegation was brought before the college authorities that Faussett was not 'a person of a chaste and virtuous life and conversation', and that in 1742 he had been rusticated for six months on the grounds of having harboured a prostitute in his chambers at University College. Faussett duly marshalled his forces for the appeal, and the file[3] opened with sundry friends and college or city officials giving testimonials of his good character, including the Rev'd John Gould Floyer, a fellow of Wadham College, who described Faussett as 'a true friend and well wisher to Protestant liberty'. But the Rev'd Joseph Wood was more truthful in stating that he, in February 1742, along with one of the proctors, had examined a woman of ill fame, whom they had with some difficulty eventually apprehended, and who accused two young gentlemen of having entertained her in their rooms. She revealed the name of one, who was duly rusticated, but was ignorant as to the identity of the other, having little recall of his person and chambers. The master of the college, Dr Cashman, interviewed a number of suspects, but secured insufficient evidence to accuse any one individual.

The accusation was corroborated by Griffin Higgs, a journeyman cook of University College, who unflinchingly recalled that just after Christmas 1742 there had been a public report around the city and college telling how Faussett had been discovered *in flagrante delicto*; and meanwhile, John Swinburn Esq, also of the college, remembered with painful clarity and in less than flattering language that Faussett 'had a criminal intercourse with a strumpet'.

In March 1743 Samuel Pegge, Vicar of Godmersham, wrote to Nicholas Toke concerning the affair, because at Godinton House, the Toke seat, were the very

---

[2]   British Library: MS Addl 5520
[3]   Lambeth Palace Library: VVI/4/5/16

documents and wills which might elucidate the true family connection. He thought fit to mention the attendant circumstances:

> Mr Faussett's design at All Souls miscarried through an accident entirely unforeseen, which I am very sorry for; but his Father has consented to continue him his allowance till he takes his Master's degree, in which I think he judges perfectly right, though amongst friends he is extremely angry and displeased.[4]

Faussett wrote to Mr Pegge from University College in October 1743, lamenting that a particular visitation containing the requisite genealogical proofs had been lost in the Great Fire; he had now received a copy of it, but it would not count as true evidence – a birth in 1496, before the time of 'Harry 8', would not have been recorded as parochial registers were not instituted until 1538. He added:

> I wrote to my Father directly, but doubt not but he is so vext at our disappointment, that he won't give himself time coolly to consider what is best to be done in order to prove it.[5]

Faussett was clearly worried about an issue of huge importance to him, and not helped by being out of favour with the college authorities as well as with his father. The fellowship now looked distinctly uncertain, as the warden and fellows of All Souls had rejected him *en bloc*, and the appeal had been fixed to take place before no less a person than John Potter, Archbishop of Canterbury, and *ex officio* visitor to the college. Francis Taylor, a senior fellow of University College, was the man who had sent Faussett down in 1742 and had also tried to block the conferring of a master's degree. He declared that,

> ... the said Faussett acknowledged that he had undergone a Punishment for some Ill Behaviour and that he complained to the Deponent, that, as there were many other persons equally guilty with himself of the Fact for which he was so punished, He thought it very hard that he alone should be censured while many others were suffered to escape.[6]

Two years later in September 1745, the matter still dragging on, he wrote to his maternal relative Nicholas Toke, then a barrister at Essex Street in the Strand, highly apologetic at having bothered them with so many requests for the pedigree:

> Kind Sir, It is not without the greatest reluctance after the trouble I have already given you that I find myself again under a Necessity of begging your Assistance. The 3 years since the Commission of the Fault for which I was refused a Testimonium (and for which I have since undergone such a series of Miseries) is now at an End; and the Fellows have all promised to do all that they can to assist me.

---

[4] KHLC: U967/F1
[5] *ibid.*
[6] Lambeth Palace Library: VV1/4/5/16

Faussett thereupon told the college that he intended to appear before them that year, but further obstacles were flung back at him – properly attested extracts of ancient records were imperative, and nothing less:

> For my own part I am heartily ashamed to have been the cause of so much trouble, but hope they have now nothing more to object against.[7]

The process of an appeal was now the logical next step, but this was hardly something to be undertaken on his own. Paternal support in kind or in money was crucial. He continued:

> And whether or no my Father will support an appeal I don't know; for I never had the favour of a Line from him since my last Miscarriage; and what is worse I have the greatest Reason in the world to fear, he will never be reconciled to me. Thus by only one false step have I forever lost the affection of a Father whom (as he himself will own) I never, either before or since, offended. All Entreaties, both of my own and of my Friends have been in vain. Tis true he has hitherto supported me; but after Christmas he is determined to withdraw my allowance and leave me to myself. This does not however much dishearten me; for, as I flatter myself I have made no very ill use of the Opportunities I have had of improving Myself at Oxford, I doubt not of getting into Orders, and of providing (however meanly I must be contented) for Myself.[8]

Ordination, then, was uppermost in his mind, and regardless, it would seem, of future poverty. His father was now 55 – how far off was his inheritance? Was he prepared until then to live the impecunious life of a curate, or perhaps, with luck and the college fellowship secured, find himself a good parish?

The following month he wrote directly to Toke at Godinton to relay sad news:

> I have just this moment received a letter from Mr Pegge wherein I am sorry to find my Father refuses to stand an Appeal. However, as to my standing, as I have already gone so far, it will be thought very ridiculous in me should I recede from my Resolution. And as it is a thing which I have so long set my heart upon, and the only hopes I have now left to regain my Father's affection or (should I miss of that) of becoming able to support myself without his assistance; I have determined to see it out.

The election was looming close and he asked Toke to supply the necessary documents. His signature revealed his nervous state – 'I am, kind Sir, with the greatest respect your infinitely obliged humble servant, Bryan Faussett.' Samuel Pegge wrote to Toke shortly afterwards on 25 November 1745:

> Mr Faussett absolutely refuses to be any ways concerned in his son's affair. I wrote this morning to Mr Faussett at Oxford to tell him I did not approve of borrowing money in

---

[7] KHLC: U967/F1
[8] *ibid.*

the manner he proposes for the carrying on the Appeal, for the better way would be to borrow it of his Father and give his Father his Bond for it, which I fancied the Father would not be against.[9]

Faussett's father was resolute: he would lend no money, not send the required family will, and in short, do nothing at all, displeased in the extreme that his son had tried to borrow money elsewhere without consulting him. Nicholas Toke, as a barrister and family member, now found himself in a difficult position in trying to act as go-between for father and son. Faussett senior had by now been persuaded to contribute to the inevitable legal fees attending the appeal, over which Toke wrote:

> The money ordered by Mr Faussett, the Father, did not satisfie the Proctor, and I had some difficulty to persuade Him to proceed. I am afraid there will be a large bill to pay; and the first Proctor had between £20 and £30. I am sorry to see that Mr Faussett is still so angry, and that in your opinion it is not without some reason. The son says He is not conscious of having done any thing lately to offend, and that the money now sent is the only money he has received from his Father since his Allowance at Midsummer. I thank Ye for your Advice about the[genealogical] papers; and have already taken care to transmit ye evidence to my Posterity. But unless College alters in many Respects, I shall not send them a son of mine.' The next thing they entered upon was the affidavits as to Mr Fosset's character, and the only charge against him was the old story of the girl; and that was supported by nothing, but Hearsay and Report, and even that not particular in any one Circumstance whatsoever. In so much that I am surprised that so much regard was shown to the affidavits, I am sure they would have been scouled in any other court of Justice.
>
> P.S. Since I finished this letter, Fausset brought me your letter to him, and I am sorry to find the Father so angry still with his son. If he will turn his son loose into the world, the least surely He can do is to set him clear in it first. This Affair has cost so much that he must soon be in jail if the Father will not assent.

The collecting of the said ancestral evidence for the appeal had, however, proceeded apace, and Samuel Pegge was careful to tell Toke that 'Mr Faussett desires above all things that care may be taken that the Archbishop of Canterbury be desired to hear this cause in a summary way.'

Faussett had been bound in the sum of £50 pending the judgment which opened in January 1746 and took some three months to resolve. Shortly before its outcome, he wrote heart-searchingly about his father again:

> … my Father still continues to be so averse to me. If this is the case, I am heartily sorry I ever took the Appeal in hand, as almost the only end for which I undertook it (namely the hopes of bringing my Father for a reconciliation) will still be unanswered. Our hearing yesterday lasted eight hours, and the Archbishop has not as yet determined the affair,

[9] *ibid.*

having took till Monday sennight to consider of it. The event to be sure is very uncertain, but I think I have very great reason to promise myself success.[10]

Indeed he would not be disappointed. He had 13 affidavits in his favour against five brought by the college. The archbishop had examined the carefully constructed pedigree and read the laboriously copied mediaeval wills and monumental inscriptions relating to the Moyle, Toke and other families, and then pronounced that here was no barrier to a fellowship. He then moved to the graver charge of the reason for the rustication, and was pleased to bring in a judgment in the defendant's favour, because, in his opinion, the defamation of Faussett's character had rested solely on the evidence and declaration of a woman of bad fame. Faussett must have smiled inwardly at this pronouncement, even though no costs were given against the Warden and Fellows, and the appeal cost him personally £200. On 28 April 1746 he was, finally, admitted a fellow of All Souls.

On that same day Faussett wrote once more to Nicholas Toke:

I was this morning admitted in my fellowship at All Souls. The Warden and Fellows have carried themselves but coolly to me, till today; when the Warden was pleased to behave in a much better way then he has hitherto done; and has put me in a much better Room than I had expected he would.[11]

But the election had not solved quite everything, for he continued:

But necessity obliges me. I have not a Crown in my Pocket, and was even obliged to borrow Money of my Friends in London, to pay my Bill at the Inn, and to bring me down; the money I had of you not being sufficient. Immediately after my going to All Souls, I find I have fees and one thing or another to pay to about the tune of 8 pound; and at University about 2 Pound more to my Bedmaker &c which would be scandalous to leave unpaid.[12]

He asked for £10 from Toke, unable to procure it elsewhere,

… for till I have it I can't shew my face at All Souls … I wrote to my Father this day, but durst not mention a word of Money to him, knowing How much it would irritate him against me. I have been laid up for about a week with a violent rash, which by venturing out too soon, I struck into my blood.[13]

Fellowship and finances presumably sorted, he could now return to work. Studies for his second degree involved church duties as well, although Oxford degrees were lax by today's standards and he could in effect do as little or as much as he chose. Clearly, though, he was well versed in Latin and the classics generally, and had

---

[10] Oxford Bodleain Library: MS Eng. Lett. d 43
[11] KHLC: U967/F1
[12] *ibid.*
[13] *ibid.*

also familiarised himself with human anatomy, a fact which shows through in the comments he would make in his notebooks on the contents of graves, where he was constantly alert to such matters as tooth wear and tooth loss, and the reabsorption of sockets as a factor in the ageing process. The Divinity School then stood in the Old Schools Quad, just a few steps from the School of Medicine, and it a safe assumption that someone of his acute intellectual interests would have wanted to learn about the mental, physical and spiritual aspects of man.

A family story relates that Faussett was once engaged to take the Sunday duty at a nearby village (possibly Horspath near Headington). On his way there he saw a squirrel's drey with several young in it, and amused himself by taking one and placing it in his deep tail-coat pocket, but then climbing into the pulpit he reached for his sermon papers and received a sharp bite to his finger. The offending creature was rapidly extracted, accompanied by an unclerical exclamation – an awkward start for a young future deacon, especially as the squirrel fell on the clerk's head and then bounded squealing into the congregation.

Whilst pursuing his classical studies Faussett became conspicuous, even in died-in-the-wool Tory Oxford, as a staunch Jacobite. His estates to which he was heir had been considerably diminished by the vengeance of parliament on his great-great-grandfather Sir Thomas Godfrey, whose fidelity to Charles I and defeat by Fairfax in the ill-fated Kentish rising had not yet been entirely forgotten in a man seemingly proud of the loss of the king and whose descendant would give free rein to political enthusiasm over the 1745-6 uprising. Also at this time Bryan senior was, despite strict surveillance by government officials, daily convening secret meetings of the local gentry at Heppington to discuss how the men of Kent might best welcome and assist Prince Charles Edward on his southward march, all the while aided and abetted by one Brett, the prince's archbishop-elect, who on these occasions assumed the insignia and ceremonies which he would normally enjoy at higher meetings.

Jacobite proclivities ran as strongly in the son's blood as they did in the father's, for whilst such cabals unfurled in rural Kent, he, along with other fellows of All Souls, was endeavouring at Oxford to organise a volunteer corps for the Young Pretender, and 'not to be behind his family ... nightly, with every glass, toasted King James on bared and bended knee'. No doubt many in the university and elsewhere looked on with bemused fascination at such proceedings.

One might wonder why Faussett took holy orders at all, other than as a victim of the unfortunate system imposed by collegiate and family reasons, rather than from a genuine vocation. A university education would have been the wholly natural precedent to ordination, yet there were no clergy ancestors, and the whole tendency of his mind was that of a dedicated scholar and antiquary rather than that of a keen churchman, who later would sincerely wish to withdraw from the profession for which he felt himself unfitted. Correspondence and papers he has left us in tolerable abundance, but here is no Kilvert's diary: there is barely a mention of religious fervour, let alone activity; no stories of parish life or the parishioners who were his nominal mainstay; all relates to genealogy, heraldry, numismatics and archaeology – the satisfactions of a keen mind greedy for intellectual stimulation and amusement.

The procession from graduate to deacon to clergyman was an unusual one for the heir of an estate, the honoured tradition reserving that employment for a third or succeeding son, and especially unusual for one whose father was comfortably off and settled almost within a stone's throw of the first cathedral city of England. Everything, surely, beckoned towards the comfortable life of an English gentleman, where he might indulge his interests and tastes to his heart's content, unencumbered by the tiresome and ill-paid duties of a succession of lowly curacies which were surely to be his before securing a parish of his own. Friends in high places, which he must have had, did not in this situation come to his rescue. Did Faussett really consider himself so badly off that he saw the church as an easy path to at least some sort of nominal income?

In the 18th century the clergy were more of a profession than the lawyers, doctors and civil servants of the day, and more or less the only one to have supervisory and disciplinary procedures. Less divided by the divisions of 'high' and 'low' churchmen than they are today, they commanded a broad national presence, standing at the forefront of intellectual, political and cultural life (the number of clerical publications at this period, covering a multitude of topics from science and politics to classics, history, antiquities, literature, music and the arts, theology and natural history, is almost beyond counting).

For the most part the clergy were conscientious, and the very fact that there is little evidence to the contrary is perhaps indicative that most people were content with their parish priest. The stereotypical view of the pastorally negligent fox-hunting parson has probably existed now for far too long – their vital role in admonishing parishioners and acting as reconcilers ran alongside being bankers, medical carers and upholders of the law, as well as key agents in disseminating religious knowledge through their rôle in catechising, promoting schools, and preaching.

Political aspirations aside, there seems to have been no other impediment to Faussett being ordained deacon on 25 May 1746 at Christ Church, Oxford, by his future ally Thomas Secker, a man of comparatively humble origins who had been educated as a dissenter before conforming to the established church, then rose to become Bishop of Bristol in 1735, Bishop of Oxford in 1737, and Archbishop of Canterbury in 1758. A year later Secker ordained Faussett priest on 14 June 1747, again in Christ Church. Two more years would follow at Oxford, Faussett undertaking sundry ecclesiastical work and no doubt looking around anxiously for preferment through one of his contacts.

This came in his presentment as Vicar of Alberbury in Shropshire, a remote rural parish to the west of Shrewsbury, on 9 November 1747. He arrived there within the month and seems to have served his time without the assistance of a curate, as the registers show a regular sequence of his own signatures. The living was, not surprisingly, in the gift of All Souls, and the transition to the far west probably a smooth, if tediously long one. The vicarage was said to be worth £40 annually in 1655 and produced gross profits of £51 15s. 6d. in around 1700. It was augmented by a grant of £400 in 1727, half of which was granted by Queen Anne's Bounty to meet a benefaction of £100 and a similar sum by subscription. At some point before 1850 the annual value was £187, but until the 18th century the greater part of the income was derived from small tithes which, together with herbage produced £26 11s. 4d., plus a further £16 3s. from Easter duties in 1700. None of these figures increased significantly during Faussett's tenure.

His Shropshire incumbency seems to have been pleasant if unremarkable, for apart from the parish register entries, the sole other tangible record of Faussett's residence at Alberbury is his recording of his herbage payments for 1748-9.[14] But how happy could Faussett be so far from Oxford, from London, and from his beloved Heppington? His incumbency there would last, astonishingly, until he resigned it on 20 September 1765, just four months after he had been collated to the rectorship of Monks Horton, ten miles south down the Roman Stone Street from Heppington. But of that 18-year tenure of Alberbury, just three were actually spent in the parish, the remaining period, typically, farmed out to two curates named Price and Roberts – an uncomfortable and impecunious position which Faussett himself would come to know only too well upon his return to Kent. If he could but have known it, the vicarial income in Shropshire was not that different from what he would receive as a Kentish curate.

But before returning to Kent, he would be married to Elizabeth Curtois, the daughter of the Rev'd Rowland Curtois, a well-descended Lincolnshire clergyman whose family had held the living of Branston near Lincoln in an unbroken succession from the reign of Charles II to at least the 1880s. All the evidence suggests that he was continuously happy with 'Tetsy' (we often give nicknames to those whom we love), but the bride brought little or no dowry, a fact that would plague Faussett for much of his married life. After ordination he had taken up residence as vicar in Alberbury, for his accounts tell us that his wedding journey back to Oxford cost him £2 4s. 0d.

The couple were married on 15 November 1748 in the imposing 15th-century chapel of Magdalen College by the Rev'd Dr Thomas West, fellow of that college. The groom was described as Vicar of Alberbury and Fellow of All Souls, the bride as a spinster of Benningworth in Lincolnshire. Faussett must have been the envy of his fellow dons in his rapid transition from bachelor to preferment to marriage. He naturally chose Oxford rather than remote Shropshire for the ceremony to suit his academic connections with the city, but it was also the case that both the bride's father and grandfather had been educated at Oxford.

The Curtois pedigree opens with Robert Curtois of Lincoln ('plebs'), whose son John was born there c.1651, educated at Lincoln College, Oxford, and Rector of Branston from 1680 until his death in 1719. His son Rowland, future father-in-law to the antiquary,

---

[14] Shropshire Record Office: 4369/Ti/2

was born at Branston in 1683, also went to Lincoln College, and was Vicar of Hainton to the south-east of Market Rasen, as well as the nearby Hatton, from 1708 until his death *c.*1723. His younger brother John, born around 1689, succeeded to the rectorship of Branston after his father's death, and to that of Hatton after his brother's death.

Rowland Curtois married Elizabeth Parish in the remote easterly parish of Well, north of Spilsby, in 1713. She was the daughter and heiress of George Parish, sometime vicar of Colsterworth, between Grantham and Stamford. Of their three children, the eldest was the only daughter, Elizabeth, born at Hainton in 1714. After her father's death she often stayed with Walker cousins at Oxford, where she probably met her future husband. After nearly four decades of a happy marriage, she died suddenly at Heppington from a paralytic stroke on 22 January 1787, 'expiring without a struggle or groan at 3pm'.

Her two brothers both continued the priestly tradition. John Curtois (1715-1801) held several scattered parishes during a long life, dying at Irnham near Colsterworth. In his will[15] he left £300 to his nephew by marriage Bryan Faussett, the attorney of Sittingbourne, son of the antiquary. His brother Grove Curtois (1721-1790), also educated at Trinity Hall, Cambridge, held a handful of scattered parishes, no doubt in plurality, dying as Rector of Benningworth and South Willingham on 27 December 1790, when he merited a mention in the *Gentleman's Magazine* as being 'of advanced age'.

We owe that younger brother Grove Curtois a huge debt for the considerable amount of light he throws on family and antiquarian matters. His evidently lonely and unrewarding parson's life in rural Lincolnshire gave him ample time to write to his fellow cleric and brother-in-law at Heppington, from which correspondence some 40 letters survive, not all dated, from *c.*1750 to 1765. One feels some pity for him, for he was clearly often enmeshed in difficult relationships when acting as Faussett's vicarious landlord. One tenant, referred to as 'an abusive and shuffling man named Oates', was behind with his payments: and clearly hard work to oversee: 'Since my undertaking the management of your affairs he has sent me half a dozen of the most uncharitable, ill-natured scurrilous letters that were ever penned.' The tenant had recently married 'a maiden gentlewoman of 50 worth a fortune of £900', but still remained obstinate about his debts. Curtois then commented:

> As to the houses you must, I am afraid, be contented with what Rent can be got for them; I have endeavoured more than once to dispose of them but all to no purpose for want of a Tithe. Would a Bond of indemnification, if it be worth while, answer the end?

Meanwhile, Mrs Parish, Faussett's mother-in-law, had died an intestate widow, and Curtois thought that Faussett might recover his money by Elizabeth taking out a grant of administration on the estate.

Curtois was next taken aback at Faussett's reply concerning money seemingly owed to him, for Curtois had intended repaying as soon as he was able and lamented that

---

[15] TNA: PROB11/1382

I did not imagine being threatened as it was my own free gift to your wife, but my sister is more to blame than you, knowing our affairs better, in letting you write after the manner you did (a manner very unbecoming you to write or me to hear, and which if opportunity offers, I'll very warmly resent) ... I'll leave you to judge which of us acted in the most scandalous manner ... I'll add more but this is dirty work unfit for a gentleman ... and you're so fond of law.

However, relationships did not take long to improve, for Curtois announced that he was coming down to visit Faussett at Heppington, and wanted to find the cheapest way from London down to Kent, perhaps by boat to Gravesend and then by hiring horses? During one winter the Lincoln roads were too bad for tenants to be visited, one house in particular, cheaply tenanted at 20s. per annum, needing to be visited. Curtois was now impecunious, needing to find £40 for a law degree.

In June 1752 a pond was being constructed at Heppington and Curtois wondered whether it was filling Faussett's mornings and giving him the opportunity of 'regaling upon cake & ale', and meanwhile lamenting that

so little stirring in this obscure scene, and that too is trifling ... since my leaving Willingham my favourite mare has had her wind broke, my favourite spaniel been bit with a mad dog, & the people lost most of their horned cattle.

Early in the following year sentiments were centred on the fortunes of being married and getting away from lonely Lincolnshire:

As more than barely living together is required to compleat the marriage state, in mutual confidence, regard & esteem, the news of your resolution to maintain them maugre the attempts you mention is a sensible pleasure to me ... I hope too, the birth of a child being reckoned the greatest pleasure that private life ordinarily admits of, you may have better luck that way then you seem to hope for. ... What a pity it is that my home should be above a weeks journey from you & in a part of the Country so circumstanced! Under supposition I ever get another Living which does not require residence, a Curacy & a snug lodging near you will be very desirable.

He had just returned from Lincoln where he tried to let Faussett's 19s. house, but without success, and so dropped the rent to 15s. a year which secured a good tenant. Winter repairs had totalled £1 5s. 6d., and his sister (Faussett's wife) had been burying her grandmother. On 5 May 1753 he congratulated the Faussetts on the birth of their new son (Bryan, born 11 April), and hoped that 'the young gentleman will live to be a comfort to you'. More family then appeared:

Tell Tetsy she has got a new sister, Billy Oats being married to an old maid of 50 [Dulcia Dymoke] with about 700l. fortune: he will scarce have 20 Boys by her; but as has not at present anything more than two Lincolnshire Curacys and her fortune to live upon that may be as well or better – To have a family without some prospect of providing for it cannot but make both Father and Mother uneasy.

Another ongoing lawsuit had now been dropped at Faussett's request as 'the attorneys are a pack of sad dogs', and one of his servants had made his housekeeper pregnant, and was succeeded by another who hanged himself in his barn. But things improved for Curtois by August 1753 when the Earl of Scarborough presented him to the living of Tealby near Market Rasen, elevating him from curate to vicar, which he considered a more certain position. Newly installed, he hoped to make £40 a year from it 'when wood and lambs bear a good price and the sheep escape being rotten'. But he was again hankering after getting down to Kingston, Faussett's current home, and regretted that he now had a vicarage and a large parish which required residence: 'However, as soon as my pockets are recruited & my livings can be servd by my neighbours, I propose stealing away'. The honey season was drawing on apace, and he would be glad of the recipe for mead. He was again strapped for cash, regretting that the Tealby living had exhausted his funds, and so could not pay another debt owing to Faussett:

> Methinks I should do well to live in Spain; one might then indulge laziness to perfection & yet be in character – Or a good Prebend or Sinecure would do better.

In August 1755 he was newly back from visiting Faussett at Charlton House, now lamenting that the present scarcity of clergy would mean no more visits. One parson named Jervas had recently walked 200 miles to serve three cures in the vicinity worth £12 each. In March 1756 his circumstances had evidently not improved, for he now regretted being a bachelor: '... a Wife, except she be a Lecturer, engages her Husband to stay at home & leisure ensues thereupon'. He now had two unfurnished houses, was almost alone except for an old woman bed-maker, and so 'was always on the rambles, being neither master of woman, dog or cat'. His schemes were all fruitless and the Faussetts the only relations he valued. The distance to Kent was too great: 'O that I had the wings of a dove!'

However, despite all this gloom, or perhaps because of it, he clearly did go out of his way to help Faussett specifically with antiquarian matters, going to Lincoln in search of Roman coins, yet exclaiming that they were of no interest to him personally:

> As to old coins they are quite & clear out of my way; I had rather be Master of one Fanny than of all of the Faustinas which the Society of Antiquarians have collected together.

A man named Arnold at Lincoln, presumably one of his regular contacts, was '... too fond of such things to let any escape. He was so indefatigable in hunting after Caesars he was so negligent of Georges that it is become unsafe for him to step out of doors except on Sundays'.

His numismatic enquiries had also taken him to nearby Ludford where he discovered that

> ... what the country People called mazzled halfpence, & you virtuosos Roman coins, [...] been now & gen found; I have sent thither to my Nurse for her to enquire whether any one have of them at present.

Curtois' undemanding employment left not a little time for him to be gossipy and vituperative. He describes three men, one a bad tenant, in less than flattering terms. The first, named Agar, had recently fled from Lincolnshire and was said by some now to be an army chaplain at Canterbury:

> He has been in his lifetime accused of forgery and slinging battle Cocks and is always plying some dirty prank or other & is not worth notice while alive. But if he should die at Canty & should chance to be hanged or shot or run through the body or, which shall be extraordinary, die in his bed while in your neighbourhood, I shall take early notice thereof as a great favour…Mr Edward Greathead is dead – Preaching a little & drinking a deal carried him off the stage. In our mobbings about the militia, George Clark of Barkwith had his ale drank very freely & was very near being pressed for a Chaplain to them. … The false brother I wrote about in my last was some time since outlawd & is at present in Lincoln Castle. It is suppos'd he will regain his liberty as soon as the Person who threw him into jayl gets possession of his living.

In December 1756 Curtois was despondent again, longing to be a regimental chaplain, as long as he could be near Canterbury 'rather than […ing] a tithe barn at Willingham and acquiring a stable at Tealby'. But more coin-collecting adventures had been pursued and information about local activities gleaned:

> I am apprehensive of being unable to contribute much towards filling your Cabinets maugre my endeavours that way. The Braziers shops at Lincoln furnished me with nothing worth speaking of; if there ever was any amongst their old stuff the Lindum Virtuosos have been before me. … One Mr Western lately opened a Hill about five miles from Tealby but I believe it did not answer his expectation, the something like an urn was, as is imagined, found. I rather supposed them to be raised by way of alarming the Country in cases of invasions.

The last extant letter from Grove Curtois to Faussett, of 2 February 1765, concerns the moving of possessions back to Heppington, perhaps after the sale of a house, for a quantity of pictures and spoons were all cased up to go to Louth and on to London. Faussett had been trying to recover a picture from a man who had proved intransigent, and was informed that 'All further intreaty will be in vain'. Such were the exigencies of being an absentee landlord.

The Faussetts' short married life in Alberbury saw the birth of their first son in November 1749 at the vicarage, an old building taxed on two hearths in the later 1600s and rebuilt a century later (Faussett in 1764 retrospectively alluded to it as 'dirty'). But the following September Bryan Faussett senior died aged 60, and a long-awaited and perhaps earnestly desired inheritance now beckoned. There was seemingly nothing to keep them in rural Shropshire, so the decision was made (and later regretted by Faussett who thought the departure had been too hasty) to make the long coach journey back to Kent. They left Alberbury on 30 November 1750, the costs of £33 10s. 7d. being added to the waggoner's fees of £2 19s. 9d. for transporting personal goods weighing a little over eight hundredweight.

Within a year of arriving in Shropshire Faussett had started a daybook of household accounts, the first of which would be virtually a married lifetime's precise and meticulous record-keeping of his expenditure and income. In all, the volumes amount to nothing less than an extraordinary cornucopia of information concerning the social conditions and daily life of an English gentleman – monies coming in and going out, incidental expenses, occasional fripperies, gifts, and the prices of a myriad of daily requisites, all recorded down to the last halfpenny.

In his time at Alberbury (then being a tenant and not a home owner) he was spending on food, clothes, garden seeds, messengers and casual labourers to a monthly total of between £1 10s. and £5. The mole-catcher charged 1s., a pair of tame pigeons cost 6d., the 1749 window tax was 4s. and land tax £1 7s. 7d. He was heavily reliant on the various church fees for income, most of which were at least a shilling, and of which there were 15 to 20 each month: a baptism was 4d., searching the registers 1s. 4d., churching a woman 1s., a burial between 10d. and 10s. 6d. depending on social class and type of funeral, whereas a smart wedding by licence in April 1749 attracted the large fee of £8 5s.

Despite having quitted Shropshire, this was not quite the end of connections with Alberbury, for in the following year a suit was commenced in Chancery which would show Faussett's litigious tendencies and constant need for funds. He claimed that although having left Alberbury, he was still entitled to the tithe or vicarial portion of all wood (except timber) and cinderwood cut or felled from within the parish. Robert Eyton of Wem, clerk, and Joshua Gee of Tern Forge, his tenant, an ironmaster, had, since Faussett's induction, held and occupied several estates, farms, lands and closes in Alberbury and other tithable places where great quantities of wood and underwood grew, and had given orders for it to be cut down in the summer of 1749 and then

> ... heaped it promiscuously to the number of 3000 long cords, 2000 and more of which comprised such wood and underwood the tithe whereof is due to me ... I was deceived and defrauded as if I had never been inducted. Not separated out but burnt for charcoal or carried off by their confederates. I have had no monetary satisfaction, and they carry on.[16]

The bill required that the miscreants should appear to defend themselves and pay Faussett what he was due, but the complainant did at least concede that he would waive all the penalties for their actions. There are no further references to the case, so we are left wondering as to the final outcome.

Affairs at Alberbury were tied up much later in 1753 when Faussett finally received £25 from his curate David Price in settlement of their business matters. In December 1765, a few months after having resigned the living, Faussett paid his successor Charles Grainger £20 in full for dilapidations.

---

[16] TNA: C12/1146/28

Chapter 4
Siblings, Curacies and Scholarship

After the return to Kent, there would be increasing reconnections with some of Fausset's extended family. It will be recalled that he was the eldest of 14 children, by no means an excessively large family for those days, but one which would see the usual proportion of infant or childhood deaths. Although he would himself die relatively young at 55, he would live longer than half of his siblings, yielding only to the greater longevity of the six sisters who survived infancy, some of whom would now take up disproportionate amounts of his ever-valuable time. But however difficult some of his siblings proved to be in their sometimes hapless and impecunious lives, Faussett seems always to have set to with relish to disentangle them from their misfortunes, even at the occasional cost of his own frayed temper.

The surviving correspondence between them is patchy, but there is enough to amplify his character and mood, and reveal the worries he had and the care that he took over the circumstances of some of his many younger brothers and sisters, deriving in part, at least, from his inheritance as his father's eldest son and heir, and a clergyman's natural concern for his close family. Eldest sons are often naturally strong, and Faussett not infrequently applied this strength of character when those close to him were in need of financial or moral support – a fortunate fact, for no sibling was his equal (and especially his brothers) in either energy or intellect.

All the children were born and baptised at Nackington, where the infant burials also took place. No two consecutive babies were born more than two years apart, resulting in 14 confinements in 19 years for a wife who had her last child at 40. Of those who married and moved away, their weddings have not all been easy to trace, even with the advent of comprehensive modern genealogical indexes. One might observe in passing that the social mobility of the 14, Faussett himself being the notable exception, was sideways at best, or not even quite that. No wedding brought a fortune with it, and the surviving sibling letters, other than Faussett's own, sometimes (and especially the brothers') show a distinct lack of cultivation. But this is not to deprecate – the earlier sections of the Faussett pedigree show an admixture of persons of all types, whereas those descended from Faussett himself display a noticeable trend towards marrying upwards, accompanied by burgeoning careers in the church and the services.

We may now tabulate his siblings.

Mary Faussett ('Molly'), the second child and eldest girl, was born 29 May 1723. She married, before 1751, William Uden, a yeoman of Elham (whom Faussett once disparagingly described as '*plebs*'). Faussett made her the gift of a guinea soon after she was married. She was buried at Elham in 1805, just before she was due to receive an inheritance of all the clothes of her sister Henrietta. There were five children including a son William for whom Faussett stood godfather in October 1753, giving two guineas for the occasion.

Godfrey Faussett (3) was born 26 June 1724 and died two years later. He would be the first of many family members to preserve the Godfrey surname as a forename.

Catherine Faussett (4) was born 19 June 1725. She married John Smith, a yeoman and butcher of Barham after 1751, and is thought to have died in 1761. There were two children, Edward and Hester.

Ann Faussett (5) was born 20 February 1726 and died in 1735.

Jane Faussett (6) ('Jenny') was born 28 August 1728 and dead by 1795. She never married, and after the death of her mother lived at Northfleet Hill and then Swanscombe in West Kent, perhaps for family or other connections, because of the proximity of the Faussett ancestral parish of Dartford just a few miles away. In March 1774 she wrote to Faussett to tell him about a business proposition at Dunstable that would bring in a good £20 a year if she remained single, with its accompanying house and £12 in ready money annually, needing only 'a surtifficat of my age' from him to complete the transaction. There was little contact otherwise between them, as she ended by saying: 'Likewise how you have had your health in regard to this very trying Winter. I have thought of you an abundance of times notwithstanding we are such strangers to Each other'.

Toke Faussett (7) was born 25 October 1729 and died in 1747. His forename preserves the venerable surname of Mary Toke, his great-grandmother, the daughter of Nicholas Toke of Godinton near Ashford. His father paid a Mr Devereux 10*s*. 6*d*. for baptising him, and 9*s*. 6*d*. in 1735 for his shirts.

Henrietta Faussett (8) was born 15 June 1731. She remained a spinster, living in Maidstone and then at Northfleet, directing that she should be buried at the latter, in the same grave as her sister Charlotte. She died in 1804 but the burial cannot be found in that parish. Her will[1] left messuages and other property to her sister Ann, jewellery to her niece Sophia Dodd, and silver buckles to her niece Elizabeth Bolger.

[1] KHLC: PRC32/67/261a

Charlotte Faussett (9) ('Charley') was born 11 July 1732. She also remained a spinster, living initially at Bearsted, then at Gravesend by 1771, and finally at Northfleet, where she died and was buried in 1795 after a 24-hour illness whilst staying with her sister Henrietta. Her estate of under £488 was administered[2] by her nephew Henry Godfrey Faussett and distributed to her surviving siblings and to some, but not all, of her nephews and nieces.

Her eldest brother came to her assistance in times of difficulty. In 1771 she was owed money by a man named Gordon from Rochester. Faussett stepped in, telling her that she should waste no time and tell him that she would expect the whole of the debt, both principal and interest immediately, and that if he did not comply 'or shuffles with her (as I know he has done before) she will sue, and tell him it is by my advice'. Here, and not for the first time, Faussett showed his predilection for litigiousness. Charlotte then told him that she had called several times at Gordon's house but found him to be away. She served him a month's notice to pay the debt of £380 at 5% plus four months' interest, thanking her brother for his advice.

Faussett had gone out of his way to try and place Charlotte's savings on a good rate of interest, but could find nobody in Canterbury willing to give more than 4%, commenting that,

> Attorneys tell me that money is plentiful but good security very scarce. As to Myself, as I have at present no Occasion for it, I do not choose to take up Money on any Interest whatever. I most sincerely, for my Part, wish you had followed my Advice heretofore, viz. in purchasing an Annuity.

Some months passed, by which time Charlotte had turned the recovery of the debt over to William Twopenny, a Rochester solicitor, who now proved his worth by collecting the balance from Gordon with full interest and placing it on a mortgage on a house and premises in Rainham at 5d. in the pound for the first year. Charlotte was now possessed of all the documents relating to the mortgage, with a bond besides. She reckoned Twopenny had treated her well in charging £2 12s. 6d. and that her expenses were £5 6s. 0d. 'and so think I am come out of it with flying Colours'.

In 1765, Robert Bass, an apothecary-surgeon from Philadelphia resident in London, a widower with a child, expressed marital interest in her, writing to invite her to spend some time together and visit the capital. Such was her agitation that she immediately sent the letter to Faussett for him to examine, adding, 'I have hear inclosed the Gentlemans own letter, as I think by that, you may be some judge, what sort of a man he is: it is the first letter I received from him'. This was not enough. She wrote again the next morning to Faussett:

> If you remember when we all meet last at Rochester, we were talking about matrimony and at the time you thought I should marry Mr Blackstoen, and I promised you I would

---

[2] TNA: PROB6/172

not him or any body else without your adwise and approbation. I now apply to you for the same on a very Serious affair which is no less than Matrimony itself.

She continued by saying that brother Harry had come to Gravesend and introduced her to Bass, who was good at business and had £91 annually for life from the Government, was of a good and sober character, and had emigrated ten years ago. 'If he settles in the United Kingdom I could be happy with him, but doubt my own courage to leave the country and my friends'.

At the same time Charlotte (along with her sister Henrietta) was attempting to move her investments in Gravesend Corporation with the help of Twopenny, who confided to Faussett that he thought Charlotte would not invest the money wisely because she had some other scheme in mind ('Matrimony, I suppose'). But now the axe had fallen on any such wedding, for Bass wrote to Faussett, having been received at Heppington as a potential brother-in-law, regretting that Faussett's proposals would not do in his opinion or in that of his friends, and that 'your care and affection for your sister I am persuaded could not make you offer less. Far be it from me Sir to cause disunion in a Family'. A subsequent letter from Charlotte to Bass clarified the matter: '... my elder Brother greatly objects my marrying you without my own little Fortune settled upon me in Case of your Death'. Thus ended all amatory matters, the sensible but firm Faussett's presence ever in the background, watching over the financial and emotional cares of his nearest and dearest.

Godfrey Faussett (10) was born 10 December 1733, and was his parents' second attempt to preserve his mother's maiden name. In 1744 his father paid a Mr Bate £42 11s. 4d. for two years of schooling. Described as a gentleman of Swanscombe, he actually died abroad in 1763 as Chief Mate of the East Indiaman *The Prince of Wales*, following his bachelor sailor's career. His first voyages had been in 1751 (when his eldest brother gave him two guineas) on the *Drake* to St Helena and on the *Essex* to China, and then to the Cape in 1752, returning to England the following year. In 1754 his father gave him five guineas before he set sail to China for a second time, and two guineas to his brother Henry who was to accompany him. Alas, he missed out on a far greater legacy of £200 from his cousin Chambrelan Godfrey, for he died in 1763, predeceasing his cousin by 13 years. Like his sister Charlotte, he left his estate to his brother and sisters.[3]

Ann Faussett (11) ('Nanny') was born 17 February 1734, and was living at Thurnham when she married Robert Rugg, a yeoman of Detling, in 1765. He died in 1791, and she was buried at Detling in 1807. There were six children, Ann, Robert, John, Patience, Catherine and George.

Susanna Faussett (12) ('Sukey') was born 14 August 1736 and married Daniel Bolger, a surgeon of Gravesend, as his second wife, in 1764. She was alive in 1805 when she proved the will of her sister Henrietta. Her four known issue were

---

[3] Guildhall Library: MS 9171/82

Elizabeth, Sophia (married George Dodd), John and Susannah Maria. Daniel Bolger wrote to Faussett in July 1771 to advise him that Sukey had just been brought to bed of a girl, and that, 'We claim your Promise as Godfather which we should be very Glad to have in your person, but if that cannot be, we must have a Substitute'. Faussett replied that he would readily stand as godfather, but as he could not appear in person, he would get a Mrs Swift to make a gift of two guineas on his behalf.

William Faussett (13) was born 13 August 1737 and died an infant the same year.

Henry Faussett ('Harry'), the last child, was born 22 October 1739 and died in 1784. Nearly twenty years younger than his eldest brother, his life looks to have been uncertain and often impecunious, facts which occasioned heated correspondence from Bryan. He followed his brother Godfrey into the navy, accompanying him as a young man to China in 1754. In February 1765, hoping to be second mate on the *Lawrence*, he was quartered at Finch Lane in the City and not in happy circumstances.

Writing to his eldest brother he told him that there was no prospect of getting out on any ship until the following season and lamented that so many young fellows were waiting at the coffee house to pick up boats. Short of money, he asked for £80 'for lodging and everything else comes dear […] and then I know what I am about at the Worst come to the Worst'. A negative reply from Faussett must have been swift for he wrote again saying that he was still impecunious and wondering how he could voyage in such a state – 'I hope you were not affraid of lossing it. You say you are very glad that I am going to sea again, but you don't know what the sea his if you did you would say otherwise'. Three days later he was on the *Lawrence* on a six-month voyage to Jamaica, having taken his leave of the Godfreys at a breakfast where 'they loaded my pockets with ½ guinea and called me couzen'.

In December 1767 he was anchored off Gravesend as fourth mate on the *Tilbury*, awaiting departure to the East Indies, when he was a deponent in a Chancery case.[4] He was back in London in early 1769, lodging at Mr Gould's tobacconist's shop at 37 Ludgate Street, and again looking for another voyage, with the hope of commanding an East Indiaman. He had been promised an advance of money from an old acquaintance towards the substantial total costs of £5000. Cap-in-hand he wrote again to his eldest brother for financial help, receiving a reply forthright in its sentiments:

Heppington, 24 April 1769

After the complicated series of base usage & undersv'd Ill-treatment which you have thought proper to bestow so liberally upon Me and mine, ever since our Mother's Death I little expected a Letter from you on any Subject; but especially on that of money. However, had I it in my Power to do you any service, I would gladly do it notwithstanding what is past. But with Regard to money I assure you I am so far from being able to advance any for you, or any Body else, that, with all the Prudence and Frugality I can use, I have very much ado to bring things round. Nor have I been able, yet, to repay all the

---

[4] TNA: C24/1763/13

Money which I was obliged to take up at a Great Disadvantage to pay your and Godfreys and my sisters Fortunes &c. And, my children being now coming out into the World will necessarily bring the family into still greater Difficulties.

That very same day Faussett wrote to his cousin Thomas Godfrey at Crutched Friars in the City, saying that he had received his brother's request for money, but had to show how unable he was to contribute, fearing that he had been misrepresented with regard to his financial circumstances and abilities to assist his brother and sisters. In continuing, a highly revealing picture of the struggling clergyman becomes apparent:

My whole Estate does not amount to more than 42pd per year […] and you may judge how much of that is sunk when Taxes Repairs &c are deducted. As to my preferment (if 2 Curacies and a small Living which I have lost money by ever since I have had it may be called Preferment) it amounts to no more than 66 Pounds a year. This is, I assure you Sir, ye true State of my Finances, except, that I am still in Debt for Part of the Money which I was obliged to take up on very disadvantageous Terms to pay my Brothers and Sisters, Fortunes &c at, or soon after my Mothers Death. My Friends and Acquaintance wd inform you that, I live in the most prudent and parsimonious Way that I decently can (and am blamed & censured for keeping no little company) and yet, I beg leave to assure you that I cannot bring matters about as I would wish. And so far am I being able to advance Money to other People, that, I am absolutely distressed … my sons now getting out into the World, and growing every Day more expensive to Me. They are I thank God very hopefull and diligent young Men, and it is my Duty to do all in my Power to forward them in their Respective Callings; but that I cannot do for them as I would, is to me a very disagreeable and melancholy reflection; but by God's Grace I mean to do the best I can. From the long Detail with which I have troubled you You will, Sir, be enabled to judge of my Ability to take care, or provide for, any but my own Household, and whether my Circumstances are such or can enable Me to advance any Money on the present Occasion. I most heartily beg a candid Interpretation of ye Liberty I have taken & the trouble I here give You which indeed, I wd not have done but I thought it my Duty to do it, it being neither my Talent to be troublesome, nor my Disposition to complain, for my Heart I thank God disdains both the one & the other.

Henry was back again in London in 1771 when Edmund Clutterbuck, secretary to cousin Thomas Godfrey, wrote to Faussett saying that Godfrey was wanting to help young Henry but was frustrated by his not passing the exam at India House. His naval career was now at an end, and he had therefore looked elsewhere and found him the offer of a place at the Poultry Compter, 'but which, upon mature Enquiry was found to be very improper for him'. However, Henry's wife understood the business of soap making and there was the offer of a manufactory at Wapping now being investigated by Mr Godfrey to fix him up, but it would cost at least £600. Godfrey realised that Faussett was distressed and this consideration was impelling him to help Henry. Faussett now replied on 25 April 1771, saying that he was not ignorant of Godfrey's help towards his brother, and that he was still hard up. His son Bryan was likely to become a member of Lincoln's Inn, and

… tho he manages matters as frugally as possible, he must spend more money than I can afford him. And, that, I am, in spite of all my Endeavours to the contrary still going backward in the world after his having servd his Clerkship with an Attorney and Solicitor in Chancery. My daughter too is growing up apace and must not be neglected.

Thomas Godfrey duly put up the £600 and Henry was installed in a soap, oil and starch shop and manufactory at Wapping Old Stairs. This would not be the end of his troubles, though. He wrote again to Faussett in April 1772, ashamed to do so, but his newly-born son had died a few days previously. His wife was all right but greatly troubled. Touchingly, he added a postscript: 'I have sent Soap. We likewise sell Starch Blue and every thing in the Oile way. The soap comes to Fifty six Shillings which his payed for.' – and indeed it was, for Faussett's account book for April 23 records paying his brother Harry £2 16s. for a hundredweight of mottled soap – no doubt a lifetime's supply!

He died on a final trip abroad, for when his estate was wound up,[5] he was a resident of Stoke Newington, but late of Bengal. He married Isabella Scott who survived him, as did a second child, Elizabeth Caroline, who was living at St Andrews in 1820.

Faussett by now was comfortably settled back in his birthplace. Earlier regets about having quitted Alberbury too hastily after his father's death had now receded; he was now no longer an heir, having come into certain inheritances, but his mother still lived at, and was mistress of, Heppington, and he therefore took up a temporary residence at Street End House, just to the south off the main Canterbury-Hythe road, where he kept a watchful eye on her until her death in 1761. But this was to be a transitory period, the demands of various curacies determining where he would live before winning in 1765 a longed-for vicarage and its concomitant stability. One retrospective view of Alberbury rankled in Faussett's mind, as recorded by Joseph Price in his diary:

Faussett most unhappy man. Talking about jointures, said 'If my mother had granted a lease (though I doubt her power to do it), of Heppington for 21 years, I would have sold the estate and it would have been better for me never to have come in to Kent, for had I stayed in Shropshire I might have had any preferment from [Richard] Lyster [M.P.] and his interest'.[6]

The neighbourhood around Nackington is still attractive today, and then, redolent with history, must have soon enthused him to go exploring. This was a rich field for the budding antiquary. A walk of 100 yards in any direction from Heppington could not fail to cross either the ancient Roman road or Saxon camp entrenchments, and just a little further was Iffin Wood which contained a well-preserved Roman

5   TNA PROB6/160
6   Ditchfield & Keith-Lucas, *A Kentish Parson:* 126

camp. His own family house, once an old castellated mansion in the reign of King Stephen, then reduced to Elizabethan comfort and shapeliness, albeit retaining its chapel, architecture and ornaments of many periods, had then been demolished by his father, once flush with money, and rebuilt in the fashionable Dutch style with high roofs and many dormers. Faussett was a mere ten-year-old when the demolition had been undertaken, but his indignation presaged a strong future interest in old things, and his account of what he saw remains most valuable.

At 29, he was lord of most that he could survey, but without employment and with a family to feed. He had married relatively young, derived but a modest income from his various preferments, and was already incurring debts. Perhaps in order to ignore, at least for some of the time, such worldly cares, this short fallow period turned him to archaeology for amusement and occupation, the seeds of which would bear such tremendous fruits in years to come.

At around this time, Faussett, having perused Caesar's *Gallic Wars*, and no doubt with the grandeur of Rome now swirling in his mind, imagined that there might be the remains of an imperial camp at Burstead Wood, a site which straddled the parochial boundary between Bishopsbourne and Upper Hardres. In 1749 some chalk-diggers had found several skeletons (each with the head to the south) and a spear-head or other weapon ('I did not see it, so only rely on the report of others'[7]), and in 1751 13 small earthen beads and a glass *patera* came to light. For reasons unknown, Faussett did not pursue the matter any further.

[The exact location has not been established; a note in the Hawkes Archive suggests that the site may have been just to the north-east in Gorsley Wood where several tumuli are still extant.]

In 1750 he obtained the curacy of Kingston, a couple of miles to the south-east. This attracted a stipend of £35 – small beer, but the beginnings of all things are small. Here, as elsewhere, he would maintain the periodic entries of baptisms, marriages and burials in the parish registers, and supervise the annual copying of the same (the so-called Bishop's Transcripts) to be transmitted to the diocesan registry in Canterbury. In rural parts this was not onerous with perhaps 15-20 entries a year – but pity someone like the vicar of Maidstone where there were 1000 and more annually.

This curacy lasted until 1756, but there was of course no residence to accompany it. In July 1751 Faussett moved to Kingston, having hitherto, presumably, ridden or been driven the few miles there and back from Heppington. But the accommodation there was not satisfactory so in October of that year he briefly took a house at St Martin's in Canterbury, then let it furnished at an annual rent of £11 and moved to Charlton House for a short period in the spring of 1752 before returning to Heppington in May 1752. The following year he let the house at St Martin's to the Rev'd Mr Simmons of Chislet for a minimum period of two years: 'He is to pay me everything & I am to be at no expense during his stay.'

---

[7] *Inv. Sep:* 36

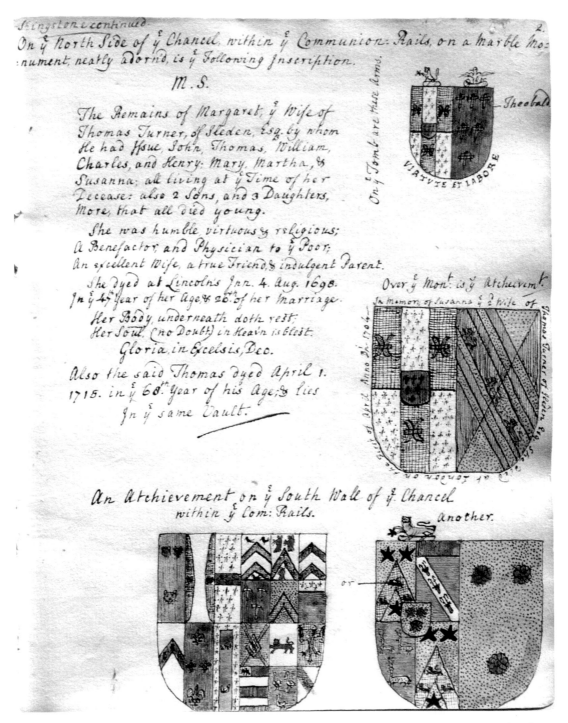

Kingston continued.

On ye North Side of ye Chancel, within ye Communion-Rails, on a Marble Mo:
:nument, neatly adorn'd, is ye following Inscription.

M.S.

The Remains of Margaret, ye Wife of
Thomas Turner, of Ileden, Esq. by whom
He had Issue, John, Thomas, William,
Charles, and Henry: Mary, Martha, &
Susanna: all living at ye Time of her
Decease: also 2 Sons, and 3 Daughters,
More, that all died young.

She was humble, virtuous & religious;
A Benefactor, and Physician to ye Poor;
An excellent Wife, a true Friend,& indulgent Parent.
She dyed at Lincoln's Inn. 4. Aug. 1698.
In ye 44 Year of her Age,& 26th of her Marriage.
Her Body, underneath doth rest;
Her Soul, (no Doubt) in Heav'n is blest.
Gloria, in Excelsis, Deo.

Also the said Thomas dyed April 1.
1715. in ye 68th Year of his Age;& lies
In ye same Vault.

On ye Tomb are these Arms.

VIRTUTE ET LABORE

Theobald

Over ye Mont: is ye Atchievem.t

In memory of Susanna ye 2d Wife of

Thomas Turner of Ileden Esqr.

Who died ye 31st of April Anno Dni 1704 ... of London.

An Atchievement on ye South Wall of ye Chancel
within ye Com: Rails.

Another.

or

Figure 10. Faussett's genealogical notes on the Turner family of Ileden, Kingston, made in Kingston church.
(Society of Antiquaries, London, MS 920/1, f.2r.)

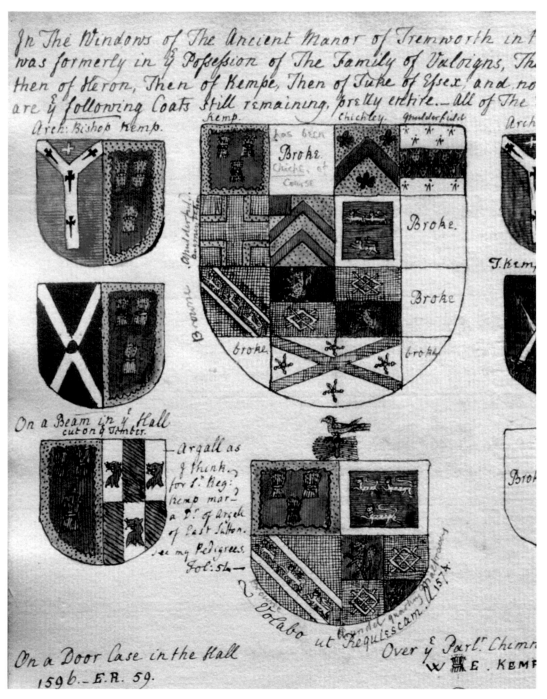

Figure 11. Faussett's notes on the heraldic glass at Tremworth manor house, Crundale. At the foot he notes,
presciently, that 'On the Down (near this Mansion), this present year 1757, I had the good Fortune to find, by digging,
a great Many very curious and well preserv'd Roman urns &c. Of which I intend, One Day, to give a full Account.'
(Society of Antiquaries, London, MS 920/3, f.20v.)

These peregrinations, derived from his accounts, are perhaps not the complete story, for the births of his children (Bryan at Kingston in April 1753, and Charles and Elizabeth at Bishopsbourne in March 1754 and February 1756) show yet further moves, but they demonstrate the uncertain existence of an ill-paid 18th-century curate, ever at the demand of his vicar. It was during this curacy, we may note, that Faussett almost daily would have seen the brow of Kingston Down and the barrows that peppered its surface, constantly wondering what might lie hidden within them.

In 1756 he moved to Petham to become on 14 February Dr Randolph's curate at Petham with Waltham, two adjacent parishes on the other side of Stone St, very close to Heppington, and from which his regular visits to his mother were made considerably easier. Here he was paid £42 annually (presumably for the two curacies), a modest sum, presumably commensurate with the light duties, but it was supplemented by the regular church fees of 1s. for churchings, 5s. for weddings and 10s. for burials, and also by the annual copying of the registers which attracted 3s. 6d. for each parish. One year he paid the well-schooled children of Petham 2s. 6d. for saying their catechism.

It was about now that he was beginning his indefatigable journeys around Kent churches to record the stained glass and monuments, much of which still remains as unique source material. Along with all this the presumably far less demanding pastoral visiting, register-keeping and service-taking continued there until 1761. Occasionally he deputed some of the work, paying a Mr Guise £5 in October 1762 for a quarter's work in serving Petham. A tangible memory of his presence there was the tenor bell of Petham church (burnt in 1923) which bore the inscription: BRYAN FOSSETT CURATE, WM FOORD CHWARDEN 1760, LESTER AND PACK FECIT.

We may now turn to Faussett's genealogical, heraldic and numismatic activities. His keenness for these subjects bordered on the passionate, easily evident from the surviving corpus of papers and charts at the Society of Antiquaries and elsewhere. (And indeed, can they rightly be called 'leisure' when they were tantamount to full-time occupation?) Five years of excursions around East Kent allowed him to amass a veritable treasure house of notes and sketches relating to monuments and epitaphs in glass and stone in some 150 churches around the diocese. Their value to modern researchers can hardly be underestimated, when one considers the rate of decay (or destruction) of such things in the 19th century, let alone of earlier ones. His accounts record a total expenditure on this work of around £15 – not large, considering the timescale, and so perhaps mostly on food and drink for long summer days, as he would have travelled around the countryside in his own coach.

All this work was achieved in the years 1756 to 1760, and thus neatly and considerably preceded his major archaeological years of 1767 and 1771 to 1773. Of the intervening period we can but surmise, but the writing-up and illustrating of so much information much have consumed a prodigious amount of time. Publication of the material, or indeed of the archaeological notebooks themselves, seems never to have crossed his mind. Ever the reclusive scholar, secreted away in the Kentish countryside, he discussed the results of his activities in correspondence with a select few, and verbally with the not inconsiderable number of guests invited to Heppington, no doubt constantly keen to show off his results to those with both eyes and mind perceptive enough to appreciate them.

Four densely-packed leather-bound volumes[8] written in Faussett's characteristically small and neat hand, and inscribed 'my parochial collections', provide the record of his church expeditions, and include additional biographical notes, coloured coats of arms, descriptions of churches and occasional notes on local antiquities. Also included in Volume 1 is a plan of a Roman entrenchment called Pond Wood at Petham which Faussett excavated in 1758, and a lengthy transcript of the account by William Warren, curate in 1712, of Ashford church, college and free school, to which Faussett added coats of arms omitted by the writer, brought the inscriptions up to date, and commented that he was surprised that many of the latter were now totally defaced or had disappeared altogether.

In Volume 3 there is an account of a dig at Linsey's chalk pit at Palm Tree Hill in Postling, when several skeletons and *fibulae* were found, some set with ivory and garnets, which Faussett immediately purchased to go alongside similar items already in his collection. In the same volume under Ash there is further material (added in 1771) on the etymology, site details and archaeological finds from Richborough Castle. In Volume 4 Faussett noted that when a cellar under the Mitre Inn in Canterbury was dug out, a tessellated Roman pavement was found in a fragmentary state, upon which 'the ingenious Mr Jacob of Faversham purchased it for 1 guinea'. Four separate indexes of parishes and surnames, minutely compiled, run to about 2500 entries.

One wonders how Faussett arranged this extraordinary programme of activity, especially as he seems to have worked quite alone. Even assuming good summer weather and light evenings, many churches were distant from Heppington and probably approaching a day's coach ride. Was he put up by friends or in hostelries? Did he spend a few days working at a group of neighbouring churches, or return home to write up his notes after a single one? Each church is dated by the year only, so we can but guess at how long each took to complete, even after taking into account the relatively fewer number of inscriptions there would have been in the 1760s and the fact that he was interested principally in the grander monuments relating to the gentry and other armigerous families.

His account books offer a few clues, of which the following are typical examples:

18 August 1757, spent at Lympne, Saltwood, Hythe and Postling 12s. 5d.
August 1758, gave the clerks at Womenswold and Nonington 2s.
September 1759, gave the clerks &c of 29 parishes around Deal £1 10s.
12 April 1760, expenses at Sandwich, Tilmanstone, Ash, Elmstone, Preston, Stourmouth, Chislet and Hoath; out 4 days, and paid for digging antiquities at Ash £3 9s. 8d.

---

[8] Society of Antiquaries of London: MS 920/1-4

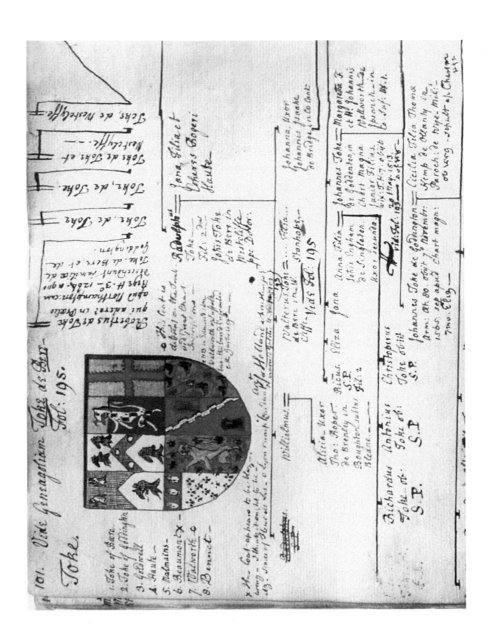

Figure 12. Faussett's construction of the Toke pedigree, descending to his father at the bottom left.
(Society of Antiquaries, London, MS 921, p.101)

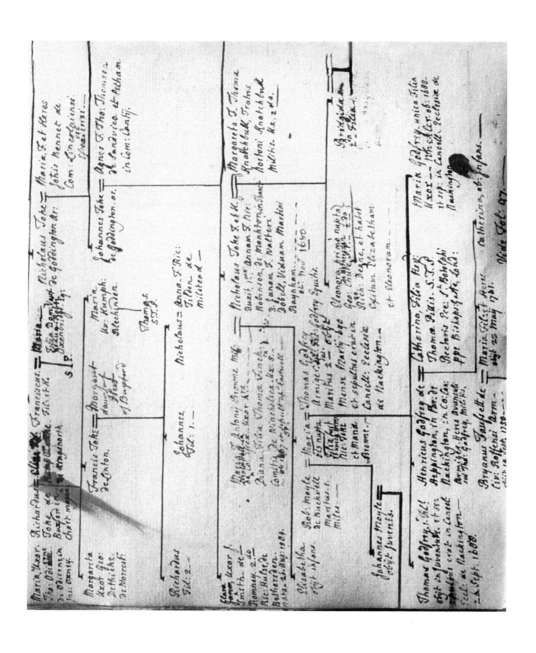

These payments one presumes to be for access to the churches, and perhaps also for practical help while engaging in recording inscriptions. The date of the last entry is interesting in that it covers both church work and digging it appears to be two days of each, the third and fourth days datable from *Inventorium Sepulchrale*.

The church visits and recording of inscriptions may be tabulated as follows:

1756: Kingston, Lyminge, Petham, Stelling, Waltham, and Whitstable.

1757: Adisham, Ashford, Barham, Bishopsbourne, Boughton Aluph, Bridge, Brook, Challock, Chartham, Chilham, Crundale, Eastchurch (in another hand), Eastwell, Elham, Elmsted, Fordwich, Godmersham, Hastingleigh, Hythe, Kennington, Lympne, Molash, Patrixbourne, Postling, Saltwood, Sturry, Thanington, Upper Hardres, Westbere, and Wye.

1758: Acrise, Bekesbourne, Blean, Coldred, Denton, Goodnestone, Great Chart, Hackington, Harbledown with St Nicholas' Hospital, Herne, Hinxhill, Hothfield, Ickham, Littlebourne, Lower Hardres, Mersham, Nackington, Nonington, Paddlesworth, Reculver, Sevington, Smeeth, Stanford, Stodmarsh, Swingfield, Westwell, Wickhambreaux, Willesborough, Womenswold, and Wootton

1758: Canterbury in its entirety: All Saints, Holy Cross, St Alphege, St Andrew, St Dunstan, St George, St Margaret, St Martin, St Mary Bredin, St Mary Bredman (undated), St Mary Magdalene, St Mary Northgate, St Mildred, St Paul, St Peter, and the hospitals of Cokyn (undated), Cotton (undated), Eastbridge alias King's, Jesus, Maynard, and St John.

1759: Aldington, Alkham, Betteshanger, Brabourne, Capel-le-Ferne, Cheriton, Deal 'Church and Chapel', East Langdon, Folkestone, Great Mongeham, Guston, Ham, Hawkinge, Hougham, Monks Horton, Newington, Northbourne, Oxney, Ringwould, Ripple, St Margaret's at Cliffe, Sellindge, Sholden, Stowting, Sutton, Waldershare, Walmer, Westcliffe, West Langdon ('ruined'), Whitfield, Wingham, and Worth

1760: Ash, Boughton-under-Blean, Chislet, Elmstone, Hoath, Preston next Wingham, Selling, Staple, Stourmouth, Tilmanstone; and also the whole of Sandwich (some undated): St Clement, St Mary, St Peter, St Bartholomew's Hospital, St John's Hospital, St Thomas' Hospital, 'Jacobs' and 'Nunnery'.

These parishes are undated: Barfrestone, Chillenden, Eastry, Eythorne, Kingsnorth, Knowlton, Lydd, Shepherdswell, and Woodnesborough.

These parishes are added much later and accompanied by sketches: Bapchild, Bicknor, Bredgar, Kingsdown, Murston, Staplehurst, and Wychling. Two further parishes: Buckland in Dover (added *c.*1774), and Staple (pasted in later).

Looking at the map, Faussett's achievement will strike us as quite staggering: somebody with a motor-car would be hard-pressed to cover the same ground of just over 150 chapels and churches. In essence the coverage is from Whitstable to Reculver, thence

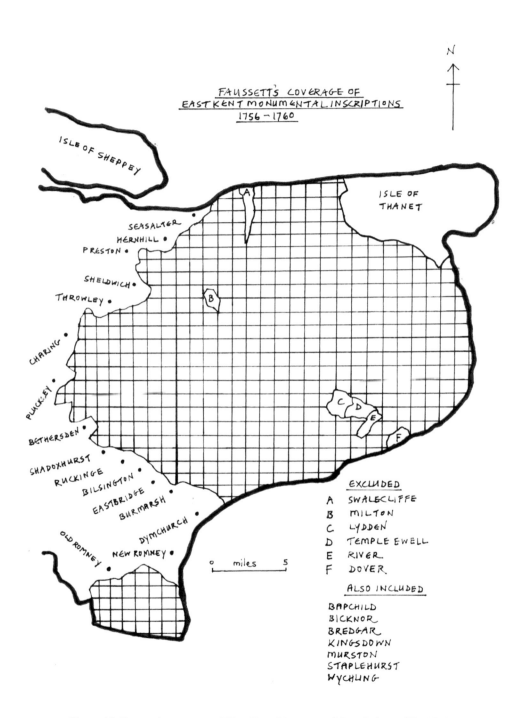

Figure 13. Faussett's coverage of East Kent Monumental Inscriptions, 1756-1760.

along the Wantsum to Sandwich, right round the coast to Hythe, north-west to Hothfield and Westwell, and then north-east back to Whitstable. Every parish within that perimeter, save Dover, Lydden, Milton Chapel, River, Swalecliffe and Temple Ewell was covered by the assiduous antiquary, together with a few outliers in the hinterland of Sittingbourne, as well as Staplehurst and Lydd where Faussett had personal connections and must have often visited. The Isle of Thanet was entirely ignored, seemingly because Lewis had undertaken similar work there in 1723 (and revised it in 1736), albeit in a fashion inferior to both Faussett and also to Cozens who covered the ground again at the end of the century.

In private hands two more associated books have come to light. The first, a slim volume, is in Faussett's handwriting, is no earlier than 1758, and has 19 pages of sketches of armorial coats from the cloisters at Canterbury Cathedral, and then, reversed, six pages of inscriptions from the same cloisters, plus a few from St Augustine's Monastery and St Martin's and St Paul's Churches in Canterbury.

The second is more intriguing. It is a fatter volume, marked on the spine 'Smythe of Milstead' and dated 1785. Investigations reveal the owner to have been Edward Smith who was Rector of Frinsted and Milstead from 1767 to 1786. Seemingly a bachelor, he left his estate[9] to Elizabeth Tylden, the niece of Mary Tylden, the mother of William Bland who married Faussett's own daughter Elizabeth. So a close family friendship is found and proven, and explains the further inscriptions from the villages high up on the downs around Sittingbourne, doubtless copied by Smythe himself and subsequently written up into the Faussett books to sit alongside the main series. The monumental inscriptions in this book cover the following parishes, some of which are dated: Bapchild, Bicknor, Bredgar, Doddington, Frinsted (1781), Kingsdown (1781), Milsted (1781), Rodmersham (1781), Wormshill, and Wychling. (There are also entries for Camberwell, Surrey, and the royal abbey of St Quintin, Picardy.)

In or around 1937, Valentine Torr, clearly enthused by the potential value of Faussett's work, transcribed them from 'five original volumes', (seemingly the four at the Society of Antiquaries plus the newly discovered Smythe volume above) into six loose-leaf exercise books.[10] Modern researchers should be aware that he copied fewer than half of Faussett's total, and even those parishes which he did include are not always complete, sometimes, for example, ignoring inscriptions in the churchyard.

Much earlier than Torr, the Rev'd Philip Parsons, Vicar of Wye, took great interest in Faussett's work, when in 1794 he published his own survey of East Kent churches. He personally visited 67 and was supplied details about a further 41 by the resident clergy of the time. Parsons was not strong on heraldry, and often omitted details about shields on monuments. Where he did include blazons, they are often not clear and the family not named. His introduction gives us a true flavour of the eighteenth-century equestrian and antiquarian parson:

---

9 TNA: PROB11/1148
10 Society of Antiquaries of London, MS 737/1-6

An ill state of health obliged me to use the exercise of a horse; by this, through the blessing of God, my illness was in a great degree removed. Still perseverance was necessary, and in order to induce it, an object became requisite. This object I soon found in the churches which frequently offered themselves to sight as I rode along; and curiosity produced amusement, continuance, and I hope, instruction.[11]

Alas, he ignored both churchyards, opining that the language of their inscriptions was in general too mean to attract attention (yet allowed that the advice they contained was excellent, if ill-expressed), and infants' tombs, of which there were too many. His greater passion was for stained glass, even if there too he might have to omit the banal 'that they lived, and that they died' type. Parsons freely acknowledged using Hasted's work in the production of his own, but even though it is clear that he was indebted to Faussett, he did not acknowledge him.

Heraldry is the comfortable bedfellow of genealogy (between which no divorce can be conceived), and Faussett did not often or for long ignore this colourful subject. A substantial volume of over 200 folios amply displays this to the full, and is summarised by Faussett's introduction which speaks for itself:

A Copy of the Visitation-Book of the County of Kent, as taken by John Phillipot [sic], Rouge Dragon, Marshall & Deputy, to William Cambden [sic], Clarenceux, in the years 1619, 1620, 1621, 1622, 1623. And also of part of the Visitation-Book of the said County as taken by Sir Edward Bishe [sic], Kt, Clarenceux King of Arms, in the years 1663 &c. Together with many additions from my own collections &c, all faithfully taken, transcribed, drawn and inserted by me Bryan Faussett, A.M. & A.S.S., Late Fellow of All Souls College in Oxford.[12]

The leather-bound volume is a fascinating medley of pedigrees, notes, bookplates and other miscellanea (including the compiler's note that through the 1634 Godfrey-Heyman marriage he is entitled to an exhibition from the King's School at Canterbury), before the principal section is reached 208 splendid double-spread pedigree charts, copiously adorned with coloured coats of arms and accompanied, predictably, at the back, by Faussett's huge and minutely cross-referenced index of some 2200 names, all in the most perfect and exact order. The whole must represent many years' and hundreds of hours of research and patient drawing – this is a dilettante's work of the highest order!

Faussett was no less keen as a numismatist and collected coins (which he usually called medals) from an early age, partly as a by-product of his other interests. Apart from direct purchases for which he occasionally gave considerable sums, he would have taken many out of the ground, although he was unable to identify, perhaps predictably, post-Roman coins, which were in any case then far less understood or desirable than classical ones. Typical entries in his accounts are:

---

[11] Parsons, *The monuments and painted glass of upwards…*, Introduction
[12] Society of Antiquaries of London, MS 921

Pembroke for coins 10*s*. 6*d*
For medals £15 6*s*. 9*d*.
Barton the gardener for old coins 2*s*. 6*d*.
Mr Legeyt for medals £1 10*s*.
Mr Loftie for a James I crown piece 5*s*.
Parker the goldsmith for a British coin (gold) 13*s*. 6*d*.
Mr Jacob for a parcel of Roman medals £2 2*s*.
Edward Jacob for some silver Roman coins £3 12*s*.
Arthur Twyman for silver coins weighing 3½oz £1 1*s*.
Revd Mr Twyman for medals collected by his late uncle, and the cabinet with them £5

Occasional references in his correspondence are proof enough that various individuals kept a lookout for forthcoming auction sales whereby he might augment his holdings. Such people included Matthew Duane, the lawyer and art patron, and one of Faussett's proposers for election to membership of the Society of Antiquaries. The furthering of his legal career had been frustrated by his catholic religion, but that was no bar to success elsewhere. Elected in 1763 as one of the two chairmen of the Society of Arts, he was described as 'the most skilful medallist in England', and was instrumental in listing Sir Hans Sloane's duplicates at the British Museum. He sold his Syriac medals to William Hunter to form, ultimately, part of today's great collections in Glasgow, and ended his life in retirement at Twickenham as a neighbour to Horace Walpole. A friend indeed to Faussett!

Faussett's collection numbered some 5500 examples of Roman and British coins, all ranged in cabinets, for which, in total, he spent just over £90 (a sum more than twice as large as those for archaeology and genealogy combined). At some point a considerable quantity of duplicates weighing about 150lbs was melted down and made into a bell which was suspended on the roof at Heppington, the chiming of which no doubt daily reminded him of his lifelong and urgent task to unearth as much as his gout-ridden and pain-wracked health would allow. The inscription was apt for those who could see it:

AUDI QUID TECUM LOQUITUR ROMANA VETUSTAS EX AERE ROMANO. ME CONFLARI FECIT. BF. ASS. 1766.

(Hear what Roman antiquity says to you through Roman bronze. Bryan Faussett had me made.)

Knowledge of the bell was perhaps more than just local, for the Rev'd Mark Noble, rector of Barming in West Kent, and historian and biographer of his fellow Fellows, noted that Faussett had accumulated so many Roman brass coins by digging that,

> … having selected a most valuable series of them, there remained as many more which he melted into a bell (instead of obliging others), which hangs in Heppington house. I was once offered a quantity of Roman brass much greater than those formed into the bell, but they were in Wales.

The bulk of the remainder of the coins, about 5000 in all, was sold by his great-grandson Bryan at Sotheby's in December 1853. During the second World War the bell was loaned by Sir Bryan Godfrey-Faussett to Hyde Park police station and used as an alarm signal during air-raids, subsequently going to the London Museum for display. Today it is back in the safe-keeping of the family.

One last aspect of Faussett's collecting fields needs recording – and this hardly a surprising one. Distinguished by no explicit mention during his lifetime, well over 100 mediaeval charters and associated documents were sold as 53 lots at Sotheby's on 25 February 1854. The charters covered many reigns from Henry III to Elizabeth I, and related mostly to Kent, but also to Shropshire, Somerset and Wales. Other items included 34 letters written by James Douglas to Godfrey Faussett at Heppington between 1781 and 1789, an order of Oliver Cromwell, an autograph signature of Thomas Wolseley which made two guineas, and a petition by John Fogge, Sheriff of Kent, to Henry VI which sold for £3 18s. The buyers were various, but the British Museum acquired the charters, now catalogued as MSS Addl 8536-8665.

Chapter 5
The First Two Campaigns

Tremworth Down, Crundale

14 June 1757 – 11 graves	24 June 1757 – 4 graves
3 October 1757 – 6 graves	23 April 1759 – 6 graves

Faussett's digging career did not actually begin with barrow cemeteries. His first independent archaeological expedition tok place on 14 June 1757 when he visited Tremworth Down in Crundale parish, a north-facing spur of the North Downs situated on the southern side of the Stour Valley at about 125 feet, with long views towards Godmersham and its prettily situated church on the sweeping bank of the river in the lee of Godmersham Down. A century later when Charles Roach Smith came to edit the archaeological notebooks for publication he ignored Faussett's chronology and placed the account at the end of *Inventorium* because most of the finds at Tremworth Down were evidence of a Roman cremation cemetery, 'and so not as important or novel as the Saxon', although he admitted that the proximity of some Saxon remains to the Roman greatly increased the value of the discoveries. Was Faussett's later view of his collections being Roman, and not Saxon, permanently influenced by this, his first formally recorded excavation?

The reasons for Faussett's visit to Tremworth Down are given by himself. He had been visiting his 'worthy friend' Edmund Filmer, the rector of Crundale, on 13 June 1757, and recollected that Dr Harris in his *History of Kent* mentioned some urns and other items found at Tremworth. That evening the two men walked out, but on arrival at the spot found it level and plain with nothing to suggest an ancient burial ground. Harris had consulted Richard Forster, the then Rector of Crundale, who had been present at the first dig, described it briefly in the first Crundale parish register,[1]

---

[1] CCA: U3/116/1/1

Figure 14. Tremworth Down, Crundale, from the south.
(Copyright Neil Anthony.)

Figure 15. Looking westwards from Tremworth Down to Tremworth manor house (exact centre, middle distance). Faussett walked down here in June 1757 with his friend the Rev'd Edmund Filmer.
(Copyright Neil Anthony.)

and recorded the location with great precision – so accurately, in fact, that Filmer and Faussett were certain they were standing on the exact site. (It is a pleasure to add here that Forster's splendid rectorial library of some 2000 books and pamphlets is now catalogued and may be seen at Canterbury Cathedral Library.)

The first discoveries had taken place in 1703 when a person walking down the hill in the hollow wagon-way spotted a skull on the side bank; an inspection then brought to light a complete skeleton, accompanied by an urn, noted by Dr Plot as being of a typically Roman shape. Nearby was a child's skeleton with a little red pot. Colonel Heneage Finch, Earl of Winchilsea, a little later in that year discovered the inhumations of two adults and one child '… lying side by side…'. They were without finds, but the same evening a fourth grave revealed a Roman pottery bottle alongside another adult inhumation.

In 1713 Harris then found some urns, all tipping slightly eastwards, after which Lord Winchilsea undertook a second campaign and found a grave dug well into the chalk and containing three pottery vessels, all of which he took possession of. Again, the Rev'd Mr Forster noted this in the first parish register and appended sketches of the vessels found on both occasions with a table of their dimensions.[2]

Harris's account had developed from a beech tree adjoining Crundale churchyard being blown down in the great storm of November 1703. Its eradication had brought up a male skeleton, well preserved by the chalk soil, which led 'the learned and ingenious Rector Mr Forster' to conjecture that either his churchyard was formerly of greater extent, as this body lay east-west, or that some suicide or excommunicant had been buried just outside the churchyard boundary. The chalk hill to the west of the church in the vicinity of Warren Wood Gate had preserved the larger bones of many bodies, in all probability for a great number of ages,

> …there being a British, or rather, a Roman or Saxon sepulture (determine it who can) on Tremworth Down against the place where the road comes out of Warren Wood, where all the bodies are buried with their feet westward.[3]

He further noted that Robert Plot considered Roman urns to be designed as receptacles for cremated remains[4] but thought that whatever Plot had meant by urns, the Crundale ones were never intended for the ashes of the dead as the skeletons were entire, in a natural position, and unburnt; and further, the Roman custom of cremation and gathering of the ashes was given up as not being the primary and original rite.

Faussett measured the site as being some 70 acres, but could find no sign of an ancient camp, even after he had asked (as was his custom) several locals, including the wood-reeve. He next consulted the parish clerk, learnt that the man had been present as one of the labourers at both the 1703 and 1713 digs, and that only a few

[2] *ibid.*
[3] Harris, *The Natural History of Kent in Five Parts:* 2, 89
[4] Plot, *The Natural History of Oxfordshire:* 328

graves had been opened, 'and even those few in a less careful manner than a search after venerable antiquity required.' Determined to try his luck, he marshalled his labourers and ordered the clerk to be with them at the site early the next morning, but not to start digging until he arrived.

Faussett must have spent a restless night wondering what might come to light. The next morning, as keen as a dog with two heads, he diverted down the hill to Tremworth manor house, accompanied by Filmer, to examine some painted windows to the Kemp family. Their prior excursion came at a cost, for upon climbing back up they found that the men had already set to and from the first grave had brought out all too hastily a large urn, a *patera* and a small footed cup of thin white glass – all smashed in the process, but Faussett saw the glass vessel as a curiosity and so later gathered up the fragments. Yet more breakages occurred before Faussett directed the labourers to deepen the holes and enlarge them by undermining so that future finds would drop gently into their hands.

Ossuaries, vases and a red urn with a rare impressed foliated ornament[5] were brought out of grave 3 and then in grave 4 a red *patera* marked with a large St Andrew's cross on its exterior. Faussett wondered for a moment whether this was a Christian symbol before rejecting the idea in favour of paganism, the cross perhaps indicating sanctification before a libation. Next he observed that small pieces of soft and rotten ivory from grave 5 soon hardened in the sun after a few hours and became brittle, and then experimented by placing glass items into warm water which, when cleansed, looked more or less just like modern glass. Some larger vessels, one inscribed *Iunius*, lent weight to Roman origins, and when he burnt some blackish wax adhering to one of them he got a strong and agreeable smell, like mastic.

As they proceeded they suddenly realised that they had broken one of their cardinal rules of digging in that they had failed to notice such soil as appeared by its looseness to have been previously dug, Faussett being well aware that chalk never united or became firm after having been disturbed. The result was that the eighth grave, lying on the side bank of the hollow road, was one previously opened by Lord Winchelsea or Richard Forster who had overlooked the contents but thrown in a mass of unburnt human bones as of no antiquarian interest. Faussett now found here a range of vessels, all overlooked by the earlier investigators, when a bystander approached the edge of the grave and inadvertently pressed down the side to reveal them.

The ninth grave disclosed yet another *patera* inscribed in Latin with the possible owner's name *Sacrina*, and then a small urn of dark-coloured earth which Roach Smith ascribed to the pottery at Upchurch (on the Thames Estuary) on account of many similar finds in that location. A knife-blade, clearly Saxon, now proved (to him) that the cemetery was both Roman and Saxon. The last grave of the day revealed an entire skeleton with its feet to the south-west, alongside a *patera* with a double St Andrew's cross. Faussett was exultant:

---

[5] illustrated in Hasted, 3: 185

> And with what I had already got, a person less enamoured of venerable antiquity than
> myself might, perhaps, have gone home satisfied. But it was not so with me: my appetite
> was not so easily cloyed.[6]

He felt sure there was more to be found and immediately sought the permission of
Sir John Filmer, the lord of the manor, to continue as and when he pleased. Ten days
later a second campaign began, doubtless after he had carefully written up the results
of the first and formulated his thoughts about the nature of the site:

> I had no doubt of these remains being Roman; but in what age they were deposited did
> not, as yet, at all appear. But I flattered myself that a further search would enable me, by
> the finding of a coin, or some such thing, to give a near guess even at that.[7]

Faussett's impression of Roman dates was clearly hazy, but tellingly, in this, his first
independent excavation, he already saw how crucial evidence for dating might be
supplied by coins.

His labourers were hard at work at six o'clock in the morning of that mid-summer's
day, soon coming across trenches and pits from Lord Winchilsea's earlier campaign.
Now came in grave 13 an undisturbed grave with an adult skeleton oriented almost
south-west, and a *patera* inscribed *Granio* and with a St Andrew's cross; other *paterae*
produced more Latin names, some of which Roach Smith recognized from his lists
of London finds.

Four months later Faussett was only too aware of the shortness of autumn
days and yet had returned for more. Now he worked furiously, only stopping when
darkness had fallen, having noted more skeletons with flints piled arch-wise over
them, one that of an old man with his teeth worn right down. This completed the
work at Crundale for the year, and he recorded in his notebook:

> 14 June 1757: paid labourers at Crundale for digging out ye urns &c 10s. 6d. and 8s.
> 3 October 1757: paid labourers on Tremworth Down 8s.

We may presume that curiosity brought Faussett back for his fourth and last day
on Tremworth Down in April 1759. A large skeleton in grave 22 with firm, strong
bones, and remarkably sound, white, even teeth allowed Faussett to extrapolate a
height of between six and seven feet. And then – revelation! At grave 24 a bystander
picked up a black urn and dropped it onto a flint, dashing it to pieces out of which
dropped a bronze coin for the younger Faustina, wife of Marcus Aurelius Antoninus.

The item would not of course prove the grave to be Roman: Roman coins are
indeed fairly common finds in Anglo-Saxon graves, but they do not seem to have
been used as currency; rather they were often pierced and used as pendants, perhaps
in an amuletic fashion, or were simply collected as curiosities.

[6] *Inv. Sep.*: 188
[7] *ibid.*

Faussett recorded his impressions:

The pleasure I felt on finding the coin may be much more easily guessed at than expressed. I had, before I found it, no kind of doubt but that these remains were certainly Roman; but I had till now met with nothing from which I could form the least guess at the time when they were deposited. But this is not only a convincing proof of their being really Roman, but, in some measure, ascertains the time of their interment. The ossuaries, indeed were a sufficient testimony of their great antiquity; urn burial, according to Macrobius, having ceased among the Romans in his time; and other writers assert that it ceased so soon as with the Antonines.[8]

Notwithstanding this assertion, he added in a footnote that he was now fully convinced that urn burial, at least in Britain, continued to be practised long after the Antonines had seen it disappear, for in 1762 some labourers digging at Frindsbury near Rochester found a large urn full of burnt bones and ashes, and under it a thin piece of ivory or bone which lay on a slab of polished marble or porphyry, between which were five copper coins of Claudius Gothicus, Aurelian, Tacitus and Probus, now all in his possession. He further adduced Dr Browne who found some Roman coins of Posthumus and Tetricus in urns at Bampeton Field, Norfolk, in 1667, and averred that 'urn-burial lasted longer than is commonly supposed, at least in this country.'

Perhaps in search of more evidence, Faussett now wandered off into a field between Warren Wood and the hollow road and noticed that the earth freshly thrown up by moles in the middle of the field was very dark or of an even blackness, whereas elsewhere the soil was light in colour and mixed with chalk. Gathering up a handful of the former, he found it full of small wood-coals and black dust, and so wondered whether it was the *ustrinum* or hearth for the funeral piles on which the bodies were laid to be burnt (as was found here in the larger urns), or just a hearth where charcoal had been made. He was undecided but elected for the former theory, as a large wood was nearby with ample supplies of timber; but upon digging no burnt bones appeared, and so he decided that even if it was the *ustrinum*, the Roman custom was to wrap up the bodies in a sheet impervious to flames so that human bones and ashes could not be mixed with the coal and ashes of the fire itself.

With probability on his side, as he claimed, he was keen to mention this point so that his brother antiquaries would never risk (or at least not in print) any conjectures on such uncertainties; and anyway, Thomas Browne, who published his *Hydrotaphia* in 1658 (which described as Roman the illustrated Anglo-Saxon artefacts), had already mentioned in it that at Old Walsingham in Norfolk there was another hearth 'which begat conjecture that this was *ustrinum* or place of burning their bodies.'[9]

He now began a summation of his first four days of independent digging, describing the site as on the north-west side of a dry and steep hill with views as

---

[8] *Inv. Sep.*: 193
[9] Browne, *Hydrotaphia*: 15

far as Sussex, and Warren Wood at its summit. It was well known that the Romans usually, if not always, made such a choice for their cemeteries, namely on dry soil, on the declivity of a hill, and by a road, 'by which means their monuments were under eye, and mementos of mortality to living passengers and might also receive their good wishes and benedictions'.[10]

It was indisputable to him that the site was Roman (or at least Romano-British) – the amplitude of stamped Latin names on the *paterae* was sufficient evidence – and that inhumation was an ancient practice as the Roman capital letters showed. Although he had not been lucky enough to find a coin with similar nomenclature, he knew that coins alone would put 'the matter out of all kind of doubt'.

He saw the contents of the ossuaries as evidence affording proof of great antiquity, and that the Faustina coin must have been in circulation around AD 180, the year her husband died. Moreover, there was a strong argument for the custom of the inhumation of the dead having been practised contemporaneously with that of cremation, as here at Tremworth, and just as he had found at Gilton, Chartham, Kingston and Barfrestone, and so perhaps some of these ossuaries and skeletons might have been deposited even long before this time. All the ossuaries were in round holes, two feet in diameter and about the same in depth, always placed centrally, one to a hole, and with the empty urns and *paterae* disposed around them.

Faussett was mystified by the feet of the skeletons lying westwards or south-westwards, at complete variance with all the others found by him which were eastwards, or nearly so, and, rarely, northwards. Did the ancients have no regard to the heavens, but merely to the situation of the earth, laying the body downward to follow the decline of the slope? But this was not the case at Kingston or Sibertswold, where the heads pointed downward.

He reflected that the Rev'd Mr Forster was probably wrong in saying that the orifices of smaller urns were deliberately placed not vertically but dipping a little to the east, as he had found none in this position – a few sloping, yes, but in various directions.

The urns and *paterae* he thought to have been made of the materials nearest to hand (except for those of white clay which appeared to have been washed over with a blackish or bluish colouring); but as for the fine coralline red earth items stamped with makers' names, and also those of similar type with no stamp, he was quite persuaded that they were of foreign manufacture.

With this Roach Smith entirely agreed, referring the reader to the first volume of his own *Collectanea Antiqua*. He also concurred with Faussett's views on burial, but saw that the Roman and Saxon graves had not been distinguished at Crundale – how could they have been when Faussett had investigated only early Anglo-Saxon cemeteries, and so been denied the opportunities of making comparisons between those and the Roman and Romano-British?

Tremworth Down, in Faussett's opinion, was a cemetery for just two or three

---

[10] *Inv. Sep.*: 196

individuals, or some small village at best, because of the relatively few skeletons. The absence of weapons and arms suggested a peaceable community, as he believed that it was a fairly constant custom for warriors to be buried with such items.

We may now summarise Tremworth Down from a modern perspective. It is one of the very few Anglo-Saxon cemeteries in Kent on the site of Roman burials, although there is absolutely no evidence for continuity of use. Faussett saw the pottery as clearly Roman, and assumed the inhumations to be of the same date, whereas some, and probably all, were Anglo-Saxon, as were all the inhumations of his career. But he would die thinking all his graves were his 'Romans Britonised' or 'Britons Romanised'. In all, he found 11 Roman cremations, as well as 15 inhumations at Tremworth, at least some of which were Anglo-Saxon. Most of the inhumations appear to have lain close to the hollow way where the initial discoveries had occurred.

A total of 25 bodies was recorded. Of the 15 graves which contained grave-goods, nine had only pottery vessels, nearly all Roman. Graves 18 (a double one) and 24 contained beads, a knife, a buckle, a Roman coin, a chatelaine and a box, and were clearly Anglo-Saxon. Those containing only Roman pottery have been considered as probably Roman, while the dating of the other graves remains uncertain. But there is a consistency of overall burial rites at Tremworth Down as all graves appear to have been aligned north-east to south-west, many had large flints in their fill, and several had coffins. It therefore seems likely that all the inhumations were Anglo-Saxon, and that the Roman pots in them had been taken from disturbed Roman cremations. The amber beads in grave 24 suggest the sixth century, but the general scarcity of Anglo-Saxon objects implies rather a general date of the seventh century or later for the majority. Alternatively, it is possible that the burials are a mixture of late Roman and 5th- to 6th-century Saxon graves.

[In 1858 there were said to have been further discoveries, including some plain urns, two circular gilt brooches with keystone garnets, 20 studs set with garnets, buckles, earrings, and 90 beads of crystal, amber, paste and glass. Somewhere in the near vicinity an Anglo-Saxon grave was excavated in 1861 and another in 1862, the finds from which were in Henry Durden's collection, now in the British Museum.]

Gilton Town, Ash

Late 1759 – a chance visit	11-12 April 1760 – 21 graves
16-18 June 1760 – 28 graves	28-30 September 1762 – 22 graves
8-10 August 1763 – 35 graves	

Not many months had passed after the final day's digging at Tremworth Down before Faussett made his first, and chance, visit to Gilton Town (the modern spelling is Guilton) in the very large parish of Ash just to the west of Sandwich. The site lay on a gentle south-east facing slope at about 75 feet, nearly on the Roman road from Canterbury to that ancient Cinque Port, and within three miles of the Roman *Rutupiae*, thus offering a high chance of success to any enthusiastic antiquary. With the practical experience of Crundale now behind him and its findings written up, he would abandon single days of investigation in favour of an opening two-day campaign and then three three-day ones, perhaps dictated here by the much greater distance from Heppington and an unwillingness to travel more often than was necessary.

Gilton was a quarter of a mile south of the main road, called Ash Street. Faussett had been alerted to a large and deep sand-pit there, for whenever sand had been dug out or frost and rain had pushed down the surface, antiquities of all kinds had been picked up by farm servants and local people, and also by men who worked at a mill standing close by, just to the west of the sand-pit. The owner's two mills appear in James Douglas's 1783 sketch of what is probably one of the earliest illustrations of an archaeological site, although by the time the scene appeared in *Inventorium* it had been romanticised and increased to a picturesquely grouped three mills. (The site today is decidedly less than photogenic.)

Faussett was at Ash copying monumental inscriptions late in 1759, and as was his habit, asked around as to whether there were any antiquities or other notable artefacts in the area. The sand-pit was quickly mentioned and then the miller's servant told him he had seen a spear-head sticking out of the ground (Faussett thought it probably a stick or root) and was certain of a grave beneath it because of the darker tinge of the sand. There was in fact some urgency touching all this, for although there was no barrow, the pit was a flat cemetery being gradually destroyed by sand extraction. Ironically, Faussett would proceed with great enthusiasm but be unaware that this was an Anglo-Saxon site, and not Roman as had been the case at Tremworth Down.

Antiquities had been systematically found at Gilton, an inhumation cemetery, long before Faussett's arrival, and would be for some decades after him. William Boys had inserted engravings of Saxon remains taken from the Gilton sand-pit long after Faussett in his *Collections for an History of Sandwich* (pp.868-9), and plates seven and 12 of Douglas's *Nenia Britannica* are engravings of objects from Boys' collections. Douglas acknowledged Boys as very much contributing to his barrow researches in that neighbourhood, and a man who had saved relics from 'the silversmith's furnace'.[11] Other finds had found their way to Edward Jacob at Faversham, ultimately to reside at the Ashmolean Museum. In the adjacent parish of Woodnesborough glass vessels had been taken in such numbers from graves that the harvest celebration on one farm was said to be toasted in ale drunk out of Saxon beakers.

Faussett's account of the proceedings grips us by its meticulous detail, graphically conveying the conditions of the time, the difficulties of the site, and, above all, the character of the antiquary himself in his powers of observation and narrative, and

---

[11] Douglas, *Nenia Britannica*: 26

in his exasperation and impatience with the workmen, tempered by cool practical sense as a novice excavator to whom *festina lente* ought to have been a constant archaeological dictum. Here we may learn exactly how he proceeded, with unlettered workmen toiling long hours to open one grave before almost falling over in their indecent haste to open the next (culminating in one day at Sibertswold in July 1772 with a total of 42).

A grave was visible in section in the side of the sand-pit, and although it was late in the day a man was bidden to fetch a ladder and

> should soon rifle it (for that was his expression), my curiosity prompted me, though at a considerable distance from home, to set them about the business and to wait the event.[12]

The miller and his companion set to work zealously and dug horizontally in a rough manner as if they were purposing an oven in the sand rock. Faussett was proved wrong as there actually was a spear head, soon to be smashed in the furore and after which a skull and some bones 'were indiscriminately cast down into the pit, without the least care or search after anything.' Standing at the foot of the pit, Faussett exploded:

> That concern, they said, they left to me and my servant at the bottom, who were very nearly blinded with the sand falling on us, and in no small danger of being knocked on the head, if not absolutely buried, by the too zealous impetuosity of my honest labourers.[13]

Would anything be rescued in one piece? It seemed unlikely without a change in tactics:

> I found, in short, that this method of proceeding would not do; but that if the grave did chance to contain anything curious, it must, most likely, be lost and overlooked. I therefore desired them to desist, and advised them rather to open the ground above, till they should get down to the skeleton, and then carefully to examine the bottom of the grave. This advice, having been used to proceed oven fashion, if I may so call it, they did not at first at all relish; but after a little persuasion and a little brandy (without which nothing, in such cases as the present, can be done effectually), they very cheerfully approved and very contentedly followed, so that in a very short time they got to the skeleton, I mean what remained of it. And though I then went into the grave myself, and very carefully examined every handful of the above-mentioned discoloured sand (namely where the body had lain and rotted), I found nothing but some soft spongy remains of decayed bones.[14]

Night had drawn on apace and brought an uninvited early conclusion: darkness and the shortening days meant that Faussett would have to contain his enthusiasm until the following spring, when he promised himself the pleasure of a return visit. For

[12] *Inv. Sep.*: 2
[13] *ibid.*
[14] *ibid.*

now he contented himself with buying a few buckles, spear-heads and beads from the miller's men (some recompense for their ordeal!), and from their master Mr Kingsford further articles including a sword-blade, some 30 inches long and two wide. His contentment was short-lived – most of the items were so rusty that all the iron artefacts shattered in the coach as he was going home.

No barrows were to be seen in or near the sand-pit as the plough had gradually levelled the neighbourhood. The two mills stood just north-west of the pit on higher ground where Faussett rightly supposed that more exciting finds would lie, but the miller, fearful of the literal collapse of his livelihood, had erected a fence against further digging. The winter would have to be borne with patience, along with the nursing of the hope of an early spring conducive to his eagerly awaited return.

By the following April 'the warm of the weather had so raised the thermometer of my impatience' that he sought permission from one Cosmaker, who was both lord of the manor and landlord of the farm on which the pit was situated, to set up camp. A large urn was soon brought out of the ground, broken in pieces, as he supposed, by those who had dug the grave, and 'a shrewd sign, surely, that this spot had been a burying place, perhaps even before the custom of burying the dead ceased.' Roach Smith noted here that 'Faussett became convinced that this notion, formed at so early a period of his researches, was correct.'[15] Faussett did, however, correctly discern Roman burials at Gilton along with the Saxon graves, belonging to the inhabitants of a *vicus* near Ash, and indeed, the prevailing Roman character and influence at the cemetery was still apparent to Roach Smith nearly a century later.

Three graves proved to be especially fruitful, but in rather different ways. Grave 66, as part of the return visit in September, revealed 18 copper weights[16] (some made of ground-down Roman coins), among the most interesting of all Faussett's finds, and probably used for weighing the various gold and silver coins in use in Anglo-Saxon England. A skeleton in grave 89 allowed him to exercise his anatomical skills in assigning it to that of an old person on account of the worn teeth. The next find, seemingly an Iron Age sword-pommel, was duly recorded by Faussett in an episode not redounding to his credit, as it may have been placed there as a joke by a workman or some other bystander. That Homer seemed to have nodded was remarked on by Jessup who opined that Faussett occasionally had a blind eye, as everyone who had seen his famous sword pommel would agree that it was nothing more than a door knob. Roach Smith, perhaps more dispassionately, chose not to excise it from the account as 'these trifling exceptions in a large collection cannot be allowed to throw suspicion on the whole.'

The final excavations at Gilton were nearly a year later in August 1763, when Faussett usefully recorded in a notebook that the three-day stint 'digging for antiquities' cost him £1 19s. 0d. Why such a long gap if the trail seemed so promising, one wonders: practical problems, too much to write up, or perhaps simply too many

---

[15] *Inv. Sep.*: 4
[16] *ibid.*: plate 17

other matters to attend to? The year's absence was worth the wait, however, for grave 94 rewarded the party with a flat circular mirror, five inches in diameter, and highly polished on one side. Such items were often found in the graves of Roman women, but their presence in a Saxon grave was remarkable, and particularly interesting in connection with the other Roman instruments and ornaments found at Gilton; thus indicative of a close chronological relationship between Roman and Saxon, the mirror was, moreover, evidence of a striking correspondence between the habits and customs of the two peoples.

In summary, Gilton was probably one of the earliest Anglo-Saxon cemeteries dug by Faussett, evidenced in part by the lack of barrows, and is to be dated to the late 5th or early 6th century. Its graves lay mostly east-west, with seven a little more northerly, and two north-west with heads to the south. These nine exceptional alignments were without coffins and poorly furnished with knives, buckles and spear-heads alone. Of the rest, about half had traces of coffins and 88 were furnished, seven richly, including many weapons. There were also brooches, pendants and other ornaments of 7th-century date.

[Gilton has excited the minds of the archaeologically curious ever since, the record of which makes for a substantial history, still not yet complete.

All the finds from the site date from at least the early sixth to at least the late seventh centuries. In 1771 labourers employed by William Boys found some items, and in the same year Douglas recorded that labourers had found a gold and garnet brooch, two amethysts, a bronze bowl and other items, further remarking that in 1773 children still looked for beads on the site near the miller's house where Faussett had found weapons. Two more graves appeared in 1783, and a bronze-gilt hair-pin surfaced in around 1831.

In 1842 Roach Smith found *fibulae*, rings and glass vessels, all some two feet below the ground surface, and in the same year William Rolfe of Sandwich acquired a substantial group of finds, including bowls, axe-heads, swords, shield-bosses, brooches, buckles, beads and crystal balls, when the miller's house was levelled to make a garden. In 1849 gravel-diggers found two glass vessels and a copper-alloy bowl in the vicinity. In 1854 Akerman, prompted by news of further finds, had a trench dug but found nothing. The 20th century saw further sundry items exhibited or illustrated, and in 1957 an iron sword in a wooden scabbard was found in a private garden. Building-work on the south side of the mill uncovered the grave of a woman in 1973, and a metal-detectorist found a sixth-century gilt-silver belt in 2003.]

Chapter 6
A Scholar and his Friends

In 1760, still curate, Faussett moved back to Street End House, ever closer to his beloved mother, who died 23 May 1761. She was buried alongside her father in Nackington chancel, having seen ten of her 14 children reach adulthood, and a substantial clutch of grandchildren. Faussett now came entirely into his inheritance, having waited 11 years since his father's death in order to walk through the portals of Heppington as his own master. But it came at some cost: he received only a small amount of personal property, and now had to disburse some £2000, left by his father in trust until his widow died, to his surviving siblings. He severed ties with Street End House in February 1762 when he paid the Rev'd Francis Dodsworth £44 12s. 0d. for the remaining furniture there.

In March 1762 Faussett was on a visit to his neighbour Mrs Milles, who proceeded to show him two Roman urns she had brought back with her from a trip to one of her estates at North Elmham, Norfolk, where, as she told him, such things were often found. They held about a gallon each and were unopened. Faussett naturally soon persuaded his neighbour of his interests, and after struggling with their narrow necks he succeeded in tipping out a mass of congealed burnt bones and ashes, some of an adult and some of a child ('I judge from the teeth and the jaws'); in each was also 'a pair of brass nippers, the springs of which had not yet lost their elasticity – they had each of them a ringle of brass wire, as if to hang them by'. Then followed part of an ivory comb, several pieces of blue or green glass, and bits of metal and glass, perhaps the remnants of some *fibulae*. Faussett noted that he had seen a similar urn from the same location in the possession of Thomas Barrett of Lee, Kent, which had also contained a pair of nippers. Despite the relatively unexciting contents, Mrs Milles was ultimately persuaded to donate the urns to her neighbour in July 1767.

That same spring saw a letter from the solicitor William Chamberlayne, one of many over the years concerning disputes about Faussett's estates and the income derived from them. From it one gains a little insight as to how trials were arranged and Faussett's procedures. The under-sheriff had summoned a jury of

> … honest Sensible Men wholly Independent of the Government. On my Wishing for some Men of Fortune upon it he said if they had been Summoned they would not Probably attend, & upon the Whole I don't know whether a Middling Jury is not the most likely to be an impartial Judge between the Crown and the Subject. I prevailed upon the Sheriff to let me have a Copy of the Jury that if any of them should be found out disagreeable to You we might be prepared to Object to them.

Chamberlayne finished by enclosing estate details and expenses, in this instance all relating to property in Essex and occupied by 24 individuals, mostly gentlemen, but also including a yeoman, a baker and a shopkeeper.

Now followed Faussett's own and personal interregnum – four years were to elapse before a long-hoped for parish would be offered to him. He would have been aware of the constant jockeying for preferment by large numbers of clergy dissatisfied with their lot, and especially their income, both in and around Canterbury as well as most of the other dioceses, so chance news about a vacant parish would mean a rapid investigation of its income from tithes and the glebe, and from 'surplice fees' – the fees for baptisms, marriages and burials. Being with a mile or two of Canterbury and the archbishop was a distinct advantage, for the prelate held very extensive patronage as a personal power, including some of the richest livings in England; and he had also the power to grant a clergyman the dispensation to hold more than one living, while his administrative staff at Lambeth controlled the system of 'scarves', or appointing chaplains to the nobility, thus allowing the chaplain to hold further livings in plurality, even if the chaplaincy itself was little more than a sinecure. Added to all this was the bonus of livings valued at £8 or less annually in the 'King's Books' which could be held in plurality without a dispensation. And even if nothing were to drop from this rich and carefully regulated cornucopia, there was the Lord Chancellor who oversaw Crown livings, and the numerous Kentish squires with livings in their personal gift, thanks to the happy foresight of their noble ancestors.

It was indeed unfortunate that Faussett lacked the distinct advantage of being related by either birth or marriage to the men, both the gentry as well as the higher clergy, in whose power lay the gifts of ecclesiastical livings; but one thing was in his favour: with his master's degree he could (would that it were to happen!) obtain two livings concurrently, a luxury afforded only to those with that higher degree. His children were now aged 12, eight and five, and the costs of their education and the maintenance of a large house now fairly and squarely faced him. His arrival at Heppington was the signal for the departure of his remaining unmarried sisters who now removed themselves to set up house-keeping at Swanscombe under the auspices of their sailor brother Godfrey – not an entirely successful venture, for when Godfrey died two years later, Faussett advised the girls to part company and seek pastures new. The many and ample rooms of Heppington would now be less crowded.

But the partly-clouded horizon of Faussett's immediate future was now to be bathed with some bright and lasting sunshine. At the Society of Antiquaries on 13 January 1763 a committee comprising the The Right Honourable the Lord Willoughby de Parham, President, in the chair, J. Burrow Esq, , T. Brand Esq, M. Duane Esq, Dr Parsons, Dr Ducarel, L. Browne Esq, and the secretary Mr Norris, sat to consider the matter in hand.

> A testimonial was presented and read recommending the Rev'd Brian Faussett MA of Heppington near Canterbury, a Gentleman well versed in the Greek, Roman and English antiquities, to become a member of the Society of which honour he is desirous; and is certified by the subscribers to be a person every way qualified to become an useful member of this learned Body. Signed by Lord Willoughby, Edward Jacob, W. D. Byrch, A. C. Ducarel, T. Tyndall, L. Browne, M. Duane.[1]

The recommendation would then be hung up for the usual period of four consecutive meetings on a certificate signed by the supporters, after which a ballot was held prior to admission in a formal ceremony.

Being 'well versed' was Faussett's passport to entry (for nobody could deny that he was essentially a local archaeologist), a clear example of the early tendency to elect men of taste rather than antiquarianism. Here was a humble country cleric carrying on the honourable tradition of field work, but an Oxford man with the additional prize of a fellowship based on founder's kin who had devoted his empty years without a clerical cure to the pursuit of heraldry and genealogy, accompanied by a stronger interest in archaeology and an almost single-handed investigation of neighbourhood sites, the future fruits of which could scarcely be guessed at. It is no exaggeration to say that the only major archaeological works of the period not represented in the papers read at the Society are the excavations of Bryan Faussett.

Most of the proposers and signatories, as one would expect, were within Faussett's sphere, sometimes quite closely. We may now show something of the various worlds that they inhabited.

Lyde Browne was Governor of the Bank of England from 1768 until his death in 1787. His wealth enabled him to amass one of the largest collections of classical antiquities in the eighteenth century and to house it in his own museum at Rome, before removing it to his country house in Wimbledon. He published in 1768 a catalogue in Latin of 130 selected objects, and in 1779 one in Italian of his choicest marbles, both of which gave provenances from well-known Italian collections and excavation sites near Rome. No less a person than the Empress Catherine the Great purchased the material in 1784 for £22,000, and it today forms the major part of

---

[1]   Society of Antiquaries of London, *Minute Books* IX: 41

the classical sculpture collections in the Hermitage and nearby Pavlovsk Palace Museums.

The Rev'd William Dejovas Byrch was a Kent man from Goudhurst, and would be buried (coincidentally from Faussett's point of view) at Kingston in 1792. His only daughter married Sir Samuel Egerton Brydges of Denton Court near Canterbury, another genealogist and writer, who was related to many noble houses and liked to claim that he had a better right to the throne of England than the then present incumbent. He fought for more than a decade to establish a claim for his brother to the recently extinct barony of Chandos, but was ultimately rejected by the House of Lords who saw in his pedigree doubtful, but more tangible, connections with yeomen grocers at Harbledown, and had not been impressed by Brydges having inserted false entries into parish registers in pursuance of his aspirations.

Like his close friend, Edward Jacob was attracted to antiquarianism as a young man, and also came from a long-established Kentish family, which included mayors and magistrates of Sandwich and Dover. He was a skilled naturalist, botanist, fossil collector and bibliophile, and on top of all these achievements, a third-generation surgeon-apothecary who ran a private medical scheme for Faversham gunpowder workers, charging 6d. a week to be on call, and four times Mayor of Faversham, a position which his father had also filled. Years of patient research bore fruit and secured his reputation in *The History of the Town and Faversham*, published in 1774, and dedicated to Lord Sondes of Lees Court, his sometime medical patient. Jacob was one of the first men to realise the significance of the rich fossil remains in the clay cliffs of northern Sheppey when he began collecting examples in the 1740s, an occupation which perhaps followed on from his first marriage at Eastchurch on that island in 1739, and led to his purchase of Nutts manor house in Leysdown. In 1754 he submitted an account of several elephant bones found at Leysdown to the transactions of the Royal Society, whilst continuing to publish on the plant life of Faversham and its neighbourhood. He assisted William Boys of Sandwich in the latter's work on shells discovered near that town, and lent manuscripts to Hasted, to whom he was a natural editor for his friend's chapters on Sheppey. He may be summarised as a Georgian polymath and a civilised gentleman of the English enlightenment.

Two weeks later on 27 January 1763 Edward Jacob spoke at the Society of Antiquaries, informing the membership about the contents of a grave that Faussett had excavated at Ash near Sandwich on 30 September 1762:

The Rev'd Mr Fausset of Heppington near Canterbury, a gentleman very knowing and indefatigable in the study of Antiquities … had examined several of the graves … and has procured a valuable collection of Antiquities from thence, part of which consists of a small pair of scales, a touch stone and a nest of weights which were found piled on one another, inclosed in a wooden case [with an armed skeleton], now decayed. As these latter seemed to be of some consequence, in Mr Jacob's opinion, in regard to adjusting a considerable point of the Roman Antiquities, he has procured their exact weights and descriptions ... He flatters himself that Mr Faussett will, at his leisure, draw up an accurate account of all that he has there collected ... He hopes that these antiquities will be accepted as a small proof of his desire of approving himself not unmindful of the obligation of being admitted a member of so eminent a body. If the drawings are not a sufficient explanation, he shall be ready to give any further satisfaction.[2]

A month later, on 17 February 1763, 'The recommendatory testimonials of Joseph Wilcocks Esq and the Rev'd Brian Faussett, MA, having hung up the limited time, were read, and their Elections severally balloted for, and they were thereupon declared from the Chair duly elected Fellows of the Society.' On 10 March Faussett, now attending, paid his admission fee and signed the obligation required by the Society's statutes, and was admitted as fellow Number 416. His accounts duly mention that the occasion cost him five guineas. With supreme irony, if only he could have known it, and now aged just 42, virtually all his archaeological work still lay ahead of him; he had indeed been ushered into a polite and recondite society on the basis of everything except that for which he is remembered today.

Faussett had now entered a world still dominated by amateur scholars and gentleman antiquaries (and none less so than he, the Georgian country parson) which would soon see the rise of many specialist fields of historical research. The histories and classification of subjects as diverse as architecture, costume, birds, insects and coins would be rigorously and exhaustively investigated, and set down in print for the delectation and approval of one's peers, and for future enhancement by the next generation of scholars. These authors were lawyers, theologians, doctors, teachers and scientists, their enquiries not distinguished from the practitioners of other forms of enquiry, and their subjects not separated from other areas of knowledge, let alone distinguished as a discipline taught in universities. Many of them were Fellows or frequent guests of the Royal Society of London, founded in 1662, and at whose meetings antiquities were discussed along with astronomy, mathematics, geology and a host of other allied and practical subjects, all to be subsumed under the umbrella of 'science' in the 19th century. Not a few would also have been freemasons, another cosy and scholarly fraternity, developed from the establishment of the Grand Lodge in 1717, which appealed particularly not only to antiquaries but also to those interested in architecture and geometry.

Another man within Faussett's rarefied circle of antiquarian contacts was Ebenezer Mussell, described as 'a skilful collector of books and other curiosities'. He was made FSA in 1760, which perhaps provided an introduction to Faussett, although he had married a Canterbury woman in 1761. The 'curiosities' from his house at Bethnal Green were sold in 1765, shortly after his death, and his library much later in 1782. Faussett visited Mussell in London in 1763, and wrote to him shortly thereafter, clearly wanting to maintain contact with a man whose knowledge and collections were at least his equal and quite possibly greater. In return for the

[2]   *ibid.*, IX: 46-7

favours and civilities received at Bethnal Green he showed off some of the artefacts he had excavated at Ash, and even offered one or two *fibulae* and beads for inclusion in the other man's collections, clearly keen to cement a working relationship:

> If you think they deserve a place in your very valuable and curious collection of antiquities, I shall think myself happy; as indeed, I shall ever do, if, in consequence of my future searches, I shall be enabled to contribute anything else worthy of your notice. The only merit these remains pretend to, is there undoubtedly being Roman, and truly genuine; which circumstances, however, make me prefer them to everything else in my otherwise trifling collection; and indeed even these I can hardly look upon with pleasure, since I saw your inestimable Museum.[3]

Faussett now turned to jewellery and his Jacobite proclivities, offering Mussell an old family ring bearing the head of the Old Pretender which he reckoned 'to be very like, and well done', a little picture of Charles II, also once part of a ring, and another item which had fallen into his hands only the previous day – a 1719 halfpenny, again with the head of the Old Pretender, found in the pocket of one of the fallen rebels at Culloden. Mussell was perhaps not too impressed by a sudden jump of 15 centuries, but Faussett was nothing if not keen to secure anything unwanted in the Bethnal Green cabinet of curiosities:

> If when you come to put your little room on the top of the stairs to rights, you meet with anything which you may think unworthy of a place amongst the many great curiosities it contains, I shall think myself greatly obliged to you for it, as I shall for any duplicates or refuse coins which may chance to come into your hands; and I shall be glad to purchase of you any such as are more valuable, of which you may happen to have duplicates.[4]

It looked therefore as if acquisition was as high on Faussett's agenda as friendship, but he did at least sign off by wishing Mussell a successful course of physick for his present ailments and looking forward to seeing him soon at Heppington, adding that, 'The four uppermost beads in the box are of amber, and on that account are more rare. I think it proper to mention to you that they are very brittle, that you may handle them accordingly.'

Mussell died in 1764, but not as an old man, as both his in-laws survived him; yet at his death he had both a married daughter, and an infant son whom he named Ebenezer George Nicholas Bryan, perhaps, one would like to think, in honour of his antiquarian friend.

It would be surprising indeed if Edward Hasted, the great Kent historian, were not to appear in this narrative. What would develop into a close friendship with Faussett started in the mid-1750s when he began to discover his true vocation as an

---

[3] Nichols, *Illustrations of the Literary History...*, IV: 32
[4] Nichols, *loc. cit.*

historian. Several letters survive from him to Faussett, in part about daily news, but much more frequently concerned with antiquarian matters, written mostly in a hand bordering on the semi-impenetrable. He stayed regularly at Heppington and it is not difficult to guess at what must have been the subject of many discussions stretching late into the evenings – on one occasion, having seen Faussett's carefully annotated copy of Harris's *History of Kent* Hasted was keen to borrow it. He was a dozen years Faussett's junior but lived on until 1812, dying and being buried at Corsham in Wiltshire. Like his friend, he inherited wealth, chiefly accumulated by his grandfather who was the chief painter-stainer at the royal dockyard in Chatham, to which town the family moved after the death of Edward's landowning father in 1740. He was educated well and then studied law, but was not called to the Bar.

The seeds for his history of Kent were planted in him as a young man when he collected material for pleasure and knowledge of the past, the hallmark of a future antiquarian seen also, of course, in Faussett's teenage archaeological expeditions. Scholarly friends encouraged him to collect systematically and then to publish his results, all of which was sustained by sufficient rents from land, allowing him the freedom to pursue his enquiries unembarrassed by the lack of the wherewithal to live – a material fact which conferred intellectual freedom. He moved between Canterbury and Sutton-at-Hone in west Kent, living at the Commandery in that rural parish, and found time to be JP for Kent from 1757, and also briefly Lord Lieutenant. Like Faussett, he counted Ducarel, the Lambeth Palace librarian, among his friends. After two months of examining source material in London archives in 1763, his *magnum opus* began to take shape, a venture which would occupy him for the best part of four decades, and one which was much delayed by his having to escape his creditors by fleeing to France as well as a seven-year spell in the King's Bench Prison for the same reason.

Alas, the punctiliousness of the first edition was not repeated in the second, which was marred by errors in the maps and elsewhere, the omission of footnotes, and considerably less detail about families and their lands, especially about female descendants – a fact of which the genealogically-minded Faussett, had he lived, would no doubt have strongly disapproved. But how could Hasted, the gentleman scholar, impoverished and incarcerated, have exercised his usual care in such matters? As some recompense, though, the general reader and the sightseer would now enjoy fuller descriptions of landscapes and no small amount of lively gossipy details which imparted a generally more popular flavour to the writing. The second edition was, despite all the caveats, a monumental achievement in its coverage of a county peppered with small manors which its unique system of gavelkind had endlessly subdivided and which had changed hands frequently. The reputation of Faussett's good friend, sometimes considered a dull and unimaginative writer, will live on, if only for his indefatigability in seeing his county history through to publication, albeit at great personal cost. (Faussett recorded in his accounts for March 1775 that he had just paid his first instalment of £1 11s. 6d. towards Hasted's book.)

In November 1763, then living at Throwley near Faversham, Hasted thanked his friend for his kind entertainment at Heppington: '… a most agreeable time. I wish we were nearer to enjoy it still oftener.' He related how he had been busy in copying Dr Plot's manuscript *Papey* which the writer had left towards a natural history of Kent. They had made for good reading:

> I dare say you will be pleased with them, tho' they are mixed with some so credulous, & childish relations, more than can well be Imagined in a person of his Sense and Experience, tho' his history of Oxfords[hire] has but too many of this sort in it.

Next he turned to another local man and mutual friend, Edward Jacob of Faversham, who had lent him Warburton's papers which he had been studying as part of his own intended county history:

> I am now Blazoning his Alphabet of Arms & tricking them all thro', which, as I am but a very beginner In Heraldry, taking me a good while in doing a very little, but I see that I shall get forward Easier & Quicker every day.

He had just had word from Thomas Astle who was now able to lend him an accurate survey of Kentish churches and castles with their elevations, after which Faussett would be most welcome to see them 'or anything else I have is at your service.' He signed off with characteristic antiquarian interest 'You have no doubt got thro' your Labour at the Barrow long […] now; I shall be very Glad to hear from you how it has turned out.'

That same year Hasted wrote to Astle, epitomising a pleasant day spent out in the fields with Faussett (the latter well prepared 'with his hollow trowel and tools proper for the purpose') at one site some two miles from Heppington, at another two fields away from the house, and at a third he called the 'Roman Camp' (which cannot be positively identified, but was probably the Roman earthwork in Iffin Wood):

> Last week spent my time most agreeably with Bryan Fosset [sic], when most of our time, indeed all that we could spare from the ladies, was spent in his study or on sallying out to find Roman camps, tumuli, etc. This we properly dressed for, and had you seen us, you would certainly have taken us for Robinson Crusoe and his man Friday.[5]

One wonders how they appeared to passers-by, doubtless dressed up to brave all weathers, unwanted spectators and other inconveniences.

Faussett now recalled the visit to the barrow in writing to Hasted a few months later in January 1764, but not in the way that his addressee might have expected. On a rare visit to London he had had his nose somewhat put out of joint by discovering that Hasted had pre-empted him in giving information about the barrow to the Society, and then not even accurately

---

[5] *Arch. Cant.* XXVII (1905): 137

I tell you that I have worked at the Tumulus, but one Half: Day, ever since I had the Pleasure of seeing You here. I was not a little surprised, on entering the Room belonging to our Society, together with Dr Ducarel, to find the Secretary reading over a Paper which made often Mention of my name; for at the Distance, at which, I, at first, was, I could hear nothing else, distinctly: but, much more so, when I came nearer, to find, that, it was an Account of this very Tumulus; of which I was very sure no Sort of Account could possibly be given, with any Kind of Exactness, or even Conjecture; especially, as, for my own Part, I am almost sure, it is no Tumulus at all; as my last search seem'd but too plainly to indicate. On expressing my Surprise to Dr Ducarel, he told Me, that, this Account came, from You, to Mr Astle; and, that, Mr Astle had communicated it to the Society; and, that, this was the 2d Time of its being read. I did not, at all, imagine, that, you sent it to Mr Astle with that View, for the reasons above given; and, therefore, desired The President to pay no further Regard to it; and, promised to send a true Acct of it, as soon as I knew what Acct to give.[6]

Hasted, inevitably, very soon got wind of the brewing storm and wrote immediately to Astle from Throwley that same week. He was keen for Astle, a formidable scholar, but also influential in the Society of Antiquaries, to try and pour oil on troubled waters as soon as he could, clearly feeling that he had trodden on Faussett's toes by misquoting him and making public what had not yet been fully and properly discussed in private:

I received a letter a day or two ago from Mr Brian Fosset of Heppington, in which he gave me an account that on his being at the Antiquarian Society when last in town, the secretary was reading the account I sent you of the tumulus that he and I had been trying to open. That he desired the President to pay no further regard to it, and promised to send a true account. There is no doubt but had I thought that letter would have been read at the Society I should have put it in better dress, but as I think Mr Fosset's behaviour had attacked the truth of it, it is incumbent on me to assert the truth of the facts there mentioned, and to declare there they are literally and minutely true. As to the conjectures, they are but conjectures, but are such as he or myself then made, and both acquiesced in at that time. I may perhaps have mistaken his words, but as you were present I hope you will let me know your thoughts of it, and if there is occasion, that you will vindicate it at your meeting, for if it is consistent with the rules of your Society and they thought the materials worth their hearing, I should insist on its being read there and a proper regard had to it, for I would sooner forgive any man's accusing me of almost anything whatsoever rather than of an untruth.[7]

Like the course of true love, true friendships can sometimes temporarily founder, clearly demonstrated in this snapshot of an *odium archaeologicum* between two scholars normally the best of friends. (It is also virtually the only reference to Faussett actually attending the Society of Antiquaries, thus briefly shedding his reputation as the reclusive Kentish scholar who seldom left the confines of his rural retreat: the

---

[6]   CCA: U11/6/3/297
[7]   *Arch. Cant.*, loc. cit.

records of that august institution do not contain one reference to Faussett either giving, or even having read on his behalf, a single paper.)

Again like true love, this true friendship was not to founder on the one rock of just one disagreement, for in 1780, four years after Faussett's death, Hasted would write to Ducarel and reminisce that,

> Our late friend Bryan Faussent [sic], who was I do think as capable and learned a man in that way as this country ever had or will have.[8]

In July 1766 Hasted wrote from Sutton-at-Hone to thank Faussett for yet another reception at Heppington, adding that he had a copy of the Horton Priory cartulary made by Prior Holbeck: 'Do come and see it at Sutton, and I will let Astle know too so he might meet you too.' In June 1769, he was just returned from northern France and gave Faussett a long description of the buildings, cathedral, food and wine to be enjoyed at St Omer. His last letter of November 1773, written at Canterbury, is short and purely business-like. He had been investigating his field at Keecold Hill at Newington near Sittingbourne and said that it had lost its ancient Roman name, being now downgraded to the appellation of 'Twopenny Hill'. The tenant could gladly show it to Faussett, Hasted also wondering whether any of his other lands might be of use to his friend. The valedictory request now followed:

> Will you be so kind to lend me, for a few Days, Aubrey's Antiquities of Surry? I cannot get them in Canterbury & I have sent to London for them, but till I get them, I must be Idle except you will oblige me in my Distress.

Thus was expressed the continuing deep and lifelong friendship between the two, only to cease at Faussett's death when Hasted, as an appointed overseer to his friend's will, would help in the winding-up of the estate. One small and endearing token of that friendship was that of Faussett's wife Elizabeth standing as a sponsor in August 1768 to the baptism of Hasted's seventh child, predictably named John Septimus.

Another of Faussett's antiquarian confidants and close friends was Dr Andrew Coltée Ducarel. He was born at Paris in 1713, and had been successively librarian and treasurer of Doctors' Commons before Thomas Secker appointed him as commissary of the City and Diocese of Canterbury in 1758. This post he enjoyed along with being the first professional lay librarian at Lambeth Palace, a position carrying an annual salary of £30 which he had obtained through the offices of Matthew Hutton and discharged for 28 years under five successive archbishops, of which Thomas Secker was his most demanding taskmaster. Elected FSA when only 24, he was active in its early meetings at the Mitre Tavern, helping on its publications committee, and so was naturally one

[8] *Inv. Sep.*: 215

of Faussett's fellow sponsors for entry to that august institution in 1763. Amongst other things, he had early seen and recognised the importance of the Bayeux Tapestry, and his 1767 work on Anglo-Norman architecture, with its appendix of drawings of the tapestry, still ranks as a pioneer comparative study of mediaeval architecture. Equally compelling for Faussett, he was also greatly interested in coins and medals, and in an age when gentlemen of leisure were in some abundance and the fruits of their research willingly shared, many would have sought friendly assistance from fellow scholars, even if (in Ducarel's case) it might not be acknowledged.

Faussett had uttered a cry from the heart in July 1764 when he wrote to Ducarel as follows:

> My good friend, I am most sincerely sorry that I ever took orders; nay, could I decently leave them, I declare to you, I would certainly do it; for thank God, I can live without them; else God help me! You know I had great hopes of getting Ripple [near Deal] in exchange for my dirty Vicarage – those hopes are vanished; for Rogers is now determined to stay in Kent. And yet what adds to my comfort, I am again threatened with a prosecution for non-residence. Indeed, these threats are annual; nor have I much regarded them whilst my friend Lyster was well, for he always stood in the gap. But he, poor man, is going. Not that I need regard even the being deprived of the living; for as I shewed you by my papers, which I received while you were here, it did not bring me 20l. last year, which by no means makes amends for the continued plague and trouble I have with it. I had, indeed, resigned it long ago, but for the following two reasons, viz, that I might possibly make an exchange; and that, after so much money laid out on my education, I might have it to say that I was not quite without preferment. But I am heartily weary of such nominal honour! But I beg your pardon for troubling you with my paltry affairs.[9]

Next he turned to more pleasant matters, discoursing on various antiquarian activities. He had been rummaging in booksellers but had no luck in finding a copy of Lewis's map of the diocese, being 'very scarce'. Colonel Sawbridge had sent him a considerable assortment of items, and affords good evidence that Faussett's collections comprised not only what he himself had dug out of the ground, but were enhanced by what might come to light through a coterie of men with similar interests and the time to go foraging.

The parcel included keys, *fibulae* and seal matrices, these last 'very fine, and as sharp as when they were first cut'. Next a copper *speculum* or mirror ('Roman', as Faussett supposed), five inches broad, finely plated and highly polished, followed by a medley of instruments construed as carpenters' gouges, punches and chisels, all of cast copper of which 'I make no doubt of their being of British workmanship'. A brass jug with a relief of Cupid followed, and then the largest sections which were of spears, darts and swords, one of brass, gilded and two feet long, glass urns and lamps, and more than 40 *paterae* and other samian ware impressed with the potter's name. All in all, it was a substantial holding:

---

[9]   Nichols, *op. cit.*, III: 556-7

These things added to my own collection, make some figure, I will assure you; and the owner of them wishes for nothing so much as to give Dr Ducarel a sight of them.[10]

The letter finished with his expectation of the arrivals of his historian friends Edward Hasted and Edward Jacob, the latter's wife 'brought to bed of a brave boy two days ago'. The final signature was typical: 'Your much obliged humble servant, Br. Faussett'.

He was in a different mood when writing again to Ducarel two months later in September 1764, lamenting both the passing of summer and the death of Mr Forster, his erstwhile university lecturer at Oxford, who was 'taken yesterday afternoon with a sleeping fit from which he could not be entirely aroused'.[11] Faussett clearly had deep and cherished memories of him from his impressionable undergraduate years:

The bell is now going for him, and as I have known him long and am no stranger to his virtues, and the goodness of his heart affects me more than I would have imagined considering I had not the happiness of an intimate acquaintance with him, which, however, I think, I was, as it were, deterred from by an awe impressed on my young clay (pardon the coxcombical expression) on hearing his catechetical lectures at University College many years ago, and which I never could somehow erase enough to persuade myself but that he was something special very much my superior, though by his now and then calling on me in his rides he seemed, as it were, to invite me to be less reserved. So strong is a prejudice of this kind early received! But, my dear friend, I grow so grave so will say no more on this subject lest I should insensibly be more so.

Now he turned to the matters so dear to his heart, and over which there were so very few with whom he could correspond. His enthusiasm bubbles though:

I have lately added greatly to my collection by the acquisition of a very fine mummy (a present from my friend Mussell) ... Mr Mussell also brought me down about 600 Copper Roman Coins &c. But as my collection is now grown pretty large I shall not be able to find among them many worth laying by except about a score very fine Greek medals, among which is a fine African Gordian. He has also brought me 6 Saxon sticas but these I have not yet seen, they being sent with his Baggage to Ramsgate.

He continued, and ended by reflecting a little on his withdrawn existence at Heppington:

I am just going to eat venison with some of my friends (such as they are) here. The best sauce to it that I [can] possibly eat expect will be some hodge podge disquisitions on horses, dogs, hunting, shooting &c. But, as it is my misfortune not to be a sportsman, it is odds that it will not be cooked to my palate. But I must bear with it, or live alone. But why do I snarl – you, my friend, are a cynic! I shall certainly drink your health'.

[10] *loc. cit.*
[11] British Library, MS Addl 23,990

Such must have been the occasional longueurs of an isolated country parson's life, always keen for recent gossip about new publications and fellow acquaintances, information on newly found antiquities, and answers to obscure points of enquiry.

He wrote again a month later in October 1764 to Ducarel, regretting that the delay in replying was because a friend had been expected to come to Heppington and take the letter with him up to London, '... but as his journey is deferred, I should count myself inexcusable if I any longer deferred paying my respects to you'.[12] Faussett had set aside some traders (or trade tokens) for Ducarel, and impatiently awaited his arrival with a learned colleague to look over them. He was equally impatient in waiting to hear from a friend of Hasted whom he was sure wanted to hire Street End, but in the meantime, when could the three keen antiquarians be together again to talk about the one subject of which they were all so fond?

In January 1765 a further letter to Ducarel presaged what would come to pass a few months later. After thanking his friend for a gift of oysters, Faussett continued:

> On the day I wrote last to you I waited (as I thought myself obliged to do) on the Archdeacon, who read to me the contents of the Archbishop's letter, so far as concerned me; and put a much more favourable construction on them than I even now think they will bear, viz "that he only wanted to be informed whether I would do the duty myself, or keep a Curate"; desired my answer, which he would send to the Archbishop that day and advised me to write to him myself. I did so, but neither the Archdeacon nor myself have had my answer yet.[13]

Further news was added about an agreement with Mr Cowland for his land 'very advantageous and convenient for us both', and Faussett then thanked Ducarel for information about the impending auction sales of Mr Mussell's coins, for

> I must depend on you only for early notice of them, as soon as the times are fixed – as also for a catalogue as soon as they come out, For please God I am well, I intend to be in town at the time of the sale of the coins at least.

He ended characteristically by appending his solution to a problem from Colchester, carefully writing out his version of a partly legible Latin inscription.

---

[12] Nichols, *op. cit.*, III: 558
[13] *ibid.*: 559

Chapter 7
A Vicar at Last

Faussett's unanswered letter to the Archbishop had clearly reached its addressee, for Thomas Secker, now Archbishop of Canterbury, came to his rescue. The prelate was described by some as a man lacking social graces, stiff and reserved, and no less a person than Horace Walpole thought him 'bred a Presbyterian, commenced a man-midwife, was president of an atheistical club, and lastly a popular preacher of the Church of England, by which means he rose to episcopacy'. But Secker was an experienced churchman: having won favour with Queen Caroline, he progressed from Rector of Houghton-le-Spring to Canon of Durham, Chaplain of the Royal Household, Rector of St James's Piccadilly, Dean of St Paul's (where, as a rest-cure, he indexed the cathedral records in his own hand), and then to the bishoprics of Bristol and Oxford before becoming archbishop in 1758. A dominating personality, although tempered by the reputation of being an impressive, if divisive, ecclesiastical leader, kept him at the forefront of public debate.

After his installation at Canterbury, he kept a close and detailed watch on his clergy (notably by regular visits), for no fewer than 72 of the 279 parishes in the Canterbury diocese were not part of a department of state under the control of the network of landowners, but lay rather within the archiepiscopal gift, together with three of the 12 cathedral prebendaries. Secker could therefore control the appointment of substantial numbers of men, and for these he drew on not only existing diocesan clergy but also on a national patronage network. Most of his men came from the professions or from within the ranks of the clergy themselves, and largely from the urban middle class – an increase in the gentry class, naturally including Faussett himself, would not materialise until later in the century.

However, nearly all the Canterbury clergy were graduates, as Secker would not promote men without a university education, many of whom would probably not have passed muster at the archbishop's assessments which required clerical testimonials and a vigorous examination from his officers. All his clergy were expected to maintain high standards, especially in preaching and the administration of regular holy communion, and in addition, curates were carefully regulated as many had not obtained the appropriate licence to officiate. Those conscientious and diligent enough to have fulfilled all the requirements tended to be promoted, and as Secker could sometimes be very generous to obscure parochial clergymen (if we may include Faussett in that category), on 8 May 1765 Faussett was collated as rector of Monks Horton, and inducted[1] five days later, his expenses for that occasion totalling £1 6s. 0d., the sequestration 10s., the land tax £1 12s. and a gift to the ringers 10s. 6d. Ah, how one wonders if Secker saw something here of a tainted chalice and how deeply the old friendship still ran, for he declared, 'I gave also Horton R[ectory] to Mr Faussett. Bec[ause] the Income was sunk so, that no body cared to take it; and he being a man of substance, was most likely to raise it.'

Faussett and the archbishop shared a personal scourge (but not one of a religious nature), for Thomas Secker was also long a martyr to the gout, so much so that he ultimately lost the use of his left arm. The laying down of wine at this period was a common practice, as was the custom of bringing 'liveries' of wine direct to the table from the pipe or tun; this, together with the fact that much Portuguese port was immature and poor, brought about its deleterious results in countless gentlemen who kept a well-stocked cellar.

The living of Alberbury was now finally and completely relinquished, and Faussett would hold Monks Horton until his death, albeit as a wholly absentee incumbent who much preferred the comfort of his own mansion to that of the rectory. He was at one point threatened with prosecution for non-residence but nothing seems to have come of it, as Secker then installed Joseph Price, then vicar of the adjacent Brabourne, as curate of Monks Horton, a position he discharged until Faussett's death in 1776, when he was then appointed rector in his place. At the same time Faussett obtained the curacy of Lower Hardres, highly conveniently placed adjacent to Nackington, but resigned it in 1772.

Monks Horton was a small parish, just over 1,000 acres in extent, delightfully situated just below the Kentish Downs. Its tiny church of St Peter, still isolated, was a little more than a mile from the remains of the Cluniac priory (whence the first element of the parish name) founded by Robert de Vere and confirmed by a Papal bull of 1144. There was no single dominant landowner, it being parcelled out to well-to-do squires who in turn let to tenant farmers. Hasted recorded that there was one acre of glebeland and that the living in 1733 was worth £100 annually. There were also 200 acres of woodland, the underwood of which in 1772 brought Faussett £75, and the timber £40. Nearby was a clutch of large houses occupied by a company of east Kent squires who, in essence, ruled the county by sitting on its judicial benches and on its parochial boards, sometimes also as the elected Member

---

[1] CCA: F/A/1765/7

Figure 16. Monks Horton church: small and humble in the trees.
(Copyright Neil Anthony.)

Figure 17. Nackington church from the south-west: Norman to Georgian harmony in flint, brick and tile.
(Copyright Neil Anthony.)

for Parliament, and all the while tied the gentrified knot ever tighter by marrying off their own daughters – alas for poor Faussett in having only the one, and she not yet a teenager. Sir Egerton Brydges' comment that 'We rarely had much mobility, but the squires ruled the day' nicely encapsulated the essence of the intimate coterie into which Faussett could not quite gain a much-desired entry.

A rather different tithe system obtained at Monks Horton to what was current elsewhere, in that farmers did not pay their rector the customary one tenth of their produce, but instead an annual sum based on the acreage of their pasture. This curious practice was established at the end of Elizabeth's reign by a decree from the Court of Exchequer, but later fell into disuse until its revival in 1723 by the aggressively litigious Rev'd Dr Conyers Middleton who, when he found mention of the former practice in his family papers, confronted the entire parish and its then rector of 48 years and swore that henceforth he would pay tithes only in the way in which his ancestors had been accustomed to. When Faussett arrived in 1765, clearly after better returns than what were on offer, he sought the opinion of Thomas Hussey, an Ashford solicitor, who encouragingly declared that the original decree was not binding upon the Rector.

Sufficiently enthused to try and raise the value of the living, Faussett filed a bill in the Exchequer against its continuation, suing the impropriator, Matthew Robinson Morris, rather than paying the expenses out of his own pocket as Secker hoped, but ceased his proceedings before a commission was issued (Hasted says that Faussett pursued the case for several years at no small trouble and expense before he dropped it). The peculiar system thus remained: the farmers paid 2*d.* an acre for old pasture and 1*d.* for new, and in addition, for the falls or casts of horned cattle, mares and sheep, ½*d.* each up to nine, but if ten or more, then in kind. Was it this additional frustration which caused Faussett to exclaim: 'I went into Shropshire a stranger, and was caressed. I come here, live upon my own estate, and in my native county, and we are all confusion'?

Joseph Price, neighbour and close friend, had come from Norfolk and, like Faussett, had through Secker's patronage as a fellow quondam dissenter obtained the vicarage of Brabourne in 1767. He resigned both Monks Horton and Brabourne in 1786 to take the living of Herne before ending his career as vicar of Littlebourne from 1794 until his death and burial there in 1807. Of consuming interest is his diary which in the main covers the years 1769-1773. Although entitled 'diary' it is not a chronological narrative, has few dates and many later interpolations, and moreover was written in a shorthand cognate to what Samuel Pepys had employed – Thomas Shelton's 'Tachygraphy', first published in 1638. The decipherment was finally achieved only in 1960, greatly assisted by its author who did not entirely faithfully adhere to Shelton's system, and who also left proper names of people and places in longhand, as at that time shorthand systems were more for secrecy and privacy than speed.

There is much information on ecclesiastical livings, bishops' and other clerics' lives (often by way of snatches of conversation), and events in London and official circles; but the author truly shines when recording details of the private lives and idiosyncrasies of the east Kent gentry and clergy, and, although an amateur with mediocre Latin, Price also achieved considerable intellectual distinction, being offered the headmastership of Wye Grammar school, and all the while collecting university gossip by virtue of the fact that fellowships were then only for the clergy. He also offers us much minute detail about household and economic matters, including many everyday costs in the second half of the 18th century, as well as detailed pictures of Margate and Ramsgate.

Tantalising glimpses have been left to us of things said by Faussett which may well go some way to explaining why his ecclesiastical aspirations foundered for as long as they did. Osmond Beauvoir now comes onto the scene, one of Archbishop Secker's inner sanctum from whom he would receive his doctorate in 1782. A former old boy, he then became headmaster of the King's School at Canterbury from 1750-1782 (during which period he instituted the school register), in addition to holding several parishes and being one of the cathedral Six Preachers. His intellectual skills and genius in the classics would also gain him membership of the Royal Society in 1785.

Faussett was considered as a candidate for Brabourne parish, but a letter written by Beauvoir in January 1767 reveals why he did not get the living:

> Mr Faussett is better, though still confined. I have not been able yet to go and see him; our snow lies deep, but nothing in comparison to what it is in the South of France, as a gentleman just come from thence told us yesterday, who in places was obliged to use six horses and four oxen to get along. Charles Norris, Vicar of Brabourne, and Curate of Nonington, really and truly died yesterday; the latter would suit Faussett, and oblige him much; but I was told yesterday, that someone has very kindly represented him to his Grace as a man subject to passion, and to utter at such times very unclerical language. He has an enemy who might not scruple saying whatever he thought proper, if he had the opportunity.[2]

Old friend as Archbishop Secker was, he was evidently swayed by the description of Faussett's occasional lapses, and did not see his way to giving Brabourne to him, it going instead to his other old friend Joseph Price, who was not above commenting that:

> Faussett most envious, disappointed man. Abuses people for getting preferment, by saying they come into life with no such hopes or expectations. Expects an Archbishop to offer a man preferment that has any estate.[3]

Learned and landed nobody can deny that Faussett was, but friendliness does seem sometimes to have been in short supply. His resentment at being ignored by some of his fellow east Kent gentry may have arisen from his partial reclusiveness, but one

[2] Nichols, *Illustrations of the Literary History...*, III: 355
[3] Ditchfield & Keith-Lucas, *op. cit.*,127

wonders if his comments about Dr Beauvoir were based less on the fees he paid him for his son Godfrey to be a King's scholar, and more on the comments in the above 1767 letter, when he described him as an 'impudent, shewy, pushing boshy, florid man'. Faussett's opinion of Beauvoir was not, however, a universal one, for Sir Egerton Brydges described him as 'one of the most correct classical scholars of his day', and Hasted considered him one 'whose great abilities brought this school to the highest degree of estimation; who united the gentleman with the scholar, one whose eminent qualifications and courtesy of manners gained him the esteem and praise of all who knew him'. (*Quot homines, tot sententiae!*)

Faussett had also locked horns with Beauvoir over the administration of Cogan's Hospital in Canterbury. It had been founded in 1657 by John Cogan, who was responsible for the sequestration of the property of the Royalists and of the Cathedral and Archbishop. He endowed it with some of the sequestrated land, which was returned to its original owners at the Restoration, an act which left the hospital with no funds for maintenance and its consequent dereliction. A public subscription of 1772 sought to raise funds for rebuilding, assisted by a modest endowment under the will of the Rev'd Dr Aucher, a Prebendary of the Cathedral, for the support of the six clergy widow inmates. Price noted here that

> Faussett does not agree long with anybody ... won't subscribe to the repair of Cogan's, because set on foot by Beauvoir, and people he does not like, and people he says that will rule everything.[4]

Faussett was indeed not above sometimes pulling rank, once describing one Thomas Denward as, 'like all people that have not had any education, talks so uneducated, strange, quaint grammatical, half-learned that it is disagreeable', and of a huntsman called Tom Randolph, he pronounced: 'God help him. He knows nothing of dogs but amuses himself. As to hunting, it is a near joke'. But occasionally, it appeared, Price concurred with his friend's pronouncements, for in July 1770 he dined with the new Archbishop Frederick Cornwallis, in whose presence also was the Archdeacon William Backhouse: 'I first saw the archdeacon at this visitation. His appearance not in his favour; it was rustic and awkward, as Faussett my rector justly observed'.

With curates effectively running Monks Horton parish, Faussett as an absentee vicar had considerable spare time to indulge his many interests. There were occasional but regular trips to London to catch up with friends, learn the latest news at the Society of Antiquaries, purchase coins and generally socialise, such trips sometimes requiring a good deal of careful organisation before the coach departed from Heppington. Some years saw just the one excursion, but there were five, for example in 1770, each costing between £12 and £80; Faussett going either alone, with one of the children, or sometimes accompanied by his wife, for periods of up to 12 days.

---

[4] *ibid.*, 128

He clearly accomplished much when visiting the capital, glad to be away from rural east Kent to enjoy fresh pursuits. We may gain some idea of his activities from a typical list of expenses: gloves, thimbles, cane-string, the barber and the ironmonger, post-chaises, salmon and oysters, theatre and chair hire at Vauxhall and the Ranelagh, lottery tickets, medals, laundry, lodgings and servants, meals (breakfast, supper, tea and dinner), buckles, books, wine and coffee, church, and the asylum.

A six-day trip in November 1766 is itemised as follows in a small leather-bound expenses book,[5] much of which is crossed through and so perhaps transferred elsewhere:

> Machine to London   £1 11s.
> Post-chaise to Sittingbourne   18s.
> Expenses there and on the roads   £1 1s. 6d.
> Coach hire &c at London   4s. 6d.
> Play   6s.
> Coach hire   5s. 6d.
> Medals   7s. 6d.
> Servants   12s. 6d.
> Coach at the Swan   4s.
> Post-chaise to Dartford   17s.
> Gave Godfrey   £5 5s.
> Gave Mr Wightman   £1 1s.
> Lottery ticket   £11 15s.
> At Dartford and on the road home   9s. 6d.
> Post-chaise from Canterbury   5s.
> Boys & c.   1s. 9d.   [Total: £24 17s. 3d.]

A gift of five guineas was no doubt looked forward to with relish by his son, while the father was no doubt equally keen to gain some return for the large expenditure on the lottery.

On 12 February 1767 Faussett was additionally licensed by Secker as perpetual curate of Nackington itself (following on from the recent death of Charles Norris), an easily accessible employment, and again holding it for the rest of his life. In 1769 the stipend was £40, not that different from his other curacies. The last register entries there in his hand are for November 1775, three months before his death. As to what Faussett did or did not do in the way of priestly duties is easily evidenced from the fact that he took every marriage and called every entry of banns at Nackington (a ten-minute walk away) between 1767 and 1775, but at Monks Horton, an inconvenient ten miles to the south, not a single similar entry is recorded by him, all such duties being undertaken by a curate. A total absence in one parish was made up for by a continuous presence in the other – how often did the parishioners of Monks Horton ever meet their rector?

---

[5]   Liverpool World Museum: MS 2002.25.20

Faussett's church expeditions were mainly undertaken from 1757-1759, some initial archaeological work in 1757, further bursts in the early 1760s and 1767, and the lion's share between 1771-1773. The period of clerical work at Kingston would therefore not have been affected by these activities at all. At Petham, Waltham and Lower Hardres he also took the majority of marriages and calling of banns, and seems to have dovetailed them with his expeditions, although of course visiting churches and digging for antiquities was not a winter pursuit. All his excavations are precisely dated and mostly in the months of June to October, thus leaving over half the year for his other demands; and indeed, nearly all the entries at Nackington are in the winter months – did he gently persuade his parishioners to avoid summer weddings in order to allow the longer days for activities much closer to his heart?

In December 1766 Faussett had the unexpected pleasure of a small legacy from the maternal side of the family. A solicitor named Joseph Pinfold advised him that 'our worthy and late relation' Mr Chambrelan Godfrey had died at home in Serjeant's Inn on 25 November, and had left £100 to each Faussett cousin, the issue of the late Mr Faussett of Kent (that is, Bryan senior, the father of the antiquary).

Soon the Godfrey pedigree would be keenly investigated by Faussett's cousin Thomas Godfrey, the attorney in London who had helped Henry Faussett, the antiquary's youngest brother, to set up in business. In January 1771 the first letter of what would be a long series of enquiries on the matter arrived at Heppington from Godfrey's office junior, Edmund Clutterbuck. After thanking Faussett for the favour of a Heppington turkey (many more, and also pigs and geese, would follow), he said that Godfrey was stuck on the descendants of Richard Godfrey (1592-1641) who married Mary Moyle, the sometime MP for New Romney. Godfrey had sought expert advice and received it in the form of Isaac Heard, the distinguished and extremely long-lived herald whose career spanned 63 years, the last 38 of them as Garter King of Arms.

A few months later, Heard was staying at Margate with Godfrey himself, and requested an inspection of such collections that Faussett might have relating to the family, adding that Godfrey was 'currently fatigued by business, but alleviated by bathing and the air of this place'. Over the coming months Heard would write with ever-increasing demands for precise information, some of it to the embarrassment of Faussett.

They agreed to meet the following week at the Fountain Inn in Canterbury (a place of rendezvous popular with other family members for all kinds of reasons), whence Heard and his wife were invited to stay at Heppington. The stay was clearly pleasurable, for Heard wrote thanking Faussett and for

> the happiness of its generous and worthy owners ... my better Part laments she lost the Pleasure of seeing & learning (from its own mouth) the Adventures of the emboxed Mummy at the Bottom of the Stairs, which happily for Candles, we were not obliged to pass in the dark...

An installation of the Knights of the Garter would now take up his time, but he was grateful that Faussett had provided the documents he needed to see. Two months later Heard was worried that there were still difficulties with the pedigree, and that he needed information from 'a Gentleman of your liberal mind, literature and ingenuity'. The coat of arms was clearly the source of the trouble, and must have touched something of a raw nerve with Faussett, the keen genealogist and heraldist, but one not dissimilar from hundreds of other 'armigerous' gentlemen:

> I must beg you will furnish me with most antient Proof, Monuml Plate, Seal &c of the bearing of Arms &c, that I may represent to my Brethren in Chapter, the Extent of a Prescriptive Right to the Arms of Faussett as borne by your family, for I do not find them legally ascertained.

He would then strive to get them inserted into the Godfrey pedigree, and now further asked about the families of Fawcett of Norwich, Forsett of Marylebone, and Forsett Esq who died in 1687, clearly casting about to find something that would fit the requirements, for 'the good Old Gent … is extremely anxious to have this Business finished'. Faussett must by now have felt more than a little uncomfortable. Quite accustomed to bearing on his silver and plate, and in his books and on his coach door, the coat of arms he inherited from his father, why should he have given a moment's thought to the fact that they were not rightfully his, as the eldest son of an armigerous father? The unpalatable fact was that the Faussett arms had never been verified, and that the antiquary supposed himself entitled to them although he could not prove the entitlement. From early times the sovereign's power to grant arms had been deputed to the College of Arms whose role was to accept legal proof on behalf of an applicant of his lineal descent from the original grantee.

Between 1530 and 1688 this jurisdiction had been formerly exercised by the heralds at the visitations, a series of tours of inspection, apparently without system, so that, for example, Kent was visited in 1552, 1558, 1570, 1634 and 1664-8, but Westmorland in 1530 and then not again until 1615. Upon arrival in a district the visiting herald would request the presence of the local gentry for the registration of their arms, a lengthy process, often skimped, as all had to be done by hand, and not many gentlemen in the 1600s would have precise details about their parents and grandparents at their fingertips, no matter how keen they were to continue displaying arms. In consequence early visitations can be sketchy (that of Kent for 1530 runs to only 22 pages, and gives hardly any dates), seldom extend beyond three generations, and often give a statement of paternity alone. This in itself was not an insurmountable barrier as the heralds were accustomed to accept arms not granted by them if they had been borne for a sufficient period and if the users were persons of gentility – that is, what was known as a right to arms by prescription, a period of never less than 60 years or two generations After the last visitations in 1688 there was great slackness in such matters. From henceforth the Officers of Arms could record the arms only of those who came to them with a request to do so.

The root of Faussett's unexpected problem was that Mary Godfrey had married his father as an heiress in her own right (that is, she had no siblings) of the elder branch of her family, and therefore, for the first time in the history of the Faussett family, brought a coat of arms to them, and indeed, a coat of arms already several times quartered through previous Godfrey intermarriage with Partridge, Toke and Pittis heirs.

What could Bryan senior have done, having no arms himself? In fact, the earliest recorded use of arms in the Faussett family are those taken by Bryan senior himself, viz. *or, a lion rampant sable overall a bend gobony, argent and gules*, and may be seen on his tombstone and his son's bookplates. This coat of arms had been granted in November 1611 by the great antiquary and then Clarenceux Herald, William Camden, to one Edward Forsett (or Fawsett) of Marylebone.[6] No descendants in the male line of this William are known, a fact of which Bryan senior may have apprised himself and so felt safe, bearing the same surname (minor variations in spelling were of little consequence), to assume them for himself. We must assume that he chose to let sleeping dogs lie, for in 1727 a search was made on his behalf at the College of Arms for the surname, but nothing found in Kent. This negative result attracted the customary search fee of 2s. 6d.

The Godfrey arms were *sable, a chevron between three pelicans' heads erased, or*[7] and had been borne by the family following confirmation to Sir Thomas Godfrey of Lydd who died in 1430 (and whose memorial at Lydd bears them), a crest having been devised in 1607 by a later Thomas Godfrey with the consent of the Earl of Northampton, in whose house and service he was then living.

At that time Bryan senior had, in common with numbers of others, the convenience of a surname not too far removed anagrammatically from a Latin word, and so took *Fauste Succedunt Qui Deo Credunt* for his motto, now appearing under the newly quartered Faussett and Godfrey achievement.

In an undated pedigree[8] submitted to Hasted by Bryan Fausset's son Godfrey, there was still displayed the erroneous descent from an Edward Forset of Marylebone, with the additionally erroneous scions of Saul Fausset of Queen's College, Oxford, and Thomas Faussett whose monument stood in the Priory Church of the Trinity of Canons Regular in Aldgate Ward, London. These false heraldic etymologies and Bryan senior's irregular assumption were all ultimately discarded in 1909 when a new grant was made by the College of Arms to all members of the Godfrey-Faussett family. In consideration of the fact that they had been used *bona fide* for so many years, the same coat was granted to Godfrey Trevelyan Godfrey-Faussett and his descendants, as well as to the other descendants of his grandfather, but with one tiny difference as identical coats can never be the subject of a second issue, and thus the colour of the bend was

---

[6] Guillim, *A Display of Heraldry*, no. 411
[7] *ibid.*, no. 225
[8] British Library: MS Addl 5520, f.46

changed from argent and gules to argent and azure. At the same time a crest was devised *on a wreath of the colours a demi-lion rampant sable supporting in the paws a Tuscan column compony argent and azure, the base and capital or.* Finishing it all off was a new and more prosaic motto: *Fortiter Si Forsitan.*

We may now return to Thomas Godfrey's investigations into the Godfrey pedigree, which give some revealing insights into heraldic and genealogical practice of the time. In early 1770 Faussett had sent Godfrey one of his ledgers to examine, the recipient then looking forward to inspecting some of the wills in them which Faussett considered 'the most curious'. Godfrey replied and said, alas, that neither he nor any of his friends could read them, and that his failing health precluded accepting Faussett's offer of looking at his collections of monumental inscriptions. He had just returned from an auction sale where he had bought a picture 'of Sir Edmund Berry Godfrey drawn after he was dead'.

The herald Isaac Heard wrote again to Faussett at Heppington in September 1771, firstly offering his sincere apologies that Faussett's career had been 'checked by so extraordinary an accident' (of which, tantalisingly, we hear no more), and then listing further queries which included the whereabouts of a missing parish register from Smeeth. (This was quite possibly the first Tudor register, still missing, with the result that today the Smeeth entries do not commence until 1662.) He realised that his requests were a Herculean labour, but encouraged Faussett, a Herculean and classically-trained friend, with

> Labor ipse Voluptas ... your affection for the Godfrey Blood & generous Freedom & Readiness of communication, that extensive Knowledge which you have gathered for bounteous Purposes.

Plans were in progress for the erection of a monument, for which Heard had two elegant vellum books ready with drafts of armorial sketches, as well as a portrait of Sir Edmund Berry Godfrey. But with regard to the Faussett arms,

> I should hardly feel a higher Pleasure than that of receiving a Commission for procuring his Majesties Fiat for your taken the name and Arms of that Family of whose blood you have a good Portion and for which you have so high a Veneration.

Faussett duly proceeded with the work and sent in his bill for 40 guineas, which was paid in August 1773 and recorded as the money received from Godfrey's executors 'as a recompense for my expense, trouble, &c on account of deducing his pedigree'.

Four days later Heard wrote concerning the Lydd parish registers:

> I am surprised we never thought of an extract from the Register of Lyd from the oldest Entry down to about 1660; for from that to the present time we can give a tolerable guess not any one of our immediate Family of Godfrey will be found there. Do you approve of my Writing to the Minister of Lyd for such an extract, or would you please to write? I am however apprehensive that there are more names of Godfrey in it than will be found of

> 6 other Families together. If the extract of all Baptisms were once certified at Bottom of
> the whole would it not be sufficient taking out the Entries in the Words of the Register?

A week later the minister of Lydd had not responded, and the pedigree was in
temporary abeyance. Four days after that, Mr Goodwin at Lydd had advised that the
Lydd registers opened in 1542 and 'would very gladly have sent you the register had
it not been what he is daily using'.

Still in September 1771, Heard now regretted the trouble Faussett had been put
to in consulting his own manuscripts for Godfrey monumental inscriptions. 'If the
artist cannot improve his time better than in taking draughts of Monuments, I'm
of Opinion he'll not make a great Fortune. Bryan Faussett has sent enough for it
to be recorded in the pedigree by the painter'. Evidently the Lydd registers were
not removed from their rightful home, for Heard continued, 'When you receive the
extracts from Lydd, I beg you will have the Goodness to select only those whom you
verily believe to be descendants of your Common Ancestor, Peter Godfrey of Lydd
who died 1566 March 10, unless you should particularly distinguish any of the Issue
of Thomas the half brother of this Peter.'

How trusting Garter was in allowing Faussett to select only those forebears he
considered truly descended from the common ancestor! The Lydd registers are
crammed with entries for the Godfrey surname, so in view of Faussett's standing
as a genealogist, we must give him the benefit of the doubt and hope that all was
correct. By the following spring the matter was still dragging on until, in April 1772,
Heard's final letter exclaimed,

> The pedigree nearly finished! There is no necessity to stimulate me to round up this
> Tedious Affair; for it haunts me in my Dreams … the Zeal with which I first engaged in
> it, in order to render all the Justice in my Power to this Family has carried me to much
> greater Lengths than few perhaps would have gone.

The matter seems to have been concluded in the nick of time, for Thomas Godfrey
died in 1772, satisfied, one hopes, with the results of such protracted and demanding
labours. And indeed, the splendid and elaborate pedigree may be seen today at the
College of Arms. Like Faussett, he was a martyr to gout, and on more than one
occasion commiserated with him, hoping that in time the physicians would perfect
a cure. His substantial will[9] directed that he should be buried at Woodford in Essex
alongside his parents.

In June 1767 Faussett was owing monies on Land Tax and there opened a
series of correspondence with the solicitor William Chamberlayne concerning a
commission and the making of an appeal. The solicitor had found three potential
witnesses, but Faussett lamented that they were aged 72, 74 and 83; he then scribbled
a note on the back of one of the letters to the effect that a commission seemed

---

[9] TNA: PROB11/977

unnecessary and, no doubt with an eye to saving money, perhaps not practicable unless suitable witnesses were forthcoming. However, by December he was in a more litigious frame of mind and had travelled to Ashford and Godmersham to consult sundry individuals in order to get matters moved on. Success was mixed as he commented that, 'Many of my witnesses are very infirm & may die before we can have the Commission in Chief.' He was diffident about troubling yet more people and once more 'recovering from a very severe fit of the gout but I am not yet down'. By March he had been left 'very weak of the Gout' but had marshalled four Canterbury men who might stand in his defence, Young Jeken, Thomas Buck, William Long and Peter Loubert. The summer of 1768 saw some progress, and in the August a solicitor's letter advised Faussett that his complaints had been laid before council, ' …. who thought it best for you to answer them, though they were frivolous…'.

Chapter 8
The Summit of a Career

Kingston Down, Kingston

14 August 1767 – 3 graves	21 August 1767 – 10 graves
28 August 1767 – 10 graves	5 September 1767 – 6 graves
7 September 1767 – 12 graves	11 September 1767 – 13 graves
16 July 1771 – 24 graves	19 July 1771 – 23 graves
23 July 1771 – 25 graves	26 July 1771 – 29 graves
29 July 1771 – 31 graves	5 August 1771 – 28 graves
12 August 1771 – 15 graves	7 August 1772 – 12 graves
2 October 1772 – 21 graves	9 August 1773 – 7 graves
13 August 1773 – 24 graves	30 September 1773 – 14 graves

A little over four years passed between excavations at Gilton and Faussett's third location, Kingston Down, part of Barham Down, in Kingston parish. He had been rector of Monks Horton for two years and now also perpetual curate of Nackington for a few months, so perhaps the regular and larger income assuaged his guilt about devoting so much time to his great passion. The site he had set his eyes on was a furlong north-east of Kingston church, about half-way to Ileden, the seat of Thomas Payler. Barham Down lies mostly in Barham parish, but its western end was just in the northern extremity of the long and thin Kingston parish. High up, close to the brow at about 300 feet and overlooking the Little Stour valley, were exposed various barrows and hemispherical mounds close or contiguous to each other, on the hanging side fronting north-west –'an aspect very frequently, if not always, made choice for such purposes'.[1]

Faussett had long been fascinated by the situation:

---

[1] *Inv. Sep.*: 36

When I was curate of, and resident at, Kingston … I had often a longing mind to open some of these tumuli or barrows; having firmly persuaded myself that this might possibly, and indeed, probably, be the very spot where Julius Caesar in his second expedition into Britain found the Britons drawn up and ready to receive him by the side of a river. (Bel. Gal. lib. v)[2]

The river would, as Faussett thought, be the Nailbourne, which still flows in these parts, although it is often dry for many years at a time – the local appellation of 'stream' is more fitting for such a gentle and usually insignificant water-course. This far-fetched theory was reinforced for Faussett by some local workmen who in 1749 had found several skeletons, a spear and other articles, and on whose report he was relying, having not been resident in Kent in that year. Additionally, in about 1751, 13 small earthen beads and some other (probably opaque) ones came to light, all likely Saxon in Roach Smith's opinion.

Had he lived another decade, Faussett would no doubt also have consulted his good friend Edmund Hasted's entry for Kingston parish,[3] where it was stated that one of Caesar's camps lay on the slope of a hill opposite the church, westwards and eastwards from which were several lines of entrenchments and many tumuli and barrows, some of considerable size, but all opened and plundered of their contents. Hasted summarised his friend's excavations, itemising the several Roman coins by their various reigns, and then drew attention to John Twyne's report of an immense barrow at 'Baramduna' located by the repeated dreams of a shepherd. It had been opened in the reign of Henry VIII at the expense of Sir Christopher Hales and by the labours of William Digges, out of which was dug

a very large urn, full of ashes and bones of the largest size, with brass and iron helmets and shields of an unusual bigness, but almost wasted away; yet there was nothing to judge by, either of its times, or whom it belonged to.[4]

Twyne wondered whether barrows generally covered the remains of giants, and so repeated an Anglo-Saxon view of mysterious antiquity. If the record is accurate, the likeliest explanation is that of a Bronze Age cremation under a barrow, with a secondary Anglo-Saxon burial inserted, but no other details or even the exact location can now be elucidated. Nevertheless, this is still interesting evidence for barrow digging in Kent as early as the 16th century, and indeed suggests that other Anglo-Saxon barrows may well have been investigated at this date, although there are no records of further discoveries until shortly before Faussett's time.

The scene was being set for Faussett's greatest campaign at one site: 308 graves in 18 days spread over four years, a substantial proportion of his grand total of 777. He had approached Thomas Barrett, then lord of the manor and the land owner,

---

[2] *ibid.*
[3] Hasted, *op. cit.*, 3: 753
[4] Twyne, *De rebus Albionicis* :75

around 1755 for permission to proceed, but was refused as Barrett thought it improper to make any further disturbances, even though a decade previously he himself had opened a few barrows at Kingston in a 'cursory and incurious manner' but found little of interest other than iron weapons and two glass urns, which he imagined were probably Saxon or Danish. When Barrett died, his only daughter married Faussett's 'worthy and learned friend' William Dejovas Byrch, who soon allowed him to excavate.

Now Faussett stated his intended method of working, nothing being left to chance:

> I now proceed to give a true inventory of the several and very curious antiquities here discovered, in which (according to my usual method) I shall mention everything just as I found it; describing and representing by a figure or a draught (after a very uncouth manner indeed, but as well as I shall be able), whatever shall stand in need of any explanation. I shall also, as heretofore, number every grave, according to the order in which I opened it.[5]

Digging was started in earnest, but Faussett soon saw the error of his ways about Caesar fighting in this location. No, it was rather

> a common burying place of Romans ... but also, if not chiefly, of Romans Britonized, and Britons Romanized (if I may be allowed the use of these expressions) till long after the Romans, properly so called, had entirely quitted this isle.[6]

Logic dictated, surely, that the cemetery was a burying place for the Romans and the local villagers with whom they had intermarried (his 'Romans Britonized' and 'Britons Romanized'), each race taking the other's customs; but what faced him was a burial place used continuously from after the Roman withdrawal in AD 410, down through the arrival of the Anglo-Saxons and onwards to perhaps as far as the archbishopric of Cuthbeorht who in 741 obtained a Papal dispensation for the provision of churchyards and cemeteries within towns and cities, thus overturning what had been the regular arrangement under the Romans who had allowed no intramural burials. (Elsewhere this regulation was further enforced by the Capitulary of Charlemagne, enacted in 789, which brought an end to burials in pagan mounds and their relocation to church cemeteries.)

But he now saw that his presumed battle graves also contained women and children, that the graves were neatly cut out of the chalk, and that most of the bodies were in chests or coffins, and burnt to make them last longer. Furthermore, nearly all were aligned to the east – hardly a Roman or a pre-Christian position – many had heaps of bones above the skeleton, indicating second or further interments, and the weapons and spears alongside were evidence of trophies and a military career, not the arms with which they had valiantly fought the natives.

The fact of almost universal eastward alignment of all the excavations (save Crundale, where the opposite obtained except for those bodies on the extreme

---

[5] *Inv. Sep.*: 40
[6] *ibid.* :37

edge of the site) was confusing; added to this, the absolute uniformity of character of the interments as he found them had to be explained away by Faussett by the supposition that coins, urns and other items were the remains of previous Roman burials which had been broken up at a later period in order to use the old graves for fresh interments.

Roach Smith thought that here Faussett's reasonings were sound up to a point and guided him away from other errors, but did not enable him to reach the truth that all was more or less entirely Saxon; later research over a wider field had proved this beyond all doubt, and thus allowed later generations to distinguish Roman from Saxon. Faussett's error was a good example of early and naturally imperfect Georgian archaeology – he had built a theory upon what was taken as fact, unaware of any evidence to the contrary.

But Faussett continued with his assumptions, seeing X-shaped crosses and, in this case, eastward alignment, as Christian ownership. Again Roach Smith clarified by stating such ornaments to be only personal decorations with Christian influence of the cross for artistry, not badges of the new faith; and indeed, similar cruciform ornaments had been found in Saxon graves elsewhere in England, all accompanied and surrounded by evidence of pagan practices, and so ornaments, and ornaments only, not Christian paraphernalia. As to the *paterae* and small urns, Faussett thought that they were overwhelmingly pagan, but could the owners have been converted, yet still retain vestiges of unbelief? Unable to discriminate the character of the pottery, he imagined it had been deposited at a date anterior to that at which the Romans had abandoned cremation. How could he have known that the Anglo-Saxons used Roman pottery, that the urns were all Saxon (or perhaps of Frankish manufacture), and that cremation did not exist in England among the Teutonic settlers?

Clarity of thought also eluded Faussett with regard to the various Roman coins found from time to time; in assuming they had been deposited at the time of their striking, or at least during the reign of the emperor who was commemorated upon them, he went grievously astray with his chronology, unaware that coins of all dates were in circulation among the Anglo-Saxons. The extreme value of numismatic evidence for dating was not yet understood and established as a standard archaeological procedure.

The finds at Kingston were many and various. A hemispherical iron shield-boss or *umbo* of a seven-inch diameter in grave 2 was the largest ever found.[7] Grave 6 produced 'a very curious *ball of native crystal*, about one and a half inch diameter', the subject of much admiration and discussion. James Douglas had found one at Chatham enclosed in silver and commented on their magical associations, seeing a similar purpose in domestic glass vessels, but his ignorance of Anglo-Saxon habits and customs led him to think that shears and mirrors were also used for divining. In point of fact, crystal balls held within a silver sling as a pendant are not uncommon,

---

[7] *Inv. Sep.*: plate 15

and appear to have had special properties to pagan eyes; they were worn on the girdle by east Kent women, and are also known in continental areas settled by the Franks.

In grave 50 were some footless goblets which always rolled over – did this mean that the contents had to be drunk straight off? Faussett wondered. The considerable rarity of an ivory or bone comb,[8] about seven inches long, was broken as it was extracted from grave 53, but Faussett found it 'a very great curiosity' and glued all the bits back together. His anatomical knowledge allowed him to comment that skulls rarely appeared with a frontal suture, as one here, and to be determined to watch out for others. Next appeared a short dagger with a spherical silver pommel, about the size of a walnut, and set with rectangles – then a new and interesting addition to current knowledge of the details of Saxon weapons, as Roach Smith commented.

September 1767 closed the first season's digging, with 54 graves excavated in a year which had been very wet. The notebooks record:

> August 1767
> Paid two labourers digging on Barham Down   4*s*. 3*d*.
> Paid two labourers digging on Barham Down   7*s*.
>
> September 1767
> Paid for digging on Barham Down   7*s*. 7*d*. and 8*s*. 3*d*.

In November he wrote to Dr Ducarel about recent events:

> I have lately dug up some very fine glass urns; a fine fibula set with garnets; a chrystal ball; two pairs of amethyst ear-rings; many beads; a Roman Lady's equipage or etwee (consisting of an ear-picker, tooth-picker &c, all of silver, and strung upon a little silver chain), a large and curious ivory comb, many silver rings &c &c &c, having opened, in all, fifty-four tumuli for them. I had almost forgotten to mention four coins, viz. one of Gallienus, one of Probus, and two of Constantine the Great. I have not yet done with this spot (which is on Barham Down); but please God I live, will at it again in the spring. You know, this is my hobby horse! I congratulate you also on your new acquisition of modern medals. I am for the ancient ones; 'cum nova tot quaerunt, non nisi priscia peto'. I write, as you may see, in much haste. Jacob and I will drink your health to night at Henfreys. So Adieu![9]

A postscript to this highly interesting letter commented on the discovery of an ancient stone cross in a garden near St Martin's church in Canterbury. Faussett had been trying to tease out its inscription, which was

> made up of barbarous monkish letters, of no particular alphabet, [and] puzzled me out of my patience; but at length our friend Beauvoir unriddled them; and they are no more

---

[8]   *Inv. Sep.*: plate 13
[9]   Nichols, *op. cit.*, III: 560

nor less than "and Alys his wife". Say nothing. Our President is to try if he can make them out.[10]

Divine providence might smile on Faussett and spare him in order to return to Kingston Down, but not in the following spring – more than three years passed before he went back in July 1771. Grave 131 contained the bones of an old person and occasioned the comment,

> Mem. That the legs of this person lay across each other after the manner of a Knight Templar; but I suppose this position of them was entirely accidental, and without any meaning or design; however, I thought proper to take notice of it.[11]

Again, Faussett was meticulous in his recording both facts, and his occasional self-declared ignorance. The next object, in grave 142, was of more than passing interest. A *concha Veneris* or porcelain shell Faussett thought to be found only in the East Indies, and thus worthy of 'a learned dissertation' – the Romans did not know those parts of the world, but perhaps these shells were found elsewhere? Roach Smith clarified the matter by adding that the Romans brought them from the orient and that they were not particularly uncommon; James Douglas thought them used as amulets around Naples by the lower classes in his own time, and originally so by the Romans themselves. Here, in a Saxon grave, however, it was probably just an amulet, although these shells, of Red Sea origin, were also used to make beads. Again, Faussett's view was in accordance with his time, and in advance of the many 18th-century collecting voyages to the southern seas and elsewhere.

The contents of grave 149 bemused him: why was a skeleton lying with its feet to the west and its head to the east, unless perhaps because of some mistake, owing to the darkness of the night when it was interred, or some other such cause? He was equally perplexed by a small chalk figure of a man from grave 167, four inches long and bereft of its hands and feet; it was certainly, he opined, sculpture, but why so deep in the tumulus if carved by a shepherd or some similar person?

For many, Faussett's reputation may well stand by the Kingston Brooch alone. It was located on 5 August 1771 in grave 205, not by Faussett himself, but his son Henry Godfrey who extracted the jewel from the earth and

> On finding it, he carried it with great glee to his father, who was in his carriage hard by, suffering under an attack of his old enemy [the gout]: his father drove off with it; and next day a report was spread around that the carriage had been so full of gold that the wheels would hardly turn.[12]

Faussett was later to describe the event in his notebook and accompany it with the best drawing he ever made. The tumulus exceeded middle size and the grave was

---

[10] *loc. cit.*
[11] *Inv. Sep.*: 64
[12] *Inv. Sep.*: 206

Figure 18. A reconstruction of grave 205 at Kingston, opened 5 August 1771. A wealthy woman, perhaps a queen, is laid to rest inside a great wooden coffin in a huge grave. She is surrounded by fine food, expensive clothing and every other luxury she will need in the after-life. Her fine linen shawl is fastened with a priceless brooch made of gold and garnet.
(Image copyright Dominic Andrews.)

larger than any he had ever opened, six feet deep, ten long and eight broad. The coffin was nearly of the same dimensions, 'much burnt and very thick'. It had been strongly bound and secured at its corners with large clasps and riveted pieces of iron. Inside was a disproportionately smaller female skeleton, but evidently a woman of high rank, for towards the right shoulder was

> a most surprisingly beautiful and large fibula subnectens: it is entirely of gold; and is most elegantly and richly set with garnets and some pale blue stones, the name of which I am at present, a stranger to; it is three and a half inches in diameter, a quarter of an inch in thickness, and weighs 6oz. 5dwt. 18gr. The acus on the underside is quite entire, and is also beautifully ornamented with garnets. I flatter myself it is altogether one of the most curious and, for its size, costly pieces of antiquity ever discovered in England.[13]

The jewel is the *ne plus ultra* of the Kentish composite, two-plate, gold, round brooches, a product of the high-status craft-working in east Kent which operated from the late fifth- to mid-seventh centuries. The Kingston brooch is to be dated to around AD 610-620, the jewellers' zenith, after which followed an inevitable decline in quality and artistry. Its rich magnificence was unrivalled in Faussett's time, and would be until the discovery of the Sutton Hoo treasure in 1939, when it would be seen that the East Anglian craftsmen had used much larger garnets and set them in cloisons of more complicated shapes, the virtuosity of the technical accomplishment and its swagger melding of red stone and gold metal having an attraction peculiarly to the taste of a modern public whose standards were by then increasingly influenced by precision machines. (Valuable comparisons may now be made with selected objects from the Staffordshire Hoard found in 2009, and especially in the near-identical stepped cloisons.)

The brooch is made of two plates of gold bound together by a strip of characteristic Anglo-Saxon beaded gold wire filigree around the circumference. The maker cleverly made the front plate convex to prevent loss of perspective when viewing its concentric design, an artifice furthered by the limiting of the cruciform pattern and by the prominent central boss. Five concentric rings of gold cloisons (stepped, square, semicircular and triangular, often following the natural lines of the garnet) form the design, each cell soldered to the front plate and to its neighbours at the points of contact. The second and fourth rings consist mainly of gold work without garnets, thus giving extra variety to the possible monotony of a uniform carpet-spread of garnet and gold, whilst the lozenge-shaped cloisons of the third ring give a chequer effect by the selective use of small squares of gold foil. A system of cleverly spaced triangular and step-shaped cells of blue glass, four (one now absent) square cells of a deeper red garnet, and a central and four satellite bosses of white shell-like material, no longer preserving their original iridescent surface, all add to the overall effect and variety. The dizzying effect of so

---

[13] *Inv. Sep.*: 78 and plate 11

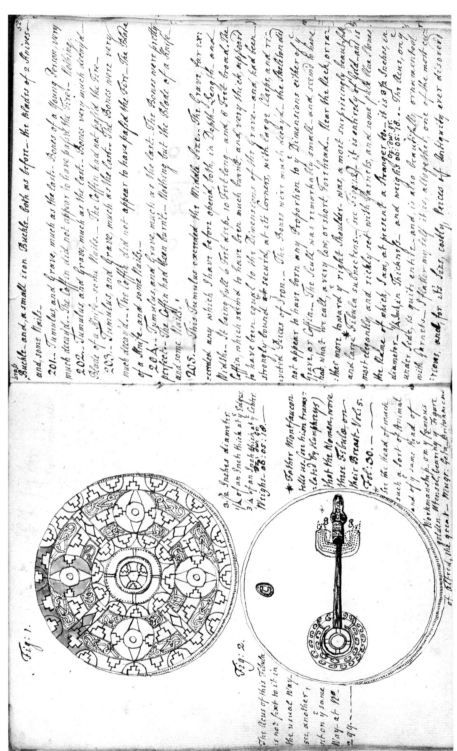

Figure 19. Faussett's sketch and description of the Kingston brooch from his archaeological notebook 'I flatter myself it is altogether one of the most curious and, for its size, costly pieces of antiquity ever discovered in England.'

(Courtesy of National Museums Liverpool (World Museum)).

Figure 20. The Kingston Brooch, *c.* AD 610-20.
(Courtesy of National Museums Liverpool (World Museum)).

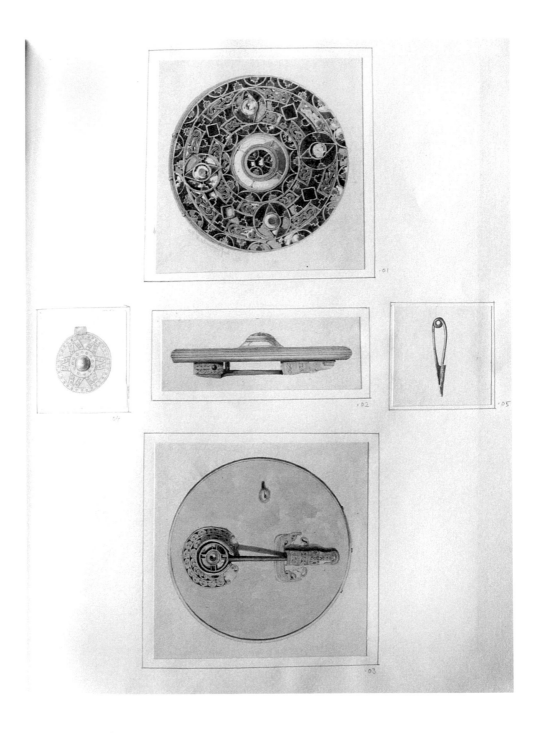

Figure 21. The Kingston brooch: Herdman's watercolour for the future Plate I of *Inventorium Sepulchrale*.
(Courtesy of the Society of Antiquaries, London.)

Figure 22. The Kingston brooch: the published Plate I of *Inventorium Sepulchrale* engraved by Fairholt. *(Courtesy of the Society of Antiquaries, London.)*

many spinning wheels is obviated by a four-armed cross dividing the entire field. The garnets, all underlain by gold foil to catch the light, were perhaps imported, ready-cut, from India, while the blue glass imitated the beautiful lapis lazuli from the same country.

Not content with the fabulous display-side, the maker lavished further decoration on the normally invisible reverse, enriching with gold wire filigree an animal-head catch-plate (carefully noted by Faussett) for the bronze pin and the drum-like head of the pin and its surround, then adding more garnets to the pin-head itself and a safety loop above it for securing the brooch to the apparel. All this would have made for a costly and much-prized personal possession and heirloom; and indeed, some of the gold is rubbed and worn through constant handling, and at one point on the circumference a repair in antiquity has patched the front and back plates together with three tiny gold clips.

Everywhere, the cloisons and filigree work excite the senses by their exquisitely fine beaded gold wire soldered to a prepared ground of gold on which the outline of the pattern had already been raised. The twisted knot and interlace pattern display to grand effect the transformation into filigree of the familiar Teutonic backward-biting (and so headless) quadruped, all enhanced to a stunning degree by an enveloping and subtle mosaic of blue glass, shell, garnets on gold foil, and gold filigree, the whole executed with consummate and precise mastery. No longer can we see pre-Christian Britain as either dark or inferior to what came later, or at least in its artistic creations – Faussett's adulation of the jewel was wholly justified and may well stand in perpetuity, Sutton Hoo notwithstanding.

What of the origins of this object? Almost all our knowledge of pagan Saxon art comes from metalwork; other materials such as leather, wood and cloth have for the most part survived badly, and the fields of sculpture and painting did not commence before the arrival of Christianity. It is to be noted, then, that pagan jewellery is not only of high archaeological importance, but aesthetically pleasing – the Anglo-Saxons tired of old fashions almost as quickly as we do, and thus their jewels are often more readily datable than most other artefacts. In the late Roman period some types of Roman brooch were taken north into barbarian homelands where they were copied and developed, many then being imported into Britain, where Anglo-Saxon versions were produced, drawing on late Roman art as the source of their inspiration for the ornamentation. No longer are the splendid jewels of the seventh century a phenomenon to be wondered at – they are the technological achievements to be expected from a people who, far from being primitive, were culturally developed when they arrived on British shores. The English nation was not a sudden flowering out of nothing in the seventh century, but the natural development of a society whose barbarian ancestors had repeatedly wished to enjoy the benefits of Roman civilization on the Continent.

The brooch would have taken a year and more to construct, the maker either being paid exceedingly well or, more likely, under the patronage of a wealthy noble. The artefact is a signal product of the period of Jutish wealth and political ascendancy in the peaceful late sixth and early seventh centuries, and but one of a group of similar and associated types found almost exclusively in this country in Kent, a fact not necessarily suggestive of local origin, as close parallels have been found in France and Germany which perhaps imply British purchase from a foreign source, or that two peoples on either side of the English Channel were of similar racial origin and responsible for their own productions. The resolution of the problem is not helped by the near-universal absence of craftsmen's dwellings and workshops, and also by a similar lack of graves containing jewellers' tools.

Sir Thomas Kendrick observed[14] that recent cleaning of the brooch had allowed a reassessment and a new fact to be exhibited. He had initially dated it to the early sixth century, rather than the seventh, on the strength of the close-set and brilliant style of the workmanship which surely could not fail to reproduce some sort of reflection of the Roman mosaic-enamel style, an inseparable part of the ornament which the cloisons of this item partly copied and entirely supplanted. But the cleaning now revealed previously hidden evidence – that the middle ring of the brooch did in fact reproduce the typical millefiori studs of the latter date with brilliant clarity.

The other objects in grave 205 were eloquent testimony of high social status. All probably had lain originally in the coffin: a gold circular pendant with suspension loop, its central boss surrounded by a six-pointed star; two remarkable Roman unilateral-spring silver brooches, probably associated with a chatelaine at the waist (described by Faussett as of 'an ingenious contrivance' hitherto unseen by him); a 20-link iron chatelaine; two large copper-alloy pans (two, and three handles) with a trivet-stand; and a green glass palm-cup. Outside at the foot of the coffin, and much more poignantly, were the well-preserved 'very fresh, white and round bones' of a child, all in a heap, at the foot of an adult skeleton in a poor state of preservation, an ensemble Faussett thought to be that of a mother and child.

Faussett must have abandoned Kingston that evening to much animated gossip and speculation about the day's events and the buried treasure. A signal day in the history of English antiquarianism was drawing to a close as, with no doubt the greatest relief, he carried his prize back home to savour its finer details and then ecstatically write up his findings. His curate Joseph Price must have had a sight of the jewel, as he recorded in his diary (with more financial acumen than aesthetic appreciation) that Faussett:

> Has a fibula of gold set with garnets and lapis lazuli (weighs £27 in money). The gold without the stones which are set is about 6oz. in weight. ... found in the parish of Kingston. Invaluable. Near 7oz. at £4 an oz. [15]

[14] *Archaeologia*, XIX (1939): 195-6
[15] Ditchfield & Keith-Lucas, *op. cit.*: 126

A week went by before work resumed. In grave 222 'a remarkably fetid smell' issued, pervading the entire site, and not helped by the day being beset by distant thunder and lightning, until at four in the afternoon a violent storm with heavy rain forced the party to decamp. Faussett wondered whether the smell was caused by the soaking atmosphere, as he had never before perceived anything of the sort.

Grave 235 produced a gold neck ornament[16] known as a *bulla* or pendant ornament, and described by Roach Smith as among the most prominent and curious items of the Kentish Anglo-Saxon jewellery.

The next year, in August 1772, Faussett had five men trying for eight hours to 'overturn a very large mound or tumulus' at the east corner of the site, close to the Kingston-Ileden road (grave 242). The barrow was 18 paces in diameter and about six feet high, but its size did not equal expectations, for half-way through the exertions Faussett found that it had been opened before and that the digger had left behind an early clay tobacco pipe of the first King James' reign. There were no contents, and as it was on the edge of the site and not of a usual shape, Faussett thought it was perhaps a rampart or protective mound. Here was a salutary lesson that such disappointments were inevitable and to be carefully balanced against the more productive days. The season was now late and the days much shortened, but October 2 was fine and sunny, and so an opportunity for a mopping-up excursion, and to find yet another barrow previously opened.

If nothing else, Faussett was thorough. Three years of excavating at Kingston and probably little prospect of anything to equal the great brooch had not, however, exhausted his optimism. A fourth and final season could surely be no more than a vain hope. He knew there was little left to check:

> Having last year opened every remaining visible tumulus, though never so small, I then imagined I could have nothing further to do here.[17]

But ever the optimist, he reflected that there could well be other graves in the area not marked by a mound or where the ground had been levelled. But how to locate them without the expensive and tedious process of trenching the entire site right down to the solid chalk?

He had already answered his own question by designing a probe, about four feet long with a three-inch lateral spur at the lower end, for discovering 'latent graves without opening the ground' (variations of which are still occasionally used to locate buried ditches, walls and other structures), and testing it at Bekesbourne and Sibertswold that summer. Now, on 9 August 1773, after a few hours' work with his new contrivance, he was able to declare that the seven graves discovered in a few hours proved that it had fully answered its purpose.

---

[16] *Inv. Sep.*: plate 4
[17] *ibid.*: 87

A polecat skeleton accompanied by the remains of its presumed last meal of birds, moles or mice was all that grave 282 contained, but grave 299 bucked the trend of an apparently exhausted archaeological site. The early seventh-century woman's burial contained a fine silver and gold *fibula*[18] further adorned with garnets and ivory, its pin unusually not fixed to go up and down like a hinge, but horizontally 'much like that on my glorious and, I was going to say, inestimable, golden *fibula*, described at No. 205.' Alongside was a brass bracelet or *armilla* worked with six snakes' heads, some shears, many Roman coins, a wooden box, another silver *fibula* with garnets and ivory, a conch shell, an ivory comb, a square, flat piece of ivory with a hole at each corner, 'an odd brass instrument' (probably part of a lock), a bell and other metal items. Treasures indeed, and all thanks to the newly invented probe.

But the riches of Kingston are not yet quite fully described, for we have the signal addition of Faussett's notebook and the expenses incurred at Kingston for six of the seven days of the third year of 1771. The entries are as follows:

16 July 7*s*. 4d
19 July 3*s*.
23 July 3*s*.
29 July 3*s*.
5 August   3*s*.; 1*s*. 6*d*.
12 August 2*s*.
12 August Paid Norrington and 1 labourer one day's work each   1*s*. 6*d*.
12 August Paid Mr Dilnott of Kingston for the horses standing &c.
    during the time of digging on Barham Down 10*s*. 6*d*.
[Total £1 14*s*. 10*d*.]

In addition, the Liverpool 1772 field notebook has this entry:

Great Tumulus at Kingston, 18 paces over by 5 feet high [7 August 1772]

Prebble 5*s*. 6*d*.	William Bushell 2*s*. 6*d*.
Samuel Vanson senior 5*s*. 6*d*.	John Walker 2*s*. 6*d*.
John Grant 2*s*. 6*d*.	James Matson 3*s*. 6*d*.
Stephen Cook 1*s*. 6*d*.	Stephen Castle 2*s*. 6*d*.
John Wood 3*s*. 6*d*.	Robert Austin 3*s*. 6*d*.
Thomas Reeve 1*s*. 6*d*.	G. Vanson junior 3*s*. 6*d*.
John Hadden 1*s*. 6*d*.	Thomas Courthope 1*s*. 6*d*.
Christopher Whitnell 3*s*. 6*d*.	W. Makey 1*s*. 6*d*.
Trice 5*s*. 6d	Servant 1*s*. 6*d*.
Hogben 3*s*. 6*d*.	D. Collard 1*s*. 6*d*.
John Ratley 1*s*. 6*d*.	W. Claringbull 1*s*. 6*d*.
Robert Dixon 2*s*. 6*d*.	[total £3 3*s*. 6*d*.]

---

[18] *ibid.*, plate 12

Twelve graves were opened on that day, but even so, the monies involved are considerable – more than twice as much as at Sibertswold. Many of the names are found also at Sibertswold, suggesting that the rates of pay were attractive enough for the men to be available at more than one site; Prebble no longer commanded the highest sum, but seems to have shared foreman's or surveyor's duties with Vanson and Trice.

In summary, Kingston produced 263 barrows and 45 flat graves, all cut into the chalk and mostly aligned east-west (one with the head to the east). The earliest, containing the garnet-inlaid brooches, were of the late sixth or early seventh century, but the site appears to have been in continuous use until the early eighth. There were 13 double burials, some of child and adult, and in others the bones of earlier burials. There were coffins in 183 graves (half of which had 'passed the fire'), and grave-goods in 214 (of which 56 contained only a knife). The site was generally not rich, although 11 graves were richly furnished and three exceptionally so. The site was at least partly Christian, as shown by two little equal-armed silver crosses in a richly furnished woman's grave.

In 1818 the Rev'd Mark Noble FSA, rector of Barming in west Kent from 1786 until his death in 1827, published his *Lives of the Fellows of the Society of Antiquaries of London*. Unsurprisingly, he had been assiduous in collecting details about Faussett's time at Kingston (for the most part lifted straight out of Hasted), whom he now summarised as:

> A learned and intelligent man, extremely well versed in Roman antiquities and very fond of exploring the remains of that people in Kent. Barham Downs have many tumuli which had generally been opened and robbed. Bryan Faussett opened 300 of them and generally enriched his valuable collection of Roman antiquities with their contents.[19]

[Kingston was still not exhausted. In 1850 a barrow missed by Faussett was dug by Wright who found in it a woman's grave with shears, a knife, and a necklace of 24 beads. Some soldiers employed in digging trenches found a skeleton in 1944, and in 1959 (the future professor) Vera Evison put down test trenches along a strip of 400 yards threatened by tree-planting – 16 flat graves were found, of which only three were undisturbed, but poorly furnished. The Thanet Water Board in 1965 cleared a strip and revealed two undisturbed graves as well as a disturbed skeleton in the top-soil, and road works continuing from 1966 produced a number of other graves.]

---

[19] Noble, *Lives of the Fellows...*, *sub* Faussett

Chapter 9
Three More Campaigns

By the end of 1770 Faussett had disposed of the greater part of his outlying estates to raise much-needed funds. As always, he had kept meticulous details of the income derived over the years, which can now be tabulated:

c. 1750, about 14 acres at Plumstead Marshes to cover funeral expenses	£600
c. 1750 lands at Eltham to cover funeral expenses	£650
1751, unspecified land at Prittlewell	£200
October 1756, lands at Prittlewell	£420
February 1758, Folly Farm, Prittlewell (the above three totalled 122 acres of woodland and farms with annual rents of £39)	£630
October 1758, house at Little Eastcheap in the family since the first Henry, sold cheaply to Mr Bignall, plumber in Eastcheap	£350
October 1760, Fullers, Iden and Wallers in Staplehurst	£2,250
April 1761, from the Government in full for as much of my estate at Purfleet in Essex as the Commissioners and Jury appointed for that purpose were pleased to take from me in order to build a magazine for gunpowder on the spot	£2,350

April 1762, eight acres of meadowland belonging to the Mills, Purfleet	£120
December 1763, my farm at Cookham Hill near Rochester	£1,500
1766 and 1770, most of the let estates at Staplehurst	£3,450
October 1770, Knoxbridge Farm, Staplehurst	£1,200
October 1770, nine acres let at Purfleet	£220

The Essex lands had clearly been extensive, as solicitors had informed Faussett in January 1761 of his then tenants in that county who occupied properties at Barking, Brentwood, Dagenham, Grays, Great Warley, Hutton, Mucking, North and South Ockenden, Orsett, Plaistow, Rainham, South Upminster, South Weald, Stifford and Stratford. In Kent there was a farm and manor at Denstead in Chartham, much under-valued for unknown reasons in August 1768 and so not saleable, and two years later correspondence itemised rents from land at Barham, Chilham and Westwell, plus marshland on Romney Marsh.

The sales brought in £13,940 over two decades, or just on £700 annually, and curiously almost exactly what his father had derived from his annual rental income just after he had married. In the middle and later 1750s Bryan's wife noted that her estate at Heppington and Stockfield was let for £303 annually. One purchase is also recorded – a collar-maker at Canterbury named John [...ager] was paid £200 in July 1768 for two houses and a forge at Lower Hardres.

Correspondence survives showing that managing estates was time-consuming and sometimes fraught with problems - a Rochester attorney informed Faussett in March 1765 that his lands at Eltham and Plumstead were depressed because the late high tide had damaged the sea wall.

Other than land and rents, like many other gentlemen, Faussett also held government stocks or consols; in 1762 he held £1200 worth, and sold some two-thirds of them to nett £770 17s. 6d. after a transfer fee of half-a-crown. He sometimes lent money to individuals, usually his siblings, but more frequently had to borrow smallish sums at interest. Each month he paid five of his sisters an allowance by way of interest on a principal sum, and occasionally was paid £16 10s. by his mother for boarding them at Heppington in the summer months.

A random selection of totals is instructive, the figures fluctuating wildly, and the income chiefly from church fees and stipends, rents, gambling and occasional sales of crops and animals. Here we can see something of Faussett's constant preoccupation with insolvency and the future selling-off of his outlying estates.

June 1755	income £3	expenditure £22
November 1756	income £7	expenditure £216

November 1759	income 4s.	expenditure £36
October 1761	income £81	expenditure £95
May 1762	income £145	expenditure £86
March 1765	income £63	expenditure £36

By the early 1770s Faussett had been keeping meticulous accounts for over 20 years – they are a remarkable and highly complete record affording us the most intimate details of the personal income and expenditure of a moderately well-off rural Georgian clergyman. Very small items (usually less than a shilling) were kept also by a servant named William who supplied monthly totals to Faussett for his own calculations. Something of them can now be given, perhaps best divided by subjects, to give an idea of the range of the items and the current prices in east Kent from around 1765-1775, all reflecting Faussett's extraordinarily busy and varied life.

Food and Drink

½lb green tea 5s.

½lb coffee 3s.

a salmon 16s. 10d.

large cod 1s.

a Ramsgate turbot 6s.

6 eels 2s. 6d.

1lb tobacco 1s. 6d.

melon & artichoke plants 2s.

a gross of corks 2s.

a gallon of Madeira 12s.

snuff and oil of rhodium 2s.

cephalic tobacco and a box of Anderson's pills 2s.

Mr James of Fleet St for tea and raisins £7 4s. 8d.

Mr Rainier, wine merchant of Sandwich, his last bill in full £86 16s. 10d.

a chicken 3d.

a duck 6d.

a rabbit 6d.

100 eggs 3s.

1lb of sausages 8d.

a fat hog £3 3s. 3d.

gallon of oysters 10d.

partridge or woodcock 8d.

butcher's bill £5-£7 weekly

hogshead of porter £2 16s.

a pot of balm of giliad 1s. 6d.

Charity and Gifts

a servant (frequent) 1s.

a distressed person (frequent) 1s., 2s. or 2s. 6d.

the poor at Bishopsbourne 10s. 6d.

Christmas box for the poor at Kingston 10s. 6d.

5 November bonfire for the boys 6d.

purses at Foundling Hospital 3s. 6d.

subscription to *Widows & Orphans* £2 2s.

subscription to Clergymen's widows £1 10s.

spent on the freeholders at *The Three Horseshoes* £1 1s.

Christmas boxes for the postman and servants 1s. each

six months' interest of the Queen's Bounty £5

Household and Personal Items

a pair of shirt buttons 2s. 6d.

a dog collar and its engraving 1s. 11½d.

paid for 3½ dozen moles caught   12*s*. 4*d*.
children's haircuts   1*s*.
inoculating the two boys   £5 5*s*.
paid Mr Hatch for mending Bryan's coral   1*s*.
a pointing dog   £3 3*s*. and 2 young hawks   1*s*.
pair of blue satin breeches   £1 1*s*.
a flute   10*s*.
6 still life pictures in oil of birds   £1 10*s*. 6*d*.
Plate Duty for one year   5*s*.
glazing and painting   £7 17*s*. 1*d*.
Mr Bolayne for drawing two of my teeth   5*s*.
chimney sweep   3*s*.
an 8-day clock   £6 6*s*. 6*d*. and a kitchen clock   £1 1*s*.
a grizel wig   £1 16*s*. and wig-combing   2*s*. 6*d*.
being shaved when ill   1*s*. 3*d*.
a pair of spectacles   7*s*. 6*d*
canary and bird seed   11*s*. 2*d*.; a canary   5*s*.
a black coach gelding   £14 14*s*.
a gross of pipes and a dozen glasses   5*s*.
a boy for informing us where the parrot was   1*s*.
expenses of the Archdeacon's visit   6*s*.
advertising for my late mother's old coach   8*s*. (sold for £26 5*s*.)
two years' Land Tax on the London House   £10
three months' Window Tax at Kingston   3*s*. 10½*d*.
Charlton Window Tax   £3 6*s*.
Lower Hardres Land Tax   8*s*.
Heppington Window Tax   £1 4*s*. 9*d*.
Nackington Window Tax   £2 7*s*. 3*d*
Nackington church sess   13*s*.
Street End Window Tax   £2 2*s*.
journey to Maidstone for the election   £4 4*s*.
subscribed to widening Bridge Hill   5*s*.
Kirby & Simmons for ½ a year's newspapers   10*s* 5*d*.
John Hitchcock of Fetter Lane for a harpsichord   £33 3*s*. 6*d*.
Andrews the tailor for a gown and cassock   £1 1*s*.
Mr Martin of Fleet St for a telescope   £5 5*s*.
a third string for the bass   1*s*. 6*d*.
Val. Picard the painter for 2 pictures   £1 10*s*. 6*d*.
ditto, for repairing the achievements   6*s*.
furniture from auctions:
      bureau   £4 4*s*.; inlaid cabinet   £5 5*s*.; hall lanthorn   13*s*.;
      pair large white china images   15*s*.; chimney glass   £2 7*s*.
paid for £1,300 share in the 4% annuities at 89¾% = £1,166 15*s*.
monthly housekeeping   £6–£7

Gambling and Amusements

play at cards and bowls – many small wins and losses of a few shillings

church concert   6*s.*

subscription to Bridge Hill bowling club   5*s.*

share in the claret drunk there   13*s.* 6*d.*

turning a pair of bowls   5*s.*

coffee house and billiards   5*s.* 6*d.*

½ ticket in the British-Irish lottery   £2 15*s.* 6*d.*

12th Night subscription   2*s.*

evenings at *The Fountain* - a few shillings

Antiquarian Interests

Messrs Flackton, Canterbury booksellers   £10 18*s.*; £20 6*s.* 8*d.*

Mr Silver the Sandwich bookseller   £1 8*s.*

Mr Jacob for antique casts   5*s.*

Mantle of Bossingham for some old writings   2*s.* 6*d.*

White the bricklayer for an antique carving   2*s.* 6*d.*

a book of gold leaf [frequent]   2*s.*

subscription to the Society of Antiquaries   £1 1*s.*

subscription to University College Hall   £5 5*s.*

subscription to Kennedy's *Antiquities of Wilton House*   7*s.* 6*d* .

ditto, its being bound   1*s.* 6*d.*

Mrs Harrison for fossils   2*s.* 6*d.*

some antiquities from Ash   10*s.* 6*d.*

one Sawyer of Canterbury for Whitstable pateras   10*s.* 6*d.*

Mr Jacob for Morelli's *Book of Consular Coins*, 2 volumes   £2 2*s.*

In February 1771, five years before his death, the reputation of Faussett having become something of a recluse occasioned some cause for comment when Hasted wrote to Ducarel:

> Your friends here are all well. As to Faussett, he is so entirely rusticated at Heppington, that he seldom stirs from thence; and his Friends are quite tired of paying visits there without any returns, so that he lives quite by himself, as much as if he was 100 miles from hence, nor do we know anything of him.[1]

Gone, it seemed, for ever were the cheery invitations to fellow scholars to visit Heppington and talk long into the night over the latest antiquarian news and fresh discoveries. Was Faussett so riddled with gout that a concomitant melancholia now supervened, or were his usual worries about money now uppermost in his mind? And yet there were still three busy years of excavating to come.

---

[1]   Nichols, *op. cit.*, IV: 69

Doubtless he still spent much of his time in his library in both writing up his investigations as well as doing the necessary preparatory work and background reading prior to going out into the field. Of his friends who would have encouraged him and discussed the findings after he had returned home laden with the spoils of the day we have seen a little already. But it is now time to consider his local antiquarian predecessors, or at least those who wrote on Kent, for what inspiration he might have derived from their lives and their publications for his own work and writing, as references survive to show his keen searching out of their works.

William Lambarde (1536-1601) was both an antiquary and a lawyer. In 1568 he was appointed Commissioner of Sewers for Kent, where he had been acquiring small pieces of land, and in which county he would marry at Ightham into the Multon family of St Clere in that parish. With notes already to hand for a topographical dictionary, he now conceived the startling idea of a systematic survey of Kent. His intended first instalment of a historical topography of England was completed in draft form in 1570 and published in 1576 as *Perambulation of Kent: Conteining the Description, Hystorie and Customes of that Shire*. The earliest county history, it was a practical guide that ran to 538 pages, written by a gentleman for gentlemen, and would afford a model original in arrangement and style for many later works of a similar nature, and based on extensive and critical reading which included Domesday and royal charters. The scope of its contents must have impressed its contemporaries: climatic, economic, social, religious and historical surveys sat alongside an investigation of the Canterbury See and a discussion of Kent's unique inheritance system of gavelkind. The period before the Anglo-Saxons did not concern him, and nor did landscape, but these failings aside, the book is crammed with a mass of fascinating and highly readable information. Lambarde's plan to publish on other counties had to be abandoned just before he learnt of the forthcoming publication (which he himself had encouraged) of his friend William Camden's *Britannia* which now covered each county, albeit more summarily than Kent had been. Lambarde's monument is in the eponymous chapel at St Nicholas, Sevenoaks, removed thither from Greenwich where he died and was buried. A distant Faussett connection was established when, in 1609, his granddaughter Margaret Multon married Thomas Godfrey, the father of Edmund Berry Godfrey, the JP who was famously murdered in 1678.

As a clergyman Faussett would have been familiar with the culminating work of the life of the cautious but brilliant scholar James Ussher, Archbishop of Armagh (1581-1656), whose monumental *Brittanicarum ecclesiarum antiquitates* of 1639, treated of the early history of Britain and Ireland and the development of Christianity from its origins to the 7th century. Today, most scholars know about his calculation of the foundation of the world, based on a prodigious knowledge of ancient languages, calendars and history, together with biblical scholarship of a depth and breadth sufficient to construct a comprehensive chronology linking biblical and ancient history, all of which made, according to Ussher, for the birth of the planet precisely dated to 23 October 4004 BC.

John Philipot (*c*.1589-1645) was a son of the mayor of Folkestone. Initially a woollen draper in London, he rose from Blanche Lyon to Rouge Dragon Pursuivant in five years, a promotion rapid enough for William Camden, then Clarenceux, to make him his deputy for the 1619 visitation of Kent, as well as for those conducted later in the north of England. Subsequently he was appointed to the remunerative position of land and water bailiff in Sandwich, later becoming that town's MP. His heraldic career culminated as Somerset Herald in 1624. In the following decade he obtained a 21-year privilege for the printing and selling of his *The new description of Kent*; it was never to see the light of day, but the 1659 *Villare Cantianum* or *Kent Surveyed and Illustrated* of his son Thomas, a poet and writer, was doubtless soundly based on his father's work. The volume comprises 401 dense pages 'Drawn out of Charters, Escheat Rolls, Fines and other Publick Evidences, but especially out of Gentlemens Private Deeds and Muniments'.

Sir Edward Dering (1598-1644), first baronet and religious controversialist, lived at Pluckley where his antiquarian deceptions were pursued with great earnestness. In 1627, keen to investigate his family and county, he had obtained a warrant by favour of the Duke of Buckingham authorising him to consult public records without paying the customary fees. In 1638 he formed an association called *Antiquitas Rediviva* with William Dugdale, Sir Christopher Hatton and Sir Thomas Shirley, whose members were to collect 'all memorable notes for historicall illustration of this kingdome', and especially for each of their four own counties. Little of this noble intention survives, alas, save for a few drafts for the preface and odd entries for the Dering family. Described as an 'excellent Antiquarye' by Dugdale, he mastered Old English and recognised its importance. He maintained a scholarly circle but, alleging that an antiquary employed by his father had once stolen family records, and so in an effort perhaps to recreate what had been lost, this did not prevent him from tampering with names on the documents in his own collection in support of a desire for the greater antiquity and importance of the Derings, as well as placing convincing fake brasses in Pluckley church ('dating' from more than two centuries earlier) to bolster his overweening family pride.

William Somner (*c*.1598-1669), a Canterbury man for the whole of his life, was an Anglo-Saxon scholar whose *The antiquities of Canterbury* of 1640 was dedicated to his patron Archbishop William Laud; the prose matched the dedicatee in describing Becket's shrine as the 'glory' of Canterbury which had been 'cut down' at the Reformation, and calling for the restoration of dedication saints for each church and chapel as were now forgotten. The volume was a bibliographical first in displaying 'An Appendix, containing such authenticall instruments, scripts and writings as are quoted and cited in the present worke' which ran to over 100 pages, starting with King Offa's charter of the donation of certain lands to Christ Church Canterbury, and all transcribed in full. The exigencies of the civil war prevented the completion of a county history, busy as he was in attempting to hide the Canterbury muniments from parliamentary soldiers and in preserving the smashed cathedral font for its reconstruction in 1660. His skills in Anglo-Saxon and knowledge of Kent's religious houses were employed by William Dugdale and Roger Dodsworth for the first volume of their *Monasticon Anglicanum* of 1659. He ended his life as auditor to the cathedral, leaving behind a well-deserved reputation based on a wide breadth of interests, linguistic ability, and publications displaying fine scholarship.

Richard Kilburne (1605-1678) was a lawyer and topographer whom Hasted in 1798 described as 'a man of some eminence ... as a lawyer, being as worthy a character, both as a magistrate and an historian'. Increasing success with his law practice brought him into contact with Kent and Sussex, and he was buried at Fowlers, an estate he had inherited at Hawkhurst. His career was rather similar to that of Lambarde whom he greatly admired, both being authors of legal and topographical works. He published *A brief survey of the county of Kent* in 1657, and then two years later *A topographie, or survey of the county of Kent, with some chronologicall, historicall, and other matters touching the same and the several parishes and places therein.* In it was depicted Kent before the Civil War, and summarily dismissed by Hasted as little more than a directory (422 pages, with about half a page to each parish), but it was of some value as the county had not been not well served by the early topographers.

Robert Plot (1640-1696) was born at Borden near Sittingbourne into an old Kent family, and lived to earn the well-deserved epithet of 'the learned Dr Plot'. In the mid-1660s he conceived a plan to travel around Britain and to collect materials for a descriptive survey of the country, greatly stimulated by earlier and similar chorographical works by Pliny the Elder, John Leland, William Camden and William Lambarde.

Optimistic intentions were severely curtailed to cover ultimately only Oxfordshire, but the success of that volume gained him a professorship and then in 1683 the first curatorship of the objects in the natural and antiquarian sciences centre which the university had created around the gifts of Elias Ashmole. In 1695 he was very briefly Mowbray herald-extraordinary before the College of Heralds made him its registrar. He was a quintessentially late-17th-century scholar, neither humanist nor modern, who provided rational and detailed accounts of things, impartial to any one intellectual system. His fame and worldliness gained him many entries to the county society whose surroundings he was so keen to record, and his writing about defined geographical areas or specific subjects encouraged other authors of the genre to tackle manageable subjects.

John Harris (*c.*1666-1719) was a writer and lecturer on science and combined that occupation with being Vicar of Icklesham and then Rector of St Thomas, Winchelsea, in East Sussex. He died at Norton Court near Faversham, then engaged in the process of printing an unremarkable but well-subscribed first volume of his *The History of Kent*, long in the making, and surely influenced by his earlier curacy of Strood and prebend of Rochester cathedral. It is a handsome indexed folio volume of 592 pages (hugely overrunning the proposed 200), listing his archive and individual sources, and containing some interesting information in the introduction about the book's difficult gestation: 'He was diffident as to whether he would answer everybody's expectations, even though he spent a good deal of the best part of his life on it. He did not fear the censure of those with greater knowledge, but rather those '*who not equally qualified to distinguish, have will and power to do prejudice, according as their passions and humours carry them. And these have indeed already shew'd their endeavours that way*'.

William Gostling (*c*.1696-1777) was another Canterbury man, and also a lifelong curate and parish priest in the mother diocese. His knowledge of Canterbury's history was equalled by few, and he was well known for guiding curious travellers around his beloved birthplace on a tour which included showing them his collections and inventions housed in his residence in the Mint Yard. His *A Walk In and About the City of Canterbury of 1774* ran to a sixth and final edition in 1825. The composer William Boyce would often consult his collections of printed music and enquire of his vast musical knowledge. Also a mechanical genius, Gostling made a model for a machine to clean out one of the Kent coast harbours, and invented a contraption for opening both parts of a sash window at one time and in opposing directions.

William Boys (1735-1803) was a surgeon and topographer of Sandwich, and descended from a famous east Kent family. His house was close to Richborough whose history he carefully investigated. His two-part *Collections for an History of Sandwich* of 1788 and 1792, in quarto volumes with splendid engravings, was based on a polymath's interests in ancient manuscripts and inscriptions, astronomy, natural history and mathematics, and his extensive collections of Sandwich antiquities. He was one of Hasted's many fieldworkers, helping to gather local information for his friend's county history, and no doubt enthusing his young grandson William Rolfe (1779-1860), also of Sandwich, who would publish the Anglo-Saxon antiquities found at Ozengell near Ramsgate, and ultimately donate his own collections to Joseph Mayer for safe-keeping and public access after he had learnt of the British Museum's rejection of the Faussett artefacts.

Richard Gough (1735-1809), like William Boys, was also Faussett's near-contemporary, busy, wealthy and the leading antiquary of his day. He never went abroad, shunned natural history and geology, and thus devoted his energies to publishing on his native land, and at first anonymously in 1768 with his *Anecdotes of British Topography*, a gazetteer of published and unpublished works of local history and topography for the whole of Britain and Ireland. Recognition of its stupendous coverage of many types of record led to a second edition in 1780 entitled *British Topography*. His two-volume *Sepulchral Monuments* (1786 and 1796) with its many valuable illustrations sought to rival Montfaucon's similar *magnum opus* in its five-century coverage, but broke new ground in concentrating on the artistic form of the monuments and their potential as sources for the study of the manners and customs of the time – now no longer would antiquarianism rely only on the authority of the written word. In 1789, whilst director of the Society of Antiquaries, and after a labour of 16 years and fact-finding travels through every county, he published a revised edition of Camden's *Britannia*. His long tenure of that important post included constant efforts to raise the standards of antiquarian work and the learning of its members, all the while seeing the recovery and preservation of national antiquities as a public service not to be compromised by private interest. Seemingly a man of trenchant opinion and decisive action (at the exhumation of Edward I in Westminster Abbey in 1778 he was caught secreting a royal finger into his waistcoat and told to replace it) he fell out with the Society, and lost his directorship into the bargain, after a row over the election of his successor James Wyatt, whose restoration of Durham and Salisbury cathedrals, the more conservative members claimed, had inflicted more harm than good.

Bishopsbourne Down, Bishopsbourne

16 July 1771 – 9 graves

Faussett paid but the one visit to Bishopsbourne, adjacent to, and just west of, Kingston, and on the same day that he dug 24 graves in that parish as well – truly a day of unbounded enthusiasm and energy. He described the site as lying on the right side of the Roman military road running from the top of Bridge Hill in a straight line, north-west to south-east, over Barham Down, and just at the corner of another road crossing at right angles (the modern Frog Lane) which ran down to Bishopsbourne church and village. From this description the certain conclusion is that he was excavating in the corner of Bourne Park, almost within sight of Kingston Down, and so easily accessible from it, even on foot, in an hour at the most. It lay at about 200 feet on the brow and upper slope of a chalk ridge, facing south-west to overlook the Little Stour Valley.

In the park he had noted nine 'fair but small tumuli', all in a line parallel with the said main road:

> I had often cast a wishful look at them, and from time to time had promised myself the future pleasure of examining their contents. But, on account of the smallness of their size and number, and their proximity to so public a road (by means of which last circumstance I knew myself liable to be pestered with a numerous set of troublesome spectators), I did not set about opening them till the 16th of July 1771.[2]

On that day he had set off rather earlier than usual from Heppington in order to continue his investigations at Kingston. On his way, and finding an adequate supply of available labourers, he set to, and in little more than two hours had opened all nine tumuli,

> during which time, it being so early in the day, we had very little or no interruption, either from the curiosity or impertinence of passengers, or other idle spectators, the

---

[2] *Inv. Sep.*: 97

teazingness and plague of whose ill-timed attendance in business of this sort is not to be conceived but by those who, like myself, have had the disagreeable experience of it[3]

Pity poor Faussett as he so eagerly pursued his exciting ends, but for the impecunious and unlettered locals what better entertainment could have been offered, and free of charge? And who would not have jumped up and wielded a spade for the day in return for being paid 1s. 6d (his usual minimum daily fee) if one man retired hurt?

The nine barrows, none earlier than the 7th century, produced ten graves set some two feet into the chalk, mostly of middle size and mostly unfurnished. All were aligned with heads to the west. Faussett was dispassionate about the absence of finds, now preferring to interest himself in many other barrows visible about 500 yards to the north-west at Bourne Place, right in front of the house itself, and of which about 100 occupied Hanging Hill. Many had large trees growing out of them and the rest had been levelled when the area had been turned into a pleasure ground or on some other occasion, 'and so now are visible only to a discerning eye'. But their quantity was compelling, and so great that one had only to dig several feet anywhere on the hill to produce human bones. Ingenuity would overcome the difficulty of location: the best way, he thought, to find the almost invisible barrows was to place his head close to the ground and look against the sun when it was near the horizon. Failing success in this way, absolute reliance could be placed on his newly invented probe, for if the soil were chalk (and chalk only), 'its sure and never failing guidance' would find even the most invisible graves.

Roach Smith noted with interest that Bourne Park was well known to the many attendants of the first congress of the British Archaeological Association in 1844 (including himself), and that, just like Gilton near Ash, it was close to Roman burial places. Lord Albert Conyngham's two attempts found little except a shield-boss, Thomas Wright opened three more barrows in front of Bourne Place in that year, and two more were investigated during the congress, one a richly furnished woman's grave protected by wooden planks.

[An aerial view taken in 1943 revealed that the site, mutilated by further excavation in 1845, was now all but obliterated by war-time ploughing, as were the well-known lynchets on Barham Down, first described by Lambarde. All had been scheduled for preservation under the Ancient Monuments Acts, but they could not be spared. Jessup noted[4] that there were ploughed-out Saxon barrows visible at many places on Barham Downs, and the wonder was that not more than a few of the hundreds that Faussett had overturned could now be seen. All that remain today are a few relatively intact barrows in a narrow strip of woodland along the western side of the Roman road which appears to have formed the eastern boundary of the site.]

----

[3] *loc. cit.*
[4] *Arch. Cant.* LVI (1943): 69

Sibertswold Down, Sibertswold

13 July 1772 – 25 graves	17 July 1772 – 51 graves
20 July 1772 – 40 graves	24 July 1772 – 42 graves
27 July 1772 – 13 graves	9 August 1773 – 10 graves

Sibertswold Down (the modern place-name is often 'Shepherdswell') would be Faussett's most productive campaign after Kingston – 181 graves in six days, one of which overlapped with one of his two days at Barfrestone, a mile to the north, and another with Kingston. The excavations of July 17, 20 and 24 were his three largest single-day totals. The site lay across the crest of a north-facing downland spur at about 320 feet, bisected by a crossroad, described by Faussett as on the left-hand side of the road from Sibertswold to Sandwich or Deal, about half a mile distant, where there was 'a pretty numerous parcel of tumuli' lying near the top of the hill and between this road and another running from Barham Down over Snow Down. Here were three barrows close together on high ground near to and parallel with the road on the left called 'Three Barrow Down' which continued onwards through Long Lane to Waldershare, from where it was one-and-a-half miles to the barrows, contained within an isosceles triangle made by the said three roads.

It can therefore be seen that there were two sites, which Faussett labelled as a lower (of 158 graves) and an upper (of 23 graves). He was alerted to the latter by a farmer who told him that his workers had discovered two Roman cremation burials there about two years previously. The items at this latter site were discovered by Faussett using his probe for the first time, and subsequently removed by him for display in the pavilion at Heppington. Almost all the datable grave-goods were of the 7th century.

Faussett duly sought permission from the land-owner before proceeding, and received a letter form Awnsham Churchill at Bath on 16 May:

> … am very glad I have it in my power to oblige a Gentleman in so laudable a persute, the Tumuli or Barrows you desire to open are intirely at you[r] service, and I sincerely wish you success in your undertaking.[5]

He finished by mentioning that a spur found previously in one of the same hillocks, perhaps inlaid or gilt, was now locked up at Shepherdswell, and would gladly be shown to Faussett when he next came to Kent. John Read of Ramsgate, lord of the manor, gave similar permission on 17 June, and on 20 July David Papillon of Acrise, seemingly with a third interest in the site, had no objections to barrows being opened and was ready to pay the expenses there, provided that 'you will only take care that the men who do it do not secret[e] anything.'[6]

Three Barrow Down was commonly also called Rubury Butts, the second element often applied to ancient burial mounds. Faussett strained etymological credulity in

[5] Society of Antiquaries of London: MS 723 f.2
[6] *ibid.*: f.4

seeing the name as a corruption of *Romes berig Butts*, and was further seduced by the Anglo-Saxon name of Sibertswold into thinking that skirmishes between Saxons and Danes (or ancient Britons) must have occurred thereabouts, and so these barrows, as well as those at Barfrestone, might well cover the casualties therefrom,

> ... and, indeed, at the time of my beginning to dig here, I was fully persuaded in my own mind that this really had been the case ... I was soon convinced of my mistake. For this summer I opened no less than one hundred and sixty-eight [actually 171] of these tumuli, and the whole of those in Barfriston adjoining, to the number of forty-eight more; yet, not a single spur or anything else occurred that seemed to have the least connection with either Saxons or Danes. But everything we met with was much of the same kind with what I found at Ash and Kingston.[7]

Once more Faussett identified the grave goods as belonging to the peaceable inhabitants of nearby villages, not warriors but 'Romans Britonized' or 'Britons Romanized', that is, those who had intermarried and adopted each other's customs. But he declared that the Romans must have been buried here long before, as was clear from the urns.

Grave 18, a large tumulus, included a copper-alloy hair-pin,[8] the top with two small animals like monkeys, holding and kissing each other. In grave 24 was a kind of brass double-cylinder with hinges and a hasp, considered by Faussett to be a child's toy whistle, but Roach Smith added that similar items found in the debris of boxes suggested that they were locks. Grave 30 contained coloured beads and also some silver rings with sliding knots.[9] His patience now snapped at grave 54:

> At the feet was an urn of black earth, capable of containing about a pint; it was broken in getting it out, having been stamped upon by the labourer who sunk the grave...[10]

And then something more exotic in grave 60 – a copper-alloy box, two inches high with a hinged handle and two small chains with pins for fastening the lid, which contained some silken strings, wool and hair, and some beads of a vegetable substance shaped like the seeds of the plant Faussett knew as the *Marvel of Peru*. Another decayed wooden box with its brass lock and key was found in grave 180, along with a rare brass pommel belonging to a sword or dagger.

Two buckles[11] were in grave 95, each having four inferior loops exemplifying the Saxon manner of fixing the buckle to the belt. In grave 98 was a decidedly uncommon barbed *iaculum* or dart, 11 inches long, and quite an Anglo-Saxon rarity on account of the thinness of the material which was insufficient to resist the decomposition so common in iron objects.

[7] *Inv. Sep.*: 101
[8] *ibid.*: plate 12
[9] *ibid.*: plate 11
[10] *ibid.*: 111
[11] *ibid.*: plate 8

In grave 103 Faussett found an iron instrument he thought looked very much like a Jew's Harp (but was actually rather similar to many other buckles found elsewhere):

> I looked upon it as a very great curiosity, and most heartily lament (as I have continual reason to do, with regard to other curiosities made of iron), that it was not made of brass, or some other more durable metal.[12]

An occasion for puzzled reflection occurred at grave 119 when in a very large barrow ox bones were found in a longish bank with hard and red dry clay to a depth of some four feet. How had the bones arrived to be buried in the chalk and with what purpose? A hole had clearly been dug in the chalk for their reception – was this then perhaps not a barrow for the dead, but rather an *agger* or defensive mound for the living? He had noted at Sibertswold that every corpse discovered had a mound thrown up over it, but of varying sizes, perhaps consonant with the rank of the deceased. Had smaller barrows been trodden flat by grazing cattle or the passage of carriage wheels, or levelled by the plough? He supposed the majority to have been levelled when larger new mounds nearby necessitated fresh quantities of earth, and so one found sherds and bones at various depths in the larger barrows, whereas small ones, being shallow, would have everything scooped up in the act of clearance.

Grave 172, excavated on the last day, proved satisfyingly rich. There were beads, gold ornaments of various kinds and, most tellingly, gold and silver coins with crosses on them, indicative, as Faussett thought, of having been struck by a Christian prince. Douglas illustrated them[13] without explanation; Roach Smith declared their presence in an Anglo-Saxon grave as first-rate evidence for the date of interment, assigning them to Merovingian France and datable to the fifth to seventh centuries. They were in fact Frankish coins of Marsal and Verdun of around AD 650, and consequently made this grave one of the key datable groups of 7th-century Kent.

In all, the large number of graves, which were mostly covered by barrows, were not, with three exceptions, particularly rich (yet worthy of several illustrations). There were many of children, and several barrows covered more than one burial. All were aligned east-west, 19 had only a knife, and 28 nothing at all; little correlation was evident between the size of the barrow and its contents. Such poor results were not helped by most of the mounds having already been levelled before Faussett's arrival in order to make 'dencher', a kind of field-dressing or manure. The site had indeed been a Roman burial ground, as evidenced by a local farmer who had often found human bones, cinerary urns and other vessels together, but all of Faussett's barrows were Anglo-Saxon.

The 1772 field notebook held in the Liverpool World Museum now affords us a singularly valuable insight into the practicalities of each day's arrangements. The tiny volume has the details for five of the six days at Sibertswold, and both at

---

[12] *ibid.*: 119
[13] Douglas, *op. cit.*: plate XXIII

Barfrestone, one being a date on which work was undertaken in both places. The details are a rough draft, preparatory to being transferred to a more formal expenses and income notebook. The later writing-up was done in summary form and exhibits discrepancies: three days are exactly the same, but for two others several payments are omitted, and for four of the five days the grave totals are slightly inaccurate – perhaps a genuine oversight on Faussett's part.

17 July 1772
Prebble of Sibertswold for beer and lodging for 5 labourers 13*s.* 8*d.*
S. Vanson 1*s.* 6*d.*
John Grant 1*s.* 6*d.*
Stephen Cook 1*s.* 6*d.*
John Wood 1*s.* 6*d.* (two half-days)
Thomas Reeve 1*s.* 6*d.*
John Hadden 1*s.* 6*d.*
Christopher Whitnell 1*s.* 6*d.*
Trice 3*s.* 0*d.* (two days)
Hogben 3*s.* 0*d.* (two days)
Paid 5 men for bringing home a very large urn 2*s.* 6*d.* [total £1 12*s.* 8*d.*]

20 July 1772
Prebble as before 14*s.* 3*d.*
Thomas Reeve 1*s.* 6*d.*
Samuel Vanson 1*s.* 6*d.*
John Grant 1*s.* 6*d.*
Robert Dixon 1*s.* 6*d.*
Christopher Whitnell 1*s.* 6*d.*
John Wood 9*d.*
William Bushnell 1*s.* 6*d.*
Trice 1*s.* 6*d.*
Hogben 1*s.* 6*d.* [total £1 7*s.* 0*d.*]

24 July 1772
Prebble 15*s.* 9*d.*
Stephen Castle 1*s.* 6*d.*
S. Vanson senior 1*s.* 6*d.*
Robert Dixon 1*s.* 6*d.*
W. Bushell 1*s.* 6*d.*
John Grant 1*s.* 6*d.*
Christopher Whitnell 1*s.* 6*d.*
Robert Austen 1*s.* 6*d.*
James Matson 1*s.* 6*d.*
Thomas Courthope 1*s.* 6*d.*
G. Vanson junior 1*s.* 6*d.*
W. Makey 1*s.* 6*d.*
John Walker 1*s.* 6*d.*
Trice 1*s.* 6*d.* [total £1 15*s.* 3*d.*]

27 July 1772, Upper Burial Ground
Prebble 13s. 2d.
John Walker 1s. 6d.
James Matson 1s. 6d.
Stephen Castle 1s. 6d.
Robert Austin 1s. 6d.
John Wood 9d.
G. Vanson junior 1s. 6d.
Vanson senior 1s. 6d.
Hogben 1s. 6d.
Trice 1s. 6d. [total £1 5s. 11d.]

3 August 1772
Prebble 12s. 11d.
Trice 1s. 6d.
Servant 1s. 0d.
S. Vanson 1s. 6d.
G. Vanson 1s. 6d.
D. Collard 1s. 6d.
R. Austin 1s. 6d.
J. Walker 1s. 6d.
John Ratley 1s. 6d.
James Matson 1s. 6d.
W. Claringbull 10s. 6d. [total £1 16s. 5d.]

Prebble presumably was foreman and perhaps also surveyor. The daily rate of 1s. 6d. must have had Faussett seeing village labourers queueing in droves to earn such relatively easy money for a few precious days until the supply of barrows was exhausted. The grand total is £7 17s. 3d., a daily average of £1 11s. 5d. These are substantial sums of money, and if extrapolated, the 46 days itemised in *Inventorium* of Faussett's digging expeditions cost him around £72 between 1757 and 1773. However, this will not square with a note in his account books giving a grand total for digging graves of £24 14s. 0d. (compare with £15 7s. 8d. for visiting churches and an enormous £90 14s. 6d. for purchasing coins).

Barfriston Down, Barfriston

27 July 1772 – 23 graves   3 August 1772 – 25 graves

Faussett had not even finished digging at Sibertswold before he became interested in Barfriston (the modern spelling is Barfrestone), as the fifth day at the former and the first at the latter coincided. The two sites were due east-west, only 160 paces apart, these 48 graves lying north of a boundary ditch and so just in the other parish. There were far fewer barrows at Barfriston, but mostly of middling size, and in a fairly regular line, with a deep wide trench to the south-west of the barrows and steep slopes on the other three sides. All the land belonged to the Bethlem Hospital and was in the tenure of Richard Harvey of Barfriston who 'civilly and readily' granted permission to proceed.

Faussett quickly observed that, in comparison with his earlier sites, the interments here were not the casualties of warfare 'as many have erroneously surmised', but rather, as he reiterated, the peaceable inhabitants he had already encountered elsewhere. In all, the graves here were typical of the late cemeteries that he had already dug, although the finds were sparser.

In grave 10 was a wheel-thrown Frankish bottle with incisions and ornaments on its belly, including, seemingly, the chi-rho, and therefore a 'plain proof' of a Christian burial. Roach Smith commented that even if it were the sacred monogram, it was no evidence of the faith of the deceased; in fact, it was a circular ornament formed of small wedge-shaped indentations, and common enough on earthen vessels of the period. But once again, Faussett is not to be censured – his accurate-enough description was circumscribed by inevitably limited experience and knowledge (and, one wonders, perhaps also by the sentiments of his ecclesiastical training and belief).

In grave 25 were three Roman copper coins of Constantine the Great, Theodosius the Great, and another bearing the head of Rome and an eagle which Roach Smith identified as of the Gothic kings in the reign of Justinian, reiterating their extreme value for the dating of the grave. Grave 47 produced several fine gold ornaments including a small black pebble, the shape of a button mould, which to him looked like a large chocolate drop; he refused to categorise it as either an artefact or a natural object, professing his inability in words wise enough and modest enough to admit defeat, or at least ignorance, and, as often, in terminology of an endearing and colourful prosaicalness.[14]

In all, Barfriston produced five richly furnished graves and 22 coffins; nine other graves had just a knife, and 14 were empty. Faussett considered the site quite distinct from Sibertswold, a view not shared by some later scholars who have treated them both as one.

---

[14] *Inv. Sep.*: 143

Chapter 10
Final Excavations

Iffin Wood

12, 16, 20, 23 October 1772

The exertions of the summer and autumn of 1772 had not exhausted Faussett's indefatigability. He had made notes on his previous excursions about an ancient camp in Iffin Wood, just to the west of Heppington across the Roman Stone Street, long intending to make an inspection, and now decided to investigate. There he had seen what seemed to be an old building looking just like a tumulus, which he viewed as the *praetorium* or Roman governor's residence, lying, he thought, within the two principal trenches and nearer to one end. Was it perhaps the summer quarters of the Roman garrison which used to overwinter in Canterbury? He doubted if it were a Roman temple ('and if ever it was, then to Diana').

The labourers set to work and uncovered east, south and north walls, regularly and neatly built of flints set in mortar, of an even three-foot thickness. There was much detritus including what must have been Kent peg-tiles, 'just as now used for country houses, with two holes in them', along with broken flints and tiles, bits of Roman brick, oyster shells, sheep bones, squared and faced grit-stone, and similarly shaped lumps of chalk, one resembling a wedge. There was no sign of any pavement or anything under it. The foundations were on loamy soil, and not lower than the natural ground surface. Part of the mouth of a large black urn was found as they cleared some five feet between the north and south walls, and then some middle-sized iron nails and a piece of iron like a *pilum* head, four inches by nearly one.

On the second day they proceeded westwards in clearing rubbish, the walls now much lower. 'That we might leave nothing for want of a proper care and a diligent search we made trenches 2 feet deep at about the distance of every 4 feet quite across the bottom which we found in every place to be sound, unmoved natural loam …'. The trenches were not commenced until they had dug and cleared somewhat deeper than the wall's foundations, upon which they found semicircular arches of flint in the lower walls, 18, 12 and five inches deep. Faussett now wondered if the site was a chantry or chapel and whether the mortar bed had served as an altar-step, or perhaps its foundation. More nails and bones came forth, along with two gallons of wood, coals and ashes, stretching a foot beneath the foundations.

The third day saw them stand 18 feet from the east wall where they found the base of a pilaster of fine grit-stone with a socketed neck, but no more architectural fragments. The inescapable conclusion was that the building, whatever it had been, was now bereft of anything worth stealing. A further ten feet of westward clearance reached the west wall.

The final day was one of summing up and taking measurements. The foundation of the north wall at the foot of a doorway was a yard thick, and apparently so all the way up. Pilasters had probably adorned the door angles. In all, the building was a rectangle some 42 feet in length and 18 in breadth – and for all the hoped-for results and careful work and measuring, a decided disappointment in terms of Roman military architecture.

Adisham Down, Bekesbourne

28 May 1773 – 22 graves	2 June 1773 – 8 graves
11 June 1773 – 6 graves	18 June 1773 – 7 graves
3 August 1773 – 2 graves	

Faussett entered his final year of digging in the late spring of 1773, now intermittently quite ill and a mere three years away from death. Just a couple of miles away from both Kingston and Bishopsbourne he had noted barrows of various sizes on the western side of the large and long Adisham Down, of which the western end lay in Bekesbourne parish and the eastern in Adisham itself, the two parts separated by a ragged parish boundary. The site straddled a crossroads on a south-east facing chalk slope, and extended from a clump of trees belonging to Sir Philip Hales for about 600 paces in length and 100 in breadth on a quiet road leading south from the said clump to Ileden on Barham Down. As Faussett had come to expect, the burial ground was on a high crest at about 175 feet, and on the usual dry and chalky soil. The sketch map included in his account allowed Roach Smith to identify the precise location, then in cultivation with no visible mounds remaining. No grave was earlier than the mid-7th century, and burials probably continued into the 8th.

Permission was forthcoming from a Mr Benson on behalf of Sir George Oxenden, as long as the tenant was given a few days' notice of the time and place. Faussett had first gained knowledge of the barrows by the happy circumstance of some of them being large enough to be seen at a distance; a few had been opened more than once, others entirely dug out and their contents carted away, as proved by the remaining gentle hollows. Another informant recalled a dozen or more barrows where the tree clump now stood, but now dug down and levelled. Faussett queried whether all this had been for making manure, but was then informed that Sir Thomas Hales, late brother of the present baronet, had removed them in order to deepen and improve the soil before planting the existing tree clump some 30 years previously. That implied that the clearance must have been right down to ground level, but in fact Sir Thomas did examine a few of the barrows, finding only bones, bits of iron and a few coins. In his last illness in January 1773, he sent word to Faussett that he knew some to have already been opened and gave his blessing for further investigations.

The new baronet did not demur either, and so Faussett 'began to break ground (to use the military term)' on 28 May. Much initial effort saw little reward, and some disappointment, when he reflected that the site was nothing more or less like all the others in that it was the burial ground of the neighbouring inhabitants, but whether his familiar 'Romans Britonized' or 'Britons Romanized', or, more likely, a mixture, was '…as immaterial as uncertain'. He could do no more than guess that the interments dated from just after the Roman withdrawal in 410, and certainly no later than the Saxon arrival of 449.

When some coins of Diocletian and Maximian were found, they suggested to him a much earlier use of the cemetery (as early as 305, the last year of the reign of the former emperor), although he admitted that of course the coins could have been buried many years later, and have continued in use long after the pagan arrivals:

> But still, I am persuaded, that the persons deposited here were not Saxons; nothing which I have hitherto met with, either here or in any other place where I have dug, having the least appearance of the remains of that people.[1]

Despite his perhaps muted enthusiasm, matters improved when in grave 7 he came across the 'very extraordinary phenomenon' of two skeletons in sitting posture, their backs against the head of the grave, and each skull with the mark of a violent cut, probably the cause of death.

A grave now appeared in the *praetentura* or retaining bank and, hoping for more, he set his nine labourers to work. In grave 30 was the medley of a piece of doubled leather, regularly cut and full of square holes (the pattern not unlike that of Roman sandals found in London), a knife-sheath (which Roach Smith considered to be part of a girdle), and the bones of a small animal,

> perhaps the remains of something of which the child was fond (having seen similar instances at Crundale).[2]

---

[1] *Inv. Sep.*: 146
[2] *ibid.*: 152

Mounting anticipation meant two long and hard days of excavating, the first with ten and the second with 14 labourers. Only nine graves were found despite Faussett having the whole bank trenched and 'turned over down to the firm chalk from end to end.' But he was still happy to record, characteristically, that,

It is, however, a satisfaction to me to be certain that I have left nothing behind me.[3]

The barrow mound over grave 41 was 34 feet in diameter and five high, and full of flints which seemed to have been brought thither, as Faussett stated that they did not occur thereabouts – a strange comment for chalk downland! Their great quantity had led him to suppose something substantial lay within, but no, only animal and human bones. Roach Smith saw that the mixed character of the Bekesbourne tumuli hardly needed comment: flints, fragments of single urns, animal bones, and the absence of anything typically Roman or Saxon indicated a Celtic origin for some of the graves and, consequently, the early appropriation of the site for burials.

Now came the largest grave of all, number 44, at 70 feet in diameter and a full ten high. Work proceeded by opening a diametrical trench through the centre from west to east, 30 feet long and 18 broad. Many scattered bones were the evidence of previous opening for fresh interments or modern enquiry. A 'substantial and sensible farmer in the neighbourhood' named Reynolds told Faussett that 30 years previously some gentlemen from Ashford had attempted an investigation: when an entire and undisturbed skeleton now appeared, he was inclined to think that the said excavators had wearied or that, 'more likely, the farmer was lying.' Nothing more conclusive than small animal bones followed.

The very last grave, number 45, was a curiosity, being cruciform in shape, 11 feet square and four wide with an arched hole at each extremity. Roach Smith thought it perhaps constructed at two periods, and admitted that the sharpest eyes and judgement were necessary for such a conundrum – even a man of Faussett's calibre might have missed something crucial, thinking, as he did, that the grave was *originally* cruciform, yet there was nothing else to prove it other than Saxon.

In summary, three-quarters of the graves were primary barrow burials, nine being located under an earth bank, and two further ones appear to have been secondary burials inserted into barrows. Faussett recorded a fairly equal division of small, middle and large sizes. 46 skeletons were found in several groups of barrows, 25 of them accompanied by coffins (nearly all burnt), and all aligned west-east. 20 graves had goods, six only a knife. Several graves and mounds contained fragments of pottery, possibly of prehistoric or Roman date, and some of the larger mounds may have been prehistoric themselves. As elsewhere, there was seemingly no relationship between the size of the grave and the richness of the contents. Faussett quitted the site, confident that he had spared no effort to make a clean sweep of all possible tumuli, having diligently employed his probe which, 'on plain ground, cannot fail to find them.'

[3]   *ibid.:* 111

Chartham Down, Chartham

13 April 1764 – 4 graves   5 October 1773 – 15 graves
13 October 1773 – 19 graves   21 October 1773 – 15 graves
[The papers relating to the last four graves, numbers 50-53, were misplaced by Faussett;
he declared that he had actually opened them on 13 April 1764][4]

Late in 1758 Faussett had recorded[5] that in the summer just past some labourers
were mending the road which led from Kenville, the seat of Thomas Thomson, Esq,
to Swadling Down, when, at the point where the road led out of the lane and wound
to the left to go onto the Down, they found a skeleton lying partly in a bank and
partly just beneath the road surface. Its head was to the north, unaccompanied by
any relics. He was puzzled as to how it had come to be there, but mused that as there
were two Roman camps nearby in Iffin and Pond Woods (both close to Swadling)
which he had recently discovered himself, he was satisfied that it had probably fallen
in a military skirmish. He accompanied his text with a sketch of the Pond Wood site;
it lay in Petham parish, and it therefore seems likely that the Swadling find-spot did
as well, rather than the adjacent Chartham.

Six years passed. Now, just two months after finishing work at Bekesbourne, and
with autumn advancing, Faussett was undeterred in continuing with what would
be his final series of excavations. It was perhaps a curious irony that this last site
had also been his first – 43 years previously, when as a boy of ten he had watched
Cromwell Mortimer excavating on Swadling Down under the auspices of Sir Charles
Fagg of Mystole House on whose land the site lay. There would consequently be no
difficulty (despite the intervening four decades) in relocating the site. Roach Smith
claimed the precise locality to be on 'Kenville' Down which adjoined 'Swerdling'
(his spellings), but, as all too often, by the 1850s everything had been subsumed by
cultivation so that even he, with the benefits of a map and descriptive text, was hard-
pressed to locate the destroyed barrows.

The site was at around 200 feet on the top and upper slope of a spur of the
North Downs, overlooking the Stour Valley, the spur facing west and the ground
sloping away to the south, west and north. Faussett opened his text by remarking
that several before him had considered the site as the battlefield of Caesar and the
Britons, but that their error was shown by what he himself had found and also from
an impartial consideration of Mortimer's account, even if

its plain drift and tendency is to confirm and corroborate that too hastily adopted
opinion.[6]

---

[4] *ibid.*: 174
[5] Society of Antiquaries of London: MS 920/1 f.15
[6] *Inv. Sep.* :160

The original manuscript was then in the hands of Sir William Fagg of Mystole House who let Faussett make a copy which he then reproduced in its entirety. The excavation account of 'the late ingenious and learned Secretary of the Royal Society' was clearly important to Faussett. He determined to transcribe it as he found it, add notes and references as occurred to him, write up an account of his exploration of those tumuli previously left undisturbed, and then compare the findings of the several investigations.

But, he emphasised, there was no possibility of any battle fought here, and especially not by Julius Caesar; no, rather the burials were of ordinary and peaceable inhabitants who lived in the period between the Roman withdrawal and the arrival of the Anglo-Saxons – the only small and conflicting evidence to this much-cherished theory was one ossuary found by Mortimer and two by himself which, to him, suggested an earlier date. (As if in need of corroboration, Faussett went and searched through the pages of *Philosophical Transactions*, thinking that as Mortimer was the secretary of the Royal Society he would surely find something to his advantage, but nothing was forthcoming.)

Roach Smith saw the value of Mortimer's account in its narration of the facts (for which reason Douglas had included it in his *Nenia*), and therefore now printed it verbatim in the *Inventorium*. But he thought it proper to omit a section in which Douglas had poured scorn on Mortimer for placing too much weight on Caesar's *De Bello Gallico*:

> There requires but little penetration to observe in this manuscript the great veneration which the Antiquaries of those days had for everything that was Roman; and but a slight reference to the body of this work to correct the animated zeal of the Doctor, when he is pleased, in the fever of conjecture, to place barrow A over the ashes of Q. Laberius Durus. As to the whole of the good Physician's conjectures, they are really too puerile for a comment.[7]

By this excision Roach Smith would render most of Faussett's censures on the errors of Mortimer needless,

> … and while this omission does not deprive our volume of one word of the journal of the facts, it keeps it clear of a discussion of a very superfluous kind, from which no information can be gained.[8]

Before itemising the more interesting or important of Faussett's own finds, all of which were no earlier than the 7th century, one might usefully look at what he had to say of Mortimer's results, taken from six barrows labelled A-F and 20 others which were merely summarised. He noted with interest crystal balls and items of jewellery including a beautiful *Roman* (my italics) silver and gold *fibula* adorned with garnets, similar to others he had recorded himself in the *Inventorium*. Mortimer had recorded

---

[7] Douglas, *op. cit.*: 107
[8] *Inv. Sep.*: 162, n.

some sets of bones as being entirely burnt, upon which Faussett remembered that he had been present at the opening

> and being then but about ten years of age, the strangeness of the thing made, as is natural, so strong an impression upon my memory that, at this day, I perfectly recollect every particular, and am very certain that none of the bones were then supposed to have had the least appearance of having passed the fire.[9]

adding that it was fairly common to find evidence of both cremation and inhumation at the same site, and even in the same grave – a manifest proof that the burial ground was so used for a long time, perhaps even over centuries.

Several skeletons within one mound puzzled Faussett. If the chalk was so hard, why then could the tumuli not have been for particular families or common tombs for 'the lower sort of people'? He also noted that certain articles such as brass hinges were found only in women's and children's graves, seemingly belonging to little boxes placed at the feet. Further comments of a general nature followed which, again, Roach Smith felt compelled to include

> All the remarks of Mr Faussett which could be supposed to explain, confirm or correct Dr Mortimer's account of his excavations are inserted. Some repetitions only are omitted; and (as I observed before), the observations in contravention to the theory of the Doctor, who endeavoured to prove the Chartham graves contained the remains of Roman soldiers under Julius Caesar, who fell in a conflict with the Britons.[10]

What Faussett found was actually something of an *omnium gatherum*. Grave 16 had a small copper alloy key (which Roach Smith considered to be Roman), and grave 26 a copper alloy instrument[11] seven inches long and nearly an inch wide at the upper end, almost certainly a writing stylus, and thus quintessentially Roman. Grave 51 was full of ossuaries, disturbed and broken, as he thought, either in an earlier excavation, or by whoever first raised the tumulus, when they destroyed adjacent ones for building material or scooped off the neighbouring turf to such a depth as to disturb the general area and then threw everything back in a heap.

This was all that survived, or could be found, following the childhood excavation of 1730. Faussett was now even more convinced that Caesar had never trod the area, such a fact 'apparent to every one who is not determined with the Doctor to persist in an error.'[12] Now it was clear that Chartham Down was too far from the Roman general's known landings, for the trinkets and ornaments and utensils all exactly corresponded with his own finds, and there were few weapons, children's skeletons or other encoffined ones. All of these things were 'of themselves sufficiently

[9]   *ibid.*: 163-4
[10] *ibid.*: 168
[11] *ibid.*: plate 12
[12] *ibid.*: 175

abundant to contradict and disprove so absurd an opinion', and further, the cross he had found in grave 9[13] put the matter out of all doubt:

> Nay, I much question if the owner of the trinkets, etc., found in the tumulus marked A, had appeared to him, and positively assured him that she really was not Q. Laberius Durus, but a mere woman, whether he would not have called her "a lying baggage", and have told her he knew better. … But I choose rather to ascribe his fondness for so unsupportable an hypothesis to the strength and warmth of his imagination, than to any desire, either of making a show of his skill and knowledge in antiquity, or of trying how far he could impose upon the incredulity of others.[14]

For the clergyman here to have been mindful of 'Let he who is without sin' would have been apposite, but now the vicious and spiteful diatribe *in Mortimerum* was at an end, as were Faussett's days of digging. The broken cinerary urns at Chartham Down were telling evidence of earlier use as a cemetery. Most of the barrows here were of medium size. About half of them were furnished, the smaller mounds containing twice as many unfurnished graves as furnished. There were no brooches, no weapons save a small javelin in a child's grave, and 14 graves with only a buckle or a knife. Three others contained pottery vesssels which may have come from disturbed Roman cremation burials. Of the 21 coffins 12 had passed the fire. A silver cross-shaped pendant, two other objects with a cross-design and the high proportion of unfurnished graves are reasonable supposition for at least partly Christian usage.

[Just to the east, on a north-west facing slope at Horton chapel, assorted finds have been located since 1987, chiefly by the Canterbury Archaeological Trust, which oversaw the discovery of an Anglo-Saxon cemetery in 2001.]

In August 1774 Faussett seems to have intended investigating Postling manor, just to the south-east of Monks Horton, for he had sought permission from its owner, Sir Edward Knatchbull of Mersham-le-Hatch, who declared: '… you are heartily wellcome to make any Researches there for your Amusement, & satisfy your Curiosity on the Spott you mention.' For the sake of the tenant Faussett had to leave the land in the same condition he found it, but other than that, Sir Edward wished him well and '… success in finding out Caesar's Footsteps…'[15]

One of the genealogical notebooks[16] includes an account of items found by some chalk-diggers in a pit at Linsey's on the western side of Palm Tree Hill at Court Lodge, Postling, on 1 August 1773, when several skeletons, a piece of gold wire, a brass buckle and two very similar *fibulae* were found, each with a central

[13] *ibid.:* plate 11; and Douglas, *op. cit.:* 67
[14] *Inv. Sep.*, 176
[15] Society of Antiquaries of London, MS 723: f.8
[16] Society of Antiquaries of London, MS 920/3: f.37

ivory hemisphere surrounded by three garnets within the usual wrought and gilded compartments.

Faussett noted that he already possessed several similar brooches 'which I have dug up at different places', but, ever the collector, still purchased this pair from the finders to go alongside his other specimens. The information from the genealogical notebook therefore confirms that they are the pair of identical keystone-garnet disc brooches (Avent class 2.1) recorded in his collection with a general provenance but no precise find-details, even as to whether the brooches were from the same context. All of these artefacts were of the mid-6th century.

Faussett's last archaeological adventure was to Petham in March 1775. It was written up by his son Henry Godfrey (and communicated to Edward Hasted who added watercolour sketches of all the artefacts), and again written up by Roach Smith.[17] The site was in a field near Garlinge Green belonging to the Rev'd Henry Thompson, and the principal curiosity, a lead coffin, had been drawn out of the ground by the action of the plough, Faussett immediately wondering how it had lain so long undisturbed at just six inches above the natural surface of the ground, and in a location under continuous tillage. It was 29 inches long, 11 broad and eight deep, entirely covered with a corded ropework design, and contained a *patera* and two empty urns, the larger of them broken by the ploughshare in the extraction, the smaller with the inscription *BIBE*, and so presumably a drinking vessel. All three were made of blackish brown earth, and Faussett pronounced them Roman without question, but was curious as to how they had survived unaccompanied by bones, ashes, coins or anything else; the finders had not thought to look further, yet of course the question might have been answered by digging around the periphery of the find-spot, as such a chest had probably been placed at the feet of an interment. That there had been a Roman cemetery there Faussett was convinced, but any other tumuli had long ago succumbed to the plough, and now the ungiving stiff clay soil did not invite a fresh assault. As he had often observed, and as it was here, Roman cemeteries were regularly on the hanging side of a gently declining hill, facing north-east, and in chalky or gravelly soil – and indeed, at the bottom of the hill was a chalk-pit.

Faussett had drawn up his will in July 1769, nearly seven years before his death. He was then just 48 and clearly in health poor enough to warrant executing the document. The gout had presumably already taken a heavy toll and probably led him to believe that the end might not be far off. And yet the three frenetic digging years of 1771-1773 still lay ahead. Was he at a temporary low ebb? Did he think that the excavation of the Kingston brooch in 1767 was the pinnacle of his digging career ? Or did he perhaps consider that he simply needed to put things in decent order in case the inevitable should overtake him unawares?

---

[17] Roach Smith, *Collectanea Antiqua* IV: 173 and plate XI

The autograph text stretched to four pages and opened with the customary declaration of sound mind and health in order that the will could not be declared invalid. A goodly paragraph was devoted to the burial arrangements, to be undertaken with as little expense as possible, and directed that he should be interred in a vault to be constructed as near as possible to his late mother in the chancel at Nackington, with the provision for his widow to be placed as near as was convenient to his right-hand side when her time came. If he died before all this could be achieved, then a grave was to be dug to the south of the ledger-stone which covered his mother and grandfather, sufficiently wide and deep to hold the coffins abreast and for other coffins to stand on them, with a brick pavement over his bones and a brick retaining wall all around. A black marble slab was to cover everything in its entirety. Faussett shared the opinion of many with regard to the efficacy of the medical profession when he instructed that there should be no burial until his corpse showed certain signs of putrefaction.

Now he attended to his worldly estate. His widow would receive, subject to remaining a widow and not leaving Kent, the majority of his estates and all the household possessions for her lifetime, and was charged with paying his three children life annuities of £40. If she could not comply, then the eldest surviving child would inherit, and pay her an annuity of £80. At her death the eldest son and heir, Henry Godfrey Faussett, would come into his inheritance and also pay £2000 (increased by daily interest of 4% from Elizabeth's date of death until the day of payment) to the other two children. It went with out saying that other arrangements assumed male precedence over female, but heirs there had to be.

His heir was to have all his books, whether in print or manuscript, but not the manuscript sermons (at last, some evidence of clerical duties!) which were to be burnt. Also to his heir would go his medals (that is, coins) and the catalogue of them, all of which were ranged in his great walnut-tree cabinet. Now followed the clause which would exasperate so many future antiquaries for so long:

> … and also all my antiquities and curiosities whatsoever, but my will is that (as I have been at great pains and expense in collecting them), that they may never be disposed of by sale or otherwise but upon the greatest necessity, but they may still continue in my Family and at Heppington; humbly trusting in God, that my posterity will some of them at least wisely prefer Polite Literature and Retirement to Ignorance and Dissipation, and Books and Medals to Hounds, Horses and Gaming.[18]

Most things were now tidied up, save goods and chattels not within the house. He now bequeathed in trust to his antiquarian colleagues Sir William Fagg of Mystole House at Chartham, the historian Edward Hasted, then of St George's parish in Canterbury, and Johnson Macaree, gentleman of St Paul's, Canterbury, all stock, crop, animals, tools, implements and hop-poles, plus ready money (if there

---

[18] TNA: PROB11/1016

was any) in bonds and securities for them to sell the same in order to pay debts and funeral expenses. If there was a shortfall, then they were to sell his marshland near Plumstead and three messuages near the church at Eltham to make it up, but if not, the said properties devolved to his widow and then to his heirs. Finally, his eldest sister Mary Uden was to receive £10.

Faussett's 'dear and most indulgent wife' was to be the sole executrix, and the three above-mentioned 'worthy and esteemed friends' overseers. Three witnesses now attested the will by signing in each other's and in Faussett's presence, Thomas Freeman, Anthony Lukyn and John Pilcher (names not occurring elsewhere, and so probably solicitors' clerks). He died 10 February 1776, and was buried in the chancel at Nackington one week later. Probate was granted rapidly to his widow on 27 February.

Thus ended Faussett's hectic, illness-prone and fabulously busy life at the age of 55. Three generations were to pass before the extraordinary archaeological artefacts, now locked up at Heppington, would see the light of day and give the world a more informed and clearer view of the riches of Anglo-Saxon England. The restrictive clause of the will would at last be loosened and allow Charles Roach Smith, an archaeologist with the vision to comprehend the treasures that Faussett had amassed, to make them known to an astonished public.

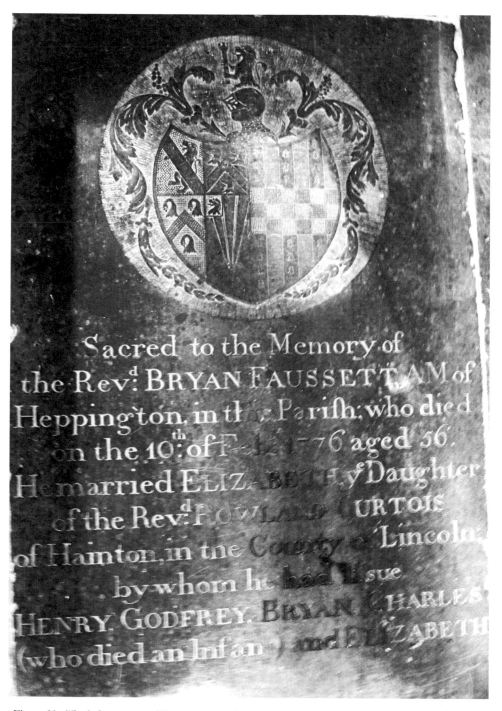

Figure 23. The ledger-stone of Bryan Faussett in the nave at St Mary Nackington. Compare the coat
of arms with that of his father.

(Copyright Neil Anthony.)

Chapter 11

A Gentleman's House and Home

It is now time to put in context Heppington House, for so long the residence of first the Godfreys and then the Faussetts. Nackington parish lies just south of Canterbury and east of the Roman road called Stone Street, which ran more or less due north for much of its route from Lympne (*Portus Lemanis*) to the cathedral city. It was never a large place or a populous one, being a little over 900 acres in extent, with 124 parishioners in 1801 and virtually the same number a century later. In 1778, writing just two years after Faussett's death, Hasted thought it pleasantly situated and healthy, then comprising 18 houses but with no village to speak of, leaving Sextries Court Lodge near the church as the major building. The vicarage or perpetual curacy had a certified value of £62 18s. 10d., and was augmented by its tithes, some of which arose from a part of the parish which was an ancient possession of Eastbridge Hospital in Canterbury, and also from an endowment of the vicarage at Blean, worth five marks. This latter portion of about 116 acres of land now belonged to the vicarage and brought in an annual rent of £42. The soil was fertile and generally worth 20s. an acre, although much was let for more, and behind Staplegate in particular it was 'very kindly to hops'.

A field called Hundred Acres, formerly Havenfield, lay in the middle of the parish, jointly owned by several individuals. There were no parochial charities, but just 8s. paid annually towards the maintenance of St Mary's church, then (and still) 'very small and kept very neat', out of an area called Willy's Lands. A (presumably) lesser mansion named Nackington House was situated at the northern end of the parish, the property of Captain John Nutt in the reign of Charles I. By descent though the Willys family, future baronets, it was sold around 1730 to Christopher Milles, Esq. of Canterbury, descended in 1742 to his son Richard, M.P. for Canterbury, and was still in that family as Hasted was writing. Today, St Mary's church preserves many memorials to them.

The South West View of Nackington Church

The North East View

Figure 24 Nackington church south-west and north-east views drawn by Bryan Faussett as a young man.
(Godfrey-Faussett family archives.)

In a King Ethelred charter of 993 the monarch granted to his mother Elfthryth certain parcels of land including *Natineddene*. In the Domesday Book the name appears as *Latintone*, in Domesday Monachorum as *Natindune*, and in the Calendar Rolls of 19 March 1247 is recorded a grant made to the prioress and nuns of St Sepulchre, Canterbury, of the gift of Eustace, the son of Ralph of *Nacindun*, raising 3*s*. rent from five acres.

The church of St Mary once belonged to the Priory of St Gregory, and was perhaps a part of its original endowment by Archbishop Lanfranc, again according to Hasted. At an early date it was appropriated to the Priory and confirmed by Archbishop Hubert Walter in the 1190s. Subsequently it was esteemed a manor, according to the priory register. The parish was in the gift of the archbishop; in 1661 William Juxon increased the stipend to £20, and in 1688 Gilbert Sheldon raised it again to £40.

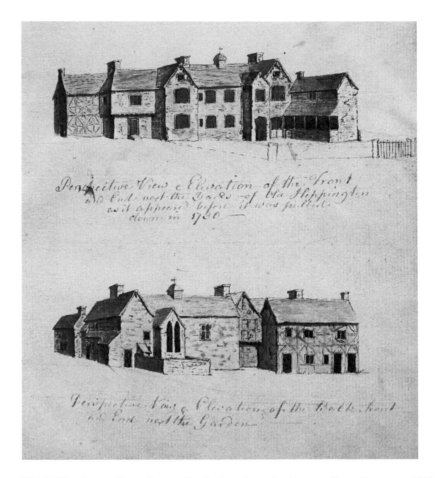

Figure 25 Old Heppington House front and back views drawn by the young Bryan Faussett, *c.* 1725-30.
(Godfrey-Faussett family archives.)

The earliest known occupants of Heppington are the Delce family, of whom William Delce in 1183 accounted at the exchequer for 40*s.* for the tenure of the land of *Hebington.* A list of fee holders for Kent in 1254 includes John de Delce holding a quarter-fee from William de Saye in *Natyndenne.* In 1272 Hamo de Forstall confirmed to W. de Delce one acre in *Hebindone* 'which I bought of Richard', and in a list of 1347 recording assessments to knight the Black Prince, the heirs of William Talbot purchased it as a fifth part of a knight's fee which their ancestor had held before in *Hebyntone* or *Hevington* of Geoffrey de Saye. From this Geoffrey may be traced a descent through the families of Clinton, Burgh, Bulkeley and Sandys to the Faussetts.

After the Delces and Talbots, the property was held by the Chiches of the Dungeon in Canterbury. The Fogges had succeeded by the 1390s, Sir John Fogge of Repton devising the estate by his will of 1491 to his son Sir Thomas Fogge,

Sergeant Porter of Calais, on whose death it went by marriage to George Pollard and Robert Oxenbridge who joined in the sale of it to John Hales of the Dungeon, one of the Barons of the Exchequer. At his death in the reign of Edward VI it passed to his second son, Sir Thomas Hales of Thanington, and thence by descent until Heppington with its mansion and lands was conveyed by an indenture of 9 May 1640 to Sir Thomas Godfrey who held it until his death in 1684. His widow Hester inherited it, and on her death in 1699 it devolved to her great-nephew Henry Godfrey, then a youth of 25 and the maternal grandfather of the future antiquary. Dying young in 1718, his widow Catherine was possessed of it for just one year until Mary, her surviving daughter and sole heiress, married Bryan Faussett senior at Nackington parish church on 4 October 1719. Heppington would now remain in the same family for a further one-and-a-half centuries until the final sale in 1874.

In the year following his marriage Bryan Faussett senior had a detailed account of his house and lands drawn up. The parchment map is inscribed:

> A topographical description of Heppington with the woods belonging thereunto as also of a certain parcel of land called Stockfield showing their abuttings and boundaries, all which are the possessions of Bryan Faussett Esqr of Heppington. As surveyed by William Brasier, 1720.

The estate then included the Heppington lands which, at 119 acres, were a little over half of the grand total of 200 acres, together with the Stockfield lands (which appear on a map of 1635), and Iffin Wood. The purchase dates of the latter two are unknown, although all three would be finally disposed of as an ensemble in 1874. Along with the house were a garden, orchards, oast-fields and hop-grounds, the boundaries of which were delineated by the Canterbury to Street End road to the east, a lane from Canterbury to Petham on the site of the old Roman road to the west, a cross-lane from Street End to the south, and a lane, seemingly then public and which later became the drive to the house, to the north. All of this was much increased in size by 1790 when Henry Godfrey Faussett, the eldest son and heir of the antiquary, purchased it, by which time it now included the North Court Farm of 100 acres.

Within a decade of his inheritance Bryan Faussett senior was clearly dissatisfied with his home, which by now was some centuries old, and no doubt at least partly dilapidated. It was pulled down in its entirety by 1730, but thanks to the precocious interests of Bryan junior, now aged ten, the little we now know about it is based squarely on his drawings and accompanying account. The sketches show Old Heppington as having a long four-gabled partly timbered façade of perhaps 100 feet in length with two main doors, varying sets of windows, all surmounted by a cupola and weather vane. Access was gained through an entrance porch with closet to find a hall with buttery, a great parlour, a smoking-room, and a great staircase to the upper floor. The servants' and domestics' quarters were made up of a kitchen and scullery, a butler's pantry, a brewhouse and other offices, and a room called Binford's. An aviary was situated somewhere in the vicinity, and is one of many references to the Faussetts' predilection for keeping assorted animals within their domain.

The account of the interior is a happy survival, and best quoted in full to show something of the future antiquary's eye for detail and interest in old things. If his aesthetic eye was a keen one, and his recording of the dilapidations accurate, then perhaps we may forgive his father for what now may strike us as the wanton destruction of a venerable building.

> Part of the house was of timber, in needle work, with overhanging chambers and floors, other parts very ancient, with very thick stone and flint walls, particularly the end to the south-east with great parlour in which appeared arrow loops filled up. The front towards the north-east had been in aftertimes put into the Elizabethan style, and the whole refaced, perhaps with additions by Sir T. Godfrey, between 1640 and 1650, who employed [Isaac] Fuller to paint the hall and staircase with various parts of Ovid's Metamorphoses – as appeared by his name on the staircase inscribed on a shield supported by a [...] on the great staircase, these being [...] on the plaister were of course destroyed. In many other parts of the house were paintings on the wainscot panels, some of which escaped destruction, viz. the Death of Cleopatra, Tobit and his dog, an old man's head with Memento Mori, many pieces of perspective, small ovals and other landscapes – the whole not doing much credit to the painter – and the upper panels of the wainscot of the great [...] contained landscapes in blue & white very slightly painted. The chimney piece of the same room was clumsy and heavy, being Portland stone, ornamented with large gilt roses, fragments of which I have seen were employed in the side wall of the staircase in the oast. The narrow pointed windows at the end of the passage leading from the front door, which part had been latterly enclosed for a small room or pantry, were fitted with painted glass, and which, as far as I can learn from my father and others who remembered, were chiefly armorial – and contained the bearings and matches of the Chiches who came into possession of Heppington temp. Richard II. They were likewise in possession at the Dungeon, where they were extinct at the beginning of Edward IV (vid. Hasted). In the beginning of Henry IV this estate passed to the Foggs, a branch of the Repton family. It is probable that this part of the house was built or at least repaired by some of the family of Chiche, temp. Richard II. Unfortunately, by the carelessness of the workmen at the time of the rebuilding in 1730 these windows were destroyed by the fall of an adjoining chimney.

George Colomb's romantically named (and written) novel *For King and Country* includes a chapter entitled 'To Heppington', all this based on 'a MS pretended to have been found in an old library in Kent', and said to have been sanctioned as accurate by Thomas Godfrey Faussett. He relates that Sir Thomas Godfrey, the purchaser of Heppington, found the property well wooded, and soon planted an avenue of limes before having the interior attended to, when he employed Isaac Fuller the portrait and history painter, recommended by Sir Henry Wotton just before his death.

Tantalisingly, there was said to have been a Van Dyck portrait of the king in armour at the upper end of the gallery but, unsurprisingly, this is not mentioned in the later inventory.

Designs for the new building had been made as early as 1723, so Bryan senior clearly did not demolish in a hurry. The architect was John Jacob de Wilstar, and the drawings reflect his Dutch origins. They were not entirely to the taste of his patron, and so considerably departed from in the actual execution of the new house. The final realised design is evident from a photograph of *c.*1873, taken just before the house passed out of the family in 1874, and reveals five bays under a hipped roof, and a front door with a Gibbs surround. Bryan senior himself laid the first brick of the new house at the back corner close to the pantry at 9 o'clock in the morning on Thursday 1 March 1733, afterwards giving the workmen 5*s.* for drink.

We are fortunate to know something about the family's tastes in art, for a catalogue (undated) exists of the pictures, listing 96 items (compare the 1750 probate inventory with its totals of 102 prints and 18 pictures). There were nine Tudor and Stuart portraits of the 1500s and 1600s (including oval ones of James II and his Queen which cost 10*s.* 6*d.* each), assorted landscapes, Dutch portraits and still-lifes. Then a good group of portraits from the Godfrey side of the family including Nicholas Toke and Robert Echlin, followed by 12 Faussett silhouettes, and paired half-length portraits of Bryan Faussett senior with his wife Mary by P. Milward who was paid £24 7*s.* 6*d.* for the same in January 1722. There were also photographs of (presumably lost) portraits of Dorothy Godfrey (d.1655) and her grandson Sir Thomas Godfrey (d.1690), the father of Henry Godfrey who inherited Heppington in 1699. The entire collection was removed preceding the 1874 sale, and subsequently dispersed around the family.

Pride of place would no doubt have gone latterly to the portraits of Bryan junior and his wife Elizabeth, measuring 30½" x 25", which were painted by Thomas Hudson 'ye limner' who was paid £30 15*s.* in February 1758 for the two pictures, their gold frames and a protective carrying box. Hudson was a Devon man, and both a portrait painter and art collector. After arriving in London he built up a circle of clients and counted Sir Joshua Reynolds and Joseph Wright of Derby among his apprentices. His career included some 400 portraits of the aristocracy, gentry, politicians, clergy and musical and theatrical personalities, among many of which Faussett doubtless felt quite at home. The two pictures were sold to the Liverpool Museum in 1989.

So much for what was hanging on the walls. The survival of Bryan senior's probate inventory, taken on 9-10 October 1750, three weeks after his death, by Thomas Strouts and Thomas Brown (whose spelling and syntax, alas, do not always equal the elegance of the contents) affords us the fullest possible picture of the contents of an English gentleman's mansion-house in the middle of the 18th century. Room by room descriptions take us through the Faussett household, minutely itemised with accompanying valuations and a grand total of £361 10*s.* 0½*d.* In summary, there were a hall, dining-room, drawing-room, two parlours, smoking-room, housekeeper's room, dressing-room, nursery, four garrets and four chambers, several closets, scullery, two pantries, cellars, men's lodging-room, laundry, brew-house, bake-house, milk-house with yard, and summer-house.

Much of this mass of detail, predictably, relates to beds and bedding, fireplace accoutrements, household utensils (notably articles for making and serving tea or coffee, some being Delft blue and white), and furniture from the humdrum to the decidedly expensive disposed around the principal rooms which included yellow, blue and green chambers. Leisure pursuits take in guns and pistols, a spinet, a backgammon set, and a library of 238 books and pamphlets. More worryingly for the future antiquary's persistent gout, one of the cellars held two gallons of red port wine and five quarts of brandy. Also itemised are six bird-cages and a parrot-cage — did their occupants contribute in any way to the many feather-beds and 'two parcels of feathers', one wonders?

The probate inventory of Bryan Faussett, senior:

His wearing apparel: Value £5.

In the best garret: 1 bedstead with striped curtains, 2 feather beds, 1 bolster, 1 coverlet, 1 half-headed bedstead, 1 pillow, 3 blankets, 1 square table, 1 hair brush, 1 fire shovel, 2 pairs of tongs, 1 pair of dogs, 1 iron hearth, 1 trivet, 1 fender. Value £4 18s. 6d.

In the blue garret: 1 bedstead and 3 curtains, 2 feather beds, 1 bolster, 1 pillow, 1 quilt, 1 blanket, 2 square tables, 1 armchair, 6 small chairs, 1 fender. Value £3 13s. 0d.

In the middle garret and closet: 1 bureau, 1 chest, 1 trunk, 1 tea table, 1 Delft basin, 1 elbow chair, 6 small chairs, 1 fire shovel, 1 bird cage, 1 Caan [cane?] couch, 8 small prints, 1 chest of feathers, 1 hearth brush & wood scales. Value £2 4s. 0d.

In the nursery: 1 chest, 1 trunk, 2 Delft jars, 1 pewter bedpan, 1 cradle with child's [ruler?], 1 parrot's cage, 1 small cage, 2 feather pillows, 1 flasket, 1 seed basket, 1 elbow chair, 2 parcels of feathers, some apples & onions, 1 bedstead & some old lumber. Value £1 12s. 0d.

In the Redwoods or housekeeper's room: 1 bedstead & drugget curtains, 1 feather bed, 2 bolsters, 1 pillow, 3 blankets, 1 quilt, 1 square table & 6 chairs. Value £2 9s. 6d.

In the maid's garret: 1 bedstead & curtains, 1 feather bed & 1 bolster, 1 rug, 3 blankets, 1 square table, 3 chairs. Value £2 0s. 0d.

Mrs Faussett's chamber & closet: 1 bedstead and blue curtains &c, 1 feather bed, 1 bolster, 4 pillows, 1 quilt, 2 blankets, 1 walnut tree escritoire, 1 case of drawers, ditto 1 hare trunk, 1 Dutch tea table, 1 easy chair, 1 square stool, 1 large looking glass, 1 dressing glass, 1 dressing box & tray, 1 spring clock, 1 brass arm sconce, 1 gloom hearth, 1 fire shovel, 1 pair of tongs, 1 pair of creepers, 1 old walnut tree square table, 2 birdcages, 1 copper coffee pot. Value £14 8s. 6d.

In the green chamber: 1 bedstead & green curtains &c, 1 feather bed, 1 bolster, 1 pillow, 1 quilt, 4 blankets, 1 walnut tree case of drawers, 1 large nest of drawers, ditto 1 square table & dressing glass, 2 stands, 1 wig block, 1 pair of glass arm sconces, 3 elbow chairs,

1 small chair, 1 picture, 1 gloom hearth, 1 fire shovel, 1 pair of tongs, green hangings of the room. Value £10 9*s*. 6*d*.

In the passage and closet: 45 jelly & sweetmeat glasses, 6 dozen of candles, 10 prints, 1 hatchment, 1 picture, 6 bells at several places in the house. Value £3 2*s*. 6*d*.

In the best chamber: 1 damask bed and counterpane, 1 feather bed, 1 bolster, 2 pillows, 3 blankets, 1 walnut tree dressing table and dressing glass, 1 large sconce glass, 1 basin stand, 1 silk easy chair, 7 small chairs ditto, 1 gloom hearth, 1 fire shovel, 1 pair of tongs, 1 pair of dogs, 1 picture, 10 prints framed, 7 ditto not framed. Value £25 2*s*. 0*d*.

In the dressing room chamber: 1 bedstead with wrought curtains &c, 1 feather bed, 1 bolster, 2 pillows, 1 cotton counterpane, 2 blankets, 1 mahogany table and dressing glass, 1 large sconce glass, 7 mahogany chairs, 1 fire shovel, 1 pair of tongs, 1 pair of creepers, 1 picture, 10 prints and 37 prints in the passage. Value £27 2*s*. 0*d*.

In the yellow chamber: 1 bedstead & yellow curtains &c, 1 feather bed, 1 bolster and 2 pillows, 1 counterpane, 3 blankets, 3 elbow chairs, 3 small chairs, 2 round stools, 1 walnut tree square table, 1 gloom hearth, 1 pair of creepers, 1 [cloop?] stool and pewter pan, 1 earthen pan ditto, 1 print and hangings of the room. Value £9 4*s*. 0*d*.

In the dining room: 1 large mahogany card table, 1 round mahogany tea table, 1 Japan tea table, 1 settee and 6 chairs, 1 pair of brass arm sconces, 2 pictures, 18 prints, 1 gloom hearth, 1 pair of dogs, 1 fire shovel, 1 pair of tongs and chimney hooks. Value £12. 8*s*. 0*d*.

In the passage at the great stairhead: 1 spinet and frame, 4 leather bottom chairs, 1 black Japan card table, 4 pictures. Value £2 0*s*. 6*d*.

On the great staircase: 1 glass sconce and Dr Pack's chart of East Kent. Value 7*s*. 6*d*.

In the hall: 1 eight-day clock and case, 1 oval table, 10 cane chairs, 1 backgammon table, box, dice & men, 1 glass lanthorn, 2 birdcages, 1 weather glass, 1 picture, 2 bucks' heads, 1 gloom hearth, 1 pair of dogs, 1 fire shovel, 1 pair of tongs. Value £8 8*s*. 6*d*.

In the great parlour and drawing room: 1 large sconce looking glass, 1 large marble table and frame, 14 chairs, 1 gilt leather screen, 1 Dutch tea table, 1 mahogany tea board, 1 brown tea kettle & lamp, 1 carpet, 1 pair of bellows, 1 hearth brush, 1 gloom hearth, 1 pair of dogs, 1 fire shovel, 1 pair of tongs, another set of chimney furniture, ditto 2 pictures. Value £16 10*s*. 6*d*.

In the little parlour: 1 marble table & frame, 1 mahogany oval table, 1 Dutch tea table, 2 glass sconces, 2 elbow chairs, 6 small chairs, 1 gloom hearth, 1 pair of bellow, 1 fire shovel, 1 hearth brush, 1 pair of tongs and chimney hooks, 1 pair of brass sconces, 1 mahogany tea voider, 3 pictures, 1 print, 1 painted floor cloth. Value £10 6*s*. 6*d*.

In the smoking room: 1 bureau writing table, 1 looking glass, 1 old gold watch, 2 swords, 1 pair of spurs, 1 round table, 1 elbow chair, 4 small chairs, 1 pair of glass sconces, 2 guns, 1 pair of pistols, 1 short pouch of powder horn, 2 belts, 1 tea chest, 1 Japan corner cupboard, 2 pictures, 1 pair of bellows, 1 hearth brush, 1 pair of dogs, 1 fire shovel, 1 pair of tongs and chimney hooks, 11 patterage of quail nets, 6 tin canisters, 27 pieces of stone & earthenware, 238 books and pamphlets, 1 deal case of drawers and some odd thing*s*. Value £23 1*s*. 6*d*.

In the smoking room closet and under the great staircase: 1 round table, 2 chairs, a large basket, 10 pewter plates, 6 drinking glasses, 1 decanter ditto, 1 tumbler, 1 glass salt, 1 vinegar cruet, 3 spitting boxes and some odd thing*s*. Value £1 0*s*. 6*d*.

In the closet in the hall: 1 case of drawers, 11 knives, 12 forks, 12 ditto for a dessert, 1 spice box, 3 sugar canisters, 1 copper lamp, 1 brass skillet, 3 tin saucepans, 4 box irons & heaters, 10lbs of unspun work, 2 coffee mills, 1 pair of small brass scales and weights, 1 lock, 1 French plate lamp and stand, and some odd thing*s*. Value £1 12*s*. 6*d*.

In the kitchen: 17 pewter dishes, 1 dozen of [snepe?] plates, 4 dozen plates, 1 cheese plate, 1 roasting jack, pulley lines & weight, 1 coal grate & fender, 1 spit rack, 1 fire shovel, 1 pair of tongs, 1 poker, 1 sifter, 2 pot irons, 2 pairs of pot hooks, 1 gridiron, 1 salt box, 2 spits, 1 pair of bellows, 3 pairs of brass candlesticks, 1 pair of brass snuffers and stand, 1 brass ladle, 4 iron candlesticks, 1 flesh fork, 1 spit holdfast, 2 iron saucers, 1 pair of iron snuffers, 1 tin pepper box and flower box, 1 frying pan rack, 1 tin colander, 1 bell-metal mortar and iron pestle, 1 chopper, 1 copper drinking pot, 3 copper saucepans, 1 spice pan ditto, 1 tin dripping pan, 1 tin [borter?], 1 tin pudding pan, 3 brass boiling pots and leads, 2 tin dish covers, 1 pot trivet, 1 warming pan, 1 long table, 1 square table, 1 form, 6 chairs, 1 fire screen, 1 tea kettle, 1 spinning wheel, 2 mugs and some odd thing*s*. Value £9 14*s*. 6*d*.

In the scullery and pantry: 1 frying pan, 1 iron kettle, 2 tin pudding pans, 1 plate rack, 1 skillet frame, 1 pail, 1 wood bowl, 1 lanthorn, 2 small stone jars, 2 earthen crock*s*. Value 9*s*. 6*d*.

In the man's pantry: 1 napkin press, 1 oval tub, leaves for a table. Value 5*s*.

In the cellars: 6 brine tubs & pork, 3 troughs, 1 safe, 1 earthern pan, 2 jars, 2 stone bottles, 1 table, 1 chopper, 1 great pewter wine measure, 3 tin funnels, 1 Delft bowl, 2 hogsheads, 2 half-hogsheads of beer, 2 scalders, 2 keelers, 1 stone jar, 10 brooms, 3 half-ankers, 9 old iron curtain rods; in the small beer cellars: 7 hogsheads, two half-hogsheads of good small beer, 3 scalders, 1 ring, 2 brass locks, 3 gross of glass bottles, 1 stone grate; in the wine cellar: 2 gallons of red port wine, 5 quarts of brandy, 20 gallons of strong beer. Value £31 4*s*. 0*d*.

In the laundry and brewhouse: 1 ash cloth and clothes horse, 1 brewing copper, 1 washing copper, 1 mash tub, 2 tin tubs, 1 bucking tub, 1 coolback, 5 keelers, 1 stirrer, 1 'gute', 1 hop basket, 1 tape house, 1 pail. Value £7 18*s*. 0*d*.

In the bakehouse: 1 beam of scales and 114lbs of gloom weights, 1 pail, 2 sieves, 1 gallon, 1 trough. Value £1 0s 0*d*.

In the milkhouse and yard: 2 charins, 2 pails, 2 milk keelers, 2 earthen pans, 1 crock, 1lb weight and wood scales of some poultry in the yard. Value £1 12s. 6d.

In the men's lodging room: 2 bedsteads, 2 beds, 2 bolsters, 3 blankets, 1 coverlet. Value £2 0s 0d.

In the summer house: 4 chairs and 2 tables. Value 5s.

The old coach and chariot. Value £10 0s. 0d.

The plate: 1 montease, 1 pair of salvers, 1 coffee pot and lamp, 1 pair of half-pint cans, 1 pair of canisters, 1 pint mug, 1 pair of small salvers, 1 pair of salts, 1 set of casters, 2 pairs of candlesticks, 1 pair of snuffers and stand, 1 punch ladle, 1 snepe spoon, 1 marrow spoon, 6 large spoons, 9 dessert spoons, 9 teaspoons, 1 pair of tea tongs, 1 strainer. The above plate 296½ ounces at 5s. 3d. comes to £77 16s. 7½d.

The china: 2 large burnt in dishes, 1 ditto blue and white, 3 lesser dishes,1 blue and white dish, 1 dozen enamel plates, 1 pair of blue and white beakers, 1 blue and white plate, a pair of burnt in bottles, a pair of snepe plates, 4 ditto blue and white, 1 small dish and 9 plates ditto, a pair of white China nuns, a pair of small blue and white beakers, 5 burnt in bowls, 2 fine blue and white bowls, 1 creckt, 1 large blue and white sugar dish, 12 chocolate cups, 2 boats, 48 assorted saucers, 6 cups and saucers, 6 in a meld tea cups, 32 tea cups, 3 blue saucers and 4 tea cups, 18 assorted basins, 2 square teapots, 2 blue and white teapots, 6 in a meld teacups and saucers, a pair of in a meld deep saucers, 6 blue and white teacups and saucers, 9 coffee cups, a pair of porringers, a pair of white mugs, 6 white cups, 1 burnt in mug, 3 milk pots, 3 white bottles and a dram cup, 2 bowls, 4 small toys, 4 small bottles, 4 small beakers, 21 pieces of broken china. Value £12 5s. 9d.

The linen: 17 huckaback table cloths, 24 pairs and 1 sheet, 10 diaper table cloths, 13 kitchen table cloths, 12 narrow cloths, 18 towels, 10 pillow beers. Value £19 18s. 6d.

Glasses in the parlour: 16 drinking glasses, 9 tumblers, 2 decanters, 2 bottle boards. Value 9s.

[An unsual and compelling postscript to the just-mentioned kitchen paraphernalia are the 'Heppington Receipts',[1] a compendium in three small notebooks, dated between 1698 and 1721, which belonged to Faussett's mother, Catherine Godfrey, and then to her daughter Mary Faussett. Carefully indexed, they contain in 465 pages some 1200 recipes for minor medicines and elixirs, and food ranging from daily sustenance to elaborate dinner parties.]

Faussett now took steps to improve the grounds of the house. In the eighteenth century, landowners sometimes built structures of large stones meant to represent Druids' temples and altars; of many examples that of Wardour Castle in Wilshire,

---

[1] Wellcome Library, *'Heppington Receipts'* : MSS 7997-7999

which included a genuine monolith from a prehistoric chamber tomb is outstanding, and, finest of all, the Druids' Temple near Masham on the North Yorkshire moors, erected around 1820 by a charitable landowner creating work for the local unemployed, which included mock burial chambers and trilithons.

In the late 1760s, his digging career in full flow, and with the increasing array of magnificent artefacts carefully catalogued and displayed within the confines of his own home, he embarked on a new venture in order to adapt certain objects from the collection to the outdoor ornament of Heppington: a garden pavilion would now house a few selected pieces, illustrative of his interests and knowledge. Visitors and cognoscenti would not only discourse about antiquities at the meal-table and be shown whatever Faussett chose to pick from his collections, perhaps to reveal some theme or argument, but might then also be invited to stroll in the grounds and approach and examine antiquities placed in individual settings with appropriate descriptions in Latin.

Here now was an 18th-century precursor of the historical museum. No longer did Faussett merely amass objects and provide clues for story tellers; he personally arranged such cherished objects as he saw fit in dedicated surroundings where each relic and its inscription contributed to an overall effect which was more than the sum of its parts. Here was no gallimaufry, no ragbag, no disparate cabinet of curiosities gathered from here, there and everywhere, united by no theme except myth and fantasy in outlandish colours and shapes, but rather a scholar's serious, hard-won and purposeful attempt to make known his act of historical retrieval through labels written in a – no, *the* – language consonant with what it described. The viewing of the past, hitherto simply the record of a personal investment in objects and their age value, was now displaying a tendency towards the accumulation and ordering of such objects in a permanent installation, that is, the museum. Antiquarian sensibility was now instrumental in the re-evaluation and representation of the past in a revelatory manner. A fresh and new view of the past was offered to those with both the eye and mind to see it – Faussett did not just passionately care for ancient and neglected objects long out of human view, but contributed positively to the dominant myth of Romantic historiography that the past should be resurrected.

Other ornaments preceded the pavilion, for Faussett recorded in 1772 that he had brought home from Sibertswold Down the cover of a Roman urn and displayed it in the garden wall, later transferring it to the pavilion. The discovery is best told in his own words:

> Having now opened all the tumuli [in the Upper Burial Ground] which appeared to be of much consequence in what I shall call for the future the Lower Burial Ground, I was so impatient to examine the contents of some others on the top of the hill, from which I had reason (as will be seen below) to expect great matters, that I resolved to defer my search into those few very small ones which remained unopened there, till after I had satisfied my curiosity there.[2]

---

[2] *Inv. Sep.*: 126

Figure 26 The Faussett garden pavilion in 1950. Some artefacts and inscriptions are still visible.
(Reproduced by kind permission of the Kent Archaeological Society.)

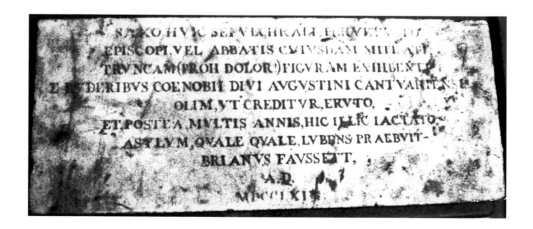

Figure 27. Faussett's Latinity set in stone: one of the garden pavilion inscriptions.
(Godfrey-Faussett family archives.)

The site was about 200 yards to the south of the lower ground, with the Sibertswold-Sandwich road running between them. Faussett thought that other areas might have had graves, now destroyed by the plough; the few remaining tumuli had been dug down or ploughed up by farmers for turf-burning in order to make dencher. All of these might have escaped his notice if it had not been for one of the farmers telling him that it was common to turn up human bones and potsherds in the course of ploughing, and that two years previously his servants had found two large jars, each of about a bushel's content, full of burnt human remains which included a skull and jaw bones – alas, the farmer had arrived too late to stop his labourers pelting the nearly intact jars to pieces.

Faussett rushed forth and proved the story to be true when he found huge numbers of sherds of *paterae* and other vessels of various colours, sizes and materials. Then the covers which had closed the jars came to view:

> There we also saw the fatal stones which had served these more than brutes as instruments to knock these precious remains of venerable antiquity in pieces with.[3]

Each was a round, coarse-grit, flat stone ten inches in diameter and three thick, '... like a small grindstone, each with a sort of pouring spout for distributing bones and ashes thereinto.' (Roach Smith adds here that the two covering stones started life as hand-mills, now worn-out, and were applied as covers in the want of anything more suitable; others have added that this crudely arranged burial was a downland peasant's version of a classical tomb, complete with its opening through which libations might be poured onto the ashes of the deceased.)

Whence the genesis of such a novelty? The pavilion was born into a background of Romanticism, but perhaps much more influenced by Faussett's close friendship with Ebenezer Mussell, the antiquary and 'skilful collector of antiquities', who in his house at Bethnal Green had laid down a courtyard of Roman bricks from Richborough and rebuilt part of the demolished Aldgate from the City of London. He and Faussett regularly visited each other's home, and so perhaps on one occasion Faussett visited this open-air museum of archaeology and was inspired to create something similar for himself; and further, he may also have seen the display of Roman tombstones in their specially constructed niches in the walls of 'The Hermitage' at Higham near Rochester (subsequently destroyed by fire, and of which nothing now remains).

The pavilion stood close to the house at the east end of a cedar grove amongst green lawns. It was small and rectangular, and of plain red brick with sandstone dressings. Vaguely Georgian, it had a large central arch, but no other features, and certainly nothing of any 18th-century Gothick about it – all was subsumed to the exhibition of relics on the interior walls, each accompanied by a marble tablet explaining its history, the texts dating from 1769 to 1775. In honour of his father,

---

[3] *ibid.*: 127

Henry Godfrey Faussett set a tablet in the gable in 1799, its sandstone of poorer quality and its lettering of a different style. One wonders how many favoured guests – James Douglas and Edward Hasted among them – must have been intrigued to gaze on the contents. The pavilion was well looked after for many years as an asset to the estate, and even survived (albeit with graffiti) the wartime occupation of Heppington, but then fell victim to the same fate as the main house, at which point the artefacts were mostly handed over to Canterbury City Council.

Faussett's noble ideal would ultimately fail, for not only did the British Museum reject his collection but even the pavilion itself was also broken up in 1950 and its component parts dispersed.[4] A talk was given by Ronald Jessup to the Society of Antiquaries in 1953 on what had remained in it until discovery and final dispersal.

Of the seven curiosities set in the walls of the pavilion, some were truly genuine relics of Roman London and 12th-century Canterbury. The quernstone lid from Sibertswold (formerly set in the garden wall) used as a cover for a Roman cremation urn has already been described.

Next were two sculptured corbels from Northbourne found in the ruins of the ancient palace in that parish; Faussett thought one represented St Augustine (to whom the parish church is dedicated) and the other King Ethelbert, an ascription based merely on the manor of Northbourne having once belonged to Ethelbert's son Ethelbald. The latter head was ultimately returned to its find-spot.

The first Northbourne head and the interesting lead font bowl were restored to Kingston church in 1931, the latter duly reconsecrated by Archbishop Cosmo Gordon Lang. The then owner of Heppington, Mr William Chapman, bowed to Faussett's opinion that the corbel did indeed represent St Augustine, and it was therefore set up in the west wall to watch over the font, just as it had in the pavilion. Modern opinion may demur on the grounds of the style of the bearded and moustached head, with its cloth hood tucked under the chin, the hairstyle and the general absence of saintly attributes. But the Norman font tub is genuine enough and distinctly unusual in being octagonal, with four pairs of sunk round-topped arches around its Purbeck marble circumference. It had suffered a common fate in being thrown out of Kingston church because of its age, and then reduced to serving as a pig trough.

Next was an 11-inch terracotta Roman relief head, excavated with other antiquities in 1773 at Gresham College, Broad St, in the City of London, which Faussett believed possibly to be Geta Caesar.

Then a section of a Purbeck marble tomb effigy of an ecclesiastic, about two feet high, thought to have come from St Augustine's Abbey in Canterbury. It had been crudely re-cut for building-stone and then suffered further deliberate damage, with the loss of the head and all below the waist, although a gloved hand survived and had been reaffixed. Nothing today of the fragments at St Augustine's Abbey can be

---

[4] *Arch. Cant.* LXIV (1951): xliv

matched to it, although the 13th- to 14th-century style, the staff and the decoration on the glove all point to an abbot as the model.

Last, and most important, there was a remarkable piece of late English Romanesque sculpture taken out of the middle of the wall of the Norman Guest House of the monastery attached to Canterbury Cathedral, depicting a head within a quatrefoil which Faussett thought represented King Canute, but was in fact a biblical prophet, and is now in the Victoria and Albert Museum. It had been found in 1764 facing downwards, in a wretched state of preservation, and was some 13 inches high and wide, and six thick. The figure was of an elderly man with a short beard, the crown on his head within a sunken quatrefoil, originally within a moulded frame but subsequently cut away, perhaps on Faussett's instructions. It bore a strong resemblance to a relief in the same cathedral's library, and in the opinion of Dr Zarnecki the pair formed part of a decorative scheme of *c*.1190. The Faussett head had been re-used as building material in the *Aula Nova* or North Hall, and it was thought that both may have been part of the decoration of the first almonry chapel.

The account may be amplified by Faussett's own words on the piece, for he wrote to Dr Ducarel on 13 September 1764 about its acquisition. Ducarel, now at Lambeth, was a former Commissary of the Diocese of Canterbury and his office had been situated in the very building where the head was found, the northern part of which was demolished in 1730.

> I have lately added greatly to my collection by the acquisition of … an almost alto-relievo of Canute the Dane, lately found, with its face downward, and covered in mortar, in the middle of a very thick wall belonging to the building where your office is kept, in the Mint Yard. This building was the Aula Hospitium … and is certainly (as you well know) a piece of Norman architecture. You will, therefore, I hope, agree with me in looking upon this piece of carving as a valuable piece of antiquity.[5]

A comparison of the two heads is instructive. The Canterbury head is better preserved in retaining the moulded frame and having a roll-moulded upper edge, but there are greater psychological differences in that the Faussett head, with its partly hidden left arm, has a calmer air than the Canterbury one, whose gesturing posture suggests energy and considerable religious fervour. It cannot be known which prophets the artist had in mind, although in both cases the coat is fastened in the classical manner on the shoulder. Despite the damage, the confident skill of the carver still comes through forcibly, and although each is a stock type, individual features convey mood and character.

One might be curious to ask how and why a scholar of Faussett's calibre mistook a prophet for a king, but alas, he offered no explanation, although it should be borne in mind that contemporary opinion would not have registered that royal figures

---

[5]   Nichols, *op. cit.*, III: 5

carved on mediaeval buildings were seldom images of historical figures, but much more commonly conventional types of prophets and the ancestors of Christ.

However, the numismatist R. H. M. Dolley argued[6] that Faussett's conclusion was not capricious but based on considered, if fallacious, reasoning. Coins of the Canute quatrefoil type have been found in smallish quantities in Kent, the majority in collectors' cabinets seemingly originating from Scandinavian hoards and not arriving for the most part in England until the later 1800s. We now know them to be fairly common, whereas Faussett would have viewed them as characteristic and unusual enough to be brought to the attention of fellow antiquaries. Dolley further defended Faussett, in connection with his opinion of the pre-Norman origin of the King Canute head, by saying that it had been found inverted and mutilated in a wall thought to be of Norman fabric, and that even today this context has to be explained as patching. Who would blame Faussett for stressing its pre-Gothic elements and thinking it Saxon when all around him he saw only analogous material? Rather than sniping, we should pay tribute to the catholicity of his antiquarianism in that he was alive to the value of numismatic evidence, even if in this instance it led him astray.

Faussett composed six Latin inscriptions, dated between 1769-1775, on the marble tablets which hung beneath each exhibit (the two heads as one). The general tenor of them was to emphasise his role in safeguarding antiquities from ancient times (the font now no longer profaned) and to preserve them from further damage in this, his rural refuge, where love of antiquity would secure them from future danger.

Discerning visitors to the pavilion would have enjoyed views of the great pond in the yard as they proceeded. Faussett seems to have had a keen interest in keeping it well stocked, for between 1762 and 1765 he was supplied with 364 tench and carp (three to nine inches long) by a Mr Hougham at Hoath Pond, taking out 200 dead ones (now six to 11 inches long) in the same period.

Life outside the house was busy. Many day-labourers and other servants (sometimes soldiers) were more or less constantly employed in planting, sowing, threshing, hop-picking, mending, cutting stakes and hop poles, and myriad other jobs around the estate, and were paid 1*s.* 6*d.* or 2*s.* a day. Ploughboys earned £3 annually, waggoners' mates £5, and gardeners £7 to £8. Faussett was constantly involved in purchasing hops, seeds, fruit and other supplies, both to feed his family and friends and also to occasionally sell surpluses of straw, wood, faggots, and animals – for example a calf for £1 10*s.*

Life inside the house was well regulated by a staff whose annual salaries were as follows: footboys 50*s.* to £3; footmen £3 to £10, plus livery; coachmen £5 to £9; and three other servants who were to earn £4 to £5 annually but to find their own tea and other household necessities. All were employed 'at a month's warning'.

---

[6] *Arch. Cant.* LXVIII (1954): 217-9

Figure 28. Heppington House garden: Victorian tranquillity. *(Godfrey-Faussett family archives.)*

Figure 29. Heppington House: the garden front around the time of the sale in 1874. Standing in front of the mature trees is Captain Bryan Godfrey-Faussett (1863-1945). *(Godfrey-Faussett family archives.)*

For 234 years there had been almost continuous occupation by the Godfreys and the Faussetts, their income derived from farming, from extending the lands, and from being the village squire or, when Bryan Faussett was also the incumbent of Nackington, squarson. Over the years there were a few alarms, as recorded by Sarah Faussett in her diaries: the nursery chimney caught fire in January 1815; in November 1820, the family, by deciding not to light celebratory fires for the abandonment of Queen Caroline's trial, had their windows broken by a mob; and in February 1826 the house was broken into, the thieves gaining entry through the little drawing-room.

Things changed in 1830 when Bryan's grandson, the Rev'd Godfrey Faussett, now Prebend of Worcester and Lady Margaret Professor of Divinity at Oxford, could spare little time to be down in Kent and so lived at Worcester or Oxford. At his death in 1853 his son Bryan, also a clergyman, succeeded but never lived in the house, instead letting it to a Mr Wallace and then probably to others as well. By then, disposal of the contents was under way, as Sarah Faussett noted in her diary 'the sale at poor dear old Heppington'. The house was now occupied only for short periods by visiting family members, and progressively emptied of its contents, so much so that at the very end it seems that the family silver and jewellery, a few miniatures, the big bell, some ancient lace and the remains of the library were all that remained.

Heppington's Indian summer had now truly passed away. It was with a heavy heart and much family grief and distress that Godfrey Trevelyan Faussett took the momentous decision to sell Heppington, owned by the Godfreys and Faussetts since 1640. He now lived elsewhere, and was prompted by a shortage of family money, the burden of the land still being heavily mortgaged, and too many rooms partially bereft of furniture after numerous sales. A lavish auction catalogue[7] entitled 'The Heppington Estates, Kent', with detailed descriptions and coloured maps (showing yet further increase in size since the purchase in 1790) was produced by Farebrother, Clark & Co of Tokenhouse Yard, Lothbury, E.C., for disposal in four lots on Tuesday, 21 July 1874 at 2pm. The four lots, if sold as one, totalled just short of 500 acres with rentals valued at £1049 5s. 4d., of which the house and grounds brought in £180, and North Court and Heppington Farms £515. The trees, underwoods and plantations, rated separately, brought in a sizeable £2132 7s.2d. The preamble, employing suitably florid terminology, enticed potential purchasers with:

> Heppington Freehold Manorial Estate situate in the parishes of Nackington, St Mary Bredin, Petham, Thanington, and Upper and Lower Hardres, only two and a half miles from the City of Canterbury. Comprising the manor of North Court with its fines, quit rents and privileges; Heppington Mansion approached by a carriage drive through a charming park, beautifully studded with forest timber of large growth, and containing excellent accommodation with the most ample domestic offices, coach-house, stabling, loose boxes, small farming &c together with kitchen garden, lawn and pleasure grounds.

[7] KHLC: U771/E57

Heppington and North Court Farms with comfortable residence most beautifully placed on the slope of the hill close to Lower Hardres church, with pleasure grounds in front having ample farm buildings and detached premises, recently erected on the most improved principles of farming; three cottages and sundry enclosures of arable and pasture land; Young's Farm, with farm house and appropriate buildings; six cottages with gardens; also a cottage at Street End with forge and carpenter's shop. The whole estate comprises an area of about 500 acres and produces a rental, inclusive of the woods in hand, of upwards of £1,000 p.a.

Voluminous further details would be supplied for those not already lured by what lay around and about the house itself. The description of the interior affords valuable comparisons with that of its predecessor. Purchasers would enter into the possession of a freehold manorial estate (a small part of which was tithe-free) comprising the manor of North Court with its fines and privileges, plus annual quit-rents of £5. The mansion-house was brick built and tiled, of handsome elevation, and entered by a spacious entrance hall of 27 by 22 feet, with ornamented ceiling. From the inner hall rose the principal staircase with balusters of solid oak, well lighted with handsome and large windows filled with Faussett armorial glass. Two communicating drawing rooms totalling 40 by 17 feet, finished with ornamental cornices and marble chimneypieces, had five windows, one of which opened onto the lawn. The dining room was substantial at 23 by 19 feet, with panelled walls and a marble chimneypiece. The library was of southern aspect. The ground floor was completed by the kitchen, two pantries, a WC, a housekeeper's room and a washhouse. In the basement were extensive wine, ale and beer, and coal cellars with a dairy and larder. For Faussett's large family and numerous guests there were in total 16 bedrooms (eight with dressing rooms) over three floors.

The outbuildings included a brew-house with laundry over, a well-house and cistern, a partly paved carriage yard with double coach-house and two three-stall stables, a harness-room with fireplace, and lofts overall. The farmery, screened off from the residence, comprised stablings for three horses, a cow-house, cart-shed, poultry-house, pump-yard, piggeries and two outdoor closets. A 'capital' walled kitchen-garden was stocked with fruit trees in full bearing, plus two outer gardens with forcing pits, root-house and shed. The lawn and pleasure grounds were 'most tastefully disposed' with parterres of flowers and choice shrubs, green rides, one terminated by a summer-house or grotto, its walls ornamented with 'relics of the past' (that is, of course, Faussett's collection of antiquities). In all, there were 21 acres, 1 rood and 10 perches lately let on lease to Captain Raymond Paley at £180 annually but with the guarantee of possession to the purchaser.

North Court and Heppington Farms offered a capital brick-built and tiled residence of neat elevation, beautifully placed overlooking the pleasure grounds, and comprising five bedrooms, two staircases, entrance hall, and well-finished dining- and drawing-rooms, all complimented by a kitchen garden, orchards and sundry outbuildings. At Street End were other extensive farm premises, newly erected,

Figure 30. The 1947 sale catalogue for Heppington House: *sic transit gloria mundi.*
(Godfrey-Faussett family archives.)

with stabling and further enclosures of arable, pasture and hop lands, and woods in hand, accompanied by cottages and smallholdings in Nackington, Lower Hardres, Thanington and St Mary Bredin parishes.

At the auction, Heppington was sold for £36,000 to the Chapmans, a wealthy family keen on horses and hunting, who had doubtless foreseen the opportunities which the estate could offer them in this regard, and had not baulked at paying such a sum, although it would have been greater, had it not been for the outstanding mortgage. They soon added a large and luxurious stable block with 16 loose-boxes and four more smaller stalls. The estate was maintained and improved, and entertainments on a lavish scale kept up for some 60 years, but the second World War and its problems defeated them, and as by now it was again empty, the house was requisitioned in 1940 as a troop-billet for the rest of the war, never again to be occupied privately.

The next sale came in July 1947, the property still attractive despite six years of military occupation. It is interesting to compare the auction catalogue description with that of the previous one. Heppington is now described as a Georgian mansion with four excellent receptions comprising library, lounge-hall, dining-room and a 39ft by 16ft drawing-room. There were 12 bed- or dressing-rooms, three bathrooms, ample domestic offices, a heated garage for six cars, four cottages, a riding-school with exceptionally fine stabling, outbuildings and greenhouses, an orchard, paddock, wood and parkland, and walled garden and grounds, in all extending to 40 acres.

The house, of brick with tiled roof and all its principal rooms of 'stately pitch', was now approached from the entrance lodge by a long carriage-drive through parkland opening onto a wide forecourt. The residence was situated in 'delightful grounds', and well protected by trees which included specimen cedars.

It was impossible for the Faussetts to buy it back, and so was purchased by a timber merchant named Green who, in a single year's ownership, cut down the trees in the park, the garden and in Iffin Wood before selling it to a poultry farmer named Hugh Finn of Vinescole House, Nackington, who, needing to expand his business, saw the adjoining Heppington lands as ideal for his purposes. It was not long now before the park and gardens were ploughed up and replaced by fruit trees. By about 1954 the splendid stables and the entire house, having offered temporary but unsuccessful accommodation for farm workers, had become a mammoth deep-litter chicken-run, prompting comment in a 1961 issue of the *Swaziland Times* (how, one might ask, did southern Africa know of such things?) that 'a stately home was now a hen-house.' A picture of the erstwhile venerable family mansion appeared in the *Kentish Gazette* of 19 August 1960.

The house stood empty in 1967, vandalised and burgled for the lead from its roof and for the valuable wood from its once-noble rooms. A local architect was called in to assess its prospects in 1968, noting that not a single fireplace-surround remained, although there was a quantity of early 17th-century panelling and a superb well-staircase. Still visible also were fine plaster cornices with leaf-brackets in most rooms, and plaster swags and cartouches in the more important ones.

Now a total liability to its owner, who was unwilling to let anybody else have occupation, demolition in the following year was unavoidable. Today only a small part of the rear of the building survives, its memory preserved in a row of cottages opposite the old lodge gates, appositely and eponymously named Faussett's Hill.

Chapter 12
A Society Reborn

At the dawn of the Hanoverian age the time was ripe for an antiquarian institution to see again the light of day. The expulsion of James II and the Glorious Revolution of 1688 had seen a flowering of clubs and societies all over the country, accompanied by greater tolerance and freedom of thought. The Royal Society, founded in 1660 in an intellectually favourable atmosphere, was the leading centre of discussion for antiquarian and literary matters, but the broadness of its interests was frowned upon by its president, Sir Isaac Newton, who naturally favoured research underlain by a more scientific basis, that is, the natural world, rather than one of human history and artefacts. The Union of England and Scotland in 1707 and the birth of the new state of the United Kingdom added not a little to national pride and a renewed vigour to the investigation of its history – the mediaeval period would now be seen not as a rude and primitive interlude between classical antiquity and the flowering of the Renaissance, but, by dint of antiquarians' careful drawings, measurements and classifications, men of taste would come to see how indebted Britain was to the glories of the gothic (and, *mirabile visu*, rebuild their own parliament house in such a style at the commencement of Victoria's reign.)

Advances in learning around the country were now obvious; there had been a great outpouring of historical books between Camden's time and the final years of the Stuart dynasty, and books which fetched substantial sums and so vouchsafed their credit and esteem with men of learning. Yet the revival of the Elizabethan antiquarian society was slow, and in no small part thanks to the difficult and often solitary temperaments of the men who knew much, but could not or would not work harmoniously with others. It was the problems of contemporary political life that led men to study their country's past under the later Stuarts, that is, an encouragement to individual work rather than corporate discussion. To take one example almost at random, George Hickes, 'the most important single figure in the latter half of the seventeenth century' was a historian and Anglo-Saxon scholar rather than an antiquary, doubtless preferring the seclusion of a scholar's eyrie to friendly evening discussion and the imparting of hard-won knowledge in a drinking-house. But as the new century wore on, with Blenheim and Ramillies now history and England and Scotland successfully united, the climate was now increasingly right for the return of that much-desired corporate antiquarian discussion.

From its very beginning antiquarianism had been concerned, as its detractors proved, with both objects as well as written texts – a fact difficult of comprehension to the scholarly culture based only on literary sources for its knowledge of antiquity, amply enhanced by scholarly contemplation, good taste, and works of art in approved styles. How could the sculpture gallery be compared with the cabinet of curiosities, when one was art, the other artefacts? The obvious step for the world of the new topographers was from museum exhibits to field monuments – documents, heraldry and other long-cherished pursuits were about to wane and their practitioners justify the title of scientist. Now the mighty Robert Hooke forcefully demonstrated the point of convergence between palaeontology and archaeology when he cited fossil shells as marks of the former extent of the sea, and Roman coins as marks of the extent of an ancient empire, and continued by placing in tandem and in parallel the 'natural antiquary' studying geology and fossils, and the student of 'artificial antiquities' whose purview was such as coins and tombs. For the first time archaeologically-minded antiquaries deliberately spurned much of their traditional subject-matter to concentrate on the actual objects of antiquity. Here, with precious hindsight, we discern the beginnings of real archaeology.

The Society of Antiquaries, the second oldest of the royal societies in England, was founded on Friday, 5 December 1707, with the noble and splendidly optimistic motto of *Non Extinguetur*, which was later to be placed beneath a drawing of a mediaeval lamp found in Windsor, the Society's future emblem. It would become the natural pioneer of archaeology and play the key role in its perfection as its fellows turned excavation away from random treasure-hunting to systematic exploration and recording, and at the same time developed stratigraphy, in close association with geology, as the mainstay on which archaeological dating would primarily depend. The principal mover, Humfrey Wanley, with John Talman and John Bagford met in the Bear Tavern in the Strand 'and agreed to do so every Friday at 6 in the evening and sit till 10 at farthest'. They were to talk about the history and antiquities of Great Britain of the period before the reign of James I, but without excluding any other remarkable antiquities that might be offered to them.

A strong nucleus, nearly all students of historical documents, rapidly developed. In 1717, after a decade of meeting informally, but continuously, it was decided to found a more formal society, with Peter le Neve, Norroy Herald, FRS, president of the first society, as president of the newly inaugurated one. He, like many other early members (in total limited to 100), was also a freemason. From then on admission was set at 10*s.* 6*d.*, plus 1*s.* payable on the first Wednesday of every month which would go towards defraying the expenses of engraving and publishing monuments and dissertations. No less a person than the great William Stukeley was the first secretary, working alongside the 23 founder members, and then busy surveying Stonehenge and Avebury. He, above all, would stress the importance of accurate drawings for posterity

With no national museums, libraries or art galleries, and no university history or archaeology departments, the field was wide open to the society and its plethora of interesting, eccentric and pioneering early members. Very soon antiquarianism would develop away from textual preoccupations and politics towards ancient monuments and archaeology, and soon it seemed that the 18th-century historian and the antiquary were further apart than their predecessors ever were. Much work of the antiquaries was ignored by the national historians, whose chief concern lay with narrative, form and style, and less with variegated primary research on a local as well as national level. History was to be narrative on a grand scale and in a polite manner, and about great events; the writer of such things was not to bother with bizarre and out-of-the-way monastic records and the laborious research that they required – these 'barbarous' materials were of no use for historical learning.

Concerned as it was with the Middle Ages, historical antiquarianism placed itself outside the context of the university which regarded mediaeval history as neither ancient nor modern. Whereas the antiquarian interest in Roman Britain to some extent stimulated the aristocratic desire to model English culture after the Romans, the antiquaries had great difficulty in justifying their intense scholarly interest in the Middle Ages to the cultured men of their own age. Far less interested than the contemporary historians in narrative representation, interpretation and historical theory, they concentrated on compiling and annotating the sources and hoped to sift fact from fiction, applying the same methods of research to classical as to mediaeval historians. This cautious and cumulative approach was not necessarily uncritical, but it more often deferred judgement to some later scholar.

Early 18th-century scholarship grew from the fateful intellectual slump of around 1730, the great flowering of post-Commonwealth scholarly activity then more or less spent as the noble line of diligent antiquaries petered out. It was still to a great extent conducted within the context of religion and politics, and in a period which did not see the origins and sudden rise of modern scholarship. Historical antiquarianism remained strongly motivated by a strong interest in the origins of the institutions of state and church, in the records that provided material for the history of the relationship between King and Parliament, and in the origin and protestant identity of British Christianity, all for contemporary ideological reasons. National concern for the *Ecclesiana Anglicana* led the antiquaries and historical editors to focus on the unexplored areas of Anglo-Saxon history and philology, constituting a revolution in scholarship. Protestant incentives aimed to wrest the church free of its catholic origins: it was necessary to de-catholicize accounts of the origin of Christianity in England in order to assert the church's identity and independence from papal jurisdiction. The origins and interrelations of the institutions of church and state were examined and given their historical credentials in old English documents, research and writing which sought to improve its method in order to defend its ideology. This new scholarship brought forth new objective insight into history as well as Tory and Whig myths; but it also inspired impolite animosity and bitter invective. Not a few scholars were inclined to disputation, and the writing of the period was to no small extent discoloured by accusations of poor use of sources and bad scholarship in endless debates about historical truth and prejudice.

A royal charter was granted to the Society on 2 November 1751, by which time it was amply clear to the members that their obligation was to protect ancient monuments if at all possible, and also to record them, a charge which rapidly led to their being held as the custodian of such relics. Their meetings continued by moving around sundry taverns, finishing at The Mitre at 39 Fleet St in 1753, in which year a house around the corner in Chancery Lane was found. In 1781 possession was taken of an entrance lobby at Somerset House (the door today on the left under the entrance arch with Newton's bust above it), highly conveniently situated for meetings of both the Royal Society and the Royal Academy in the same building, many of whose members belonged to two, or all, of the three societies. Greater financial outlay, a corollary of much larger accommodation, soon led to few or no limits on membership numbers, which multiplied nearly fivefold in a quarter of a century. This was now a time when the society's membership moved slowly from fewer gentry and professionals to increasing numbers of artists, writers and politicians; but contemporary taste still preferred classical objects with a respectable veneer to homespun artefacts dug out of native soil, and the public reputation of antiquaries as gullible and short-sighted was one difficult to shake off, crisply reflected in some of the vicious cartoons of the period.

Now came nearly a century of stability until a reluctant move, but into much more capacious accommodation, was made to Burlington House, the present address, in 1875. The library on the left-hand side of the forecourt facing the Royal Academy is today the finest of its kind in the British Isles. The magnificent high-ceilinged room, resplendent with its white and gold Corinthian columns, holds 20,000 volumes (there were around 3000 in the first catalogue of 1816) comprising incunabula, early printed books, rare archaeological and antiquarian volumes, manuscripts, prints and drawings, proclamations and broadsides, the best collection of brass rubbings in existence, lantern-slides, seals and seal impressions, all complimented by a museum of antiquarian objects (donated from the earliest days to one of the few national organisations then collecting such things), paintings and oil portraits. The value of the museum objects alone speaks for itself: in 1851 the collections of the Society of Antiquaries of Scotland passed into government hands to form what is today the National Museum of Antiquities in Edinburgh; a move to make a similar transfer to the British Museum in 1901 was heavily defeated at the Society's Anniversary

Meeting, and so today at Burlington House there remains a collection supreme in its importance not only as a learning resource but also as a paradigm for the history of collecting in Britain.

By the later 1700s the Society of Antiquaries had grown by leaps and bounds, in no small measure thanks to its publishing activities from about 1770 (drawings were highly important before photography) and its sponsorship of scholarly works which brought considerable repute. Members could meet informally with other members, the naturally ensuing ripple-effect of which would speed the dissemination of news and opinions across social life. Such success with its accompanying reputation for smartness brought pressure to expand: the membership, limited to 100 in 1720, grew to 180 in 1755, 386 in 1784, then soared to over 800 at the start of the 19th century, and to some 2300 today.

Increasing numbers meant some dilution in the nature of those keen to join. In the 1840s Edward Hawkins, treasurer of the Society, said that there were three classes of member: real antiquaries; those of high rank and eminence who gave *éclat* to the Society and whom others liked to have an opportunity of meeting; and the *plebs contribuens*, or people of fair standing in society, with a reputation for general knowledge and a liking for antiquarian research.

Women members were first admitted in 1921 following the 1920 Sex Disqualification Removal Act which made illegal the exclusion of women from, *inter alia*, 'any Incorporated Society, whether incorporated by Royal Charter or otherwise'.

The barrow was the most common of all the national ancient field monuments – a long or circular grass-covered heap of earth or stones marking the burial place of a prehistoric aristocracy. In terms of quantity, the barrow cemeteries of Wessex are supreme, followed by those of the Cotswolds, the Peak District, Devon and Cornwall. Other parts of the country have few or none because of destruction by the plough and other agents, or because locations were unsuited to early settlement. Some barrows, particularly in Derbyshire and Somerset, were investigated by curio-collecting Romans, but for the most part all lay undisturbed for a millennium and more until mediaeval treasure-hunting, often at the behest or sanction of royalty, began to reveal promising avenues of exploration. William Digges of Barham (adjacent to Kingston where the eponymous brooch would one day be found), on the instructions of Henry VIII, opened a large mound on his estate close to Watling St where he found an urn of bones, brass and iron helmets and shields of 'an unusual bigness'. In the late 1500s the Sutton Hoo ship barrow in Suffolk was cut into, but after the central shaft had nearly penetrated the relic chamber, the diggers lost heart – to the undying gratitude of all later archaeology.

Other than these stumbling forays, barrows were merely noted by certain writers. But in the wake of the Renaissance, men were stimulated to be aware of the prospects of new antiquities, perhaps to be found in the local neighbourhood, and thus a keener sense of history and the recording of ancient earthworks were the natural concomitants. Some saw barrows as of military origin and that they would contain the remains of those slain in Romano-British or Saxo-Danish conflicts; John Aubrey in his *Monumenta Britannica* referred to them as 'the mausolea or burying places for the great persons and rulers of the time', although elsewhere he considered them to mark battle sites.

By the early 1700s barrows were perceived as the tombs of the ancient Britons, but as few had been penetrated for the information on their origins and affinities which the grave-goods might reveal, a general ignorance supervened as to origins and antiquity. William Stukeley began to throw some light in the course of his fieldwork in the 1720s and 1730s by the tremendous collection of notes and sketches which accompanied them; his pioneering observations and recordings hugely encouraged an incipient interest in such studies, despite his later life being clouded by a druidic obsession and its cult (he even turned his field notes into religious tracts) which would obfuscate the next century of archaeological thinking and progress. In his sketching he attempted to classify barrows by shape, but employed a bizarre and religious-based system of descriptions whereby one barrow was that of a king, another that of an arch-druid, and a third that of a priestess. Matters were not improved by a series of bronze axes which he assigned to a class of Druid mistletoe hooks, so giving full vein to those who would summarise him as an acute observer tainted by ridiculous hypotheses.

His work in Wiltshire, where he set out to oblige 'the curious in the Antiquitys of Britain' was based on acute perception; with the financial assistance and moral encouragement of Lord Pembroke he carried out the first objective barrow diggings on record at Stonehenge and Avebury, and on Salisbury Plain in the 1720s. Hired labourers would relieve him of some of the digging, and allow him to note, for example, 'how the body was posited', although he still failed to note its location and thereby let the significance of primary, secondary and intrusive interments pass him by. That notwithstanding, he stands as the bridge between interested theory and questing investigation.

The latter part of the reign of George III saw the great age of barrow digging beginning to wane, and Faussett did indeed not long predecease it. Over the course of several centuries thousands of barrows had been opened across England by a cross-section of the society of the times: merchants, clergy, soldiers and landowners on whose work so much of our knowledge of Neolithic and Bronze Age society is now so firmly based. Would that all those who preceded him had excavated, sketched and recorded so punctiliously as Faussett did; but no, it was he who more or less single-handedly ushered in a precious, if premature, scientific approach to the interpretation of the country's hidden past. The long line of his predecessors had each worked to his own decidedly imperfect and acquisitive system, their techniques improving with painful slowness, and only the very last would see the importance of recording a barrow in plan and section. Thousands of hours of labourers' exertions had left no paper record of the pillaging of countless mounds, all too often undertaken at great speed, the precious finds squirrelled away with equal alacrity into gentlemen's collecting cabinets. Never again would rich and leisured landowners have the time or the wherewithal to practise their depredations on barrows there for the opening.

Within or shortly after Faussett's lifetime adventurous researchers initiated excavation at prominent sites elsewhere. One of the first was Pompeii, first investigated in 1748 and continuously for long after, its extraordinary artefacts shedding wondrous light on ancient Rome. At Huaca de Tantalluc in Peru a mound was excavated in 1765 and its stratigraphy well described. But the credit for what has been called 'the first scientific excavation in the history of archaeology' goes traditionally to Thomas Jefferson, third American President, who in 1784 dug up a trench or section across a burial mound on his property in Virginia to try and confirm or disprove speculation that hundreds of unexplained mounds known east of the Mississippi river had been built not by the indigenous American Indians but by a mythical and vanished race of Moundbuilders.

Ahead of his time, Jefferson worked scientifically by testing ideas about the mounds against hard evidence, that is, by excavating one of them. He was careful enough to recognize different layers in his trench and to see that the many human bones present were less well preserved lower down, from which he deduced that the mound had been reused as a place of burial on many separate occasions. Humble enough to admit (correctly) that more evidence was needed to resolve the Moundbuilder question, he saw no reason to doubt that the ancestors of the present-day Indians could not have raised the mounds.

As the 18th century moved on, knowledge of antiquities based on fresh finds gradually accumulated and with it an antiquarian awareness of how much could be learnt from physical remains upon which the written sources were silent. Gough himself, although acknowledging his debt to the great Montfaucon in France, commented on the latter's failure to use the monuments he recorded for anything other than a history of the rulers of France, ignoring the manners and customs of past societies, and drawing no comparisons with them in terms of style and representation. It is probably true to say that before Gough's time almost all scholarly interest in tombs had focussed on the individuals commemorated rather than the monument itself as a work of art. Now Gough, with selected others, would develop a comparative and critical approach towards a 'system' of Gothic styles as evidenced by architecture and sculpture; and at the same time an empirical and comparative approach would be applied to the excavation of the physical (and not textual) remains of the past, this leading to the critical use of 'antiquities' in the manner of modern archaeology. Artefacts henceforth were 'facts', and when properly assembled could yield historical truths which would more than compensate for the annoying lack of ancient records – in the early part of the following century William Cunnington would be aware that his physical evidence was 'at war against preconceived opinions gathered from books'.

In 1775 the *Antiquarian Repertory* claimed that 'without a competent fund of Antiquarian knowledge no one will ever make a respectable figure'. Gough now shared the assumption of his own circle that antiquarianism was suited only to gentlemen of education, for appreciation demanded learning, and the ever-present issues of property and genealogy rendered the subject the natural preserve of the upper class. And yet the greatest and most significant of the contributions to eighteenth-century antiquarianism appeared not in the pages of *Archaeologia*, but in the (literal) fields of local history and topography, the fulsome evidence of which is apparent in the large numbers of county and urban histories published at this time (among whom is included the great Hasted, even if his pedigrees could be muddled and his church monuments notable by their absence). Faussett and many other gentlemen of the period would gladly pay several guineas for county histories and other works whose text they might not read, but which were well illustrated with engravings, for now the recognition of the value of monuments and artefacts as potential 'texts' integral to the history of the country was greatly enhanced. Men of Faussett's calibre were increasingly receptive to the possibility of illustrations as evidence in their own right, rather than their merely corroborating a written text. The accumulation of information for its own sake and the uncovering of lost details was truly, it could not be denied, a pleasure, and one enhanced by the belief that it was a useful and rational pursuit – a society still grounded upon a precedent and authority of the past could not but benefit hugely from antiquarian studies in its legal processes and conduct of public affairs.

Fresh threats faced mediaeval buildings by the reign of George III, when it was now realised that their survival was as much in danger from the way they were restored as from total destruction. The architect James Wyatt gained an unwelcome reputation for knocking down buildings when he restored Salisbury and Durham cathedrals with 'startling thoroughness' between 1780 and 1800. His work at the latter in particular provoked an outcry from the Society of Antiquaries when drawings commissioned by it revealed Wyatt's rebuilding of the east front and demolition of the Norman chapter house. But this first preservation battle was in part vindicated, as Wyatt's design was not taken through to completion, leaving the Galilee chapel unscathed and the crossing tower uncapped by the intended octagonal tower and spire.

By this time county histories were long established as an important department of the antiquarian world, although their compilers received far less than their due and had all too often been passed over by both literary men and historians – Dr Johnson's view that 'Great abilities are not requisite for an historian, for in historical composition the greatest powers of the human mind are quiescent' was a typically Johnsonian *aperçu*, and followed by later professional historians who tended to skirt by these men in silence (or ignorance), barely condescending to allow them as amateurs useful for recording minutiae, far distant from any concept of a 'proper' historian. And indeed, even today, the *Oxford Dictionary of National Biography* summarises many such men as 'antiquary' or 'topographer', but hardly ever as 'historian'.

The English county, one cannot deny, is all too often an irregularly shaped and unsystematic product of historical accident, but nevertheless not entirely devoid of attraction to the budding recorder. Its size beckons as encompassing a whole geographical district, but small enough to lie within the ambit of a single scholar. If a topographer, he can know the lie of his land and most of its minor antiquities; if a herald or genealogist, a mastery of the nobility, gentry and yeoman families is attainable; and if a political historian, the fullest details of commercial, industrial and agricultural life can be more or less fully gathered. How great is the range of skills and knowledge required to write a county history! And that is why few men have been equal to the task, and why the history of such works has for the most part been parcelled out among teams of scholars, and typified, for example, by the *Victoria County History* whose Berkshire volumes took nearly 60 contributors and 21 years to complete. Breadth of scope and design were now compromised by the loss of the perfect unity arising from the work of a single author.

The advantages of many minds are evident, but it has meant the disappearance of the *historian* as an individual responsible for solving the major problems of scale and the organisation of a large work. And so the best and most satisfying of the classical county histories were written between the mid-1600s, just as the full scope of the art began to be grasped, and the late 1800s when the enormousness of the task dictated by a plethora of sources encouraged the writing of specialist monographs.

Edward Gibbon had single-handedly brought the decline and fall of the Roman Empire within the compass of one monumental piece of writing; but no longer could such an enterprise be the preserve of one individual.

In terms of human history, what was wanted was a brave attempt to synthesise the accounts of the separate parishes and manors given patiently by such writers as Dugdale and Thoroton, and to weld them in some introductory chapters into a unified history of the county as a whole. The problem was far from simple and very long in its solving, if indeed it can be said ever to have been solved. James Wright, in his book on Rutland of 1684, prefaced his text with a short essay 'of the county in general', followed by assorted accounts and lists of persons extending to sixteen pages – a modest but useful beginning. But the first serious attempt to grasp the nettle was John Hutchins' 1774 *History of Dorset* with an introduction of 70 pages covering archaeology, ecclesiastical and natural history, fairs, markets and roads, all usefully supplemented by the Domesday survey.

The county historian John Nichols broke new ground with his *History and Antiquities of Leicestershire* of 1795-1815. Not a scholar himself, his forte was in assembling a team of writers and welding their disparate results into a unified whole. It is perhaps because he was a literary man and expert journalist, and not a scholar, that he discerned so clearly what needed to be done, standing back to see the wood and not the trees. His methods were not consonant with his aim, for the book is a flitting ragbag marred by the reproduction of overlong original texts, but the scene was now set and the book duly influential, in no small way because of a valuable innovation – illustrations.

The early histories were each adorned with a map (Dugdale's *Warwickshire* had a series of them, together with many engravings, mostly of church monuments). Views of some of the places mentioned in the text soon began to creep in, and from Wright's *Rutland* onwards it was customary for a county history to include engraved plates of country seats. Economics played a part: those whose house was illustrated felt obliged to accept the dedication of the plate offered by the author or publisher, and to subscribe for at least one copy of the book. Nichols now improved on this: his book contains traditional full-page plates, but the chief element in the illustration was now a long series of whole-page plates depicting sundry objects, all connected with the parish to which the plate referred. And so the church, drawings of tomb figures, depictions of minor manor-houses and other archaeological miscellanea, all enclosed within a border of appropriate family shields, would soon become *de rigueur* - an artistic mess but historically more valuable than a mere gentleman's estate. Nichols knew what antiquaries and historians would like to see, and the more of them the better, so he provided what they wanted, and in doing so he preserved much that we should not otherwise know.

Faussett and Douglas appeared in the middle and later 1700s respectively as the schoolboy enthusiasts of their time, bent on dispelling the darkness which had for so long befogged the nature of the barrows in south-eastern England, and pursuing their researches almost entirely among the then many vast Anglo-Saxon barrow cemeteries. Each, in his own way, was far ahead of his time, notwithstanding that until this date the historical resources remained the only ones available, thus ensuring that Anglo-Saxon studies were virtually static for around 1000 years; now that impasse was about to be breached, and the myth that the Anglo-Saxons were incapable of producing high-quality work soon shattered.

Faussett, like others, was acquisitive, but what he did acquire would be described and recorded in a fashion centuries ahead of his contemporaries; this careful and painstaking observer sought to satisfy a thirst for knowledge, trammelled, if only he had known it, by no cogent chronological framework with which to date his finds. His fascination and keenness (sometimes shared with others) to move rapidly from one barrow to another in pursuit of yet more finds resulted in too many results in too short a space of time – and yet (nobody can deny it), he miraculously recorded every single artefact and all of his 777 graves in well-nigh perfect order and with exemplary clarity. Monetary expense was soon forgotten in the enjoyment of boyish enthusiasm and the exercise of pure intellectual pleasure. At his death a lifetime's collection included no fewer than 400 Anglo-Saxon jewels alone, many of consummate beauty and the highest archaeological interest. The torch he had so bravely and pugnaciously lit would be soon fanned to a blazing flame by James Douglas a few dozen miles away in the Medway valley.

The work of both men was carried out only in pagan Anglo-Saxon tombs, but still represented the first full-time and systematic effort to glean knowledge of the past by the opening of hundreds of burial mounds, and despite their joint imperfections, the work was crucial for its own sake (too many of those barrows have long since been destroyed, and the contents of others disposed) in stimulating later antiquaries into an interest in the field monuments of their own county or locality.

Pace Faussett and Douglas, the half-century after Stukelely saw little progress in the study of English barrows; interest in the early 1800s probably arose as an offshoot of the Romantic movement which, with its expressions of individuality and intense emotion, tended to encourage an already existing morbid interest in mortality and the impedimenta of the grave. England's intellectual climate was fast succumbing to the 'Gothick', and barrows on lonely or blasted heaths were now objects for aesthetic satisfaction or speculation. Prehistoric bones merged seamlessly with other aspects of rugged landscapes so beloved of the Romantic mind; classical learning and archaeology now had a rival study, and one which could be conducted entirely at home.

It has been suggested that the 19th-century barrow-diggers took no less than a morbid delight in skeletons, graves and mortality, the sum of which was an exulting in the paraphernalia of the corpse, closely allied to the psychological phenomenon which was being exploited in contemporary literature and art. Was this why barrows underwent wholesale assaults whilst living sites seem to have been quite out of range? Were the latter now hard to find but the former easily recognized and so easy to attack and rifle? Paper-free archaeology played second fiddle to the swift and silent acquisition of colourful baubles to tinkle in private candle-lit studies and libraries, while historical importance might well be trodden underfoot in the rush .

By the time that the Regency drew to a close, British archaeology had emerged from a composite patchwork of intellectual endeavours which characterized the Enlightenment. No true and concerted progress towards emergence is really discernible, and no individual scholars' efforts can be easily threaded into a continuous and seamless whole. By their nature such men worked in seclusion from the universities, their investigations quite divorced from the classics. Although many would have met at the Royal Society and the Society of Antiquaries and corresponded quite freely, they were essentially lone workers who for the most part operated in a highly individual way, secure in the belief of a benevolent God whose crowning achievement had been the creation of man. By their work they would reveal Him, and in a fashion far removed from the modern view of archaeology. In troubled times, with the constant threat of invasion from across the English Channel, they forged the understanding of antiquities as a solid means to the study of the past, defining a sense of patriotism and national identity in an age marked elsewhere in Europe by political and social upheaval.

Chapter 13

Three Pioneers

In 1780, writing just a few years after Faussett's death, Richard Gough, the wealthy and leading antiquary of his day, noted that:

> The Rev. Mr Brian Fausset of Heppington, near Canterbury, was long engaged and indefatigable in researches after the Roman antiquities of the county [of Kent] and has left a most learned and ingenious account of them, and the places where they were found, with his arguments and proofs drawn from thence, and his own observations of the Roman transactions there ... But both his collections of antiquities, as well as his papers relating to them, and his transcript of the monumental inscriptions throughout the diocese, are locked up by his will, so as to be of no use to anyone.[1]

Gough doubtless voiced the frustration of other scholars; and he clearly had knowledge of who was important in Kent, for he had itemised Hasted's local sources, which included the late Dr Lewis of Margate, Mr Hall of Harbledown, Dr Brett of Wye and Mr Austen of Sevenoaks. His comments on the Faussett collection reached other high places, including the College of Arms, for in 1794 Sir Isaac Heard, Garter King of Arms (who had had much dealing with Faussett himself), sought permission from Henry Godfrey Faussett on behalf of 'Mr Townsend, a brother officer' to be shown his 'late and honoured father's collections'.[2]

Half a century later the antiquary and clergyman Frederick Wrench noted in his history of Stowting parish that the best collections of Anglo-Saxon artefacts were those formed by (in this order) Bryan Faussett, Sir John Fagge, W. H. Rolfe Esq, Lord Albert Conyngham and the Rev'd William Vallance of Maidstone.[3] As a local

---

[1] Gough, *British Topography* I: 446; 492
[2] Society of Antiquaries of London, MS 723: f.10
[3] Wrench, *A Brief Account of the Parish of Stowting...*, Introduction

man, Wrench was probably only too aware of what still lay locked up at Heppington.

But it is principally thanks to one man that the initial impetus which would lead to knowledge about the existence of the Faussett collection was born. As a young man, the Reverend James Douglas (1753-1819) worked in a cotton manufactory in Lancashire, and was then briefly travelling in Europe, where at Tongres in the Low Countries his interest in antiquarianism was born, before returning to England to go up to Peterhouse, Oxford, in 1778. He left with no degree in the following year, but on the basis of his reputation as a skilled draughtsman and knowledge of fortifications, soon accepted a commission in the Corps of Engineers and was put to work fortifying and remodelling, over some 20 years, the huge defensive chalk earthworks protecting Chatham Docks and the Medway Estuary known as the Chatham Lines.

It was during this lengthy employment, while stationed at Fort Amherst, that he first came across barrow clusters, constantly disturbed in the course of his work, from which he would amass, by courtesy of unlimited free military labour, a collection of carefully recorded Roman and Anglo-Saxon relics, his initial curiosity about such things born in Flanders now greatly awakened. By 1782 he had supervised the excavation of over 80 barrows and flat graves in the area. An association with the collector and antiquary Sir Ashton Lever led to the development of his interests, his election as FSA in 1783, and subsequent ordination, whereupon he became chaplain-in-ordinary to the Prince of Wales' Regiment of the 10th Royal Hussars before a series of benefices around southern England, never gaining preferment, and ultimately residing at Preston near Brighton.

His archaeological and theological interests were uneasy bedfellows in the eyes of his contemporaries, and led to his connoting the Saxons with pure barbarism before their conversion to Christianity, ignorant of art and so incapable of producing the objects he had discovered. He further saw a Byzantine character in the ornamentation and concluded that it must be the work of artificers who came to England with Theodore the Greek in 668, and so was drawn inescapably to assigning Christianity to pagan peoples long before their actual conversion and the subsequent injunction concerning the attachment of cemeteries to the early churches. To the unbiased observer everything, of course, was wholly pagan. In a paper read to the Royal Society he promulgated the 'heresy' of mammoth bones found at Chatham some 12 feet deep as being of a great age and so precluding the idea of a universal deluge. A Church that took Archbishop Ussher's dating of the earth seriously could hardly tolerate one of its own fold turning established belief on its head, and led, inevitably, through continuing disfavour to a retirement of secluded writing and picture-dealing. His monument in Preston church near Brighton is inscribed with a gentle (Latin) caveat: 'He was a disturber, though not without reverence, of other men's sepulchres. May he, in his, rest quietly.'

Faussett's excavating had preceded that of Douglas by a generation. Both in no small measure had begun digging as a consequence of the widespread quarrying for sand and gravel in Kent which had revealed such rich grave-deposits, especially at Ash near Sandwich, which became a focus of early archaeological activity and was investigated by Faussett, Douglas and Roach Smith. The pair were the earliest schoolboy archaeologists in Britain, and by a strange coincidence the younger man would make practical use of the discoveries and field work of the older. Hasted described the young Douglas's cocksure beginner's attitude thus, although today we can see that he was right, even if his methods sometimes gave offence:

> Captain Douglas, who is just entered on the study of Antiquity, and is complete an Enthusiast as ever I met within my life; for he despises all the Roman remains in this Country so late as Caesar's time, before which, you know, there was none here. He seems beginning where he should leave off, and talks much of criticising on the conjectures of our late friend Bryan Faussett, who was, I do think, as capable and learned a man in that way as this country ever had, or will produce.[4]

Whereas Faussett had been content to note merely whether a grave was small, medium or large, Douglas, as a trained surveyor, recorded the exact measurements and composition of the mounds, never abandoning the rigour of his military training. Interestingly, he noted that 'These tumuli … seldom exceed 33 feet in diameter, the smallest 13, the medium 23; and the largest 33,'[5] figures that seem arbitrary in their regular increases in size, but are in fact exactly the same figures as given on the 1730 sketch map[6] by Jared Hill of Cromwell Mortimer's excavations at Swadling Down. Are they truly arbitrary, then, or perhaps the averages of many careful measurements? It is known that Douglas appears to have kept detailed records of his digging, but nothing has survived.

Around 1780 Douglas told his friend Henry Godfrey Faussett (the late Bryan Faussett's son and heir), whom he had met for the first time a few years earlier on Chatham Lines, that he had very nearly completed a general history of the funeral customs of the ancients (his forthcoming *Nenia Britannica*), and to that end he had examined a profusion of materials and spared no effort to achieve a rational and concise system whereby the history of barrows, kistvaens and cromlechs might be ascertained. Far in advance of most of his contemporaries, he realised that the relics of antiquity were not mere decorations to be viewed in a collector's cabinet. He had prepared about 100 drawings and hoped to publish them as aquatints, averring that his object was not material gain but the pure pleasure and amusement in such preparation, and that all would be subservient to hypotheses founded on reason and practical observations rather than the time-honoured speculative fancies of the past.

What Douglas craved, if not outright purchase, was at least access to the collections at Heppington, for some of the Faussett items would clearly be indispensable as part of the story, and no less so if they could be illustrated. A correspondence

---

4 Nichols, *op. cit.*, IV: 648
5 Douglas, *op. cit.*: Introduction, 1
6 British Library, MS Addl 45,663

survives from Douglas writing at Rochester, alas one-sided, but from which one may gain something of the progression from keenness to coolness to a final but polite snubbing from Faussett. Douglas opened in the guise of an intermediary:

2 April 1781

A gentleman high up in the estimation of the antiquarian world and who has himself a great and valuable collection of antiquities, has delegated me to treat for your cabinet should you have any desire to part with it? I am therefore to request of you the sum, which you would set upon it, provided you would listen to a negotiation from me – you will acquiesce with me in supposing that antiquarians do not scruple in making bargains for antique rust, therefore any delicacy on this subject would be ridiculous – however if you have any inclination to listen to proposals, I make no doubt but what I shall be able to introduce your cabinet of hastae, umbonae, fibulae etc to a good antiquarian market.[7]

The intending purchaser was Sir Ashton Lever who had in fact neither visited Heppington nor made an offer. Douglas seems to have been dissimulating, although there was perhaps another purchaser in the wings:

4 May 1782

I should have no manner of objection in treating you with concerning your collection of things found in barrows, etc. If the value set upon them is compatible with reason and the scarcity of money in general, indeed I should say the poverty of time. Permit me now to tell you that I am empowered to negotiate with you for the purchase but also not to exceed a certain price; the person is not a very moneyed man, yet if you conclude the disposing of them he will remit you their value on the immediate conclusion of the bargain. Whatever transpires with me, I give you my honour shall remain a secret, but indeed I see no reason why you should have the least reluctance to make your intention public of disposing of them, since it happens every day that the first families in the kingdom are selling their collections of pictures, gems, antiquities … I believe I could enumerate many families that do this, not through distress, but merely owing to their fancy changing on other matters – I find Dr Jacobs has sold his collection of medals &c which he has been much disappointed in; they fetched a mere trifle indeed. I apprehend you have no objection to permit your manuscripts that is your father's to go with the things - it would be extremely awkward to have the collection without them.[8]

What was Faussett to make of all this? Was a small fortune lying hidden at Heppington? Could the sadly depleted family fortunes be suddenly wrested from further disaster, the terms of his father's will notwithstanding? Douglas had surely visited often enough to have formed some shrewd idea of what sums might be involved, but seemed reluctant to put anything into words:

[7] *Inv. Sep.*: 215
[8] *ibid.*: 216

30 May 1782

If you have any serious intention of disposing of your cabinet mention your sum and an opportunity will present itself to you which you perhaps will not so sooner meet with again to sell it into private hands ... It is you Sir to mention your price – it is impossible that any other person can make you an offer. If your terms will meet with approbation I will have the pleasure to wait upon you and conclude everything to your perfect satisfaction.[9]

What are we to conclude other than Douglas's sole wish to acquire everything, collections and manuscripts, for himself? Faussett was legally trained and a man of business – could such a subterfuge possibly get past him? But with no idea of the value of his assets, and out of pure curiosity, why not tease his correspondent into naming his price? There was no compulsion (or indeed, sanction) for him to sell, and anyway, how could Douglas possibly afford an outright purchase? But there was an easy way to stifle any further negotiations: stipulate that a condition of the sale would be to include the enormous collection of Roman coins and medals. Now he had called Douglas's bluff:

18 June 1782

I had the pleasure of your favour setting forth your intentions not to part with your collection, unless the medals were to accompany it. As the person who is willing to purchase the cabinet (and who by the way is well acquainted with the particulars) only collects barrow curiosities he will therefore not accept of coins etc. ... so much of this – now to my own proposal – I have very nearly completed a general history of the funeral customs of the antients, having for that purpose made acquisition of a profusion of materials ... I have made drawings of the most material part of my small researches ... my proposal is to request the assistance of your collection – which as it will ornament my work to a great degree I have not the least doubt of its making it known to the world, and as I shall have an indubitable proof of appreciating their value, by an elaborate description of their justly to be admired antique estimation, so I think as you will have an easy opportunity of communicating the discoveries to the world, you will at the same time ensure yourself a channel of making their value known.[10]

There was no point in any further bargaining. The artefacts and the notebooks would be kept well and truly secure from public gaze for another half-century and more. But scholarly friendship meant that before long Douglas paid a series of visits to Heppington and busied himself in examining and making notes of selected items, and, it seems, cheerfully assisted by Faussett, an excellent draughtsman himself. Of the illustrations which subsequently appeared in the *Nenia*, excellent as they are, there is no common agreement as to the authorship, whether Douglas or Faussett.

[9] Society of Antiquaries of London, MS 723
[10] *Inv. Sep.*: 217

Slight clues elsewhere in the volume hint that Faussett's policy was for himself to draw everything that he allowed Douglas to illustrate, thus keeping a controlling hand by allowing nothing to leave Heppington – and anyway, what would his father have said about such a practice?

19 July 1782

Far be it from my thoughts to entertain any idea of making extracts from your manuscripts … I am perfectly contented with yr. permission to make drawings of those things which I may find serviceable to my plan … but I do not wish by any means to give you any trouble to draw them yourself.[11]

But this was the procedure, and Douglas executed only the *aqua tinta* for the *Nenia*, the coloured engravings from Faussett's original drawings, so it does seem that he actually never gained free access to the collection. Naturally, the rich Kingston grave 205 with the brooch and associated articles would be high on the list of desiderata:

4 February 1785

I shall readily accept your offer of the drawings of the rich barrow with the description of the relics as they were found – and from which I shall make an engraving which I mean to inscribe to the owner.[12]

These would become Douglas's handsome sixth and seventh plates. Faussett was duly thanked for his labours on 25 April:

I thank you much for your drawings – I have prepared all things for engraving and if I could only commune with you – you little know, the good you would infuse into me for my studies.[13]

In 1786, with the first part of the *Nenia* then published, Douglas gently reminded Faussett that he would welcome criticism – a guarded way of saying that what he wanted more than anything else was a further selection of items from the collection in order to establish (as he tactfully put it): 'some literary truths which I think in a great measure depend on the relics which are in your possession'.[14] He was now treading on shaky ground for Faussett had already disapproved of some of Douglas's comments, sensing them as disparaging to his father's memory, and for the time being allowed no more illustrative material to be taken away.

Douglas had drunk deeply from a rich well, the results of which would occupy a substantial part of his forthcoming book. But it seems that his overwhelming

---

[11] Society of Antiquaries of London, MS 723
[12] *ibid.*
[13] *ibid.*
[14] *ibid.*

thirst had not been slaked – future and repeated enquiries for more material, sometimes unwelcome and to Faussett's offence, were to follow in the next few years as Douglas began, *faute de mieux*, to include sketches of his own to supplement those from Heppington. When he was accused of reading and quoting from Bryan Faussett's excavation diaries, access having been expressly denied him, he responded ingratiatingly by asking Faussett for advice and help, and in March 1788, as publication of the *Nenia* instalments progressed, a final letter enclosed a proof of one plate for Faussett's approval:

> … taken from my sketch book; the rapid production of a few minutes on a cursory survey of your cabinet; and I am reluctant to make out the description from my own notes which I can not well trust to.[15]

The relevant plate xviii of the *Nenia* shows sketches clearly based on Douglas's work and not the much higher degree of accuracy which Faussett would have ensured. From this one can but conclude that only those items from the Faussett collection illustrated in the *Nenia* drawn by Henry Godfrey Faussett himself can be relied upon for historical verisimilitude. [The fate of the pictures which Douglas selected to reproduce is, seemingly, unknown, as they are not at the Liverpool World Museum and were not included in the later sales of the effects of Joseph Mayer.]

In 1785 Douglas had published *A Dissertation on the Antiquity of the Earth*, a weighty discourse on geology evidenced by three 'cases' and an appendix remarking on previous geological theories, in which he drew attention to the relics from a barrow on Chatham Hill opened by him in 1779; a group of artefacts from a Kingston barrow which Faussett had dug in 1771; and fossils collected by himself and Sir Joseph Banks on the Isle of Sheppey. The then prevailing belief that the Noachian flood was a fact drew him up with a start, for it was now clear to him, if to nobody else, that the Sheppey fossils proved (Genesis notwithstanding) that there had been some sort of inhabited antediluvian world full of animals (and human beings?) subsequently destroyed by a global catastrophe, perhaps along the lines of a great inundation.

At the end of the 18th century the unspeakably vast age of the earth could not even be guessed at, but Douglas made four cogent points, not unique to him, but far-reaching in their intellectual significance: fossilised animals and plants, even if tropical, had lived where they were found; the climate was then much warmer than in his own day; a flood of biblical duration would not have sufficed to carry animal remains over great distances; and that the earth must have some interior power by which such remains had been fossilized.

Douglas had had the advantage of exploring more widely around Kent than Faussett had, and the even greater advantage of being able to study the other man's collections. He had also dug elsewhere in England as well as on the continent. No

---

[15] Society of Antiquaries of London, MS 723

one saw more clearly than he the errors of his predecessors and contemporaries, and nobody was more painfully aware than he that 'confusion lies under the stroke' when the ignorant labourer cheerfully smashed an artefact in its extraction, and that most finds from casual excavations were rapidly lost or scattered. He correctly identified his (and Faussett's) finds as Anglo-Saxon, and used coins to date the majority of the artefacts to after the Christian conversion at the end of the 6th century. But he was shaky in positing magical uses for some grave-goods and, like Faussett, saw far too much of a Christian character in many of the graves.

He was puzzled by the exact significance of the orientation of graves and of the presence or absence of grave furniture. He saw occasional traces of cremation as 'attesting that a succeeding people had buried near one of a more ancient date, when cremation had been used',[16] and was well aware of the difference between cremation urns (or 'ossuaries' as they used to be called), and those placed, for whatever mysterious reason, with the inhumed skeletons. He noted that swords in his collections had no guards, and understood (as Faussett did not) the use of the handle-bar of the shield crossing the hollow of the *umbo*.

Concerning that commonplace of Anglo-Saxon graves – coloured beads – he was almost modern in remarking that they were in all probability imported into England by barter from Marseilles (although many others were probably of insular production). And of the origin and affinities of tomb furniture in general, he asserted that

> ... the nature of the arms, the most convincing proof of a parity of custom, found in the barrows, affix them to their Saxon owners...[17]

thus ridding the mind at one fell swoop of any Roman connections, for

> The Roman claim to these sepulchres, notwithstanding their coins have been found, must be totally out of the question.[18]

The fact that he doubted the power of the native Anglo-Saxon craftsmen, in the early days of settlement, to execute fine work need not count against him, even after the treasures he had excavated, for others were of the same opinion including Akerman, who, having illustrated a number of superb jewels in his *An Archaeological Index* of 1847 still thought that 'the more costly articles of personal ornament were generally imported'.[19]

Let us now examine his (flawed) masterpiece. *Nenia Britannica: or, A Sepulchral History of Great Britain, from the Earliest Period to its General Conversion to Christianity* (the sub-title runs to 100 words), dedicated to the Prince of Wales, had a protracted and

---

[16] Society of Antiquaries of London, MS 723
[17] *ibid.*
[18] *ibid.*
[19] Akerman, An Archaeological Index...: 128

trouble-stricken 12 years of difficulties between its initial concept and the publication of the 12th and final part, by way of five-shilling instalments, in 1793; the sum total of its constituent parts was 197 pages of text and 36 extraordinary folio plates.

The many remarkable aquatint illustrations in the *Nenia Britannica* cost Douglas his health, and especially his eyesight, which was irreparably damaged by the acid fumes necessary for the engraving of the copper plates; but now, for the first time, these took precedence over the narrative, and included the earliest ground plan of an excavated tumulus known to English archaeology[20] – a skeleton surrounded by its grave found near Rochester in 1779 – and the first sections and plans of a grave in British field archaeology.

Douglas's personal copy, a sumptuous and magnificent volume,[21] may still be seen: the freshness of the colours will delight those used only to consulting other copies with their dull and murky hues, as will the original watercolours for each plate (three by Henry Godfrey Faussett) and a further range of annotated watercolours of similar objects by Douglas himself which were never engraved (and include a partly broken skull with an inquisitive mouse perched on its jaw). As to the Douglas collections, they were sold by his widow to Sir Richard Colt Hoare, who presented them to the Ashmolean Museum in 1829. At that time, nobody in Oxford, or indeed anywhere else in England, had ever seen comparable archaeological material.

The volume consisted chiefly, but not entirely, of Douglas's own archaeological reports. They are not error-free, but sound and logical with a clear perception of the points of dissemblance between the different classes of antiquities he considered. In all, the work attempted a general history of funerary customs of the ancient Britons, and described his own excavations at the Chatham Lines, elsewhere in Kent, and further afield, as well as the contents of many small barrows recognized for the first time as being Anglo-Saxon and not Roman. Alas, his text includes the details of only a few of the graves which he excavated, and is further marred by his assumption that all graves were covered by a barrow mound; the consequent general epithet of 'tumulus' leaves us quite unclear as to how many graves were actually so covered.

Douglas was the first to notice with understanding and to record 'the marks of a factitious earth in the native sand', that often elusive clue on which the value of modern excavation so largely depends. He further saw that the coins and Christian artefacts from some of Faussett's graves indicated the burial sites of the first Christian converts, between the conversion of the Roman mission under St Augustine in the late 500s and the transfer to intramural and churchyard sites in the 8th century.

Of the 19 sites described (none, alas, accompanied by an adequate plan of his field-work), one was at Ash near Sandwich, where he knew that Faussett had found many items, some of which had fallen into the hands of Edward Jacob, and were now in Douglas's own cabinet. The range of locations itemised and the approach to their illustration allowed the reader to make valuable comparisons of the artefacts.

---

[20] Douglas, *op. cit.*: Plate 1
[21] British Library, G6863

This was supplemented by notes of Roman graves in Britain and at his erstwhile sojourning place of Tongres in Flanders (where his study and description of the famous Roman burial-mounds instilled a prescience crucial for his future work), and a detailed analysis of Stonehenge. In contrast to Faussett who had dug boldly, Douglas confirmed by close study and application what he had observed, always working with appreciation.

The work did itself no favours with a verbose title and perhaps too many illustrations, and was typical of its time in incorporating a vast amount of lore, mainly as footnotes, but all had been carried out in a scientific spirit, and was vouchsafed by the bold statement that:

> The inscription or the medal are the only facts which can obviate error, and produce the substitutes for deficiency of antient records; when these are wanting, in vain will the human mind be gratified by the most acute investigating; incredulity will arise in proportion as the judgement is matured. By contemplating the relics discovered in our antient sepultures, the historian may have an opportunity of comparing them with similar relics found in different places, and on which arguments have been grounded by authors who have written on the antient inhabitants of Britain … the most trifling fact will invalidate many received opinions, and history reduced to a more critical analysis … the reader may frame his own conclusions without any apprehension of being involved in the confusion of self-opinionated theory…[22]

Not popular at the time of publication, contemporary antiquarian opinion was unprepared for a work which replaced dependence upon early literature in favour of the tiresome scientific necessity of practical observations. Its pioneering importance as the first successful attempt in Britain at the systematic recording of archaeological material was recognized only a decade and more after the author's death – even Colt Hoare, who adopted his idea of classifying barrows, rejected Douglas's Anglo-Saxon dating for barrows of the 'small conic' variety.

It perhaps hardly needs to be iterated that scientific methods of excavating until this time were, to say the least, superficial. Chance finds were not publicised, comparison with other objects was well-nigh impossible, the importance of context was unknown, and dating methods hopelessly inaccurate. For the most part it was labourers who uncovered objects, unsupervised and unaware, keen only to remove bullion and coins and make off with their spoils. But now at least the humble skeleton whose sex and stature had once been guessed at, and then disarticulated and tossed to one side, was now receiving more scientific analysis.

Douglas's estimation of the Faussett father and son as archaeologists was a high one, and he did not forbear from alluding to them when describing Chartham Downs:

---

[22] Douglas, *op. cit.*: Preface

Mr Faussett of Heppington was with me, whose father was present at the opening of these barrows, and who had opened some himself on the same Downs. The experience of his son, who has great knowledge and taste in the cabinet of tumuli treasures, which he possesses from his father, has confirmed me in the assertion of these relics being found in the graves of women.[23]

How could he possibly not write thus, when some of the glories of the volume were not even his but plagiarised? Crucial to his narrative, he had also incorporated the work of his contemporaries, and so when he came to illustrate his tumulus XIV, opened at 'at the end of the race-course' on Barham Downs, Kingston, it was none other than Faussett's grave 205 which had contained the Kingston brooch, and on which he now proudly commented that,

I am favoured with the drawings of the magnificent relics found in this tumulus by H. G. Faussett Esq of Heppington in Canterbury who inherits from his father, the late Rev. Bryan Faussett, a fine collection of sepulchral remains, and I may, without any accusation of flattery, say that the son is possessed of a knowledge and taste in the study of the antiquities of this country to render himself worthy of such inheritance.[24]

He then devoted two pages of text to a description of the Kingston brooch and an entire plate to it and the accompanying gold pendant ornament, glass bowl, iron chain and iron box-hinges.[25] An increasingly curious and discerning public could now see Faussett's *clou* 60 years before it would be published in *Inventorium Sepulchrale*.

The fame of Kingston Down as the finest Anglo-Saxon grave-site in England would stand until the Sutton Hoo treasure was unearthed in Suffolk in the 1930s. Faussett's vague theory that his graves and their contents were Anglo-Saxon, unresolved and unproven at his death, could now be seen in its correct light, and valuable comparisons now made, firstly by Douglas, and then by a wider and more discerning circle, through the itemised sites and clear illustrations of the *Nenia Britannica*.

As has been stated, despite his being given access to the Faussett collection, it has never really been clear to what extent Douglas was enabled to make use of it; for it seems that he selected what he thought immediately necessary for his work, and then either made drawings himself or was supplied with them by Henry Godfrey Faussett. The manuscripts were not made available to him, and it seems likely that Faussett himself had some idea of publishing them,[26] especially as there were in Mayer's papers outline sketches of most of the antiquities, grouped as if arranged for being engraved. (A further letter[27] shows that Douglas had not abandoned the idea of removing the collection from its obscurity at Heppington.)

[23] Douglas, *op. cit.*: 22
[24] *ibid.*: 37
[25] *ibid.*: Plate 10
[26] *Inv. Sep.*: 219
[27] *ibid.*: 221

Now in a footnote Douglas sings the praises of Bryan Faussett and laments his early demise:

> The late Rev'd Bryan Faussett acquired the name of our British Montfaucon, a title which implies a respectful homage due to his diligent and learned enquiries into the antiquities of this country; if his life had been spared and he less afflicted with bodily infirmity, he might probably have favoured the world with the result of his labours in this study. I presume to say, if he had done this, he would not have handed his name down to posterity by a vast amas (sic) of confused antique remains as we see in Pére Montfaucon, but have concentered a great collection of facts for the advantage of literature, and a more clear exposition of the antiquities of this country than has been hitherto established.[28]

He continues by giving an interesting and, probably, the earliest overview of Faussett's collection and scholarly attainments:

> His collection consists of tumuli relics discovered chiefly in Kent, and which were minutely explored; many sepulchral urns from Tremworth, or Long Port Downs, near Crundale in Kent, a Roman burial-place; and which by a manuscript in my possession of the late Heneage Finch of Longleat, Earl of Winchilsea, was first discovered around 1703. His Lordship opened a few of the interments, which were finally and wholly explored by Mr Faussett. The other part of his tumuli collection consists chiefly of the contents of the smaller conic barrows found in clusters similar to the specimens which I have here described, and to which he had prepared a description neatly drawn up in manuscript. Beside a collection of medals which he had diligently and choicely amassed at a great expense and in which he was uncommonly skilled, he bestowed much labour on the ecclesiastical history and genealogical records of families in Kent; which studies, united to the best of classical learning, accomplished him for an excellent antiquary. These particulars I have taken the liberty to record, lest accident, or the many unforeseen chances of life, should conceal the name and abilities of a learned and diligent antiquary from public memory.[29]

In the library of the Society of Antiquaries is a pen and ink caricature[30] of around 1787 which, on the basis of its accompanying inscription alluding to a soldier-parson-antiquary who concerns himself with both the living and the dead, was probably executed by Douglas himself. The graveside scene is of six gentlemen holding arrows, pickaxe, shovel, sieve, magnifying glass or skull, nicely depicting 18th-century amateur enthusiasm in shades of sepia, grey and black. The scene may actually show Douglas digging on Wimbledon Common (in which case he is the man holding the pickaxe), when he recalled that he was joined by a Quaker and then called for a sieve to explore the grave contents with more accuracy – true enthusiasm indeed. If one were to substitute Faussett and his son Henry Godfrey here, a true picture of how work at Kingston and the other sites proceeded would emerge.

---

[28] Douglas, *op. cit.*: 37
[29] Douglas *loc. cit.*
[30] illustrated in *Making History, Antiquaries in Britain 1707-2007*: 101

Between them, Douglas and Faussett bequeathed a magisterial legacy of recorded excavations and artefacts. In combination with a small number of other records from the 18th century, notably of Edward Hasted at Eastry and of William Boys at Sandwich, by 1800 a total of 29 Kentish cemeteries, burial sites and find-spots had been registered, precisely ten per cent of the modern total. Thereafter the pace would measurably quicken, but the standard of recording would for too long sadly not exceed that of the two pioneers.

The antiquarian decades of the half-century between James Douglas and Charles Roach Smith would be spanned by the collaborative efforts of two men who would raise barrow digging from an art to a science, albeit an inexact one. William Cunnington (1754-1810) and Sir Richard Colt Hoare (1758-1838), one the barrow-opening supervisor, the other a munificent provider of labour and capital, would in a relatively short joint career open 465 mounds and barrows. Their collaborative work stands as a landmark at the exact end of the 18th century, marking the end of a tradition going back to Camden, and forming its last expression. It also heralds a break from one approach to the historic past, that of the antiquaries, to a new one, that of the archaeologists allying themselves for the first time since the Restoration with the sciences as they joined with the geologists to determine the antiquity of man.

Cunnington came from a humble Northamptonshire family, had no chance of higher education, but fortified an active mind by wide reading. He set up business as a wool merchant, mercer and draper in Heytesbury near Warminster, and sought relief from increasing ill-health by riding out onto the Wiltshire Downs where he gained an interest in the many barrows peppering the landscape and thereby cultivated the friendship of local antiquaries. He was busily digging by about 1800, where his capacity for thorough exploration and attention to detail, coupled with carefully written notes, was unparalleled for its time. A landmark meeting in 1803, where the baronet was so impressed by Cunnington's digging methods, led to all future work being underwritten by Hoare. A firm and lasting friendship was born, more or less free of disputes, and led ultimately to Hoare's two-volume *Ancient History of South Wiltshire*, the first part of which was dedicated to Cunnington (Hoare's 'Arch Druid') on the grounds of his pioneering work and extensive personal collections (which Hoare would later buy from his widow for £200, and are now in the Devizes Museum).

Hoare's background could not have been more different. He was a fabulously wealthy landowner and banker who as second Baronet inherited Stourhead, ten miles south-west of Heytesbury, in 1785, and then severed all links with the family bank except as a customer. No antiquary had ever enjoyed such means or such opportunities, these gifts perfectly complimented by their bearer's great taste, sensibility and charm. His wife died within a year of marriage, and so for solace he turned to travel, easily affordable on his five-figure annual income. In a Grand

Tour of six years he moved from being a tourist to a systematic antiquary, roving through Holland, Germany and Italy, where he settled at Siena to locate the major Etruscan sites, continuously impassioned by the classical authors. Home by 1791, he never went abroad again, but rather made annual forays through the British Isles, particularly to Wales, always a favoured haunt of any antiquary. At Stourhead he could withdraw to his extraordinarily complete library in its opulent and atmospheric purpose-built surroundings, where most documentary sources needed by him and his collaborators lay ranged on mahogany desks and tables supplied to order by the younger Thomas Chippendale. Research into the history and archaeology of Wiltshire could not have been more pleasurable. After his death his collections, then at Stourhead in the cellars, were loaned in 1878 to the Devizes Museum, and purchased outright for £250 in 1883.

Hoare's aim was unprecedented and wholly admirable: his team of Cunnington and two trained diggers, Stephen and John Parker, would effect a sudden access of primary evidence, on a scale hitherto unthought of, deliberately sought as a means to increase knowledge, and all recorded with detail at a new and unheard-of standard. Not only were the grave-groups from the barrows described and preserved as units rather than disparate curiosities, but new plans of hillforts and settlement sites were produced for the first time. Alas, such achievements must be placed in context: today we can see how lamentably inadequate were the standards of technique and scholarship within which the work was necessarily conducted, and marred further by a complete absence of plans, drawings or sections.

Cunnington always took charge of the spadework, seemingly seldom encountering difficulties with permission to proceed, and would file written reports on his findings, while Hoare planned each season's activity with military precision and oversaw the surface activity and general descriptions. Affluence allowed him not to stint on the expenses of each year's many expeditions, even when too many sites were empty or barren of interest. His first, of two, noble folio volumes of 1810 is portentously sub-titled (in capital letters) 'We speak from facts not theory' and announced in its preface that he hoped 'to throw some new light on the history of those Britons who formerly resided on our hills'. His introduction confirmed that the text would therefore include only indisputable information supplied by the pair's researches, and

> ... neither shall I place too much reliance on the very imperfect traditions handed down to us by former antiquaries on the subject. I shall describe to you what we have found; what we have seen, in short, I shall tell you a plain unvarnished tale, and draw from it such conclusions as shall appear not only reasonable, but even uncontradictable.[31]

True pioneering work had opened a new area of antiquarian study based squarely on practical research and not from the clues and inferences gleaned from classical

---

[31] Hoare, *The History of South Wiltshire* I: Introduction

learning. To this would accrue many excellent maps and sketches of the barrow groups accurately pinpointing what had been opened. But alas, such noble parameters still did not allow them to discover the origins of the barrow builders of the Stonehenge plains, starting, as it did, with so little to guide them, for after a decade's labours all-encompassing ignorance still reigned and the supposition that the barrows were sepulchral monuments of the Celts and other early colonists, one epoch merging vaguely into another, held doubtful sway. The two men were not fated to perceive the apparent contemporaneity of pre-Roman burials, which remained in their eyes as 'Ancient British' and to be dated roughly from 1000 BC down to the time of the Roman invasion.

How easy now it is to see their procedures as childlike and uninformed, but Cunnington and Hoare must be judged by their times and their necessarily primitive ways of working. A gang of labourers would carry out the preliminary digging, followed by either a central shaft-excavation down into a barrow, or a trench driven in laterally to the centre, sometimes prolonged to the opposite edge. Although not comprehending how they had been built, Hoare distinguished various barrow types, and less fancifully then Stukeley had done (although he echoed him in employing 'Druid'), describing and illustrating his long, bell, bowl, Druid, pond (or saucer), twin, cone, and broad types, some sub-divided if with an accompanying *vallum*. He also classified pottery, naming the beakers as drinking cups, the miniature ones as incense cups, and the third main type as the sepulchral urn. The first two labels remained in use until the late 1800s; the last is still current.

Of the 485 barrows investigated over six years, 86 were unproductive, often after much labour and expense. Where Stukeley failed, they succeeded in realising the distinction between primary and secondary interments, and Hoare noted that a skeleton near the top clearly showed a later deposit, but, and despite Douglas's important Kentish work, could not appreciate that some burials were Anglo-Saxon, even when the evidence of the illustrations in *Nenia Britannica* for comparison with the Wiltshire artefacts was fully available to him – like Faussett he employed the term 'Romanized Britons' to describe the Anglo-Saxons. Skeletal remains were regularly jettisoned, depriving later generations of important study material, as Hoare commented on them only when appearing unusual or out of the ordinary; smashed victims of the pickaxe or naturally crushed remains were likewise ignored. It is mystifying as to why extreme carefulness and wholesale neglect were randomly exercised in equal measure as they proceeded from one grave to the next, even after Hoare had lamented the 'imperfect and unsatisfactory' methods of Stukeley – the history of error is as instructive in science as is the declaration of truth. A valuable trend was started, however, when dated tokens or coins were left in a grave as they moved on from one to another.

Their signal lack of insight concerned the long earthen barrows scattered across the Wiltshire Downs whose secrets they never fathomed despite the outlay of so much money, effort and time – often a whole week at one site. They were too often puzzled by what lay in a barrow and disappointed by what did not, their frustration compounded by what struck them as the irregular and muddled positioning of bodies; but in Hoare's defence, he was able to discern that the black loam of the lower and middle parts of the mounds was a constant structural feature, and also that the dumped construction of some of the long-barrows originated in the piling of heaps along a chosen axis.

Some of their many excavation parties probably attracted spectators, only too keen to see what might suddenly be pulled out of the ground, and other expeditions may well have become almost social events patronised by the local aristocracy, antiquaries and others, prompted by curiosity to lodge for the week at nearby Amesbury.

To summarise: Cunnington and Hoare's six-year collaboration marked the first serious attempt to investigate the origins of the prehistoric barrows in any part of Britain, and was underlain by strenuous investigation, continuous refining of method, diligent writing-up and careful preservation of finds. Their researches gave them an inkling of the idea of a threefold classification of burials and artefacts into separate ages, an idea anticipated by Douglas, but one which would be expounded only much later on in the century when Archbishop Ussher's idiosyncratic dating of the world (bone and stone for the primeval, savage and Celtic peoples; brass originating from Africa and exchanged with the Belgae; and iron arising just before the Roman invasion) had lost its grip on human belief. Their legacy was a cornucopia of antiquarian literature and a collection of prehistoric material which would have a profound influence on Bronze Age archaeology, but *South Wiltshire*, although encapsulating the state of knowledge of prehistoric Britain reached, after unprecedented effort in the field by the antiquaries of the day, constitutes little advance over the views of Stukeley in the 1720s – and indeed, the model of the prehistoric past as presented at the end of the 17th century would remain, with only minor improvements, essentially unchanged until well into the reign of Victoria when General Pitt-Rivers would revolutionise techniques of excavation and set them on a recognisably modern footing.

Just before leaving Georgian Wiltshire, a small but important postscript must be added. Dr John Thurnam (1810-1873) followed closely in the wake of the two Wiltshire pioneers. He dug widely and became famous as an intrepid interpreter of barrows and their contents. His two-part monograph *On Ancient British Barrows, especially those of Wiltshire and the adjoining counties* are the basis of all subsequent study because they assessed the information given in every previous publication and analysed the mound-types and their relics under a series of headings, all distilled from long and penetrating study.

By profession a doctor, archaeologist and craniologist, he was also medical superintendent of the Wiltshire County Asylum at Devizes from 1851 until his death. He exacavated intially at Driffield in the East Riding, but in a hasty and uncritical way, soon becoming more thorough and systematic and chiefly concerned with the recovery of skeletal material, this with the sole aim of attempting to relocate burials recorded, but then reinterred, by Cunnington and Hoare. Earthen long-barrows were his especial interest and in a little over a decade he dug 22 of them in Wiltshire, that at East Tilshead (south of Devizes) producing eight skeletons densely packed together in a small space, and allowing him to opine that it could hardly be an original burial site but must have followed a prior interment which had been moved thither after the decay of the soft parts and separation of the bones.

Thus was born the theory of long-barrow burials being stored elsewhere before the final interment, backed up by later observation (and the first recorded) of missing bones and limbs which gave rise to the current partial belief that long bones were abstracted for magic or ritual purposes, a fact backed up by their presence in the ditches of causewayed camps in southern England. His other obsession was with that of 'cleft skull human sacrifice', deduced from broken skulls whose owners he felt had been sacrificed at the death of a chieftain, but in fact a phenomenon relating only to disarticulated burials where damage could have occurred during disinterment and collection for reburial, or perhaps from the collapse of the mortuary container or building. Such was his zeal for these matters that he was constantly on the lookout for skeletons left behind by Cunnington and Hoare, and sometimes found examples in graves pronounced barren by the earlier men.

His theses on barrows were learned in the extreme, but sadly did not preclude his adhering to the central-shaft method of opening round barrows which preserved the external shape at the expense of understanding stratification and the high probability of subsequent burials. So rigid was he in this that he criticised other diggers in Dorset for following the much more costly and tedious method of cutting a trench right through the mound as this defaced the general outline and was unnecessary for a full disclosure of the contents. But he rightly castigated his contemporaries for not restoring the mounds after they had finished.

The first few decades of the 1800s saw the true beginnings of modern archaeology. Already there were crucial developments in the newly developed science of geology, for in 1785 in his *Theory of the Earth* James Hutton (1726-1797) had studied the stratification of rocks and established firm principles of excavation. Hutton showed that stratification was due to processes which were still going on in seas, rivers and lakes. The theory was furthered by Charles Lyell (1797-1875) in his *Principles of Geology* of 1833 which argued for geologically ancient conditions being in essence similar to those of our own time; this was applicable to the human past also, and marked one of the fundamental notions of modern archaeology – that in many ways the past was much like the present.

The antiquity of mankind, for so long unfathomable, would now soon reveal its mysteries. In France the customs inspector Jacques Boucher de Perthes (1788-1868) published in 1841 convincing evidence for the association of hand-axes and the bones of extinct animals which he had found in the gravel quarries of the river Somme, arguing that they were proof of human existence long before the biblical Flood. Now it was agreed that human origins extended far back into a remote past, thus overturning anciently held views of the age of the earth as just a few millennia. This would harmonize well with Darwin's findings, where in 1859 his *On the Origin of Species* would establish the concept of evolution as the best explanation for the origin and development of all plants and animals. The idea of evolution was not new – earlier scholars thought that living things must have changed – but what Darwin demonstrated was *how* this had occurred. Now 'natural selection' was seen as the true process of evolution, and that the human species had emerged as part of this process. The search for human origins in the material record, by the techniques of archaeology, could now begin.

As early as 1808, Colt Hoare had recognized a sequence of stone, brass, and iron artefacts within the barrows he excavated, but this was first systematically studied by the Dane C. J. Thomsen (1788-1865) when he published his guide to the National Museum of Copenhagen in 1836. There he proposed that the collections could be divided into those coming from a Stone Age, a Bronze Age, and an Iron Age, a classification soon found indispensable by scholars throughout Europe. This Three Age System established the principle of a chronological ordering through the study and classifying of prehistoric artefacts accompanied by comments on the various periods in question. Archaeology was now moving beyond mere speculation about the past, and becoming a discipline involving careful excavation and the systematic study of articles unearthed. The system remains fundamental today, although in part superseded by advanced dating methods.

Chapter 14

From Heppington to Liverpool

In the later 1700s and early 1800s significant changes in the physical appearance of the British landscape had taken place as result of the enclosure movement, the building of infrastructure for a transport network, and increasing industrialisation. The Enclosure Acts, lasting nearly a century, had effectively privatised large tracts of what had hitherto been common land, and the newly created landlords now saw financial incentives in making agricultural improvements in such things as drainage, fences, the removal of old trees and boundaries, and peat extraction. Agriculture was now intensifying in the wake of enormously increased urban populations. The overall result of all this was to make large parts of the countryside now freely accessible to ordinary people for the first time; if Napoleonic warmongering had prevented most European travel, then the curious could now roam freely in searching out domestic antiquities. Gentlemen's summer excursions to ancient sites, the visiting of private collections and active scholarly enquiry into local finds were now the order of the day.

Metropolitan development in the wake of commercial prosperity meant both the random discovery of structures and objects as well as the destruction or disturbance of stratified deposits on a large scale, chiefly from new sewers, deep cellars, railways, canals and roads, and the widening and deepening of the Thames (whose adjacent wet and boggy soils were so conducive to preservation), facts which early on turned Charles Roach Smith to rescue archaeology, actively investigating and recording finds, and alert to the fact that chance finds were important for building up a body of reference which could lead to more intensive investigation or excavation of a site. The principles of stratigraphy were now becoming recognised as an aid to forming a chronological framework for artefacts, slowly displacing evidence afforded only by stylistic comparisons, and this, coupled with Victorian progress in investigation and recovery techniques, meant that unstratified objects in existing collections could now be looked at afresh.

The half-century preceding the accession of Queen Victoria had seen a burgeoning of scholarship and the rise of many specialist fields of historical research. Even though amateur scholars and gentleman antiquaries still held sway, the history and taxonomy of architecture, painting, the decorative arts, coins and other artefacts had made huge advances, and the publications of these years still form the bedrock of modern scholarship. But despite the example and legacy of Cunnington and Hoare, much digging was still careless and indiscriminate, the period having ushered in the gentleman dilettante whose disinterested labourers plundered in wholesale fashion to fill their employers' cabinets and showcases with ever more curios. All too rarely were such finds published or even recorded, leaving increasing quantities lost to posterity.

By the 1830s and 1840s a great impetus in digging was taking place, so much so that mere rumour of a virgin site might attract the curious almost overnight. The subject was rapidly in danger of assuming the appearance of a field sport and it would not be until the 20th century that the term 'archaeologist' replaced 'antiquary'.

[A Kentish example may be adduced: between 1858 and 1874 a combination of railway construction and brick-earth digging virtually effaced the exceptionally rich Anglo-Saxon cemetery at King's Field, Faversham, a grievous loss to posterity of a site which, with the small exception of the efforts of John Brent in 1874, was completely unrecorded by the assorted antiquaries and collectors who visited it. All that remains today is an impressive (but widely scattered) collection of jewellery and glass vessels, every piece lacking a contextual record.]

Wyatt's 'restorations' of Salisbury and Durham cathedrals in the 1780s and 1790s had threatened the survival of many mediaeval buildings in the succeeding century. Augustus Pugin and John Ruskin had each displayed passionate interest in mediaeval architecture, and especial concern about the deceit of restoration. This provoked William Morris into forming the Society for the Protection of Ancient Buildings in 1877, just at the time when the threat of Sir Gilbert Scott's attentions to Tewkesbury Abbey was being reported. The original remit of protecting mediaeval buildings was soon overtaken by concern for other periods: in the City of London the parish church of St Mary-at-Hill was saved when seven other Wren churches disappeared between 1884 and 1896. Morris's comment that old buildings do not belong only to the present age but also to the past and the future had struck a chord; each succeeding generation was but a trustee for those who would follow.

The Society of Antiquaries had regretted there being no legislative machinery for the conservation of monuments, leading to various bills being introduced into the House of Commons from 1873. In that year the future Lord Avebury, Sir John Lubbock (1834-1913), put up a Private Members' Bill, only to be opposed by the many with landowning interests who saw unwarranted interference in their private estates; this notwithstanding, Lubbock's bill was passed in parliament in 1882 as the

Ancient Monuments Protection Act. The Commissioners of the Board of Public Works could now, with the owner's consent, take into guardianship, or acquire, and maintain at public expense, any monument included in a short-list or 'schedule' of 68 monuments in the British Isles, all but a few of which were of prehistoric origin: Avebury, Old Sarum, Silbury Hill, and a number of megalithic monuments in Derbyshire, Cumberland and Westmorland.

But the Act offered protection to monuments that were for all practical purposes useless, and were therefore least likely to be restored or removed at a whim. Ecclesiastical buildings still in use were specifically excluded. Vandalism by members of the public was now punishable, but the owner of an ancient monument was still at liberty to destroy or neglect his property; and further, nothing in the Act compelled the owners to hand over the guardianship of monuments to the Commissioners, or to ensure their upkeep. Nevertheless, this ground-breaking Act would spawn many successive ones after 1900 and lead to the present century's zealous concerns for the past.

Instrumental in this happy sequence of events was the career Army officer, General Augustus Lane Fox Pitt-Rivers (1827-1900), whose daughter Alice had married Lubbock in 1884. An inheritance of vast estates in Cranborne Chase near Salisbury allowed him to excavate many of the prehistoric monuments he now had the supreme good fortune to own. In so doing, he invented some of the most advanced techniques of archaeological fieldwork of the century, and then published his results in remarkable and well-illustrated detail. The general was by far the most obvious and available man to become England's first Inspector of Ancient Monuments, based on an annual salary of £250 plus travelling expenses. Neither was necessary, but he wholeheartedly threw himself into touring the country to promote the 1882 Act and take sites into voluntary 'guardianship', whereby they would be maintained and information signs erected at public expense. In time, this would lead to the sweeping Ancient Monuments Consolidation and Amendment Act of 1914, the first effective legal system for protecting the country's heritage of historic buildings and monuments.

The greatest archaeologist of his age, Charles Roach Smith (1806-1890) left his native Isle of Wight to work briefly in a solicitor's office and then, after apprenticeship, to start in business as a chemist and pharmacist in Founder's Court, 48 Lothbury, in the City of London (a fact for which the socially exclusive Society of Antiquaries, looking askance at his trading origins, would initially blackball him in 1836). In that year of 1834 he would start to witness the greatest destruction of the capital's historic fabric since the Great Fire, and also be happily placed to see the excavations for the Bank of England's new extension.

He was only too aware that the large-scale redevelopment of urban areas with the concomitant destruction of ancient monuments and historic buildings was bringing

Figure 31. Faussett's saviour: Charles Roach Smith, the greatest
archaeologist of the 19th century.
(Reproduced by kind permission of Mr Michael Rhodes.)

rapid and increasing concern in the antiquarian circles who were at the forefront of
the growing preservation movement.

Busily rescuing and recording objects taken out of metropolitan sites before their
imminent redevelopment, his work enabled him to suggest the development of the
Roman City and to demonstrate the survival of Roman monumental buildings and
Roman work within the City walls. He worked steadily with the threefold intention
of understanding how London had begun and grown; founding a City museum to
house and exhibit his finds; and preserving the ancient monuments of the City. His
lifelong dictum was:

> Nothing that relates to the knowledge of the human race, can, indeed, be unworthy [of]
> the consideration of man.[1]

---

[1] *Inv. Sep.*: ix

And all the while, in two decades of frenetic activity between the 1830s and 1850s, he was amassing what would be the first reference collection of pre-Roman, Roman and mediaeval antiquities: here were flint tools, potsherds, leather shoes, trade tokens, coins, pottery, jewellery and stone sculptures, meticulously disposed to parade the past centuries of the capital's history. Exceptional Bronze Age items sat alongside comparable artefacts of the Romano-British and later eras, ultimately to be the bedrock of four departments in the British Museum. Here was the first man to see that it was really only coins that could allow a conception of the Romano-British period ('No work of art is more significant of civilisation than coins'[2]), that legionary stamps on tiles could elucidate military history, and that makers' marks on Samian ware could provide evidence of massive trade between Britain and Gaul. The English capital was for ever to hold Roach Smith in its debt, for nobody after him could equal his example, and record and illustrate the finds of the Victorian era uncovered in a period of accelerating rebuilding and expansion. And by now the public was ever keener to inspect new finds: the discovery of the Roman pavement between Bucklersbury and Poultry in 1869 created an archaeological frisson, and when the Guildhall Museum was rebuilt it included a museum in its basement with part of the pavement incorporated into the wall of the new exhibition room.

Some 5000 objects were collected, not by active acquisition but rather by a reliance on donations and the occasional purchase of the odd outstanding item of artistic merit (large profits were available to those prepared to exploit their finds), when he would gather as much background information as was possible, ever aware that his prime duty was publication and not salvage. In this regard, his long admiration for James Douglas's early practice of substituting ' ... a clear description and ample illustration for vague generalities and theories sparingly supported by facts'[3] must have been ever uppermost in his mind.

His collections, assembled not for their artistic or monetary value but to illustrate 'the institutions, the habits, the customs, and the arts of our forefathers'[4] were freely available to public enquiry at his museum, and published in 1854 as a *Catalogue of the Museum of London Antiquities*. Once in print, with clear descriptions and many illustrations, the cries of his contemporaries for the material to be saved for the nation grew ever stronger (despite the constant opposition of the City Corporation who complained that Smith had reprimanded them for far too long over their laxity), as did an unsurprising new demand for, and trade in, freshly discovered artefacts, where dealers might smash objects in preference to being undersold or to losing them to be melted down for bullion.

The collection, the largest, most representative and choicest of its kind, and even then recognised as of superlative scientific value, was offered to the City Corporation, who were not interested, and then to the British Museum in 1855 for £3000, but

---

[2]   *ibid*.: xiv
[3]   Roach Smith, *op. cit.*, II: 156
[4]   *ibid.*, IV: App. 46

(and strangely prescient of the Faussett fiasco) rejected because their policy hitherto had been to acquire only foreign antiquities, and then those of particular artistic merit. The ensuing outcry from the press saw that a late offer form the Museum of £2000 was accepted in 1856 (a sum far greater than that offered for the Faussett collection, and indeed a large proportion of its annual budget), thus ending a long and hard-fought campaign, even though Smith could easily have achieved £3000 at auction.

Thus the first national department dedicated to British antiquities would soon be founded in 1860 under the keepership of Sir Augustus Wollaston Franks, an assistant appointed with special responsibility for British material. In his tenure of the newly formed British and Mediaeval Department the systematic treatment of British antiquities began, leading to the overthrow of the policy operating since 1826 of a single antiquities department (including ethnography!), under the keepership of the numismatist Edward Hawkins and his staff of six, again all numismatists, whose purview encompassed little nearer than the Mediterranean and Near-Eastern countries. However, at least initially, most museum purchases were still for civilisations under threat, any spare money for native objects being available for gold items only. But Franks did much to encourage gifts from private collectors, recognizing that the scientific value of British antiquities depended upon the reliability of associated records, and that the antiquities obtained from dealers would always be deficient in this regard. In an article of 1853 he lamented ominously that 'additions to the Saxon antiquities have not been very numerous, and that branch of national archaeology is the most deficient in the whole collection'. It was manifestly obvious that Franks would have done anything within his power to acquire the rich prize of the Faussett collection.

This public acquisition was an important step in Victorian archaeology for it forced recognition on the central authorities that scientific archaeology as practised by amateurs was growing strongly, and pointed out the need for greater representation in national collections of national remains curated by specialist staff.

The bachelor Roach Smith retired to Temple Place, Cuxton Rd, Strood in 1856, having seceded from antiquarian circles by haughtily resigning from all subscribing societies in order to prove that he could further his own way without the aid of those to whom he was now annoyingly accustomed. Subsequent work in Kent and elsewhere led to many publications, including his 1850 *The Antiquities of Richborough, Reculver and Lymne,* financed by public subscription, which was the first systematic survey of the Roman forts of the Saxon Shore. Retirement brought new interests too: now bereft of his great collection, he devoted much time to gardening and fruit plantations, was recognized as an expert on apple-growing, the outdoor culture of vines and champagne-making. He also proposed planting vines along railway lines – a practical idea spurned by the English but taken up by the French and Germans.

Roach Smith was further instrumental in discoveries at Sarre Mill on the Isle of Thanet in 1860. His finds, along with those of previous digs, could now but confirm it as the site of an Anglo-Saxon cemetery, and most usefully the property of Lord Conyngham, who in 1863 allowed John Brent two years of excavations on behalf of the newly formed Kent Archaeological Society. Some 272 graves covering a period of four centuries produced large numbers of artefacts including many swords and imported items. Nothing comparable would be found or recorded on such a scale in Kent for nearly a century. (Lord Conyngham's connection with this narrative is still not ended, for Thomas Godfrey Godfrey-Faussett, great-grandson of Bryan, excavated on his land at Bifrons, Patrixbourne in 1867-8, recording and publishing the results of 91 graves of the 5th and 6th centuries.)

The extreme value of Roach Smith's work rested upon the principle of dating by association with objects of known date, an axiom first propounded by Douglas. Having ascertained the means of dating Anglo-Saxon burials, he then set about identifying and describing the varieties of objects which they contained. Early work in this field included his tripartite classification of Kentish circular brooches, based on their construction. His limited experience of excavation taught him how important it was to note the position of things *in situ* to determine their use; but his greatest contribution to Anglo-Saxon cemetery studies lay in his recognition of regional differences in brooches and other goods, for until 1847 most of the known Anglo-Saxon material had come from Kent, and any hope of distinguishing regional tribal characteristics depended upon new discoveries outside the county. The only other substantial groups of finds were from the Isle of Wight, prompting him to remark on their close affinity to the Kentish groups (having been born on that island, nobody was better placed than he to observe this fact). When in 1847 a substantial Anglo-Saxon cemetery was excavated at Fairford in Gloucestershire, he saw immediately that two shield-bosses were of a form not yet recorded in Kent, and in 1850 when the Marston St Lawrence, Northamptonshire, finds were exhibited at the Society of Antiquaries, he commented that, unlike the Kentish burials, these did not include swords, and the brooches were of different forms.

His comparative work on Dark Age antiquities was not restricted to England; he achieved much in placing Anglo-Saxon remains in their European setting and became aware of close parallels between English and continental discoveries almost from the beginning of his career. Indeed, the importance of studying continental parallels to Anglo-Saxon materials had been stressed at the 1844 Canterbury Archaeological Congress when a Dane remarked that some Saxon remains in the Canterbury museum bore a strong resemblance to others in the Copenhagen museum, and suggested that they belonged to Germanic invaders from Jutland.

The Society of Antiquaries' portrait medal of him is the one presented to Smith by his fellows a few days before his death 'in recognition of life long services to archaeology'. The medal shows a handsome profile, perhaps happily consonant with his energetic and industrious nature. He died alone and in poor health, when the *Archaeological Review* of 1890 described him as 'the Nestor of the Southern Antiquaries ... full of years and learning.'

Roach Smith lived long enough to see the telling move from uncoordinated 18th-century antiquarian zeal to early modern scientific archaeology. Excavations in Greece, Mesopotamia, Egypt and South America had discovered new civilisations and brought their exotic remains back to northern Europe. Lyell and Darwin had revolutionised human understanding of itself and its relationship with the planet, society and God; and Roach Smith himself, by his formative archaeological work, had been instrumental in promoting and co-ordinating the scientific and systematic study of native antiquities by making them ever more popular to an interested but ignorant public, and by forcing attention about their significance into the eyes of long-disinterested national authorities.

His methods of exploring still strike us as adventurous and colourful, being not just an excuse to get out of town, but rather a series of archaeological excursions throughout the environs of the London metropolis; in a time when publications and museums were rarities, personal exploration backed up by diligent reconnaissance was by far and away the best method of discovery. By 1839 he had combed much of south-eastern England and often visited France in search of parallels to local antiquities, the first person to do so. Always greedy for information, hearsay and gossip was gathered, newspapers scoured, and all leads followed up by a visit. His careful notes concerning long days of walking, and staying at inns where the keeper would be questioned, shops investigated, and local antiquaries visited, afford a valuable insight in to 19th-century antiquarian provincial practice.

In early 1841 his curiosity was raised by seeing some of Douglas's finds at the Ashmolean Museum, and in that summer he travelled down the coast from Gravesend to Reculver and on to Canterbury. He then set out down the Roman Stone St towards the fort at Lympne, already aware of the existence of the Faussett collection through both James Douglas and Edward Hasted. Nothing had been heard of it for many years, and he now seized the opportunity, for Heppington was but a stone's throw off his route, where he made the acquaintance of the Reverend Dr Godfrey Faussett, the grandson of Bryan, and then owner of the manuscripts and 'vast collection of Saxon sepulchral remains'. As Lady Margaret Professor of Divinity at Oxford, he was seldom at home, and then only for short periods, so Roach Smith could not have been too hopeful, armed with the knowledge that the collection was shown with reluctance, if at all. He walked up the drive,

> ... for I had no introduction to Dr Faussett; and I heard that he had an objection to showing the collection. As I walked slowly onwards, I reflected; paused; turned back; and went to the house. I was courteously received. Dr Faussett said that it was partly true what I had heard; and at the moment it would be rather inconvenient for him to shew me the collection; but that there would be no difficulty at some other time...[5]

---

[5] Roach Smith, *Retrospections...*, I: 67-8

Walking back down the drive, his mind must have been in a state of torrid excitement as to what lay in the near future; and now something local of consuming importance was about to happen. The following spring Lord Albert Conyngham presented a paper to the Society of Antiquaries on his recent barrow excavations at Breach Downs near Barham, just five miles away. These were the first Anglo-Saxon barrows to be reported in Kent since the time of Douglas. A rich collection of grave goods was obtained and John Yonge Akerman, Lord Conyngham's secretary, having studied *Nenia Britannica*, considered that the barrows were probably of the 5th or early 6th century. Roach Smith illustrated them in *Collectanea Antiqua*, afire with enthusiasm, as he recalled seeing similar objects in the collection of William Henry Rolfe, the Sandwich antiquary; he rapidly requested them for exhibition, and with his comprehensive knowledge of Roman small finds, the Rolfe items were instantly remarkable when displayed in March 1841:

> ... thus the two discoveries will be mutually illustrative, and furnish a store of facts, from the general and distinctive features of which deductions may be drawn with greater certainty towards a classification of the remains ascribed to the northern tribes, who successively over-ran Britain after the withdrawal of the Roman forces. As these nations have a near relation one with the other, with similar habits and customs, the correct appropriation of their works of art ... can only be expected to be fully accomplished by a patient and systematic arrangement of the materials themselves, and the circumstances under which they are presented to us.[6]

These words were prophetic, for by an extraordinary and intuitive flash of inspiration, the future path and aim of European Dark Age studies for the next two decades and beyond was laid bare. In the last chapters of the *Nenia* Douglas had discussed the problems of establishing the ethnicity of the sepulchral remains of the northern tribes but failed to propose a solution; Roach Smith could now see that a beginning could be made by determining regional differences within burial groups of the same period based on the compilation of accurate data from which the general characteristics of the various groupings could be derived. After a long and stumbling birth-process, the science of true and accurate classification was now born. Roach Smith duly recalled his gratitude to Rolfe when dedicating his *The antiquities of Richborough, Reculver and Lymne in Kent* of 1850 to his friend and colleague: ' ... for his zeal in investigating and preserving antiquities around Kent, and his liberality in giving access to his collections and encouraging others.'

When Roach Smith paid his second visit to Heppington on 17 October 1841, bursting with enthusiasm to make now an informed study of the Faussett collection, everything that he saw far exceeded his expectations (there were some 400 jewels alone), even though the tantalising glimpses he had obtained from *Nenia Britannica*

---

[6] Roach Smith, *An Account of Some Antiquities Found in the Neighbourhood of Sandwich, Kent* in *Archaeologia* XXX (1844): 132-6

had led him thither confident in not being disappointed. Dr Faussett confirmed that nobody, save family and a few friends, had been allowed access for 40 years and that it was Roach Smith himself who was the cause of its being opened up and rearranged. The almost palpable excitement of his visitor led him later to comment to Rolfe that a full week was the minimum in which a proper consideration of the many riches could be made. But now, after so long, a critical and antiquarian examination, albeit too brief, had at least been made.

By this time Roach Smith had probably examined more small British antiquities than anyone else, alive or dead. His superlative gifts were rewarded by being made secretary of the London Numismatic Society, and by a position on the council of the Society of Antiquaries, even if its journal *Archaeologia* never pleased him because of its verbosity and lack of illustrations. He therefore commenced his *Collectanea Antiqua* which placed an emphasis on the illustration of minor antiquities, and in turn reflected his collecting interests and his recent perception that even humble artefacts might be used to characterize ethnic and regional affinities. For this he won the accolade of 'the British Montfaucon', previously given to Faussett, a tribute which reflected the labours of both men in emulating the French Benedictine whose great study of classical antiquities became the principal textbook in the study of Romano-British antiquities for over half a century.

The formation of the British Archaeological Association in 1843 by Roach Smith and Thomas Wright (1810 1877), an Anglo-Saxon scholar, had been impelled by the birth of a similar institution in France to safeguard, survey and publish the nation's monuments. It was a society founded, like that of the Archaeological Institute, by men possessed of a particular view of antiquity in which the national past was accorded a greater significance than had been acknowledged by the majority of their antiquarian predecessors or was yet recognized by the public at large. The first meeting was at Wright's house at 14 Sydney St, Brompton, Chelsea, where he was writing busily on historical subjects to support himself in the absence of a private income, and perhaps as socially excluded as Roach Smith was. His precocious literary skills saw a huge number of publications come from his pen, partly fuelled by the patronage of Joseph Mayer, and generally of broad but not deep scholarship, the work of an intellectual, but not a stolid antiquary.

Both he and Roach Smith men were greatly concerned about the general levels of archaeological destruction in the country and by the fact that the Society of Antiquaries had neither encouraged rescue archaeology nor pressed for government action. Wright had seen the pressing need for a national museum of antiquities when he wrote:

> In the British Museum, our native antiquities appear to be held in very little esteem … It is discreditable to the Government of this country that we have no museum of national antiquities.[7]

---

[7] Wright, *The Archaeological Album*: 149

The BAA was underlain by a distinctly popular approach to national archaeology, and saw a clear split from the Society of Antiquaries in its local activities and annual congress in provincial centres, and the encouragement of active amateur interest in artefacts and finds. Lord Albert Conyngham of Bourne Park, Bishopsbourne, himself a keen amateur digger, agreed to become its first president, Wright its editor, and Roach Smith one of the secretaries. Even before its first congress it leapt to prominence in June 1843 in defence of archaeological monuments in Greenwich Park when the building of a reservoir was proposed which would necessitate levelling Anglo-Saxon barrows mentioned in Douglas's *Nenia Britannica*. The affair proved to be a nine-day wonder, earth was replaced on the barrows, and considerable public sympathy accrued to Roach Smith and Wright.

Roach Smith now wrote promptly to Dr Faussett asking if a visit to Heppington might be possible as part of the association's forthcoming congress in September 1844 at Canterbury (a venue considerably facilitated by the new railway). Some reluctance was voiced from Heppington because of the fragility of some of the items and how those not under glass might be protected from the incursion of a group of strangers; and the coins, he added, would be strictly off-limits. The visit duly took place at 2pm on the third day of the proceedings, Wednesday 11 September, the curious filing in by detachments under Roach Smith's personal guidance to the small room where the collection was displayed, and all amid tight security with policemen on guard outside the house. Wright noted that,

> On the present occasion, Dr Faussett received his visitors with the greatest politeness, and a room adjoining to the hall was abundantly stored with refreshments.[8]

By now Dr Faussett was justly proud of his collections, prizing them highly and only too aware of their increasing importance; but he had little time to develop the incipient antiquarian tastes he had inherited from his father and grandfather, and by now could see that family considerations would render a sale desirable in order to avoid dispersal by public auction and loss in transport (the common grave of antiquarian collections), thereby all the better honouring the memory of his illustrious and reverend grandfather.

This was in fact just one part of an immensely successful series of events marking a watershed in British archaeology, when all things Anglo-Saxon, and especially the Faussett collection, were now the archaeological centre of attention. The public was now being brought into rapid and illuminating contact with a mass of materials hitherto hardly known or studied – Lord Londesborough (1805-1860) FSA, politician, art connoisseur and first president of the BAA, would soon keenly excavate Kentish barrows, the splendid contents of which would afford valuable comparative opportunities to those capable of appreciating their affinities, and John Akerman FSA, secretary to that society, would write in his *An Archaeological Index*

---

[8]   *op. cit.*: 10

(whose colour plates were as magnificent as any yet published) that 'The ridicule which once attended the prosecution of this study is hushed'. Nearly 200 delegates had attended a rigorous series of lectures and other more light-hearted entertainments amid full press coverage – so much for those detractors who had scorned the popular appeal of the proceedings. So pleased was Wright that he recorded how the Faussett collection had changed people's view of the Anglo-Saxons:

> … we are accustomed to regard them as half-savages, without refinement, rude in their manners, and skilful only in the use of their weapons. But the followers of Hengist and Horsa seem to rise up before us … our previous notions vanish … we see at once the refinements of Saxon life … and the skill and taste of Saxon workmen.[9]

A further day's excursion to Breach Down at Barham to observe Lord Conyngham's recent excavation of over 60 barrows (despite the accompanying thunderstorm), prompted one of the party to recall movingly,

> Mere fibulae without a robe to clasp,
> Obsolete lamps, whose light no time recalls,
> Urns without ashes, tearless lachrymals.

In the wake of the Canterbury congress Wright published in 1845 *The Archaeological Album: or, Museum of National Antiquities*, attractively illustrated with many engravings and vignettes by Frederick William Fairholt (1814-1866). The first chapter described in some detail the activities of the inaugural congress, adding that Canterbury had been well placed and the event successful 'in spite of the fears and misgivings of many'. The rest of the book was no more than a wretched miscellany with dull chapters on old punishments, the history of art, the Romans in London and suchlike, not at all to the liking of the more serious-minded, and the prompt for the many disaffected within the newly founded association to secede forthwith and set up their own institution.

After a while, Dr Faussett announced that for family considerations he felt that the collection must be removed from Heppington and wished to consult Roach Smith about the best way to proceed to keep the material intact. A seed had thus been sown, and at the end of the congress Roach Smith moved a vote of thanks to Dr Faussett, saying that,

> … the visit to Heppington had been one of the most important and interesting achievements of the meeting. By the kindness and liberality of Dr Faussett, they had been permitted free access to a museum of local antiquities which, he considered, was unrivalled in the value of the objects themselves, as works of ancient art of a particular epoch, and in the admirable manner in which they were arranged, classified, and illustrated by the skill and judgment of the doctor's ancestor.[10]

---

[9] Wright, *loc. cit.*
[10] Dunkin, *A Report of the Proceedings…*: 362

The excursion to Heppington would bear great fruit. Roach Smith had noted that the collection contained weapons, personal ornaments ('many of the richest and most costly description'), toilette articles, glass vessels, copper and brass, coins and other items. They were mostly Anglo-Saxon, together with a valuable group of Roman and Romano-British antiquities, and a small but no less valuable collection of Celtic implements and weapons, all from within a 12-mile radius of Canterbury. He inspected Faussett's notebooks, observing with extreme interest that every artefact had been numbered and described, and that most of the barrows on Barham Downs and some elsewhere had now been obliterated by ploughing and other means. He further noted a collection of Anglo-Saxon antiquities, handsomely donated by Sir John Fagg, which had been excavated in 1730 and now lay ranged alongside the main series of exhibits in the house museum. The clarity and excellence of the layout with full provenances prompted Roach Smith to reflect that at Brompton (near Gillingham) where James Douglas had opened so many barrows and obtained correspondingly large numbers of treasures, now in the Ashmolean Museum at Oxford, all tradition of the individual circumstances had perished, and that in the week preceding the Canterbury congress he had been at great pains in trying to trace the exact spots where Douglas had excavated.

Next he turned to Faussett's coin collection, quoting Hasted:

> … the curious and numerous collection of coins in the possession of Mr Faussett of Heppington near Canterbury were almost all dug up in its close vicinity. They were so numerous that his father who collected them sorted but one most capital series from the rest; and the remainder, which would have been an exceedingly good collection in the hands of anyone besides, and together filled more than a bushel measure, he caused to be melted into a bell, which now hangs in the roof of his son's house.[11]

[Dr Faussett, writing to Roach Smith in January 1845, considered, however, that the coins so melted to have been only rubbish.]

He was then proud to continue by announcing that Dr Faussett had intimated that if at any future time the association should feel disposed to publish his grandfather's manuscripts illustrative of the collection, every facility should be afforded towards effecting this object – Roach Smith could now do nothing but wholeheartedly agree, although, alas, the Association had neither the time, nor the money or vision to undertake the work.

A man of Dr Faussett's scholarly nature would have been only too aware of the importance of the collection, and also why his grandfather had been able to amass so much material of outstanding quality. Kent was, after all, the first established Saxon state, and it was therefore hardly surprising that so many remains of the first settlers lay in the ground, almost waiting to be excavated from within the groups and clusters of shallow circular barrows, found in no other parts of Britain. Dr

---

[11] *ibid.*: 187

Faussett received a Danish visitor who had lately seen some of these sepulchral remains in the museum in Canterbury and alerted him to the existence of others in the museum in Copenhagen, declaring that the Kentish relics did indeed derive from the Germanic invaders.

Dr Faussett counted among his fellow clerical colleagues Professor William Buckland (1784-1856), who, when he was not engaged as a canon of Christ Church, Oxford, and Dean of Westminster, practised his skills as a geologist. In his 1819 inaugural lecture at Oxford, Buckland had tried to reassure his audience that the facts of geology were consonant with the Biblical record; such a reconciliation was of course impossible, although he did make acceptable the concept of deep time, then acceptable to the Oxford Anglican establishment, and thus paved the way for the Darwinian revolution. The popularity of his showman lectures, enlivened by jokes and impersonations of the gait of extinct animals, was compelling enough for Charles Lyell, the future leading geologist of the mid-1800s and mentor of Darwin, to attend them.

Buckland had also been on the excursion to Heppington and had expressed his high admiration of the artefacts:

> ... a collection equal to, if not exceeding in interest even Sir Richard Colt Hoare's inestimable illustrations of the antiquities of Wiltshire. Mr Bryan Faussett's merits in illustrating an obscure but most interesting branch of the history of our country are known to the public only through a note in the Nenia Britannica. His collection is unique in the number, variety, and beauty of its Saxon sepulchral remains; and these have been most accurately catalogued and carefully described by their discoverer, and illustrated with exact tracings and drawings, in a manuscript catalogue of six volumes, which Dr Buckland considered a most valuable document relating to the history of England, the publication of which, in the complete state in which it was left by its author half a century ago, he believed to be the greatest desideratum in the history of the antiquities of our country.[12]

That Dr Faussett was fully cognizant of the provenance of his collections he made clear in a letter to Buckland of 26 November 1844:

> Douglas's sketch of the barrows on Chartham Down, was, I perceive, copied from my grandfather's. The barrows must have been completely disturbed, and ploughed over before his [Douglas's] time; certainly since. Sir John Fagg's collection was made for his ancestor by a Dr Mortimer in 1730. My grandfather (then ten years old) was present, and about forty years afterwards, he obtained permission form Sir John's Grandfather to open those which Mortimer had omitted, and I have no doubt he did so, so far as his experienced eye could detect them. He opened more than two hundred on Kingston Down which forms part of Barham Downs, and from these some of the choicest specimens came. But above five hundred more were opened elsewhere, the chief localities

---

[12] Dunkin, *op. cit.*: 111

being Crundale near Wye; Ash near Richborough; Sibertswold, called Shepherdswell; and Barfreston. I suppose about fifty were opened by him on Chartham Downs, and a few in the parishes of Bishopsbourne and Beakesbourne. I know of no barrows now near Bridge, except those in Bourne Park. By a note in my grandfather's manuscript it appears that he considered there might be nearly one hundred there, but I presume he was not allowed to touch them. I do not know at all what the plough has done at Sibertswold, but I dare say my grandfather explored the barrows there pretty thoroughly, as I have many things marked as from there.[13]

It was after the 1849 BAA congress at Chester that its co-founders Roach Smith and Wright became friendly with another bachelor, Joseph Mayer (1803-1886). He was the son of the mayor of Newcastle-under-Lyme, and after attending that town's grammar school was apprenticed at Liverpool as a jeweller and silversmith, later establishing his own shop in Lord Street. His natural flair for business brought early rewards and allowed him to indulge his passion for archaeology and collecting. As a non-conformist, and a radical one, he was a natural patriot and realised the value of cultivating learning and the arts among all classes, with the express purpose of public enlightenment and benevolence. He had played an important part in organising that 1849 Chester conference, had exhibited at the Great Exhibition of 1851, and enjoyed a rich circle of cultured and distinguished friends, including Sir Augustus Wollaston Franks. He was an early systematic collector of ceramics, particularly of Liverpool porcelains on which he wrote a history, and discovered the vast hoard of documents relating to Josiah Wedgwood, now housed at Keele University.

In middle life he began to apprehend 'modern' archaeology, having withstood the religious and mediaeval elements in high Victorian art, and founded the *Historic Society of Lancashire and Cheshire*. He became an assiduous collector of finds from the mediaeval village of Meols on the Wirral estuary, and also profited in similar fashion from the digging of the railway line to Lancaster. In 1852 he opened his Egyptian Museum in Liverpool's Colquitt Street, inspired by the British Museum's new Egyptian Gallery which had opened in 1846. Here now, far from London, was a study resource with scholarly publications which would ultimately be presented to the city in 1867 in his usual actively benevolent and philanthropic way (the collections were then valued at £80,000). In 1857 Mayer commissioned Wright to print a vocabulary of the 15th century, which Roach Smith considered 'a valuable volume, printed at his entire cost, and one of the chief contributions of the age to archaeology'. In the 1860s he moved to *The Pennants* in Lower Bebington on the Wirral. This property he extended and re-named *Pennant House*, soon to be endowed with a free library, gardens, lecture-hall and picture-gallery. There are telling figures for the popularity of the library: in the first 12 months 700 tickets were issued and 12,190 books borrowed; in 1877 these had risen to 5263 and 30,872 respectively. After retiring in 1873 he devoted himself to a history of art

---

[13] *ibid.*: 112

in England, and the compilation of a catalogue of the gems and rings in his collection.

Although the BAA had shown no interest in the Faussett collection since the 1844 congress at Canterbury, Roach Smith had not forgotten Dr Faussett's offer to allow publication, and shortly before the latter's death in June 1853 he offered to publish it. Faussett refused, probably because he was considering the disposal of the collection 'consistent with the preservation of its integrity, and the interests of his family'. His will, proved in August 1853,[14] carefully specified the system of tail male for certain of the benefits to his seven surviving sons, and then proceeded to bequeath Heppington in trust, and 'the bibles containing the family registers and the manuscripts relating to the antiquities at Heppington' as well as the antiquities themselves directly to his eldest son Bryan, another clergyman and then at Oxford, but who would retire to Herne Bay and die there just two years later at the age of 43.

It seemed that some progress might now be made, and Roach Smith described what now happened:

> Consulted on the subject by the Executors, I immediately advised that the antiquities and the manuscripts should be valued and offered first of all to the Trustees of the British Museum. In consequence the Executors, very considerately and commendably, gave the Trustees the power of acquiring this extraordinary collection of Anglo-Saxon antiquities, at a very moderate sum. That the Trustees might have a full chance of understanding the value of the treasures placed within their reach, the officers at the head of the department of Antiquities made a personal examination of them; and the six volumes of manuscripts were forwarded for their examination, and study, if necessary. This was in August 1853. The Trustees declined the offer. The officers, backed by the antiquarian societies, continued to importune them to purchase; but still they refused. In this fruitless negotiation, six or seven months were consumed … At length, however, the Executors received a final refusal, and Mr Mayer immediately became the purchaser.[15]

However, the executors were empowered to sell or dispose of such property as was necessary to settle debts and charges, and it was they who would decide the fate of the collection. Dr Faussett had nominated his widow, his second son Godfey (another clergyman), and his cousin William Bland as executors, the latter well-known to Roach Smith who had assisted in the excavation and publication of the Roman villa at Hartlip. None of the three would have gainsaid Roach Smith's advice which was that the collection should be valued and offered to the British Museum. A few days later Edward Hawkins (1780-1867), a numismatist, Vice-President of the Society of Antiquaries, and Keeper of the Museum's Antiquities Department for 35 years, went to Heppington with the express intention of securing a collection that was 'of the highest importance to the Museum', and arranged for the manuscript volumes to be forwarded to London in order for a mutually agreed dealer to make a

[14] TNA :PROB11/2177
[15] Roach Smith, *The Faussett Collection* in *Collectanea Antiqua* III: 182

valuation. This was done by William Chaffers (1811-1892), a numismatist, antiquary and antique collector (and, once again, a friend of Roach Smith) who had been an exhibitor at the 1844 Canterbury congress and would soon act as intermediary in the forthcoming negotiations. Chaffers had a slight Kentish connection in that he had received his early education at Margate; his later studies developed into his becoming an authority on hallmarks and the markings of pottery and ceramics.

On 20 September 1853 Chaffers submitted his description and valuation, here quoted in full.[16] The comprehensive list is valuable for a glimpse of how Dr Faussett held the collection at that time, and, one presumes, how Bryan Faussett himself had perhaps also arranged it.

Mr Chaffers's Valuation of Mr Faussett's Antiquities. Sept.20/53
Inventorium Sepulchrale, in six volumes, being a MS. descriptive of Discoveries in various parts of the county of Kent, of Roman and Saxon Remains, with numerous etchings and coloured drawings, by *Bryan Faussett*, Esq., of Heppington:

> Vol. 1. Tremworth Down, in Crundale, 1757 and 1759.
> Vol. 2. Gilton in Ash, near Sandwich, 1760-2-3.
> Vol. 3. Barham Down, Kingston, 1767-71-2-3; Bishopsbourne, 1771.
> Vol. 4. Sibertswould, near Sandwich, 1772-3; Barfriston, 1772.
> Vol. 5. Adisham Down, in Beakesbourne, near Canterbury, 1773.
> Vol. 6. Chartham Down, near Canterbury, 1730 and 1773.

A quantity of amber beads, and two variegated ditto, found at Stapleford.
Two amethyst necklaces, containing about 100 beads, Kingston and Barfriston.
About 370 variegated glass beads discovered at Ash, Kingston and Beakesbourne.
A large quantity of coloured beads in a drawer, Sibertswould.
Thirteen Venetian glass beads (modern).

Drawers:
> No. 1. Various bronze implements, Kingston.
> No. 2 Iron implements, ditto.
> No. 3. Pins, tweezers, styli, needles, &c.
> No. 4. Twenty-four gold bullae, having loops for suspension of circular, oval, triangular and other forms, set with stones and gold filigree ornaments, and various silver ornaments.
> No. 5. A speculum, bronze rings, beads &c.
> No. 6. Roman keys, styli, and various implements.
> No. 7. Twenty bronze Roman keys, and 26 bronze and other rings
> No. 8 Fourteen bronze fibulae of curious forms.
> Four silver clasps, with gold filigree ornaments.
> Silver clasp and buckle, and four bronze buckles.
> No. 9. About 80 bronze and silver buckles and clasps.

---

[16] Liverpool World Museum, file

No. 10 Two sword pommels (inlaid with gold), armillae, two boxes, glass
        bead, portions of scabbards, &c.

No. 11. Four bone combs (fragmentary), &c.

No. 12. Various beads, padlocks, dice, ivory, &c.

No. 13. Beam and scales, with coins adjusted for that purpose.

No. 14. Portions of shields.

No. 15. Unique Saxon gold brooch, inlaid with garnets and blue stones,
        the interstices or compartments having raised vermicular
        ornaments of exquisite workmanship; on the back is its acus,
        also richly ornamented, and a raised loop for suspension. This
        gem is $3\frac{1}{2}$ inches in diameter, and weight 6oz. 5dwts. and 18gr.,
        found in a tumulus on Barham Downs.

        Nine Saxon brooches of gold, or of silver and bronze, with gold
        plates, richly worked and set with stones in elegant designs, some
        enamelled.

        Three smaller gold fibulae, set with garnets.

        Five others, equally rare, of inferior metal.

        Cross, rings and beads on a card, two bronze potter's stamps.

        Crystal ball found in a tumulus, and various other things.

No. 16. Variegated Roman bead, two bronze club-heads, two key-rings,
        portion of inscribed tile, shells &c.

No. 17. Various fragments and coins found at Reculver.

No. 18. Scales and weights in a case (temp. Charles I), various bronze
        fragments of the Byzantine and Saxon era (curious), 10 gypsieres,
        spurs, crucifixes, &c.

No. 19. Fourteen bronze celts, spear heads, &c.

On the Mantel-piece:

Fourteen Roman terracotta lamps, Roman sword of bronze.

Eight Egyptian porcelain mummies, 11 bronze lares.

Five mediaeval bronzes, and bust with stone eyes.

Roman tile, and two hollow flue tiles.

Two inscribed monumental tablets.

Two boxes, containing 16 treen platters (temp. Elizabeth), painted and gilt in fruits, mottos,
&c.

Fragments of pottery &c. in basket.

Marble sarcophagus (inscribed) containing bones.

Eight Roman funeral urns.

In Glazed Cabinet:

Eleven Roman urns.

Eighteen ditto (some broken).

Seventeen ditto.

Eight rare and perfect Saxon glass vases, of curious forms, with spiral ornaments, &c.

Ten others, imperfect, but equally rare and curious.

Two Roman glass vessels (octangular bottle and bowl).

Twenty-six earthenware urns (two with handles).
Sixteen Samian paterae (perfect).
Four bronze vessels, with tripods, handles, &c.
Earthenware vessels.

In small Glazed Cabinet:
A large and curious collection of Saxon weapons from Tumuli, principally of iron, consisting of seven umbos of shields, spear heads, &c., &c.
Six Samian paterae.

The antiquities in the foregoing list belonging to the Rev. Godfrey Faussett, of Heppington, have been valued by me, this 20th of September 1853, at the sum of Six hundred and Sixty-five pounds.

£665. 0. 0.   (signed)   *W. Chaffers,*
                                         Numismatist and Antiquary,
                                         No. 20, Old Bond-street, London.

Unsurprisingly, the executors thought the sum rather low; and in addition they had not seen the six notebooks which had for some time been kept at Oxford, and so asked Hawkins to send them for inspection before deciding on whether to proceed with the sale. This done, they agreed to the figure of £665 at the end of September, the notebooks to be included. The trustees of the British Museum considered the offer on 8 October, listened to a report from Hawkins which commended the collection as 'probably the most instructive and interesting ever formed of such objects', and with every item 'ticketed with the name of the place where it was found', but declined to purchase on the grounds of insufficient funds. A month later George Vulliamy wrote to the trustees on behalf of the Archaeological Institute of Great Britain and Ireland, saying that the committee viewed with lively satisfaction the setting aside of rooms at the British Museum for collections of national antiquities, and sincerely hoped that the Faussett collection '... of greater importance, probably, than any other now existing'[17] might soon be housed in such propitious surroundings. But on 15 November the opportunity to acquire the material was again turned down, and there was some consternation as to whether it might be sold to the French. Sir Henry Ellis, secretary to the Society of Antiquaries, opined to the trustees, 'that such removal will be a confirmation of the truth of the allegation, that while England collects the antiquities of every other nation, it neglects its own.' Roach Smith declared that:

> Foreigners had long reproached us for the neglect with which we treated the valuable remains of ancient art illustrative of our history ... They asked, when they visited the British Museum, for the halls and chambers consecrated to British, to Romano-British, to

---

[17] British Museum, *Reports, Memorials &c. on the subject of the Faussett Collection:* 4

Norman and to English Antiquities; and were astounded when told that such apartments existed not.[18]

In November 1853 Hawkins, in the chair as vice-president of the Society of Antiquaries, exhibited the Faussett notebooks which he wished the Society to encourage the British Museum to buy along with the collection. 'Faussett', he declared,

> ...opened about eight hundred Anglo-Saxon graves in about eight or nine parishes in Kent. The contents of each grave were minutely recorded; every object capable of preservation was carefully secured, and drawings made ... Perhaps so instructive a collection was never formed. It does not consist of rare, valuable or beautiful objects, picked up or purchased from dealers at various times and in various places, with little or no record, or perhaps false records of the discovery; but it consists of all the objects found in all the graves of a particular district...'.

Scholarly concern was now rising and various private collectors expressed interest. It is possible that Roach Smith, Wright and Mayer met in Liverpool in October to discuss tactics, but the correspondence is yet to be traced. Mayer was then unknown to the British Museum's officers, but put himself in their debt by gifting 25 Wedgwood plaques and a remarkable 14th-century astrolabe. He then expressed his interest in the collection to Faussett's executors and was promised first refusal, quite probably because of his assurance that the material would remain intact and as a discrete entity. It was now imperative for Roach Smith to see the Faussett notebooks and for the first time to make a proper inspection of them. As they were still with Hawkins at the British Museum, Roach Smith sought, and was immediately given, permission by Dr Faussett to borrow them. Hawkins flatly refused to let them out of his sight, objecting strongly to Roach Smith's request, but as it had been on the direct advice of the latter that the collection was on offer to the Museum, the slight was a pointed one. Mayer was nothing less than disgusted by the entire proceedings and withdrew immediately his proposal of giving the collection to the Museum.

The Archaeological Institute met on 21 November and minuted the opinion that,

> The want of such a collection is daily more felt, and the complaint of such deficiency in the Museum of this country alone, if of all European nations, is loudly expressed by all English archaeologists, and is a subject of sincere remark and disappointment amongst the scientific visitors from the Continent.[19]

Hawkins had exhibited the Faussett notebooks to the Society of Antiquaries in November, and its officers now wrote to advise the trustees that if they accepted the collection, W. M. Wylie, author of the *Fairford Graves*, would make a gift of his

---

[18] Roach Smith, *The Faussett Collection*, loc. cit.
[19] British Museum, *op. cit.*: 6

own collection (Wylie had signally advanced 19th-century antiquarian progress by publishing the results of the excavation of that individual cemetery). Twice more, on 10 December 1853 and 14 January 1854, did the British Museum officers convene, and twice more the same answer came back: the true significance of the refusal was now patent to all, for the trustees would not even attempt to raise the money. The problem was not money; it was complete disinterest. But Mayer's unabated enthusiasm shone through when he wrote on 24 November 1853 to Augustus Franks saying, 'Hurrah! For the Faussett collection. I hope you will get them … I wrote to the Rev. Faussett to ask about them if you refused them – but of course nothing more as they should be yours but if you refuse them they shall not be separated if I can help it.'

Any remaining doubts as to whether the lack of finance was an excuse for something else were rapidly dispelled when a sub-committee of the Museum trustees met on 10 February 1854. The agenda was on the estimates for the coming financial year, and it was agreed to seek a purchase fund of £4000 if the Faussett collection were to be purchased, and £3500 if not. By now, whatever remained of Dr Faussett's long-held patience had evaporated, and he wrote on 18 February 1854 to Mayer saying that he and Hawkins had agreed that if the treasury had not responded by then, he would withdraw the offer. The following week Mayer, accompanied by Chaffers (whom he had met at the Chester congress) went to Heppington and bought the collection for £700; in addition, and typical of his generous nature, he paid the full cost of the valuation, whereas the Museum would have paid just half.

Mayer declined to buy the coins and seals which were immediately consigned to Sotheby's along with Faussett's papers (the 5000 and more coins, many seemingly rare or unique, were pronounced as 'more numerous than valuable'). Roach Smith was naturally anxious to know if there was anything else relating to the Saxon antiquities, for the papers had included important correspondence between Douglas and Dr Faussett which Chaffers managed to secure for Mayer. But the coins were a different matter; Smith was forced to contact the successful bidders directly and was rewarded by the discovery of six Saxon weights made from coins which had previously escaped attention.

And so the fate of the Faussett collection, for too long the subject of invective, wrangling and exasperation, as well as total disinterest by those who should have known better, was at last settled. But the aftermath was unexpected by many, and its final resting-place unknown by all, except one.

Chapter 15

Publication and Adulation

The purchase of the Faussett collections was duly celebrated with a lecture on Anglo-Saxon antiquities by Wright (rather than by Mayer himself) to the Historic Society of Lancashire and Cheshire at the Philharmonic Hall in Liverpool, when the items, having been sent thither by rail, were placed on display to the participants and Mayer was presented with an address in recognition of his services to scholarship. Reviews were predictably fulsome, and related how Wright had had before him 'the contents of 700-800 hundred graves which had furnished an almost indefinite variety of articles, less but for the perishable materials'.

Wright did not demur from recalling the erroneous opinions that both Douglas and Faussett had held on material of this period, but swiftly added that a careful comparison of the artefacts showed how little was then understood of the degree of civilisation existing among the Anglo-Saxons before their conversion to Christianity. He proceeded to emphasise the ethnological importance of the collection, and by way of example adduced Kentish *fibulae* as being for the most part circular, and thus distinct from the cross-shaped ones of East Anglia. He concluded in adding his voice to the many others who lamented the rejection of the collection by the British Museum, and considered that the Faussett material 'should be considered as, in the highest sense of the term, a national monument'.

Roach Smith was not shy in putting into print the topical argument of classical versus native art and architecture. It was true that the glories of Greece and Italy and Egypt were available for all to see at the British Museum, but was this all?

Yet not only does the Government begin with gathering the monuments, ancient and modern, of all foreign countries, but it ends there also. Our national antiquities are not even made subservient and placed in the lowest grade; they are altogether unrecognized and ignored; and that, too, within an English metropolitan museum, surrounded by an English population, and paid for, with no stinted liberality, by English money.[1]

He did not stint in continuing:

Although I could not be ignorant of the indifference with which our national antiquities have been and are regarded by the Government, I thought it possible that what could not be looked for from good taste, or from patriotism, might be conceded to dictation or to interest...[2]

A modest sum had been asked of the British Museum, so modest that three other persons showed willingness to purchase if the trustees were to reject a collection which was

in every point of view truly valuable, and which, as purely national remains of historical importance may be considered priceless.[3]

The government was to be held fully responsible for the fiasco,

... and be reckoned among the numerous inconsistencies and deficiencies which it has manifested and for which it will have to answer to all who desire to see our country respected and honoured. When our Government shall be composed of statesmen instead of placemen; of men who look to the credit, the prosperity, and the glory of the country, more than to the maintenance of themselves in power and their connexions in places and pensions; then, and then only, may it be expected that our national antiquities will be cared for and protected; and that, at the same time, the ancient national literature will be appreciated and its students encouraged.[4]

The news of Mayer's acquisition met with rejoicing on the part of societies and the press alike, and universal condemnation of the British Museum's trustees. Roach Smith condemned the board members as a 'monstrous anomaly' to shame them and demonstrate that the great and good were really quite ignorant of the articles in their charge. Many of the 47 trustees held post by reason of their position (the Archbishop of Canterbury and the Speaker of the House of Commons included) and never attended a meeting, and nor did the nine family trustees. Board members elected their own kind and so maintained an intimate coterie of like tastes and outlook, and as many meetings numbered as few as half a dozen, the onus of great decisions fell on the very few – principally a small clique of three comprising Sir David Dundas, the Duke of Somerset and William Hamilton, who, although an antiquary of some distinction, defined fine art as Greek art. Roach Smith fulminated:

---

[1] *Inv. Sep.*: x
[2] *ibid.*: v
[3] *Inv. Sep.*: vi
[4] *loc. cit.*

It is no discredit to the prelates, noblemen and gentlemen who figure in this list that they have no taste or feeling for the antiquities of their country: eminent in other ways, all certainly honourable men or men of business, and can therefore afford to be ignorant of the archaeology of England. Could even three out of forty-seven distinguish Anglo-Saxon from Chinese works of art? So they are appointed by the Government, people of a nature not adapted to discharge duties by education, taste, or scientific and antiquarian knowledge; but positively disqualified by their important state offices and other engagements. How many of the twenty-three official trustees know or care anything of the British Museum? How many of the elected ones are competent to attend and comprehend the business of the Institution? The constitution of the entire board is a monstrous anomaly, and its existence detrimental to the British Museum's best interests – they will not grant the necessary trifling sum for purchase but rather lavish it on objects of very secondary consideration.[5]

Who was to agree with them that the collection was not high art? It was a matter of scale and context and relationship, he continued, and yes, there were other uncouth and monstrous forms in the halls of the British Museum allowed to stand as worthy of their type. If the Britons had left us no literature, then their rude works became precious memorials without reference to high artistic skill – a misshapen coin of King Alfred was as valuable as the most finished production of a later mint. As works of high art, 90 per cent of the early and mediaeval antiquities of our country would be excluded. Roach Smith knew only too well that if the British Museum had acquired the Faussett collection, then the chances of publication would have been negligible; Joseph Mayer had preserved its integrity, and his liberal and enlightened care would make it publicly accessible by printing the manuscripts and illustrating them fully.

All of this was compounded by no museum officers being allowed to attend the meetings of the trustees, the upshot of which was that arbitrary decisions were almost the order of the day. Yet two years before the rejection of the Faussett collection, the trustees had agreed to spend £200 on a collection of Latvian grave-goods, and (with extreme irony) because the material was regarded as being of especial scientific value because it was well documented and supported by details of find-spots!

Following the purchase by Mayer, two other men were then persuaded to seek another archaeological beneficiary. W. M. Wylie, who had published *Fairford Graves* in 1852, offered his collection to the British Museum on condition that they bought the Faussett material; their refusal led to the Ashmolean at Oxford receiving it instead. W. H. Rolfe, the Sandwich antiquary, grandson of William Boys, and a great friend of Roach Smith, sold his collection to Mayer in 1857; this was a considerable loss to London as the collection consisted largely of objects from Anglo-Saxon cemeteries, including Gilton where Faussett had also excavated, as well as a large collection of mediaeval antiquities. Rolfe also had an important holding of coins, but these were

---

[5] Roach Smith, *Collectanea Antiqua:* III

not really within Mayer's area of interest or expertise, and so went elsewhere.

The *Art Journal* of 9 April 1854 threw in its own twopenn'orth:

> Such men as Mr Mayer become public benefactors, and present valuable examples of affluence acquired by industry, directed to the noble end of promoting science and popularising intellectual pursuits. One such person does more real good than the entire body of British Museum Trustees. We have little hope for the future good fortunes of the "National Antiquity" department there, or for the energy of officers crippled by such means; and still less faith in the judgement of those whose fiat is law in Russell St. Unfortunately, many of our public institutions are ruled by men of rank, and not by men of that peculiar knowledge which must be necessary to qualify such place-holders, if he would not be rather a hindrance than a help to science. This has proved to be the grand error of our own National Gallery ... Our public institutions should at least be on a par with the general scientific progress of the nation.

The archaeological fraternity was of the opinion that:

> The recent fate of the invaluable Faussett Museum has shown in too strong a light how disadvantageous to science is the want of enlightened intelligence in the administration of the British Museum. ... The "Faussett Collections" comprising a richer and more instructive assemblage of Roman and Anglo-Saxon antiquities, than might be ever attainable from other sources. The family of the late possessor of this valuable collection had shown the utmost liberality impressed with the desire for its permanent preservation in the National Depository... [6]

Parliament came off worst of all in the imbroglio for not keeping a closer eye on the composition of the board, for it was clear that major decisions about purchases should have been delegated to curatorial staff. Roach Smith cried for parliamentary reform, but the composition of the Board of Trustees remained essentially unaltered until 1963. He summed up matters following the purchase by Mayer who had

> ... lost no time in arranging and throwing open his important acquisition to the public, and at once decided to print and illustrate the manuscripts as soon as possible, wishing to show that he had purchased with no selfish or restrictive feeling what the public voice and opinion of our most eminent antiquaries had declared to be of national importance ... a painstaking and truth-loving investigator, and 'a conscious steward' of the treasures he had brought to light. [7]

One wonders at the degree of public embarrassment that the trustees underwent. But when Roach Smith's own collection was offered to them in 1855, this further and genuinely unrepeatable offer was still the victim of anti-British bias; however, the prospect of further public outcry made the trustees see better of it and they

---

[6] *Archaeological Journal* (1854): 91; 402
[7] *Inv. Sep.*: i

backed down by making a bid of £2000, even though it was somewhat below the figure of an independent valuation. Roach Smith graciously accepted, making a personal sacrifice in order to preserve the integrity and scientific value of his collection. Just at this time Anthony Panizzi, a man of Greek taste, succeeded Augustus Franks as Principal Librarian at the British Museum, an appointment which would see a gradual improvement in the quality of decision-making; in future neither the trustees nor Panizzi could ignore the need to collect British antiquities, this policy doubtless undergirded by Franks' development of the British and mediaeval European collections into a museum resource of major international importance. Panizzi, having vainly tried to purge the Museum of British material, relented in 1866 and accepted the inevitable by creating the Department of British and Mediaeval antiquities.

But antiquarian ill-feeling towards the British Museum was still not exhausted, and collectors continued to refuse to bequeath their objects, preferring to sell privately or donate elsewhere. The Mayer purchase soon encouraged the idea of a national archaeological museum in Liverpool, and the philanthropist duly obliged when he donated his collections to Liverpool Town Council in 1867. Although they did not expand to become a national series, their national significance cannot be denied, and today the names of Mayer and Faussett are inextricably linked at the Liverpool World Museum.

Mayer lost no time in displaying the Faussett collection to the public; but he was equally anxious to publish the manuscripts for two reasons: respect for Bryan Faussett's memory, and to underline his munificence. And after all, if it were not for the six Faussett notebooks, much of the collection would have lost all archaeological value and been reduced to *objets d'art*, the majority being more *objet* than *art*. He therefore asked Roach Smith to edit the work under his direct sponsorship, and for Frederick William Fairholt FSA (1813-1866), an artist and antiquary of Prussian descent, to be brought in as draughtsman and engraver.

The book would be provided with 20 exquisite monochrome, sepia or coloured newly engraved plates based on Faussett's original sketches, and ample proof of Fairholt's reputation as the best archaeological illustrator of the day, for he had already illustrated Roach Smith's *The Antiquities of Richborough*, and was a regular drawer and writer for the Society of Antiquaries, and the British Archaeological and Numismatic Societies. Having started life as a drawing-teacher and scene-painter, he moved on to colouring prints and soon was much in demand for his skills at draughtsmanship, and also for his antiquarian knowledge, especially of things mediaeval, for which learned publications sought him out. Such was his skill with the burin that he could etch freehand straight onto a plate.

The six manuscript notebooks, the direct source for *Inventorium Sepulchrale*, are of paper with vellum bindings, some eight inches by five, and have copious indexes loose at the back, greatly expanded in the printed work. Each has several dozen pages followed by many blanks. In general there are a good many more sketches and watercolours than Roach Smith utilised (although, alas, far fewer than one would have liked of the graves themselves). The sixth book has five final folios of watercolours which 'contain sketches of the antiquities discovered on Chartham Downs by the Rev. Bryan Faussett in 1773, and described by him in the preceding pages', as penned by his son Henry Godfrey in 1785. The final colophon reads: 'The following sketches of the antiquities found on Chartham Downs referred to in the margin of the Rev. Mr Faussett's copy of Dr Mortimer's manuscript account and now in the possession of Sir William Fagg of Mystole Bart were taken by his permission by Henry Godfrey Faussett', and is followed by 14 pages of watercolours.

Roach Smith might have wondered, as we do, why Faussett himself never considered publication. The six notebooks are in good order, a well-nigh complete record, and, as its editor immediately saw, virtually ready for the printer. Was Faussett worn out by grinding ill-health, too tired and too world-weary to contemplate such a venture? Was there still enough of the solitary and rural antiquary in him wanting jealously to keep to himself and to his family the extraordinary fruits of his excavations? For after all, he had never given a paper at the Society of Antiquaries on what he had discovered, never published locally, and never made anything known except by way of occasional letters and by informal conversations with house-guests at Heppington. To this conclusion one is inevitably drawn, and confirmed in it by the terms of his will, by which the collections were bequeathed to his descendants in the hope that they might divert them from more frivolous entertainment and lead them to deeper learning.

Mayer was not one to delay: the proofs were ready in 1855 and the volume issued to the subscribers (329 are listed at the back of the book – more than the print run) and underwritten by him in April 1856. The printer was Thomas Richards of 37 Great Queen Street who invoiced Mayer for 300 copies of *Inventorium Sepulchrale* with plates interleaved at £20 12*s*. 6*d*., and 19 large paper copies of the same for £2 12*s*. 3*d*., a total of £23 4*s*. 9*d*. Roach Smith soon commented that

> No expense was spared, as the work will show, and when I and friends advised three guineas as the price for the subscribers, Mr Mayer would allow only two. He presented me with 200 guineas; had I made a charge for it, it would have been not more than a quarter of that.[8]

He considered that his accompanying introduction and commentary was warranted by the unusual importance of the collection, the obscurity it had lain in for so long, the sudden notoriety of its rejection by the British Museum, and the approaching publication of the manuscripts under Mayer's auspices – in all, it was 'One of the chief *discoveries* of the day', and a counterblast to the sad fact that the contents of hundreds of tumuli were unpublished and unprinted, despite the increasing popularity of antiquarian research. The Society of Antiquaries 'with their £7000

---

[8]   Roach Smith, *Retrospections...*: I

or £8000 in the three per cent Consols, and a vast annual subscription' were not interested, for they 'did not profess intense zeal in antiquarian science, nor warm admiration of national antiquities.'

Hindsight allows us to see that the Faussett collection fared very well indeed after its sale: a good home (albeit far from London), where the curious could go freely to examine it, and the *ne plus ultra* of a comprehensive and magnificently illustrated catalogue, available at a reasonable price to all who were interested. By comparison, other Anglo-Saxon material which went to the British Museum, such as the Gibbs collection from Faversham and the Taplow Hoard, had a long wait before full publication.

He was now reinforced in his view that the British Museum would not have proceeded with publication because, as was now only too clear to him, such publication was minimal: Faussett's six notebooks had been largely copied by him word for word, merely excising the odd repetition and clarifying occasional textual obscurities and blunders; he then gently modernised spelling and punctuation, rejected irregular capitals and put figures into words, and by the further addition of his own generally concise amplificatory points, all was done and ready for the printer.

The introduction would place the collection in its historical context as far as that was then understood – and the fact that *Inventorium Sepulchrale* is still so important is the legacy not only of the collaboration of Mayer and Roach Smith but also of Faussett's superbly accurate and clear account. The book was in proof form by December 1855, a rapid process, clearly underlined by the fact that Roach Smith's task had not been an arduous one, for he printed Faussett's text *in extenso*, omitting only footnotes and references judged by him as based on mistaken views, and material intended to illustrate but which actually produced a contrary result or none at all. To the occasional detractor who thought Faussett's writing a little over-detailed and sometimes lacking in archaeological weight, the editor's response was that to abridge it would have meant the loss of authenticity and fidelity; so keen had he been to preserve the integrity of the text that he not only included but also illustrated two post-mediaeval sword-pommels and a knife-handle, even though he believed them to have been placed in the graves by Faussett's friends as a joke. His only substantial alteration was to place the Crundale antiquities last since, unlike the other finds, these were Roman, a fact which had escaped Faussett. The book was rounded off by a preface summarising the history of the collection, an introduction with full bibliography which discussed Faussett's discoveries in the light of contemporary knowledge, stressed by the inclusion of cuts borrowed from many previous works on Dark-Age cemetery finds, and an appendix of transcripts of pertinent correspondence.

Fairholt's reputation stood firm in the high-quality tinted engravings, of which seven were exquisitely coloured, and unsurpassed in an English publication. His final bill to Mayer in February 1857 was for £221 10s., over half of which was

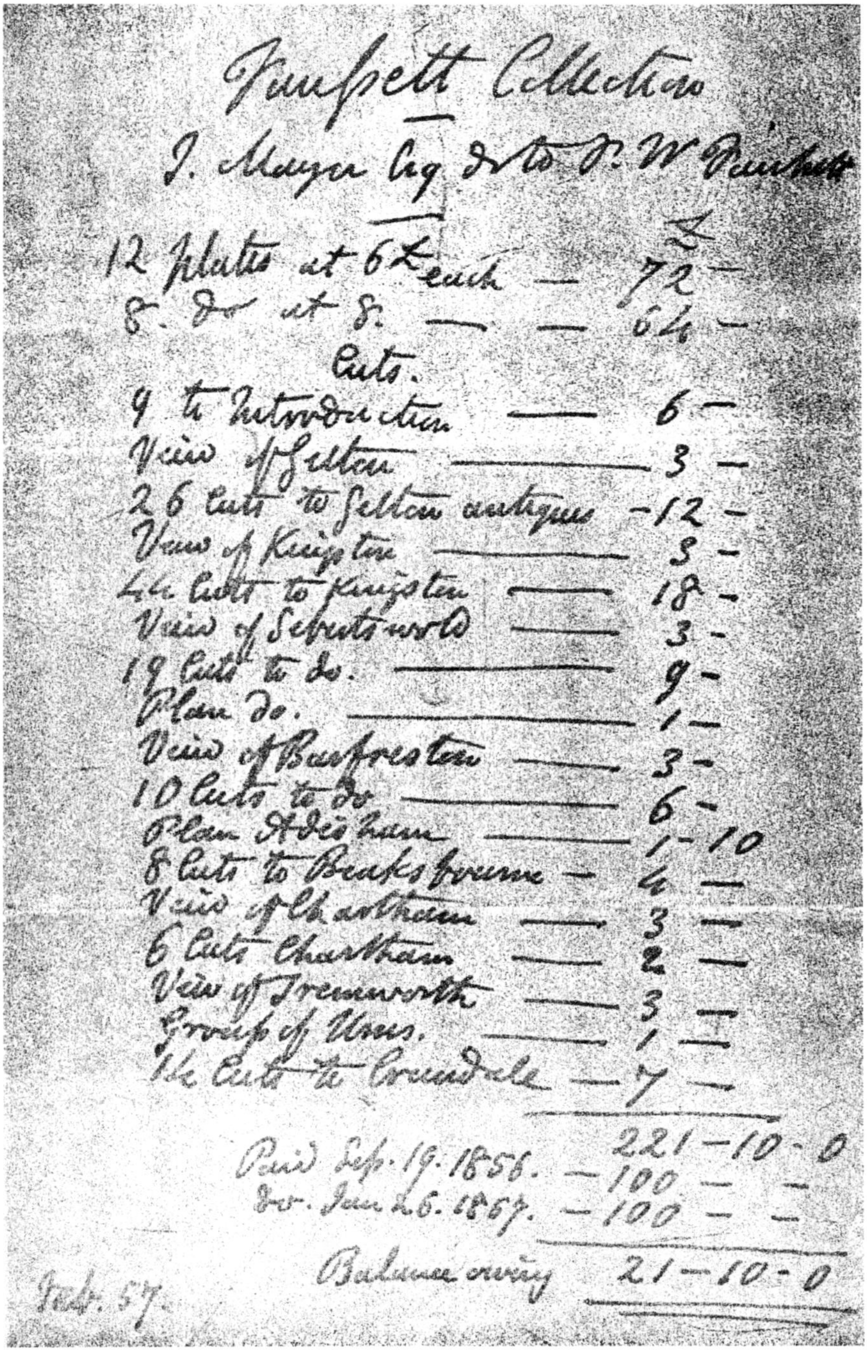

Fausett Collection
J. Mayer Esq Dr to F. W. Fairholt
£
12 plates at 6£ each — 72 —
8. Do at 8. — — 64 —
Cuts.
9 to Introduction — 6 —
View of Gilton — 3 —
26 cuts to Gilton antiques — 12 —
View of Kingston — 3 —
44 cuts to Kingston — 18 —
View of Sibertswold — 3 —
19 cuts to do. — 9 —
Plan do. — 1 —
View of Barfreston — 3 —
10 cuts to do — 6 —
Plan Adisham — 1 - 10
8 cuts to Beakesbourne — 4 —
View of Chartham — 3 —
6 cuts Chartham — 2 —
View of Tremworth — 3 —
Group of Urns. — 1 —
16 cuts to Crundale — 7 —
221 - 10 - 0
Paid Sep. 19. 1856. — 100 — —
Do. Jan 26. 1857. — 100 — —
Balance owing 21 - 10 - 0
Feb. 57.

Figure 32. Frederick William Fairholt's summary final invoice to Joseph Mayer for illustrating *Inventorium Sepulchrale.* The illustrations would speak for themselves. *(Courtesy of National Museums Liverpool (World Museum).)*

Figure 33. Joseph Mayer: every inch the Victorian philanthropist.
(Godfrey-Faussett family archives.)

for the plates which cost either £6 or £8, the other smaller cuts, plans and views costing a few pounds each. There were inevitable worries about rising costs, for which Fairholt had to promptly reassure Mayer of the kudos which would ensue to the noble publisher. This being perhaps not quite enough, Mayer proposed that his portrait should also be included, whereupon Roach Smith favoured its being circulated privately among friends, but when the *Inventorium* finally appeared in April 1856 the portrait, engraved by John Henry Le Keux (1812-1896), was firmly bound into every copy, opposite the dedicatory page fulsomely penned by Roach Smith:

> To Joseph Mayer … this volume, descriptive of a large and important collection of national antiquities, preserved by his liberality and patriotic feeling for public purposes, after being rejected by the government, is inscribed with sincere esteem and friendly regard, by The Editor.

As the price was set at two guineas rather than the three which could have been asked, this was presumably not too much for Mayer to have demanded. Publication brought Mayer the recognition he had so keenly sought and led directly to membership of, or high office in, the Royal Society of Northern Antiquaries, the Ethnological Society and other learned bodies. He commissioned two marble portrait busts of Roach Smith, presenting one to its subject with a cast of his own portrait and a bust, and further paying him the large sum of 200 guineas, perhaps in compensation for the losses incurred by Roach Smith in underselling his own collection to the British Museum.

The Society of Antiquaries possesses a larger and de-luxe edition of the *Inventorium* presented around 1897 by no less a personage than Sir Augustus Wollaston Franks. Typically, for a high-Victorian publication, the title and dedication pages are enhanced with colour to resemble a mediaeval manuscript; but the real treasures are at the end in 72 pages of original drawings, watercolours and engravings by Fairholt and William Patrick Herdman, all ranged alongside the published plates, from which one may get some idea of the genesis of these beautiful images from manuscript to print (for example, the seven published coloured plates are accompanied by both the drawings and also the engraved plate in monochrome, and there are also many other images not selected for publication).

Plaudits were loud and ubiquitous. Roach Smith wrote to Mayer on 20 February 1856, responding to a letter of his on the expense incurred in the purchase of the collection, that

> … if I did not feel that the work will inevitably bring you great returns in honourable fame, I should regret them. I am sure of this: many will envy you: and many will regret they are not in your position. There are chances, my dear Sir, which occur only once in an age, & the Faussett collection was a chance of chances.

Thomas Wright passed on a request from the eminent archaeologist l'Abbé Cochet that he would like a copy and that he would be prepared to exchange any of his own publications for it, and Wright himself declared that Mayer should be immortalised, if only for his most munificent gift to the town of Liverpool. Franks wrote from the British Museum to congratulate Mayer, adding that he had surely conferred on English archaeologists a great and valuable boon, and that the publication was the only thing which in any measure reconciled him to the loss of the collection to the National Museum.

The lavishness of the volume did not escape the press. The *Oldham Chronicle* observed that 'its beauty, and the costly way in which this sumptuous quarto is got up make it in itself a rarity in these days of cheap literature', whilst the *Derby Telegraph* of 4 October 1856 thought it

> ... is the most carefully prepared; the most beautiful in its style of "getting up"; and the most elaborate and exquisite in its illustrations ...Three men better known in the world of literature, archaeology, and art, at the present day, do not exist, and anything with their joint names attached must of necessity command the best attention.

The philologist and historian John Mitchell Kemble (the son of the actor Charles Kemble) reviewed the work and thanked Mayer for his efforts in preserving the collection, while noting the views which archaeologists throughout Europe held towards the British Museum. He reminded his readership that antiquarian research in Faussett's time was characterised by a wild spirit of reckless theorising where vague traditions based on no sound historical grounds were assumed to account for whatever was exhumed. Comparative archaeology necessarily did not then exist and nor was history pursued critically. It was Faussett and Douglas who first deserted this unsatisfactory course and founded a school whose first principle was patient observation and the conscientious collecting of facts. If Bryan Faussett had lived another 50 years and been able to reduce his own observations to order, the spirit of systemising, and the anxiety to win results from the phenomena collected, he might have been seduced into adapting his journals to a form less satisfactory than their present unadorned and, as it were, spontaneous record:

> We follow him now from grave to grave, and see how in every case the details of the interment presented themselves to his eyes upon the removal of the superincumbent earth... The position of the articles upon the skeleton teaches, for the first time, what was their actual use, and puts an end to a good deal of unprofitable speculation, as to the modes of their employment.[9]

The influence of the *Inventorium* on Anglo-Saxon studies since its publication is perhaps not easy to determine. It no doubt reinforced the best contemporary practices of observation and documentation, of which Roach Smith's standards of excavation and recording stood supreme. But he cannot be compared with modern

---

[9] *Archaeological Journal* (1856): 298-302

archaeological methods which have moved on considerably. Faussett's method of presentation by way of a dated inventory of graves had in any case wholly superseded the contemporary diary format of general discussion and excavation; his importance was, and is, emphatically supported by the information he recorded so meticulously.

The depredations of the 1941 blitzing of Liverpool, when the museum in William Brown Street took a direct hit, are a salutary reminder of the value of publishing, as some of the Faussett collection, chiefly the metal vessels and pots, and also a few Crundale items, was destroyed, making Fairholt's illustrations (for example, Plate 9, a supplement to the earlier work of Henry Godfrey Faussett in Plate 7) all the more valuable.

The present-day rarity of *Inventorium Sepulchrale*, now a collector's item, was made clear some decades ago when the need for a new edition was realized, underlain by the cogent point that Kent is exceptionally rich in Anglo-Saxon cemeteries and that systematic excavation from Faussett's time onwards has provided a great mass of finds which reflect Kent's close political and economic ties with the Frankish world in the fifth to seventh centuries. In all, over 1000 graves have been excavated and the findings recorded in either *Archaeologia Cantiana* or *Inventorium Sepulchrale*.

In 1961 the need to re-publish the material to modern standards led Sonia Chadwick Hawkes of the University of Oxford's Institute of Archaeology to undertake the publication of Kentish cemeteries as the first stage of a national monograph series, the *Corpus of Anglo-Saxon Graves and Grave-Goods* or, in deference to Faussett, the *Novum Inventorium Sepulchrale*. Work proceeded on around 1140 graves and large numbers of unassociated objects from Bifrons and Sarre (whose finds are in the Maidstone Museum) and the seven Faussett sites, resulting in an extensive archive of descriptions, drawings, photographs and x-rays. From 1963 to 1971, when the items were not on display at Liverpool, they were sent in batches to Oxford where, with a grant from the British Academy, they were recatalogued and provided with new drawings (by Marion Cox) and photographs.

Publication would therefore include the results of modern research and excavation whilst retaining, as Roach Smith did, the integrity of the Faussett notebooks. New drawings, photographs, X-rays and metallurgical analysis would lead not to a mere catalogue of survivals, but the reconstruction of the grave-groups by employing the new illustrations alongside the drawings of the two Faussetts, Douglas and Fairholt, whilst discussing the graves and their contents in a modern and wholly up-to-date fashion.

By 1993 editorial and financial problems had slowed down the entire process, and Hawkes' death in 1999 brought the project to a standstill.

Her literary executors donated the Hawkes archive of notes, index cards, drawings, images and X-rays to the Institute of Archaeology at Oxford. In 2000 the catalogue of the Bifrons cemetery was published, and in 2004 an application was made to the Arts and Humanities Research Council to realise the potential value of the Hawkes Archive as an international research tool in the light of the great advances in the study of Anglo-Saxon cemeteries of the last 30 years. In consequence, the website (http://we.arch.ox.ac.uk/archives/inventorium/index/php) of over 150 X-rays, 1500 drawings, 300 colour photographs and 2000 black-and-white negatives materialised in 2007 to make the archive widely available for the first time.

Here the researcher may now see a transcript of Faussett's text accompanied by facsimiles of the published and manuscript illustrations, updated by Hawkes' annotations, subsequent references and, where available, augmented with photographs and line drawings of the surviving artefacts.

As we have seen, Roach Smith's incisive mind made light work of moving Faussett's work from manuscript to print. His valuable (but now long out of date) introduction brought him considerable acclaim: the *Art Journal* of 1856 commented that

> For the first time he has enabled us to classify the somewhat chaotic mass of Saxon antiquities discovered at home and abroad; and by the careful comparison of their peculiarities, and the thoughtful testing of the historic record, made one illustrate the other so completely, that we may safely refer certain ornaments to certain tribes, who had settled in various parts of England.

He had had ample time to observe and reflect on what had been Faussett's regular practice: although lacking the innovation which James Douglas had shown, he was nevertheless a practical and sensible novice excavator, constantly present and supervising each dig, with the result that nothing would have escaped his attention. Except for sketch-plans of the barrow-groups at Sibertswold and Adisham Down, he made no properly surveyed plans of his cemeteries, and, perhaps more surprisingly, not even of the major graves; but this deficiency was amply compensated for by enthusiasm, patience, dedication, keen observation and painstaking recording. Each grave was dated, numbered and measured; the presence or absence of a coffin and its state of preservation noted; and then the condition of the skeleton, its age, sex where determinable, and anything else noteworthy. The grave-goods with their positions and an occasional accompanying sketch were placed on the blank reverse of the opposite page. The descriptive terms of 'small', 'medium' and 'large' which Faussett applied to the barrows had been confidently interpreted and enlarged by the findings of both Douglas and later excavators, so that his terms now acquired greater dimension and structural character. A few descriptive terms which he employed wrongly, such as *hasta* and *pilum*, were corrected for publication, as were some scattered erroneous observations. Those artefacts which he could not identify have for the most part now been correctly ascribed, thanks to Fairholt's engravings and subsequent research, so that today very little of importance remains mysterious.

Minute accounts of the researches were registered on the spot by Faussett at the time of excavation, often with line drawings (some are, admittedly, a little amateurish) in preparatory field notebooks. Of these there are but a few precious survivals which include other interesting miscellanea; for the bulk of the record we are dependent on the six formal journals which are the basis of the *Inventorium*. Such meticulous work meant that there was a rich plethora of facts for comparison, and especially in relation to the practices of cremation and burial – cremation was the traditional rite of Germanic people, and by inference, where inhumation was practised, it represented a subsequent development – thus the co-existence of both was evidence of high importance.

Faussett made it clear that most of the Kentish burials were aligned east-west, with the head at the west. Anglo-Saxon cremations are extremely rare in the county, and many of the skeletons were found in wooden coffins, some of which showed traces of burning and had probably passed the fire, as a symbolic rite, although he thought the coffin was burnt to make the wood more durable. In digging the graves, earlier cremated burials were sometimes disturbed, and cases are on record of a broken cinerary urn of Roman date being included in the Jutish grave, the burnt bones being readily distinguished from the later interment. In Kent a large number of the burials were below small barrows or grave-mounds of circular outline, but there were also cemeteries with no indication on the surface, the graves being arranged in rows side by side with the same orientation.

Save the odd episode of antiquarian over-hastiness and occasional cursory recording, all of Faussett's work had proceeded with care and circumspection, neglecting no observation which might authenticate and elucidate discoveries, especially with skeletons where he often posited a woman's or child's grave, and noted the condition of the surviving teeth, where the re-absorption of the sockets offered evidence of the ageing process (a point which particularly interested Roach Smith who had rarely found decayed teeth, even in a skull which showed signs of advanced age). Faussett knew whether coins were common or scarce, but could not identify post-Roman ones. He sometimes conjectured that articles might have been children's toys, and frequently made comparisons with objects found elsewhere by him. He also noted whether graves, for example at Kingston, had homely characteristics such as toilet or similar articles.

He was honest in saying that he found some things so perished that accurate identification was impossible (some small bodkin-shaped objects thwarted him), always gave exact measurements and full coin inscriptions, admitted that many graves contained just a few bones (recorded as 'nothing') and that, alas, too often, artefacts fell to pieces at the slightest touch, especially iron ones which had perished under the blistering effect of sand.

The excavations were conducted under Faussett's personal supervision and, while verified by all the details and facts he could collect, his narrative was not injured by preconceived or hastily formed theories; on the contrary, he went to his work with a truth-loving spirit, with a desire to record what he saw that others might understand. His remarks were characterised by good sense, and if occasionally his opinions were erroneous, it was chiefly because in his time the means of comparison were not so plentiful as they were now.

Today we should perhaps admire his tenacity when dogged by poor health, and his optimism in the face of the unknown, for at this date Anglo-Saxon antiquities were then hardly understood at all. Really rich graves of this period are decidedly uncommon, and in fact many of his contained little of financial value, or, as often, nothing at all. It was of no matter – his ardour was never quenched, his curiosity never dampened, he would battle on with his self-imposed task, indefatigable almost to the very end.

Initially, Faussett had been puzzled by the possible Roman nature of the graves at Chartham (childhood memories of Cromwell Mortimer still perhaps too strong to be quickly dispelled), but by working carefully and reasoning acutely he saw the truth, ever amending his opinions as new evidence was forthcoming, and ultimately fell not too far short of a correct understanding of the character and epoch of his discoveries. Dating them to the earlier fifth century following the Roman withdrawal, and to peoples he called 'Romans Britonized or Britons Romanized', he erred by a century in the true age of his finds, blissfully unaware of the true Anglo-Saxons, and thinking that such burials had continued long after the full Roman withdrawal, and even after the arrival of the Saxons themselves.[10] Careful always to guard himself from the obvious inference of the graves being at least partly Anglo-Saxon, he insisted more than once that nothing he had found in any one of them had the least suggestion of such a provenance. He stressed the point at Adisham Down:

> But still, I am persuaded, that the persons here deposited were not Saxons; nothing which I have hitherto met with, either here or in any other place where I have dug, having the least appearance of the remains of that people.[11]

In Faussett's time Saxon antiquities were then hardly recognized, let alone understood – it would not be until James Douglas began his work that all this would change and the fashion for seeing ancient art as merely collectors' pieces, rarities in themselves without adaptation to historical uses, would start to fade. Now, and not before time, collectors and owners of ancient baubles, erudite as they might be, would become cognizant of different epochs and peoples.

So much for Roach Smith's observations. Today, two centuries and more after Faussett, a much clearer picture of the historical background to the graves which he investigated and the people which created them is now available. The three centuries following the gradual collapse of Roman occupation were of the greatest importance for an incipient nation, and would decide the cultural and linguistic make-up of the

[10] *Inv. Sep.*: 38
[11] *ibid.*: 146

future English-speaking peoples as a whole. By the middle of the 7th century the Anglo-Saxons were established as the dominant political group and their English tongue as the dominant language. The England they inhabited in about 750 was a markedly different society from that which the Anglo-Saxons had found upon their arrival three centuries earlier. Today we no longer see them as a motley group of incoming tribes sandwiched between the civilised and clever Romans and the rough and exciting Vikings, even if at their height they produced objects as exquisite as the finest Roman mosaics and at their worst were as savage as any Viking marauder. Their long period of being overlooked or disregarded is now truly history.

In the 1st and 2nd centuries AD the predominant funerary rite in Kent was cremation, with burnt remains usually being deposited in domestic (rather than specifically funerary) pottery or glass vessels. During the third century, for reasons as yet imperfectly understood, cremation was replaced by inhumation as the dominant practice. It was at some point in the fifth century that the Germanic immigrants entered Kent to find a landscape with an ancient history of settlement, development and exploitation, and the substantial and visible remains of Roman civilisation in the forms of structures, roads and material culture, all, to some degree, peopled by a proportion of the late Roman population. Of the presently recorded 290 identified Kentish Anglo-Saxon sites, 232 are in east Kent, and comprise over 5400 graves from 77 cemeteries, 90 burial sites and 51 find-spots. West Kent, although a third of the size, has proportionately far smaller figures.

We now know that east Kent cemetery archaeology for the 5th and 6th centuries is fundamentally different from that of the western half of the county. It is an irony that so much more is known about 5th-century burial from a handful of sites in west Kent than from all the sites recorded east of the Medway. The east is characterised by the development of a distinctive 'Kentish' material culture, commonly typified by gilt cast silver, a feature which later spread westward. Cremations, whether in a pottery urn or organic container, are extremely rare east of the Medway at this date. In terms of material culture, although both 'Saxon' and 'Anglian' influences are present among the earliest burials in east Kent, a significant south Scandinavian element in the form of distinctive brooches, small gold pendants and hand-made pottery is found. This, however, is complicated by a major presence of Gallo-Roman and Frankish cultural material in the later 5th and most of the 6th centuries; and indeed, it is through a combination of Scandinavian and Frankish elements that the uniquely blended Kentish tradition emerges during the 6th century, culminating in its fullest development during the 7th.

East Kent burial sites provide the bulk of the archaeological evidence down to the 8th century, although few have been adequately published. Fifth-century burials tend to be less well furnished, with fewer dress fittings, weapons and other finds compared with graves of 100 or so years later. The cemeteries containing finds attributable to the later 5th and early 6th centuries share a broadly coastal distribution, extending from Chatham Lines through to Milton and Faversham, with many more sites east of Canterbury along the rivers that feed the Wantsum channel, such as Westbere, Howletts, Bekesbourne and Bifrons, together with Thanet sites such as Sarre. Further south, Finglesham, Mill Hill and Buckland also reflect this coastal pattern. The range of 5th-century objects recovered indicates mixed immigrants including Saxons, Angles and south Scandinavians, the latter particularly interesting because of Bede's account of the settlement by Jutes from mainland Denmark.

The outstanding feature of Kentish fashions in the 6th and 7th centuries is the fusion of Scandinavian forms with continental modes of decoration, exemplified by the addition of garnets to certain types of brooch, and related to the use of luxury materials, rarely available elsewhere in England. Gold became available in increasing quantities from the later 500s, making possible the production of the elaborate jewellery that typifies Kent in the first half of the 7th century. The ability to acquire luxury materials and prestige items is what marks out east Kent from its Anglo-Saxon neighbours, as the more prosperous Kentish households could emulate their continental neighbours in displaying their status and wealth in death just as they had in life. It is noticeable that the richest burials in east Kent cemeteries during the 6th and 7th centuries are appreciably better furnished than their equivalents elsewhere in England.

Cemetery organisation and social structure in east Kent is in need of further research, as adequately published plans are rare; but one noticeable feature is that cemeteries are frequently focussed on Bronze Age barrows. The wealth in terms of gold and silver jewellery, and imported fittings including amethyst beads from the Faussett sites of Kingston Down, Barfrestone and Sibertswold, make it clear that these communities were even more prosperous than those in the prime arable regions to the north and south of the Downs.

The different objects deposited in the various graves of a cemetery, it is generally accepted, reflect less a command of resources between households and families, and more a ranking within such households. The married couple that headed a household was buried with the fullest honours in terms of grave dimensions, with a barrow or other substantial above-ground marker. They were dressed in their best clothing, perhaps lying on bedding, and accompanied by items indicative of their status, including imported vessels form the continent of bronze, glass or wheel-thrown pottery. Other members would be buried according to their standing within the household, slaves and servants being given the simplest treatment.

Within the boundaries of the ancient county of Kent nearly 300 definite or possible Anglo-Saxon burial sites have been identified. In total they have yielded in the region of 6000 graves excavated between Faussett's time and the present, most of which have been recorded. The proximity of Kent to Europe made it a conduit for the flow of materials, people and ideas from the continent for much of its history. Its sea-girt situation afforded isolation from the rest of southern England and the production of a culturally and politically distinct region, culminating in political independence as an Anglo-Saxon kingdom between the 5th and 8th centuries, a period during which historical and archaeological evidence combine to suggest the exercise of a dominant power in southern England for long stretches in the 6th and 7th.

The quality and quantity of grave-goods found in Kent for this period, both local manufactures as well as continental imports, imply a society materially and culturally wealthier than its neighbouring regions. For much of the 6th and 7th centuries Kent appears to have held a virtual monopoly over many types of imported items and to have enjoyed close political and cultural links with the Frankish kingdoms, thus producing distinct archaeological and historical differences in comparison with its Anglo-Saxon neighbours.

The cemeteries of Kent, whilst throwing light on aspects of northern European Germanic culture, are essentially the burial places of the local inhabitants, an aspect in the past often ignored at the expense of discussions about migration, trade and ethnicity. It was as repositories for the disposal of the dead of the surrounding communities that they were established and used, and whatever the ultimate ethnic and cultural origins and affinities, for most of the period in question their identity is 'Kentish'; it was the inhabitants of that county who attended and performed funeral rites, and who were buried in them, often accompanied by the rich paraphernalia which today offers crucial information about Kent and its inhabitants for the first four centuries after the Roman withdrawal.

Earlier cremated interments appearing in a few graves containing unburnt Saxon skeletons were as a rule recognized by Faussett as former survivals but he drew no chronological or racial inferences from those facts. Constantly misled by coins, one of Justinian in grave 41 at Gilton (for example) led him to infer only that his supposed 'Romans' of Richborough continued to bury there 'even to the very dregs of the empire'.[12] In great contradistinction, James Douglas would have seen at once the clue for the dates of the objects found with the coin and, inferentially, to the whole cemetery or group of cemeteries, a period circumscribed by the accession of Justinian in 527 and a decree of 742 forbidding the further use of suburban cemeteries. Thus, if pagan, the graves dated from the year of that accession to the conversion of Kent by Augustine 50 years later, and if Christian, then down to the mid-8th century.

Douglas had viewed Faussett's graves at Sibertswold and Barfrestone, as well as those at neighbouring villages, as all being Saxon, and said that,

> The discovery of coins, the workmanship of the relics, arms, and nature of the burial places, either considered externally or internally, show them to belong to a people in a state of peace, and in general possession of the country. Their situation near villages of Saxon names, their numbers proportioned to a small clan of people existing at a particular area, afford the critical evidence of their owners. [13]

---

[12] *Inv. Sep.*: 19
[13] Douglas, *op. cit.*: 177

Faussett had been impeded by being a parochial archaeologist, never leaving the county, or even east Kent, to gain the wider picture of what was being discovered elsewhere in England; inspection of Roman and Romano-British finds would have allowed him to surmise that the weapons, tools and ornaments that he found, but unaccompanied by indications of contemporary cremation, must have originated at a date later than he ascribed to them. Coins would have helped, but alas, only made him assume all was Roman, for he could not recognize post-Roman ones. The lasting value of his collections would lie in that bedrock of all sound theories: a rich supply of comparative material as evidence of identical practice and usage in graves, and identical or similar remains, thereby demonstrating common and contemporaneous parentage.

Both Faussett and Douglas, as men of their time, had the advantage of working on sites known as those of ancient cemeteries through the ample evidence of burial mounds on the landscape, and they proceeded with care and deliberation. Many cemeteries discovered accidentally were pillaged at hazard and the contents dispersed with no proper record having been kept. Even the best of the old explorers, and some modern ones, have paid far more attention to the single grave than to their connection and place in the cemetery as a whole, and in this way too much valuable evidence has now been irretrievably lost. Almost all the larger cemeteries had clearly been in use for a considerable period of time, and the digging of the graves for successive generations of the deceased must have proceeded according to a certain system. Either the burial ground was extended in concentric fashion around an original centre, or it was enlarged progressively in one direction or in two. Whichever method was pursued, if known, would offer a valuable indication of chronology; but failing that, the scheme may be inferred from the appearance in this part or that part of the area of objects, the approximate date of which is otherwise known.

If a number of graves in one part contain early tomb furniture and a group of others in another part late objects, while transitional pieces occur in-between, there is already a basis for a hypothesis of the history of the cemetery, and if this can be established there is acquired a means for arriving at the date of things for which a chronology has been hitherto uncertain. It is of the utmost rarity that graves have been divided up in this way by their explorers into groups from a chronological aspect.

Chapter 16
Anglo-Saxon Death and Burial

Having analysed the background to Faussett's work on east Kent barrows and the methods by which he proceeded to excavate and record them, it remains to look at what his reputation in many people's eyes truly rests on – the extraordinary array of Anglo-Saxon artefacts he accumulated, described, catalogued, housed and exhibited at Heppington. Of his naturally limited and partial comprehension of their nature enough has been said. But before the collection itself is considered, it remains to ask how and why such objects, some of the highest cultural and artistic value, were consigned with the bodies of the deceased to the gloomy earth, and then to look at the nature and variety of such artefacts for the light they throw on 6th- and 7th-century Kentish society. The Anglo-Saxon cemeteries of Kent represent one of the richest and most important sources of archaeological material in pagan northern Europe (and indeed until the late 1840s almost all published Anglo-Saxon material was Kentish). Notwithstanding the sheer number of sites, graves and finds, and the disparate and often confused or inaccurate state of the historical records relating to their discovery and excavation, they form a large, important and integral part of the burial archaeology of Anglo-Saxon England.

A preponderance of the locations is in Thanet, the hinterlands of Deal and Dover, and along the Canterbury-Dover road. The favoured positions were on the end of a ridgeline or projecting spur, and on slopes where there was a marked preference for higher rather than lower ground, thus giving uninterrupted views of the community they served and no doubt also ensuring maximum visibility to passers-by. Gentle declivities were decidedly preferable to steep ones for the practicalities of digging graves. Most faced to the south, south-west or south-east, and over half lay, not unpredictably, within a half-mile of a known ancient route-way, fresh water, or of a parish boundary or parish church, but no especial correlation with the coast seems apparent. Just over a quarter are associated with a prehistoric or Roman round barrow or barrows, an observation consonant with the general distribution having been primarily affected by settlement patterns. Ease of access, the availability of fertile land and a desire to visibly signify and legitimise possession of both territory and the past made for the conscious and deliberate founding of a site.

Common to Kent and elsewhere in southern England is a virtually total absence of large purely cremation cemeteries, and where cremation does occur (albeit occasionally in locally large numbers) it generally forms a comparatively minor component in cemeteries that consist predominantly of inhumation burials. On the other hand, it is much less easy to interpret with confidence the meaning of the mixed cemeteries.

As the centre and focus of the Saxon Shore, Kent with its principal fortifications at Reculver, Richborough, Dover and Lympne would have been subject to some degree of assimilation. Any barbarian settlement in these parts must have been effectively controlled from the beginning and maintained thoroughly; Germanic burial customs would be rapidly adapted to contemporary British models, and material equipment of many kinds would take on forms perhaps hard to distinguish from those prevalent in the Romanized towns, villas and villages of the Kentish countryside.

There are a few early Kentish cremation cemeteries, but 5th-century inhumations in Jutland and Friesland and the later preponderance in Kent of inhumation and not cremation is evidence of little direct Roman or British influence. But the county does offer much clearer signs of some genuine continuity with the social conditions of the Romano-British past than are evident in other areas – the open country of east Kent has produced a striking concentration of early Germanic remains from Thanet, the two Stour valleys, and the area between Watling Street and Richborough, which include many of Faussett's sites.

Faussett found many graves which he described as 'having passed the fire'. The process of cremation involved laying the corpse on the ground or in a shallow trough, piling up a great pyre above it, and then setting it alight. After the fire had burnt itself out (women's fattier bodies would be consumed more rapidly), the bones were gathered together and as a rule placed within an earthenware urn, either an ordinary cooking pot or one made especially for the funeral. Occasionally the cremated remains were placed in another receptacle, usually a bronze bowl, and sometimes also in the ground without an urn (this last practice possibly more common than has been hitherto observed, as un-urned cremations are hard to recognize). These receptacles were then placed directly in holes in the ground which gradually accumulated into large cemeteries which were not infrequently laid out into rows.

It is not known whether the burial practices of Kent differed in any way from those elsewhere in the country after the change to the use of churchyards, perhaps in part influenced by Christianity. The historical record from Anglo-Saxon Kent remains sparse in comparison with later periods, and offers little relating to burial grounds and practice. In Kent, where the Christian religion took root early, the custom of depositing grave-goods at the time of burial was the most prolonged and elaborate in Anglo-Saxon England.

Was the Anglo-Saxon funeral both a social and ritual event where the disposal of the physical body was but one part of the proceedings? The provision of grave-goods, the construction of barrows, the evidence of coffins and a variety of other treatments of the body and grave suggest that no one single aspect is dominant, and that complex social and ritual messages were conveyed by way of the obsequial passage.

The social nature of the funeral will have implications for the interpreting of burial remains. Were the deposed objects intended for use in the afterlife? Ancient Egypt may here cloud our thinking, for if this were the case one might reasonably expect to find greater quantities of functional items, such as food vessels or tools, than is normally the case; what normally obtains is a great quantity and variety of individual objects but a far smaller range of artefact types. The two largest classes are dress fasteners and ornaments, not devoid of functional purpose, but more indicative of a greater concern with display and status in the present life than in the hereafter; and then weapons, far more common than tools, but often non-functional when found in the graves of children or handicapped persons. Here, too, acts of social display and perhaps also power seem intended.

Funerals would not have been the only social occasion in the Anglo-Saxon year; weddings, religious events and rites of passage would carry equal importance, and ones where material culture might also play symbolic as well as functional roles, even if the meanings conveyed varied over time and space. No doubt such meanings were underlain by sets of unwritten rules of behaviour and communication, complex in themselves and liable to frequent change.

In the face of so many variables, perhaps the best way of assessing Faussett's collections is to immerse oneself in the totality of the available evidence for Anglo-Saxon society and to be concerned with significant patterns of similarity and difference in the nature and use of material culture, ever mindful that an Anglo-Saxon grave represents merely the tangible remains of a funeral, itself only one social and ritual event. The situation is further hindered by a large percentage of sites and burials not having been recorded to modern standards, the result of which is a partial – even highly incomplete – set of data of enormously varying quality with which to unravel the mystery of a long-extinct society and its customs. Informed inferences may well long prevail over precise analysis, and partial guesswork over rational theory. Anglo-Saxon society is still reflected darkly through the glass of the mortuary rite, and even then not life, but death.

The significance of cremation is not easy to discern. The process demanded huge quantities of wood for the pyre and left a body transformed or utterly destroyed, and in complete opposition to the bodily intactness of burial. The Anglo-Saxons were extremely fearful of hauntings, so the releasing of the spirit, on the whole, seems to have been the idea behind it, in order that the body would no longer be troubled by its presence. This may explain the provision of little glass windows in some early Kentish urns, but the problem of why miniature combs, tweezers, shears and knives were made for the funeral (when it would surely have been far easier to use old, ordinary-sized ones) and placed in the urns after the bones had cooled, nobody has yet explained. Cremation was a social rite, and a skilled task, perhaps in the hands of special families; more certain is that its practice implies a settled community, with time to spare for social protocols such as the collection of wood and provision of urns, and thus cremation burials are rarely isolated events – and if they are, further research would almost certainly discover more.

Among the Anglo-Saxons burial was the most usual rite, perhaps because it demanded least time and equipment. Like the inhumation burials of the Romano-British and post-conquest mediaeval periods, those of the Anglo-Saxons are usually extended or loosely flexed. A great proportion of the heathen English graves, though by no means all, are furnished with grave-goods, a deliberate social practice fortunate indeed for those investigating them, and one whose main role was in reinforcing the social position of the deceased's kin in a period when a new social order was being established. Even in early cemeteries a large number of graves are unfurnished, but in the rest are found imperishable articles characteristic of what the person would have carried when alive: a knife (the most common), then belt-buckles, jewellery (usually with women), warriors' weapons (these last hardly ever found in a cremation) and finally rough pottery accessory vessels, elegant glass beakers, bronze-bound wooden buckets or elaborately ornamented drinking-horns. These last were possibly deposited after being filled with drink, a theory strengthened by occasional accompanying articulated animal bones, which must have been buried while still covered with meat – eggs, nuts and unopened oyster shells sometimes also imply a more varied funerary diet. All of this would imply a fairly comfortable standard of living, even in the pagan 5th and 6th centuries, for at least some people.

Cemeteries provide important evidence for the assimilation of Christianity in pagan England, although a mixture of traditions makes them tricky to evaluate in terms of belief or the origins of the population, and there is no evidence of any initial impact of Christianity on the deposition of grave-goods. The evidence from Kentish cemeteries suggests that Anglo-Saxon burial practices continued almost unabated until the mid-600s, whereas objects of Christian significance were used as grave-goods in the 'pagan' 5th century. Such objects, however, may have had little or no religious meaning for their owners, and they provide a useful caution against accepting as evidence for Christianity the objects bearing Christian symbols such as Faussett found, and which appear in Kentish and other cemeteries after the Augustinian mission.

All of this might suggest that the person inhumed was much more the inhabitant of the grave than the one cremated, and that the hovering spirit could partake of the food and equipment provided – or were they really only marks of respect, just as we place flowers on a grave? Against this view is the fact of inhumation cemeteries being as a rule in open country, away from settlement, and the occasional decapitation of skeletons, such mutilation stopping the re-animated corpse from straying to harm its erstwhile relatives, especially if the character had been awkward or bad-tempered in life. The prevention of the walking dead is seen also in the skull found beside or between the legs. There is some slight evidence from both Kent and Surrey that on occasion a wife or female slave was forced into a grave and killed, the skeleton usually lying in a contorted position and pushed down across the man's. Horse and dog skeletons may also be occasionally found sacrificed to accompany their owner.

The idea of constructing their own barrows, rather than using existing ones, does not seem to have occurred to the Anglo-Saxons until the late 6th century. This development is marked by a correspondingly progressive reduction in grave-goods, probably indicative of the wish for the grave to be seen by the many, rather than its contents by only the few. The Kentish barrows share a peculiarity with those of the Isle of Wight and Surrey in being clustered together in groups instead of found singly as they are elsewhere in the country. The considerable effort and time needed for the construction of a mound was not the preserve only of the rich, for many have been found (as Faussett knew only too well) quite devoid of grave-goods.

From time to time two or three such rich graves are found close together, but tumular cemeteries are found for the most part only in Sussex and Kent, the latter notable for exhibiting no correspondence between the size of the barrow and the richness of the deposits – the most splendid contents as a rule being found in middle-sized tumuli, not in particularly small or large ones. Kentish prosperity and power at the end of the pagan period may have been responsible for the gradual spread of barrow burial away from the south-east.

It would appear that barrow burial effected an even greater belief that the deceased dwelt within than it did with inhumation, for the goods on the whole are richer, and a visible memorial more of an incentive for the spirit of the dead to attach itself to it. Often situated on the false crest of a hill, within sight of the settlement below, it would stand as a beacon to the deeds of the deceased. Some excavated barrows have contained no bodily remains at all, the person commemorated perhaps being killed far away in war and buried elsewhere, but a splendid heathen funeral and memorial barrow were still perceived as desirable.

Children seem often to have been buried more simply and with fewer grave-goods than adults, probably because a short life had acquired fewer of them. They are found buried with women and also with armed warriors, and so perhaps were related and carried off by the same disease or accident; or perhaps as infant mortality was so high they were simply placed in the grave of any adult dying at the same time. For reasons unknown the bodily position sometimes differs from that of the adult, one being prone and the other supine, for example.

The deceased were laid out to rest honourably and comfortably, the barrow constructed, its grave-goods provided, the whole ensemble in a visible position to remind the living of the dead. Good care was taken to keep the spirits of the deceased at a respectable distance from the dwellings of the community by either cremation or the siting of a cemetery well away from the village. All was done to the greatest glory that the Anglo-Saxons knew – the praise of their followers and descendants after death.

Because historical sources remain unsatisfactory, how accurate is the surviving material evidence? It comprises almost entirely the finds from graves, of which there are nationally over 50,000 from 1500 burial grounds, and which have produced tens of thousands of articles deposited for the after-life. Useful and informative as these graves are, they pose problems of their own when it comes to interpretation. Not only have the goods been naturally selected by time (which has chosen to destroy certain materials by the actions of the soil and weather and by the random chance of discovery) but they have been selected in the first place by the bereaved themselves. Objects deemed suitable for use after death are not necessarily those indispensable during life; many would have been heirlooms, perhaps a century and more old when deposited, whilst others seem to have been made especially for interment. Old objects of little use were put to the service of the dead, some perhaps in traditional forms no longer in everyday use. All of this makes for difficulties in dating and even greater difficulties in interpreting. Are a few Saxon brooches found in one area the result of being brought by an incoming population, or by a trader, or did they arrive soon after manufacture, or reach their final resting place a century later?

Pottery is especially fraught in this context. By its nature often well preserved and susceptible to predictable and regular changes of fashion, it is also the archaeologist's standby. Pagan settlers made their pots by hand and decorated them very simply, so no two are likely to be identical – did some styles remain in vogue longer in the colonies than in the homeland?

Can any pagan artefacts be dated with confidence? For the Roman period coins can be used to give dates to objects associated with them and to mass-produced artefacts such as pots which were widely traded and often subject to short-lived but traceable fashions. Kent is particularly fortunate in that there are parallels with coin-dated continental graves which now allow some graves in the east of the county to be dated confidently to within two or three decades. Documentary sources and inscriptions are also valuable for dating. But in the 5th century Roman pottery and coinage disappeared from use and inscriptions ceased except in the extreme west. Clues may therefore be sought on the continent from Roman objects found in association with barbarian artefacts, and in addition, as Frankish history is well known, objects of that culture can be readily dated.

The general conclusion now accepted is that the incomers arrived from a number of areas on the continent and quickly interacted with each other and the British population to produce a new culture. Different, mixed tribes coalesced into established regional identities during the 6th century, probably determined by the characteristics of a dominant group – hence the Anglian, Saxon and Jutish/Kentish identities that had fused by the 7th or 8th centuries to inherit the 'Englisc' or 'Anglo-Saxon' nomenclature, and one carefully to be distinguished from the 'British' or 'Weallas'.

They were primarily farmers, arriving here with few possessions other than the clothes they stood up in, and perhaps also with a few family heirlooms. They would have realized the sense in farming the old estates rather than breaking the established system of land tenure, but generally chose to erect their own dwellings instead of inhabiting derelict Roman villas. Such practices were extended to their cemeteries, for although some, but by no means all, were sited outside Roman towns (or indeed close to major Roman settlements), the cases where late Roman cemeteries continue in use as Anglo-Saxon ones are exceedingly uncommon, and really only exceptions to prove the rule. By far the great majority of early Anglo-Saxon cemeteries were established on new sites, such moves to new burying places standing as marked examples of cultural discontinuity. Unbroken use of sites and deliberate continuity are far more difficult to prove, although it is indisputable that some of the earliest Anglo-Saxon finds in England have indeed come from sites which include Roman burials.

England in the 5th and 6th centuries would have been awash with Roman material culture in the same way as we today may find Victorian coins and pottery in fields and gardens. The Anglo-Saxons were great collectors of such things, along with fossils and prehistoric objects, and clearly had a concept of the past and a desire to connect with it. Commonly found are glass vessels and complete Roman pots, either acquired directly from their original owners or, perhaps more likely, found lying around abandoned. Most are objects of adornment such as brooches, pins, beads, bracelets and toilet articles, and also items extremely rare on Roman settlements, such as mirrors, *paterae* or bronze saucepans, and ornamental bronzes.

Roman coins, too, are frequently found in Anglo Saxon graves, despite the fact of no more Roman arrivals much later than about 400 AD, and their no longer being in use as currency a generation later. Many hundreds have been found covering a wide range of dates, but whether they were found by chance or kept as heirlooms cannot be ascertained; however, their retention may imply a degree nostalgic indulgence for the Roman past from which their ancestors had hoped to forge both their present and their future. Such aspirations must account for the popularity of Roman coin designs as models for the first Anglo-Saxon coinage types of the 7th century.

The Faussett cemetery locations were evidence only of populous areas and wealthy inhabitants (but without the assistance of any nomenclature), whilst Gilton and Kingston had produced grave-goods most indicative of powerful early settlers. The Anglo-Saxon graves were sometimes contiguous with or surrounded by Roman or Romano-British burials, but more by accident than design; Crundale stands out as a noticeable red herring among some 300 sites in Kent in that it happens to have been placed on the same site as a Roman cemetery, rather than indicating a rare archaeological type. Faussett's artefacts, to a certain degree, suggested that Roman art and taste had influenced some Anglo-Saxon personal ornaments, but there was little strong evidence that he had found a single intact Roman grave – so many Roman and Anglo-Saxon graves had been ransacked by his time that meaningful evidence or proof had not yet been come by.

Chapter 17
Treasures Indeed

Roach Smith gave a summary description and assessment of the Faussett collection, indexing the grave goods of each site (that of Sibertswold, for example, runs from 'amber beads' to 'urns') and then indexing the contents of each of the twenty plates in the *Inventorium* (some 220 objects). He noted, in passing, that a few artefacts sketched by Faussett had not survived, or at least had disappeared.

Before the time of the Kingston brooch lay two centuries of developing art, an area of human endeavour essentially abstract and one from which historical inferences are notoriously difficult to make. The limited nature of surviving early Anglo-Saxon art extends to jewellery and metalwork, and also to stone and bone. Of leather, wood, cloth and other perishables there is almost nothing. And there is, crucially, no painting, wood-carving or monumental art in the first 250 years until the coming of Christianity which would produce sculpture and manuscripts. Naturalism is entirely avoided, and replaced by a kaleidoscope of sinuous lines and broken, twisted and dismembered animal forms, completely divorced from contemporary Mediterranean work.

We may now examine the classes of artefacts which Faussett discovered, and note with more than a tinge of regret that for all the references he made to skeletons, not a single one has come down to us. And with even greater regret should it be said that archaeology can rarely tell us what a person thought or believed when they were making or using such artefacts as are still being found today.

Coins

The early Anglo-Saxons did not make of use coins until the advent of a village economy in the 7th century when an urban economy could no longer exist on barter. Until the 6th century the only coins coming into England were the occasional stray and exotic gold pieces which were valued for their metal content and ornamental qualities: a wide range of coins so used has been found, including Byzantine, Frankish and Roman, pierced for suspension or mounted in a gold collar with a loop as a pendant. Roach Smith knew the extreme value of coins in archaeology when he wrote that 'No work of art is more significant of civilisation'.[1] Other evidence and deductions had placed Faussett's graves as no earlier than the 5th century; and so the Roman coins could offer no testimony as to the date of the interments – they were curious only in showing the prolongation of old customs, and not as ornaments or objects hoarded as rarities, as Roman coinage was relatively plentiful in Saxon times before the native mints came into operation. The lack of dates on most and the many long reigns also precluded a precise chronology.

Daily articles and toilet apparatus

Many such items would have been deposited in graves as a survivor's duty to the deceased. Bronze basins were probably for the table rather than the fire as the handles were soldered or enamelled. Buckets were used for carrying ale or wine to the hall.

Combs were common in Anglo-Saxon England, and similar to both Roman and modern ones other than being made of bone or ivory. The earliest and commonest type was the double-sided form, the single-sided hump-backed design arriving in the 7th century. Some were plain, but many enhanced with engraving. Bone keeping-cases are known.

A bronze mirror with a separately cast handle from Gilton was one of the most remarkable items in the collection, one side highly polished for a reflecting surface. Common in Roman tombs, mirrors are highly unusual elsewhere. Douglas had illustrated a metal *speculum* in the *Nenia*, and also a circular one, this latter probably Faussett's. Ancient writers had attributed magical and divinatory uses to them, an inference Douglas chose to repeat at some cost to his reputation. Bone dice from Gilton were evidence of gambling propensities.

There were many small sheet-bronze boxes, sometimes with a simple repoussé design and sometimes gilded, and often with remnants of linen, wool, thread, or scraps of fabric inside (on which see below). The tall case from grave 222 at Kingston contained two 7th-century needles. Douglas thought they had amuletic purposes, but in reality, as the contents showed, they were workboxes or receptacles for daily articles; chains were evidence of their being suspended upon the person, probably from the girdle. Keys and padlocks were often strikingly similar to modern ones, sometimes very large, and mostly of iron.

Larger square wooden boxes, or more often their constituent handles, hinges, hasps, locks, bolts, corners and clasps of iron and bronze, were found at women's

---

[1]   *Inv. Sep.:* xiv

feet. The contents included pieces of jewellery, large amulets such as the cowrie shell, combs, spindles and spindle whorls. The last-mentioned objects were naturally housewifely accoutrements, made of bone or clay, and circular, flattish or perforated. Whorls were occasionally fashioned from pieces of broken pottery and include Roman survivals. Grave 172 at Sibertswold produced two large glass ones.

In the absence of pockets, girdle fittings were worn by most people as an everyday practical article in the 6th and 7th centuries, their designs much influenced by individual wealth. Large elaborate buckle suites inlaid with gold, garnet and glass pastes were used to fasten wide waist-belts of material or punched leather; smaller buckles would secure the straps holding stockings or shoes, and became more popular in the 7th century. Grave 94 at Sibertswold produced a bronze buckle[2] unique among examples of zoomorphic ornament in this country in having a pair of animal heads at the lower end with protracted jaws so elongated that they allow the lower to be coiled backwards below and across itself until the tip protrudes at right-angles above the upper jaw. Decorated pieces of bronze or silver were riveted to the ends of belts and straps to prevent fraying.

Châtelaines or girdle-hangers were composed of iron chains or small link chains, rarely surviving intact. They extended in two lines from hips to knees, with objects such as tooth-, ear- and nail-picks, latch-keys, amulets, purse and workboxes attached at the lower end. Buckles and girdle ornaments formed one of the most striking components of the collection, being abundant and often richer than those found elsewhere. Frankish girdle buckles presented many analogous features to Anglo-Saxon ones, especially in the mode of construction, although the material and workmanship were usually inferior. The position of some small items in assorted graves suggested that they had been kept in leather or cloth bags hanging from a belt at the waist. Such organic material would of course have soon perished, leaving traces only in metal mounts or associated fittings (the extraordinary Sutton Hoo purse-fittings make a valuable comparison).

Tweezers, pincers and shears commonly survived, and in modern shapes. A pair of scissors (which Faussett called 'pincers') from a male grave at Sibertswold more resembled modern clippers or hedge-shears, and would have cut material, thread and hair.

Pot-hangers and hooks, consisting of iron chains and attachments, would have suspended food and pots over a fire. Cup mounts were fitted onto turned wooden bowls or cups and made of bronze strips, one gilded example having a repoussé design. Faussett uncovered two sets of weights and scales, and six other weights were found among the coins after the auction sale. All of these items were Roman, and considered by Roach Smith as being found only in Kent.

---

[2] *Inv. Sep.* plate ix

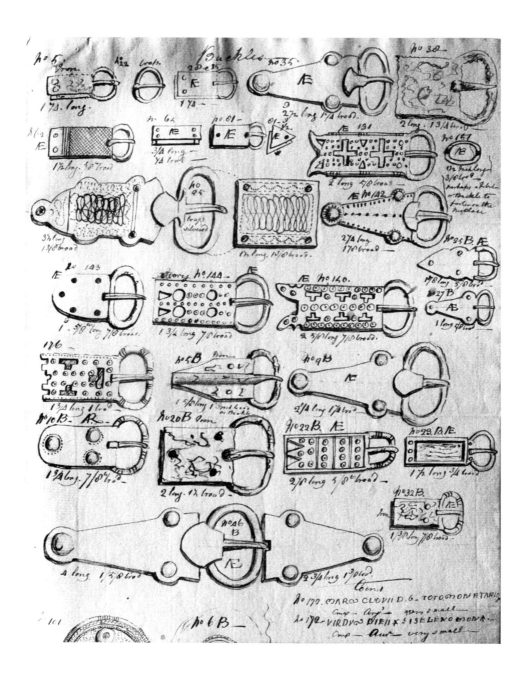

Figure 34. Buckles and brooches: unpublished ink and pencil drawings by Henry Godfrey Faussett,
together with notes on the Roman coins from Sibertswold and Barfriston, most of which can be
identified in *Inventorium Sepulchrale*.
(Courtesy of the Society of Antiquaries, London.)

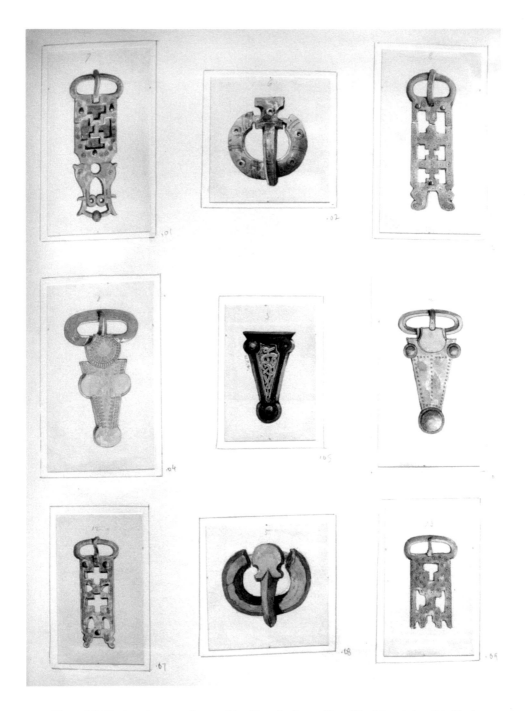

Figure 35. Herdman's watercolours of buckles, the future Plate IX of *Inventorium Sepulchrale*.
(Courtesy of the Society of Antiquaries, London.)

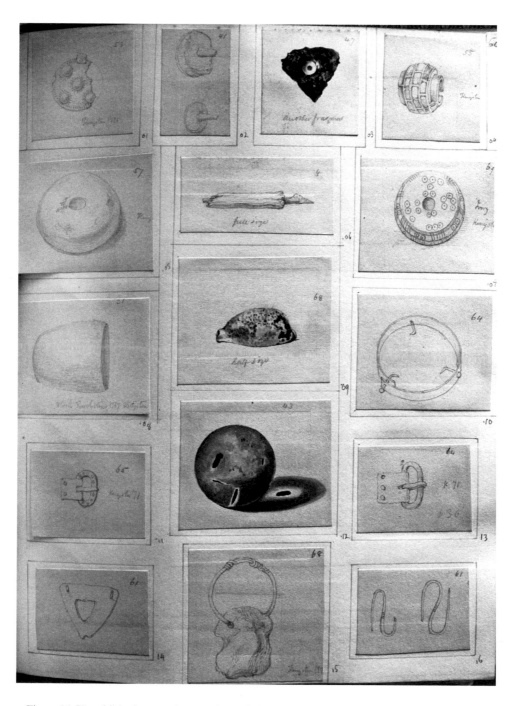

Figure 36. Unpublished watercolours and pencil sketches, perhaps by Herdman, of shells, buckles, fibulae and ornaments.
(Courtesy of the Society of Antiquaries, London.)

Glassware

Glass produced some of the most remarkable and interesting Anglo-Saxon vessels (the majority of which have been found at Faversham where there was a probable production centre). It was delicate and of a high order (as was Roman glass) and continued to be made in the same way and using the same sources of raw material as the Romans had. It was the ordinary household ware of the wealthy, not produced specifically as grave-goods, and mainly drinking-vessels, although some may have been used as lamps. In contrast to their Roman predecessors, the Anglo-Saxon glassmakers employed a limited range of techniques, shapes and decorations, resulting in just 11 basic types being known from Britain and the continent, only two of which were in common use: mould-blowing to produce an exterior ribbed pattern; and trailing, which effected a raised pattern by running a thin ribbon of glass around the outside (*Beowulf,* line 983: 'the twisted ale-cup'). A claw beaker from Gilton was a fine example of the Roman technique of the applied claw or prunt – after being blown and trailed, blobs of glass were applied to the vessel and drawn out with pincers as re-blowing proceeded.

The centres of glass manufacture in the 5th to 7th centuries are still a matter of discussion, but much of the glass in use in this country was produced in either the Rhineland or north-east France and Belgium. Bede mentions that in the 7th century glass-workers had been brought over from France to Northumbria because the art was unknown in this country, but that possibly related to window glass, for which the artificers were in great demand. Some types of bottle, and others items in a distinctive blue colour, are found exclusively in south-east England, and were probably made somewhere in Kent. Native glass also had the peculiarity of the round or tapering bottom, denying verticality other than when held; the imbibing of the contents was thus necessarily brief, and the glass then returned upside down to the table, a story fitting well with the general view of hardened Saxon drinkers – and indeed one which caught Faussett's imagination.

Jewellery

Little is known of the mining or extraction of precious and semi-precious metals, although gold and silver were probably imported as coins, plate or ingots. Pre-eminent were the circular *fibulae* or brooches, one of the mainstays of the Faussett collection, and, along with the other jewels, totalling over 400 items – a supreme delight to both archaeologists as well as the aesthetically minded. These discoveries alone would have secured his reputation: Fairholt's virtuosic engravings of the best pieces for illustration in the *Inventorium* exceeded any possible physical description in Roach Smith's opinion, who thought that at the time they had few continental equals.

Jewelled disc-brooches are found almost exclusively in Kent, and so presumably made in local workshops, although not one has ever been discovered. Frankish

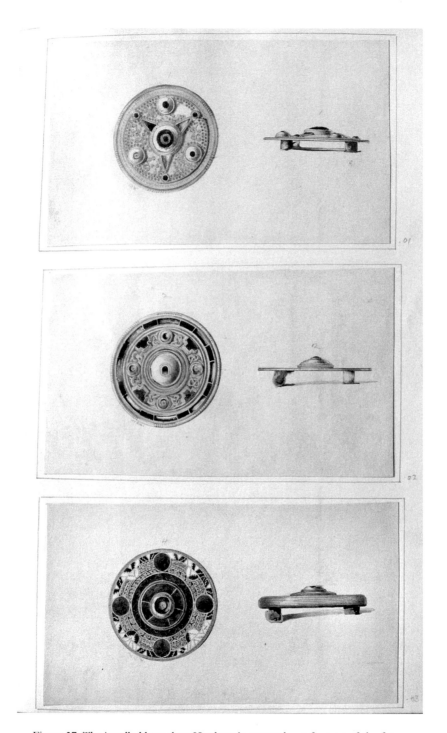

Figure 37. The jewelled brooches: Herdman's watercolours for part of the future
Plate II of *Inventorium Sepulchrale.*
(Courtesy of the Society of Antiquaries, London.)

presence in Kent since the early days of settlement accounts for a variety of splendid objects including many of the brooches, first copied from Frankish originals around AD 525, but when the Franks lost their domination of the markets around the mid-500s an artistic flowering in Kent accompanied by an increasing love of gold and garnets in stepped cloisons culminated in such achievements as the composite Kingston brooch. In all, the disc-brooches are one of the great glories of English art and have been catalogued in a corpus to a high degree,[3] which defines seven classes of keystone garnet disc-brooches, seven of plated disc-brooches, and four of composite disc-brooches, all three classes being further subdivided, and spanning the late 5th to mid-7th centuries.

The brooches date from the mid-6th to mid-7th centuries and comprise three groups, plus a smaller fourth of miscellaneous which do not quite fit with the other three. The commonest are the keystone garnet disc type, cast in one piece of silver-gilt or gilded bronze with zoomorphic chip-carved designs between raised cast settings which hold inlays of garnet, shell or glass pastes, usually arranged in threes or fours around a central ornament, and with an inlaid perimeter of niello. The fastening on the back (integral to the original casting and not welded on later) consists of a simple iron pin with a spring hinge and a catchplate. The extraordinary skills employed in the production of these brooches were extended to other objects such as pins and pendants.

Next are the plated disc type, those constructed of a thin plate of silver-gilt or gold decorated with filigree work and cells to hold inlays of garnets and opaque blue glass in step-pattern cloisons, soldered to the back-plate of a cast disc of silver or bronze. The inlays are held in place by cement or the inturned edges of the cloisons, and gold filigree decoration replaces the chip-carving of the first type. Shell decoration has usually superseded niello inlay. The back of the plate has the usual type of spring fastening.

The rarest and most elaborate are the composite type, thicker than those in the preceding two groups, and consisting of two thin metal plates bound with a decorative strip and filled with a white cement-like substance, the upper surface covered with a network of cloisons containing garnet, shell, glass paste and filigree work. The fastening on the back-plate consists of either a spring or pivoting hinge accompanied by a catch-plate. The Kingston brooch is the finest example of this category, and predates the 7th-century drying-up of the gold supply and its replacement by silver. Earlier shortages of gold and the breakdown in trade links with Indian sources for garnet and other semi-precious stones in the 560s led to the later versions of such brooches adopting copper-alloy frames to house tiny recut garnets.

Kent seems to have been the first area to import square-headed brooches, in part contemporary with cruciform ones, and developed from Roman bow-brooches.

---

[3] Avent, *Anglo-Saxon Disc and Composite Brooches*

They are found in silver or bronze, and early examples were probably brought to Kent by women from the Rhineland before the end of the 5th century. Typically they display an ornamental device of a crouching animal with human head. They were copied by jewellers in Kent for several generations, but the more elaborate examples lasted here and elsewhere well into the 7th century, still the ordinary jewels of the peasant agriculturist. One from Gilton had a disjointed design of face-masks and was probably cast in a sand-mould, the details of the design then improved by chasing and gilding. Other brooches were mostly of late Roman date and had probably been found by their new Saxon owners. Simpler in design, they were flat discs of bronze, the face often gilded or silvered and enhanced with a basic punched ornament.

Brooch fittings were a key feature of female costume in Anglo-Saxon Kent, serving as functional dress-fasteners as well as decorative fittings. Their value to archaeologists in seeking to establish ranking in society and relative dating of burials can hardly be exaggerated. A wide range of brooches was imported from the Frankish world to Kent from the late 5th century onwards.

Earrings, popular throughout human history, were simple in comparison with the brooches, usually made of silver (sometimes gold) wire strung with a single bead of glass or amethyst. Some had large blue glass drops, probably in imitation of amethyst, the most popular stone for the Anglo-Saxons after garnet, but too expensive for the majority of people. Finger-rings were equally simple adornments of twisted bronze or silver wire, and common down to the 7th century. Those of silver were perhaps also worn as earrings or necklace spacers. Faussett had one unusually large silver ring minus its setting, which may have been of amber.

There are no known elaborate bracelets or armlets from the Anglo-Saxon world, perhaps for the good reason that their long sleeves would have rendered them invisible. The rich Kingston burial (grave 142) included a simple bronze bracelet in the box at the feet of the woman, and also an ivory bracelet, perhaps rather part of a purse framework, but the positioning of short strings of beads elsewhere suggests that they were not bracelets. Hairpins found near the head were probably used for pinning the hair worn in braids on top of the head or for keeping a head-covering in place, larger pins for clothes-fasteners. Most were made of metal or bone, and simple in design, although two silver ones had cabochon garnets set either side of the head and gold foil beneath.

Necklaces, like earrings, were perennially popular, and ranged from basic ones of a handful of glass beads up to the most expensive of gold pendants set with garnets, amethysts and glass mosaic-work. Strings of amber and polychrome beads in the 6th century were gradually replaced by monochrome glass ones in the 7th. Beads came in a multiplicity of materials: silver, Baltic amber, oriental amethyst, and glass, amongst others. Those in polychrome glass were often the most elaborate, those in silver or gold the most variable in form, the latter metal including continental coins mounted in a collar or pierced for suspension. Long ropes of beads and pendants

Figure 38. Pendant ornaments: Plate IV of *Inventorium Sepulchrale* engraved by Fairholt.
(Courtesy of the Society of Antiquaries, London)

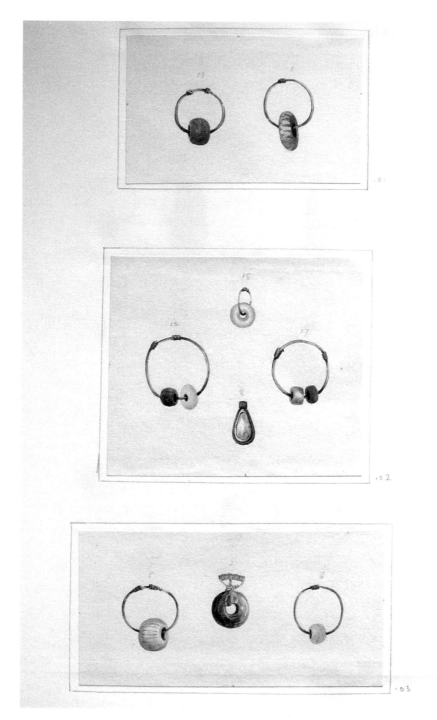

Figure 39. Pendant ornaments: Herdman's watercolours for part of the future Plate VII of
Inventorium Sepulchrale. *((Courtesy of the Society of Antiquaries, London.)*

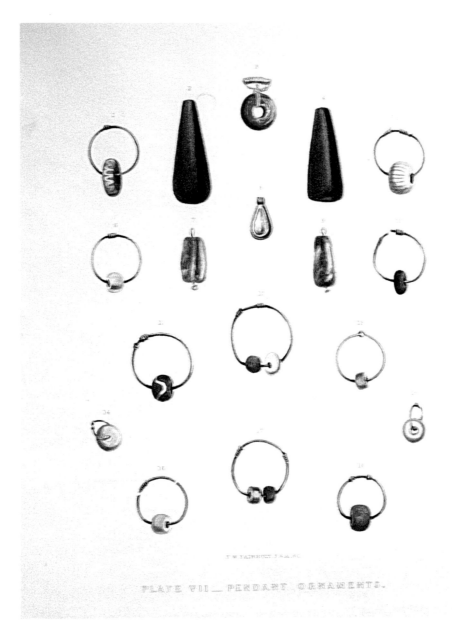

Figure 40. Pendant ornaments: Plate VII of *Inventorium Sepulchrale* engraved by Fairholt.
(Courtesy of the Society of Antiquaries, London.)

would have been worn around the neck or folded up and fastened across the breast by large pins or pairs of brooches. The S-shaped pieces of bronze found near the neck of a female at Kingston may have formed a fastening for a necklace, or were perhaps used as earrings.

Of pendant ornaments there were many, of great beauty and variety, the most interesting those consisting of coins for suspension on the person, and known from the collections of Lord Londesborough and William Rolfe. A crystal ball mounted in silver bands was similar to one found at Chatham; Douglas had argued a magical purpose for it, but if other goods had a common usage, should this be any different?

Pottery

Faussett found only sherds of cinerary urns, probably the result of anterior interments. None of his wide-mouthed pots seemed to have been used for cremation, the inference being that in Kent cremation had ceased as a general practice before the burials uncovered by him had started. The vessels illustrated were quite similar in form, especially the bottle-shaped ones, and in the character of the ornaments, but quite different from others found elsewhere in England – it was apparent, then, that Kentish funerary pottery exhibited the peculiarities of local parentage, close in form to Roman items, but of inferior manufacture and with graceless and crude ornament.

Pottery vessels would have originally contained a food-offering. Both wheel-turned and hand-made objects were found, sometimes in a fragmentary state. Many had a simple geometric repeating pattern, but nearly all were lost in the Liverpool blitz of 1941 which destroyed the museum. A limited range of simple hand-made pots with repeating patterns of stamped decoration was the norm in England until wheel-thrown pottery was imported from the continent in the later 7th century.

Textiles

These comprise home-produced linen and woollen cloth and are of signal interest, even if their survival rates are minimal and generally evidenced by spindle whorls and loom-weights. Faussett had noted and commented on textile evidence on a number of occasions, a fact not generally recognized, and, much more unusually, watercolours of some had been executed by his son where such remains were indicated by cross-hatching. Not only was the presence of textile remains recorded, but also frequently their position, and a conjecture as to the type of material. The amount of details included may well make his accounts rare, if not unique, for this early period.

Some 27 metal objects from all the sites except Bishopsbourne and Crundale had traces of textile material present on them, including string with four threads or strands suspending a brass ornament or pendant in grave 94, and a 'small wheel-like

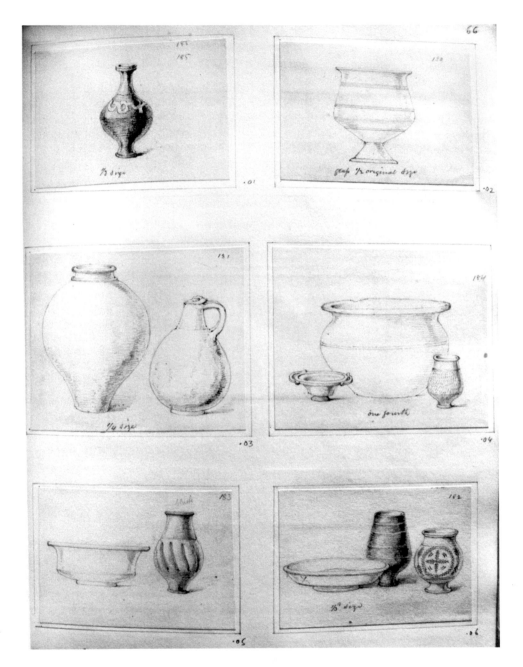

Figure 41. Pottery: unpublished pencil sketches, perhaps by Herdman, of flasks, dishes and pots.
(Courtesy of the Society of Antiquaries, London.)

brass thing' threaded with thread or string in grave 151, both at Sibertswold. In grave 241 at Kingston he recorded:

> …what is rather remarkable, the double thread on which these beads were strung was not only very distinguishable in the ends of the two silver ones, but was as white as if it had been just new, and strong enough to bear being pretty strongly pulled.[4]

But most noteworthy of all was a small collection of threads from inside the relic box in grave 60 at Sibertswold, seemingly consisting of string or thread and woven textile fragments, and described by Faussett as: '… some small silken strings, of two sizes, some raw silk, as it seems; some wool, and some short hair.'[5] All of these remains were probably preserved as a result of metal corrosion on the iron weapons and other artefacts.

Faussett gave no technical details but his descriptions still allow much to be deduced. He noted the coarseness of the fabric and sometimes suggested the fibres used, and the fact that most was preserved on the iron objects lends credibility to his account. He deduced that many of the iron weapons preserving coarse cloth were actually deposited outside the coffins in the graves, so the textile remains resulted from the practice of wrapping the weapons rather than textile clothing – another tribute to his meticulous observation and recording, especially as the practice of wrapping grave-goods, such as weapons, is now well attested. Objects other than weapons may also have been wrapped: grave 83 at Kingston contained

> At the feet, and on the outside of the coffin, were the remains of what I took to be an iron trivet; … it had been wrapt up in some coarse cloth, as appeared from the marks of impression of it on the rust.[6]

Other textiles preserved on metal objects may have been the remains of clothing. A coarse cloth on some iron chain-links found near the neck in a female inhumation grave, number 59 at Kingston, was possibly the remains of a cloak, and a brass buckle there in grave 65, that of an 'elderly person', had some linen cloth on the inside, perhaps what was left of a tunic fabric. Faussett also noticed some pieces of textile-making equipment, but not for what they were: in a relic box in grave 222 at Kingston was

> … a brass pin … Here also was a small brass cylinder; in it were two brass needles, gilt; and a small piece of linen cloth, which had served to keep the head or end of it tighter on, was found, fresh, white, and strong.[7]

Finally, he had observed spindle whorls, such as one in grave 29 at Bekesbourne which he described as a kind of disc or quoit, found only in the graves of women or children.

---

[4]   *Inv. Sep.*: 83
[5]   *ibid.*: 112
[6]   *Inv. Sep.*: 56, n.2
[7]   *ibid.*: 81, n.2

The Manchester Textiles Project, proposing a catalogue of all British mediaeval textiles between AD 450 and 1500, re-examined the material in 1998 to test the usefulness of investigating such early archaeological collections for vestiges of textiles. The main problem was not exposure to the air for over two centuries, but more that the labelling and storage practice of the metal objects by 19th-century curators had detached many of the objects from their original context, leaving exact provenance difficult to ascertain. After acquisition by the Liverpool Museum, the artefacts were cleaned and conserved, highest priority being given to the metalwork objects, thus accounting for their storage out of archaeological context. Today, only a small collection of textile material is clearly identifiable, but does fortunately include both string binding and woven textile fabrics. Some textiles were probably missed by Faussett; more distressing is that other material has been removed or lost as a result of cleaning and conservation and from the deterioration of the ironwork subsequent to the original excavation.

Weapons

After wood, iron was the most important material for the Anglo-Saxons, although little is known about the mining or collecting of the raw material, and no anvil or major piece of equipment has ever been found. Weapons were essential symbols of a warrior society and also important heirlooms, and men were usually buried with those which they had been entitled to bear when alive. A few individuals of high rank wore the long two-edged sword, whilst most free men carried a spear, small knife and shield, and a third group also carried the shorter, slightly curved, one-edged sword or *seax*, all now bereft of their scabbards of iron, bronze, bone, wood or leather. (*Beowulf,* line 3089: 'and drew her seax, broad, brown-edged'; line 5400: 'drew his deadly seax, bitter and battle-sharp').

The social significance of such articles meant that they were buried over a long period, even continuing after nominal conversion to Christianity. All were made of wood and iron, two materials far from imperishable, the result of which is that, unlike other types of material, few weapons can be ascribed to a correct site and grave-group, and do not help in dating a grave to closer than about a century.

Most Saxon swords (the warrior's most treasured possession and often passed down to a son) had a blade about 31 inches in length, as did the few Faussett ones. None had a surviving pommel (a valuable dating feature), although two *seax* pommels were found, one of bronze, the other of silver inlaid with niello. Some swords from Gilton had ornaments on the handles and sheaths (*Beowulf,* line 1346: 'gave his ornamented sword, the costliest of steels'; line 3228: 'and the hilt also, with treasure variegated'). One interesting iron fragment from Kingston was inlaid with silver wires in a stepped pattern with a central garnet set in shells, surrounded by a bronze collar and beaded silver wire, and was possibly a sword decoration or scabbard. Another silver object set with shell or chalk in a cell-like pattern was once thought to be the pommel of a short sword, but was more likely a decorative 'sword-bead' attached to the hilt by a thong, or perhaps acted as an amulet.

Spears normally had ash, hazel or oak shafts, with a socketed iron head and iron or bronze ferrules. Conservative in their designs, they are usually dated by reference to associated objects, and in particular shield bosses. Faussett found a good number of javelins and spears of assorted shapes and sizes, many having the strange characteristic of a longitudinal slit in the socket to receive the wooden staff, which was afterwards fixed and closed with iron rings, string and rivets. Some of what he called arrows were probably small darts or spears; arrowheads were rarer, but as a common weapon, must have generally disintegrated.

An intact Anglo-Saxon shield would be a marvellous find. Common in the 6th century but rarer later on, their component parts have ensured virtually no intact survivals – a regrettable fact as modern typology can now date them fairly closely. Of leather-covered limewood (the Beowulf *lind* or linden-wood shield) with a rim metal-bound for extra strength, an iron hand-grip on the reverse was riveted across a central opening and perhaps augmented by a leather shoulder-strap for suspension. On the front a central boss, or *umbo* (once called a "Roman helmet"), protected the hand and the hand-grip, and was probably surrounded by decorative bronze or silver studs. Earlier 6th-century types were in the form of a shallow cone, those of the 7th century in a more pointed shape known as a sugarloaf.

Faussett found only iron bosses and studs, and parts of iron handle-fastenings, their positions often suggesting circularity and a diameter of about 18 inches. Iron decomposes rapidly in air, and so nearly all ancient weapons and tools are badly oxidised and misshapen. Teutonic weapons are thus found only in iron-protecting conditions; if they do occur elsewhere in graves not affording such conditions, then it is hard to say to what age and people they might be ascribed. Roach Smith saw these graves as offering valuable collateral evidence which limited enquiries and permitted statements of some certainty.

Chapter 18
The Descent of Genes

As has been already shown, Faussett's material possessions were firmly secured at his death, but this of course was no barrier to the descent of antiquarian genes to his descendants and in-laws. We may now draw together the many threads which continued for a century and more after his death and see how one man's scholarship imbued the hearts and minds of some of those who followed him. Here, it is granted, were no dynasties of Huxleys or Darwins crammed with geniuses in every generation, but the annals of Kentish history and antiquarianism (as well as the church) would be all the poorer but for the many descendants of Bryan Faussett.

Henry Godfrey Faussett (1749-1825)

Faussett, always concerned for the welfare of his many younger siblings, no doubt rejoiced when he and Elizabeth started their own family a year after their marriage. Thirteen grandchildren would come in the next generation, but none to be born in his own lifetime. The majority of the present-day family descends from the eldest son and antiquary, Henry Godfrey (confusingly sometimes called 'Godfrey') Faussett.

He was born 18 November 1749 at Alberbury vicarage, Shropshire, during his father's first incumbency. In celebration of the birth of a first child, the local ringers were paid 5s. A few months later his father expended the princely sum of a guinea on his first pair of shoes. He had not seen his first birthday before Faussett had learnt of his own father's death, the consequent inheritance and a swift return to Kent. He won a Heyman scholarship in 1758, and entered Ashford school in July of that year, his father paying a Rev'd Mr Barrett the entrance fee of two guineas, on which occasion his grandmother gave him 10s. 6d. The first half year's board was a substantial £12 13s. 3½d. Smallpox visited Canterbury in 1760 when Faussett paid a Mrs Cullen in St Mildred's churchyard six guineas to nurse his promising first two sons, and a further five guineas for inoculating them both a few weeks later. The boy clearly had some artistic as well as professional skills, for when he was about 16 a Mr George Philpot, dancing master at Ashford school, taught him that subject for two years, receiving £7 6s. 6d. for his efforts. Like his father, he seems not to have attended the King's School, but did join the Feast Society around 1766 and was a steward in 1771.

In November 1766 he was articled to William Chamberlayne of Crane Street off Fleet Street at a fee of ten guineas, followed by admission to Lincoln's Inn in 1771, for which his father paid 11 guineas. There he became a man of business but was not called to the bar. In November of that year, writing from the Rolls Building,[1] he was enjoying correspondence with his sister Elizabeth and asking about yet another bout of his father's ill health. He had just returned from a trip to France and found the current talk to be of the death of the Duke of Gloucester and fears for the imminent demise of the Princess of Wales. Neither (he hoped) was true, for if it were, general mourning would be problematical as 'I should appear very oddly at Hall and at Westminster among the students.' He was enrolled as an attorney in 1776, and became Deputy Lieutenant for Kent in 1795.

This eldest son was almost born and bred an antiquary – he accompanied his father when very young on digging expeditions, and later would boast that he himself had lifted the Kingston brooch from the earth as he superintended the opening of that now justly famous barrow, carrying it with glee to his gout-stricken father propped up in his carriage, and no doubt craning to see what had been discovered to elicit such rejoicing. Faussett had then immediately driven off with the delectable prize, only to read the next day a report of his carriage being so full of gold that the wheels would hardly turn – a predictable comment, perhaps, and one that reflected the astonishment and prejudice suffered by antiquaries at that time.

By the terms of his father's will the Heppington estate went to his mother for life and then to him, but he inherited the books, antiquities and other collections immediately in 1776 at the age of 27. His father had inculcated into him his own passion for antiquarian matters, and along with his skills in legal practice he was a practised draughtsman. Many draft layouts of illustrations for a folio publication, not dissimilar to Douglas's *Nenia Britannica*, together with finished watercolours of the objects his father had discovered and finds from the 1730 excavations on Chartham Down, are at the Society of Antiquaries. The latter he painted at Mystole House before the Fagg family collections were dispersed, and later inserted them into his father's manuscript notebook, thereby preserving them for posterity in the absence of the original objects.

One might wonder why, after a good education and expensive legal training, he did not proceed to a full career in the law. Had his father overspent in excavating and feared that the son might copy him, or was one son practising as a solicitor enough? Might

---

[1] KHLC: U771/C9/1

Henry Godfrey instead enter the church, or think that his inheritance and interests did not necessitate full-time work and that he was far better suited to putting back into good order the estate that his father had allowed to diminish to what it was now? Perhaps he also harboured plans to arrange the collections of antiquities with a view to publication, his father's testamentary injunctions notwithstanding, and augment such a work with watercolours and paintings, of which he was such a skilled exponent.

He was generally healthier than his father, but although he too would suffer the tribulations of gout, he was more affable and thus better-known to other antiquaries, growing to be the intimate counsellor and brother-labourer of both James Douglas and Edward Hasted. From time to time he would add objects to his father's collections, but he wrote little and so remains a shadowy figure today. He seems to have lived almost continuously at Heppington, looking after it for his mother in her widowhood and enjoying a quiet country life in managing the estate, seldom travelling much further than Rochester, where he was part of a literary circle, and occasionally to London. In 1790 he purchased the manor of Lower Hardres from Henry Coope of Nottinghamshire, a court baron still being regularly held there. A substantial picture collection added to his daily pleasures. His father's early death bequeathed him property and possessions which his practical education made him ideally suited to take care of, but which would soon be gradually encumbered with increasing debts and funeral expenses, leading to his selling off all the remaining outlying property, including what remained of family lands at Eltham where two houses raised £400, the *King's Arms* £250, and marshland at Plumstead £600.

One wonders if he could have known the long-term value of his father's work, especially, it has to be admitted, as most of the artefacts were not intrinsically valuable and their significance not yet fully appreciated. The recent sales of the Eltham and Plumstead estates perhaps brought home to him at what cost the collection had been formed, and the fact that neither he nor his brother was sent to Oxford at great expense, but that both rather entered the law, a profession which too often drew their father's litigious tendencies and cost him hard-earned income, is perhaps reflected in Henry Godfrey's keenness to restore and maintain a family estate which his father had allow to languish and disintegrate.

In 1779 he married at St Mildred's, Canterbury, Susan, the only daughter of Richard Sandys Esq, four years his junior, who brought with her shares in the Northbourne estate, inherited from her father (and concerning which trunks and portmanteaus of writings and receipts arrived at Heppington in 1789, 'the keys of these several boxes given to Mr Faussett upon an iron ring'). They were happily married for a decade before her premature death at the age of 36, leaving eight children, the youngest a tiny infant. She was described as being of delicate health with a loveable personality, never once leaving Kent in her many visits and calls, undertaken mostly on horseback. Two years before her death, her children were being amused by Lieutenant James Sandys, her brother, who had instituted 'The Honourable and most flattering Order of Merit for the encouragement of good behaviour in all his nephews and nieces at Heppington'. He was the patron, their father the president, and the children elevated to knights and ladies of the order, each proudly wearing a garter blue ribbon with a silver medal attached. Susan kept a diary for the duration of her short married life, much of it of a domestic nature, but we do learn that she regularly hosted the 'Oyster Club' for supper followed by cards, and in March 1789 went with her husband into Canterbury to see the illuminations on display for the King's recovery.

A man with as many commitments as Henry Godfrey had would have little chance of looking after eight children, the eldest only nine when he was widowed. However, this he seems to have managed, probably with the help of the family, until he remarried in 1798 at St Martin's, Canterbury, an heiress four years his senior, Sarah, the daughter of Fettiplace Nott Esq, of Marston Hall, Warwickshire, the High Steward of Lichfield. She predeceased him by nine years, Henry Godfrey himself dying in 1825, when his daughter-in-law noted in her diary that she had now lost her 'poor dear father-in-law'. His will[2] reveals that his six surviving younger children were entitled by virtue of a settlement made with their mother to £2000 and to her shares in the Northbourne estate, as well as a further £6000. His eldest son and heir, Godfrey, now 45, was to inherit Heppington and the estates scattered around Nackington, Petham, Lower Hardres, Upper Hardres and St Mary Bredin, Canterbury. The inheritance was non-specific, making no mention of the library, antiquities and other collections, all of which had been secured by the terms of his father carefully-worded will. A sum of £50 was also left to the Kent & Canterbury Hospital, a very short distance away in St Mary Bredin parish. In all, he is fondly remembered by his descendants as a considerate landlord, an active and kind-hearted magistrate, a zealous and successful promoter of agriculture, benevolent and energetic in all his duties.

His eight children were all born within a decade at Nackington, four of them, curiously, having birthdays in one week in August.

Godfrey Faussett, the eldest son and heir, was born 27 August 1780 (on whom see below).

Eliza Faussett was born 21 August 1781, and died unmarried of a lingering illness in 1819.

Ann Faussett was born 9 November 1782. She remained a spinster and spent the last decade and more of her life as an inmate in the Ticehurst lunatic asylum, where she died in 1862 aged 79.

Susan Faussett was born 19 June 1784 and died unmarried in Canterbury in 1861.

Mary Faussett was born 29 May 1785, and buried, unmarried, at St Giles, Oxford, in 1830.

Robert Faussett was born 30 October 1786. He entered the King's School at Canterbury in 1796 and left in 1799 to embark upon a colourful and adventurous

---

[2] TNA: PROB11/1699

but short life as a midshipman in the East Indies, rising to Lieutenant RN before dying in 1818 aged 32.

Henry Faussett was born 28 August 1788, and followed his elder brother to the King's School from 1797 to 1802. He was trained to be a solicitor with his uncle Bryan, but an early death cut short a promising career when he died at 20 in 1807 and was buried in the family vault at Nackington.

Emma Faussett was born 25 August 1789, lived in Holy Cross parish in Canterbury, and died unmarried in 1850.

Godfrey Faussett (1780-1853)

Today, the numbers of Henry Godfrey Faussett's descendants are considerable, but they all descend from his eldest son (the other seven producing no children) and the next to enter the church, Godfrey (nicknamed 'Muskin') Faussett DD, who was schooled at Ashford, ordained in 1805 and, after his degree at Magdalene College, served his curacy at Holton near Oxford before becoming Vicar of Cropthorne near Evesham. He was Public Examiner of Oxford in 1809 and Bampton Lecturer by 1820; but in 1827, no doubt by now well-connected, he was elected Lady Margaret Professor of Divinity at Oxford, a position which carried with it a Canonry of Worcester, commuted in 1840, largely by his own exertions, to that of Christ Church, Oxford. He corresponded with Newman and others and published many pamphlets and leaflets. A few days after his death, the *Morning Herald* in its obituary of 30 June 1853 stated that,

> During the past twenty years more especially the name of Dr Faussett has been associated with the most formidable dangers to which the University has been exposed [...] Dr Faussett stood forward, the bold and hearty uncompromising champion of the Church of England, the able vindicator of its creeds and formularies.

Others comments followed: 'Dr Faussett's share in the matter is intelligible; hating the movement in all its parts he struck with the vehemence of a mediaeval zealot'.

Such busy employments meant that he had little time to indulge his hereditary tastes, acting rather as a caretaker of the collections, although he would gladly admit the curious when he was at home. He visited Heppington infrequently, and when he did, in something of a rush. In 1809 he spent Christmas Day in Kent. His return journey involved departing from Faversham on the Thursday morning, breakfasting in Sittingbourne, dining and sleeping in Dartford, and passing through London without stopping on Friday to sleep at High Wycombe, which still left a further 20 miles for Saturday. The coach roads must have been unusually clear, considering the time of year.

In March 1829, when busy at Oxford, a letter was delivered to 'Mr Faussett Esq, Street End, Nackington'. Far away as he was, he could not have been unaware of the current rural unrest surrounding the Swing Riots, and despite the two bracketed phrases, the sketch of a gallows at the bottom of the sheet must have struck a chilling chord in the family:

> Sir, we the determined men for want of work, food and raiment, and owing to the price of bread that we have been this winter just starved but nevertheless we have taken a solemn oath that you farmers (not you in particular) do not bring the corn to market and sell it if not done before a month that we will set fire to the barns and stacks of corn (not yours alone) and slay your sheep and oxen for 20 miles around, for we 12 men of courage will live on you having property. "Live and let live". You farmers have not lost sheep enough, you will lose more before it's done. Reward will be no use for none will split. We are Sir and call ourselves "The Kentish Gang".

Like his father, he married twice, and like his great-grandfather he produced 14 children, ten boys and four girls, seven by each wife. The eldest were born at Holton, three at Harefield, two at Nackington, and the last four at Oxford, a varied route reflecting their eminent father's busy life and career. Four sons would enter the church, one rise high in the army, one (Thomas Godfrey, *q.v.*) become a noted Kent antiquary and FSA who excavated Bifrons at Patrixbourne, and the youngest a civil servant, member of the Inner Temple and Keeper of Oxford University Archives. His will,[3] made in 1851 two years before his death, entrusted his manuscripts to the care and discretion of his eldest son and heir Bryan, also a clerk in holy orders, who also received personal articles from the Canonry House at Christchurch, including plate, watches and trinkets, bibles containing the family registers, and the manuscripts relating to the antiquities (which merited no further description). He was buried at Christ Church, Oxford, his spiritual home for a quarter of a century.

Bryan Faussett (1811-1855)

Godfrey Faussett's second son, but the eldest to survive, was another Bryan, born 20 December 1811 at Holton during his father's curacy. He was very poorly as a teenager in January 1824, causing his mother to keep him away from church to put leeches on his chest for a severe cold and difficulty in breathing. After Bedford Grammar School and the customary two degrees at Corpus Christi, Oxford, he was ordained in 1834 and served his curacy with his father at Cropthorne. He married at 26, but not happily, to Helena Caroline the daughter of Sir John Trevelyan of Nettlecombe Court, Somerset. Divorce was to follow and, it seems, a lessening of ecclesiastical duties, for he was to inherit Heppington, if only briefly, at 42, and die a year later when living in Herne Bay. His two small children were entrusted to a chronological succession of younger brothers, excepting William, the Army Major, who 'from his professional pursuits may be absent from the country'. He was buried in the family vault at the crossing in St Mary's Nackington in 1855, occupying the last available space.

---

[3] TNA: PROB11/2177

Godfrey Trevelyan Faussett (1840-1915)

Son of the above, Godfrey Trevelyan Faussett, was born prematurely on 28 February 1840 at the Royal Western Hotel in Bristol. Sometime of the Gloucestershire Artillery Volunteers, he rose to be a Major in the 76th Regiment. On retirement he took a farmhouse at Corwen, practising his considerable skills as a botanist, fisherman and lover of shooting. After his death he was taken back to Nackington to be buried alongside so many others of his ancestors. It was to him that fell the task of selling Heppington in 1874.

Bryan Faussett (1753-1808)

The antiquary Bryan's second child, Bryan, was born 11 April 1753 at Kingston. That same month his father paid £1 11s. 6d. for his christening cake. Such was his father's pride in the venerable Godfrey surname that it would be his second son, and not his first, who would carry his own name into a third generation. His elder brother groomed to be the heir, the young boy was destined to enter the law, and not the church as one might have expected; there was no other son who might become a clergyman, but Faussett, perhaps reflecting on his own circumstances, was thinking more of financial security for his son than spiritual progression. He was duly sent to Ashford Grammar School in July 1761, his father paying the Rev'd Mr Barrett the entrance fee of two guineas. Half-a-crown pocket-money would be his occasional reward when he saw his father. He entered the King's School at Canterbury in 1766, upon payment of five guineas for entrance and an initial half-year's schooling and boarding for £14 13s.

When Bryan junior was just 12 in 1765, his father was corresponding with W. Chamberlayne, a London solicitor, who opined that 'I should Endeavour to Convince him that it is as much for his Interest as mine to apply himself to business'. A month later in July 1765 Chamberlayne wrote again to Faussett in a more encouraging manner:

> You certainly do right in letting Master Faussett apply himself to the Law hands though there is no reason for his deserting Greek & Latin, for though he may have enough & more than most of our Profession, Yet depend on it, it will always be of Use to him. My constant usual Forms have been 200 guineas & if Master Faussett was to come, the best time would be after Christmas as articling a Young Gentleman in Summar is apt to give him an Habit of idleness at the first Setting out the long vacation.

Bryan left the King's School in 1768 and entered legal training. In May 1769 Thomas Collins, a proctor at Doctors' Commons, wrote to his father approving the behaviour of young Bryan, but declared himself unable to continue their five-year contract over the boy's clerkship as he feared such a service would not enable him to become a proctor. Somebody else would have to be found, and in June it was to be Mr

William Geering who would take the teenager for 200 guineas, but could not offer board or lodging. Geering was vouchsafed of good character by his colleague Dr Thomas Bever who said that 'the young Man's behaviour is very good, that he shews a very diligent attachment to business, and gives hopes of answering the warmest expectations of an affectionate Parent'.

With his son's articling now under way, in July Faussett had to estimate what the expenses might be after seven years' clerkship, taking into account that Geering's attendance fees on the future proctor's admission would be £70-80, a high sum in his opinion, and one which he swiftly communicated to Doctors' Commons, adding that 'but others have paid 200g, and I can take no clerk for less', and so, ever careful, he finished by securing the guarantee of a refund if Geering were to die before the conclusion of the term.

Faussett now approached Dr Bever about securing a foundation for young Bryan at Oxford. Bever replied, regretting that he was a stranger to most of the electors, but would go to Oxford and speak in favour of his son. The outcome was sadly negative, for a Thomas Smith of Messrs Smith & Williams of Dartford wrote to Faussett of their regrets over '… your son's disappointment at Oxford. We could be happy in so good a young man, but have already too many young ones to do him justice'. Faussett must have felt this keenly, being so attached to Oxford himself. Bryan junior seems to have been withdrawn from his London training, as in March 1770 he was articled to John Hinde, an attorney at Milton-next-Sittingbourne, at a cost to his father of £150 plus duty of £7 10s. 0d, followed soon by further expenses of £12 2s. incurred by his son on business in London, all of which were generously repaid to the newly-fledged solicitor, including the costs of the journey. Now set up for his future career, the young Bryan was given a silver watch-chain and seal, a pair of boots and a 'case of drawers' to see him on his way. Once fully trained he set up in practice in Sittingbourne, remaining there for the rest of his life, and owning a freehold house and land. In addition to his legal work, he was also appointed clerk to the Canterbury Militia Division in 1803. The poll books show him as also owning a freehold house and land at Bearsted, occupied in 1790 by a man named Usher.

In 1778 he married Dorothy, the daughter of the Rev'd John Smith, Vicar of nearby Borden, and Rector of Skirbeck in Lincolnshire. A frequent visitor to Heppington, he died 23 September 1808 at 55, the same age as his father, and was buried in the south transept at St Michael's, Sittingbourne. The position is marked, not by a chaste white marble Grecian tablet as would have befitted the date and his social standing (although the testimony is: 'an affectionate husband and indulgent father'), but by a large black ledger stone, very similar to that of his father save that the lettering is of decidedly inferior quality. He left £1627 each to his widow and two daughters. His widow Dorothy followed her third daughter down to Bideford and was buried there in 1831 aged 74.

They had four children, irregularly spaced:
Elizabeth, baptised 24 July 1781 and died January 1800, unmarried.

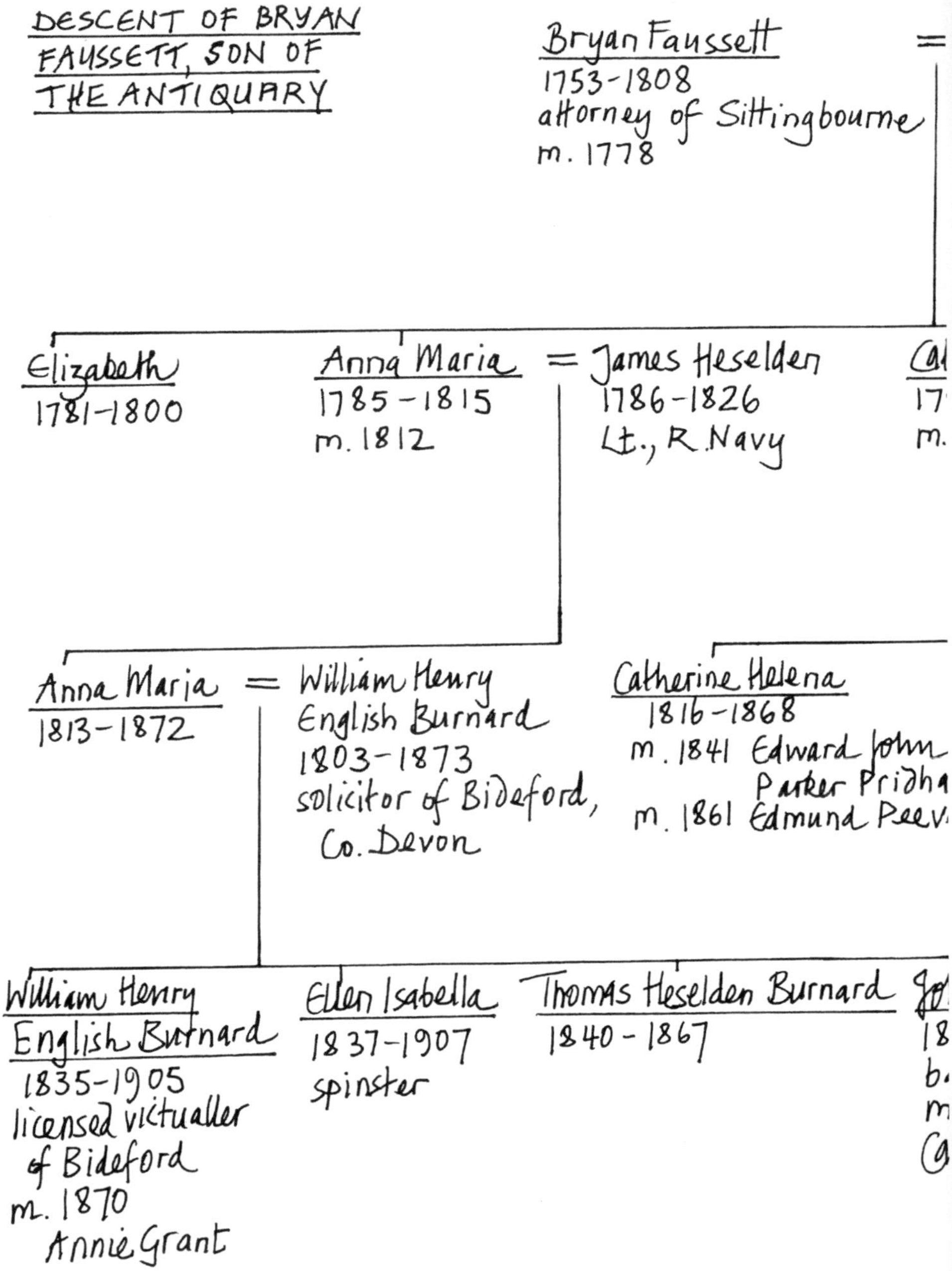

DESCENT OF BRYAN
FAUSSETT, SON OF
THE ANTIQUARY

Bryan Faussett   =
1753-1808
attorney of Sittingbourne
m. 1778

Elizabeth
1781-1800

Anna Maria   = James Heselden
1785-1815   1786-1826
m. 1812   Lt., R. Navy

Ca
17
m.

Anna Maria   = William Henry
1813-1872   English Burnard
                      1803-1873
                      solicitor of Bideford,
                      Co. Devon

Catherine Helena
1816-1868
m. 1841 Edward John
            Parker Pridha
m. 1861 Edmund Peev.

William Henry
English Burnard
1835-1905
licensed victualler
of Bideford
m. 1870
   Annie Grant

Ellen Isabella
1837-1907
spinster

Thomas Heselden Burnard
1840-1867

Jo
18
b.
m
Ca

Figure 42. The descent of Bryan Faussett, son of the antiquary.

= Dorothy,
daughter of Rev'd John Smith
1757-1831

'herine Helena = Francis William Pridham   Bryan Faussett
92-1858   1775-1831   1797-1798
1815   surgeon of Bideford,
              Co. Devon

Mary Elizabeth   Frances Isabella = Thomas   Anna
1818-1855   1821-1885   Summerfield   Maria
   spinster   m. 1852   Hilton   1824-1853
m   Twyman   spinster
er   1824-1889
                                   Captain, Indian Navy

hm Edward Burnard Catherine Mary Minnie Helen   Francesca
43-1904   1855-1942   Rose Ann   Helena
ank clerk   spinster   1858-1930   1865-1919
. 1878   religious   spinster
therine Manning Williams

Anna Maria, baptised 1 September 1785 and married in 1812 James Heselden, Lieutenant RN of a family from Barton-on-Humber, who died in 1826 at Canterbury. She died 9 April 1815 and was buried alongside her father. Their only child, Anna Maria Heselden born in 1813, followed her aunt down to Devon, and married a Bideford solicitor named William Henry English Burnard.

Catherine Helena, baptised 12 October 1792 and married in 1815 Francis William Pridham, a surgeon, also of Bideford, whither they returned to produce four daughters. She died in 1858.

Bryan, baptised 8 August 1797 and died the following year.

Charles Faussett (1754-1755)

Faussett's third child was Charles, the first occurrence of that name in the family. He was born at Bishopsbourne 2 March 1754, the delivery undertaken by a Mr Loftie who charged four guineas. At his baptism three weeks later the Rev'd Mr Tucker was paid a guinea. He survived until just after his first birthday, when his father now paid the Rev'd John Gosling 10s. 6d. for the burial service and John Couchman £1 5s. 6d. for the burial fees. Faussett also paid Ann Clarenbold a guinea 'for her extraordinary trouble and attendance upon Charley during his illness and before it.'

Elizabeth Faussett (1756-1789)

For a man as uxorious as Faussett, and still mourning the death of his last child, the gift of an only daughter must have been a joyous event. Elizabeth Faussett (frequently called Bessy or 'Spickct') was born 11 February 1756 at Bishopsbourne. She was educated at a Canterbury boarding school run by a Mrs Taylor of St Margaret's parish, her father paying two guineas for entrance in June 1767. A succession of private tutors lectured her in writing and casting accounts, amongst other things, before she left at the age of 14, then to start learning the harpsichord, and be presented with a silver watch and chain for which cost her father £3 14s. 6d. She had been inoculated three months prior to arrival at the school, Faussett no doubt solicitous for his daughter's health now that she was away from the rural safety and seclusion of Heppington. She had a happy adolescence, five shillings each birthday from her father, a good social life and several suitors, the first of whom was a future cousin by marriage (probably Richard Tylden, Rector of Milstead and Frinsted), to whom she had been introduced by her brother Bryan.

There was to be no love-match. She recorded in her account book for June 1781:

Received my letter &c from [Anuntor?] in return for his which I had sent back by Bry and with them a letter that has harrowed my heart. Oh, why did I listen to my mother &c &c to accept Mr Tylden whom I had refused on A's account but by their over persuasions did at last accept, and as I then had and still have a very good opinion of him, vainly hoped, to [...] buried all thoughts of A in oblivion, but the vanity of that hope, this letter alas proved and told me that I am a wretch. But I am doomed to be the wife of Tylden and of course unhappy, yet I will try all in my power to be a good one and look on death as my only refuge.

In the following December she wrote:

Dear Bry: As I find Mr Tylden has made me an offer with settlements in a letter to Godfrey, and as I can never (after what has passed) entertain a thought of accepting him, I think it is highly incumbent upon me to let him know my sentiments on it as soon as possible. Therefore shall be much obliged to you to tell him from me as soon as you can that I have looked on our engagement as at an end ever since he was last at Heppington and as I can never think of renewing the connection, I hope he will lay aside all further thoughts of it and let the subject entirely drop. I heartily wish him well and happy, and a much better wife than I have the vanity to think of ever making.[4]

Around 1785 Thomas Bland, the brother of her future husband, wrote expressing his continuing love, even after his distress at the rupture of their engagement and her preference for his brother, signing off as 'Your once dear Tom'.

Over the summer of 1786 that brother, William Bland, would write often from Sittingbourne to Heppington, ever anxious to assure her that after some years of estrangement his fortune was now sufficient to keep them above want, 'his feelings for her having lain dormant for many years'. Elizabeth replied and expressed pleasure at seeing him again:

I flatter myself that my heart has never yet been another's, though I blush to own my hand was all but gone, thank God however I escaped, tho you had very near been the cause of my making a sacrifice of myself to please the ambition of some of my relations, a sacrifice that I can't think of to this moment without the greatest horror.[5]

Elizabeth had known the Bland family from at least as early as 1775, for in that year her father wrote to her when she was staying with the Rev'd Thomas Bland at Tunstall, the father of the two brothers. Faussett was relieved she had arrived safely at Tunstall and was among good friends. He was obliged to Mr Bland for all his civilities to his daughter, and in particular for his requesting 'your so long continuance there as a month'. However, this could not go on, and she was permitted to stay another fortnight and no longer, after which her brother Bryan would conduct her home. His paternal concern for a daughter not yet 20 was evident, and he duly signed off, 'Dear Bessey, your most affectionate father, Br Faussett'.

Elizabeth kept a minutely detailed account book[6] of her income and expenditure during the decade leading up to her marriage, all written in a tiny and neat hand. The income was almost entirely derived from her annuity which was paid often

---

[4] KHLC: U771/C9/8
[5] KHLC: U771/C11/2
[6] KHLC: U771/A28

in small amounts totalling between £110 and £176 annually, and was balanced by outgoings of between £21 and £31, leaving ample funds for her many and varied interests. One of the earliest expenses is a guinea in March 1776 for a mourning ring in memory of her father who had died on the eve of her 20th birthday.

There were regular expenses for such quotidian matters as canary and bird seed, poultry, her chestnut horse named *Forrester* of seven years and 14 hands (bought from her mother for £8), and later a bay mare of eight years and 15 hands, the cleaning of her watch, turnpike charges, a half-crown after the communion, the state lottery, being let of blood, postage for correspondence and brown paper for parcels, concert and theatre tickets, card assemblies (from which she had regular winnings), sundry gifts to boys and men and the poor, drinks for the coachmen (who often stabled her horses at the *Fountain Inn* in Canterbury) and an auction at Hardres Court. She often purchased toys for small children, and was not averse to lending her brothers money at interest. The more feminine articles included frequent bills from the shoemaker, milliner and hairdresser, needlework and clothes-making (including 12 feet of whalebone), perfumes, flowers, a book on the maxims of whist, eatables at the pastry cook's and numerous excursions to Schnebblie's in Canterbury.

[There is an antiquarian connection with this last-mentioned emporium: Jacob Schnebblie (1760-1792) followed his father into the confectionery trade, firstly in Canterbury and later at Hammersmith, but then abandoned it to become a drawing master. He executed many of the drawings for Richard Gough's *Sepulchral Monuments of Great Britain*, and also engraved plates for the publication of the spectacular Cornish Trewhiddle hoard, no doubt finding such work more remunerative than baking. One wonders whether he and Faussett would have exchanged antiquarian news whilst eating and drinking in Canterbury, or whether Elizabeth brought back snippets of information after each excursion.]

After an attachment of some 15 years, Elizabeth was married at 11am on 2 January 1787 at Sittingbourne to William Bland, the groom's financial worries now past, following his father's death in 1776. After the wedding there was a large dinner party at Heppington and a still larger crowd for a dance which went on to well past midnight. At this time William was living at Trott's Hall in Sittingbourne and farming 100 acres there, together with the greater part of his grandmother Elizabeth Tylden's moiety of the Hartlip estate, of which he had recently taken possession. How happy Faussett would have been to see his only daughter so comfortably settled!

There would be one child to the marriage before, tragically, Elizabeth died in 1789 at 32 and was buried in the Osborne family chapel at Hartlip church. Her sister-in-law Susan Faussett recorded in her diary that 'Mrs Bland expired at 5pm so calmly that she more ceased to live than died'. She predeceased her husband by 44 years, leaving him to raise their only child William Bland, junior, who was born at Sittingbourne 21 January 1788, and would become the heir to his father's estate, a magistrate, and (if only Faussett could have known) something of an antiquary in his own right.

Of his antiquarian activities, more shortly, but a digression is now necessary to say something of his interesting pedigree with which, displaying its many Kentish lines and armorial bearings, Faussett would no doubt have been fascinated.

William Bland senior, who married Elizabeth Faussett, was born at Sittingbourne in 1752, the fourth of the seven children of the Rev'd Thomas Bland and his wife Mary Tylden. Thomas Bland was Vicar of Sittingbourne from 1742, and Rector of Little Warley in Essex, until his death in 1776 when he was then resident at Tunstall House, just to the south of Sittingbourne. There he enjoyed such creature comforts as extensive lands planted with walnuts, apple- and other fruit-trees, and a scholarly library with manuscripts. His origins around 1715 have not been traced, but it is his wife's parents of Tylden and Osborne who are of greater interest. Her father was Richard Tylden of Hogshaw's Court, the manor house of Milstead, descended from a venerable Kentish family, long-established around Wormshill, Tunstall and Milstead, the Tylden chapel of the last-mentioned church fairly overflowing with their monuments. He was another gentleman enjoying a fine library which went, probably, to his eldest son, another Richard whose 'mind was highly cultivated; ever ardent in the pursuit of literature', and one from whom a younger son, son-in-law, grandson and great-grandson would be successive rectors of the parish of Milstead for over 70 years. Like many other families concerned with inheritance, they augmented their surname, one branch becoming Osborne Tylden and another Tylden-Pattenson.

William Bland's grandmother was Elizabeth Osborne who would ultimately inherit, and then devise, Hartlip Place by fascinating and convoluted family relationships. The Osbornes had been at Denne Hill and elsewhere in the parish back to at least the fifteenth century, visibly evidenced by brasses in the Osborne chapel at St Michael's church. Anciently they had been at Nutts in Leysdown and Eastchurch on Sheppey according to Faussett's own notes on the subject. Elizabeth was the daughter of Thomas Osborne, a major in the militia, and the third of his eight children by two wives (a third marriage was childless). By 1719, six of her siblings had died either as infants or survived only into their twenties and thirties, leaving no male heirs. And so at 32, having lost her last brother and now comfortably married to Richard Tylden, she came into the Hartlip estate, enjoying it for 47 years until she died in 1766, 'much advanced in years'. Her husband had died three years previously, leaving a silver flagon of one quart valued at £15 to Milstead church, and to his wife 'ten books from my library as she shall choose.'

She had produced nine children, six dying young with no male heirs. This left Hannah and Richard, both of whom now died just months before their mother, and so the last surviving child, Mary, already married to Thomas Bland and with a family of her own, inherited under the terms of Elizabeth's will.[7] The probate document is a lengthy affair, requesting burial in Hartlip chancel (alongside her father and

---

[7] KHLC: PRC17/97/380

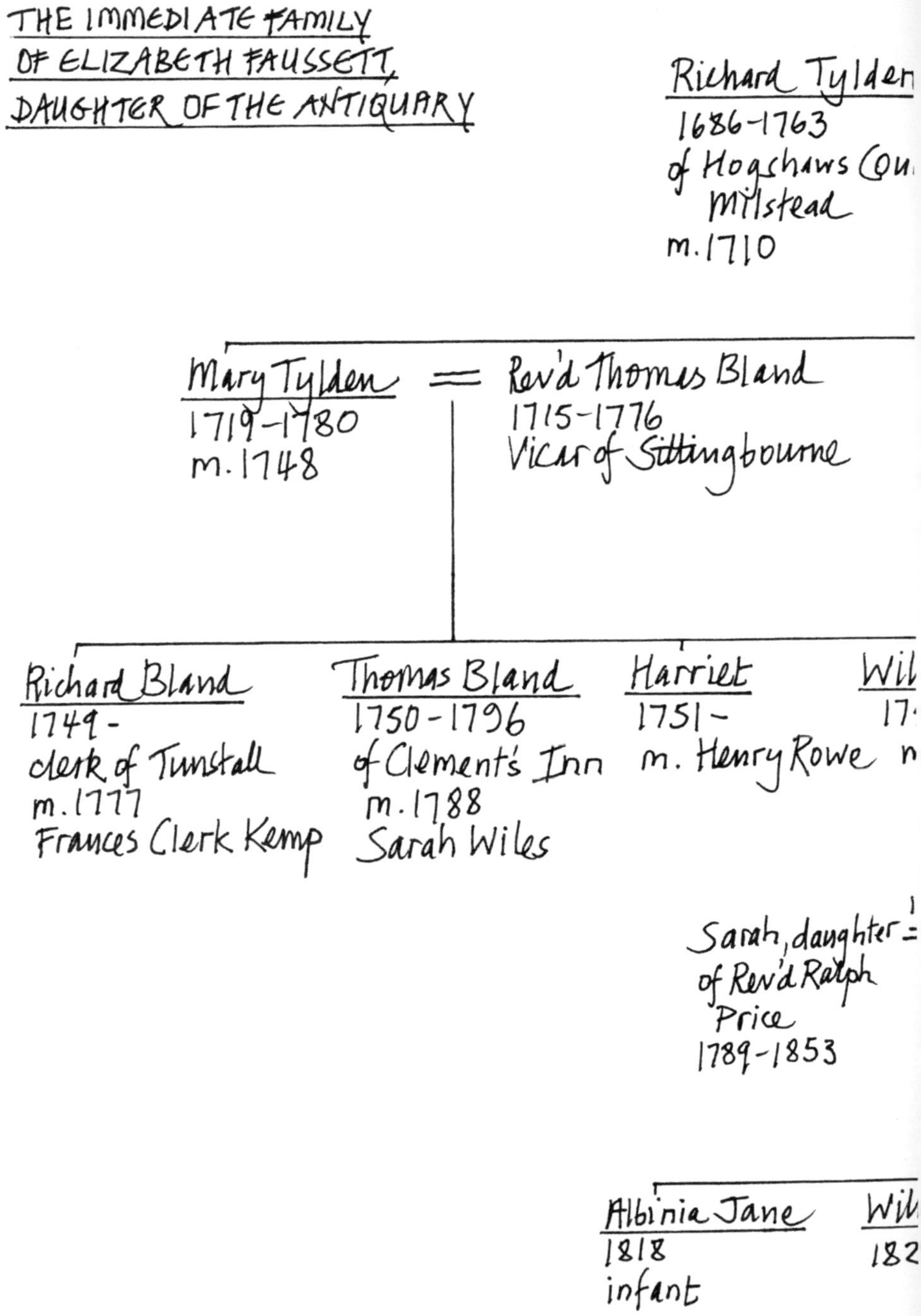

THE IMMEDIATE FAMILY
OF ELIZABETH FAUSSETT,
DAUGHTER OF THE ANTIQUARY

Richard Tylden
1686-1763
of Hogshaws (Ou.
Milstead
m. 1710

Mary Tylden = Rev'd Thomas Bland
1719-1780   1715-1776
m. 1748   Vicar of Sittingbourne

Richard Bland   Thomas Bland   Harriet   Wil
1749-   1750-1796   1751-   17·
clerk of Tunstall of Clement's Inn m. Henry Rowe n
m. 1777   m. 1788
Frances Clerk Kemp Sarah Wiles

Sarah, daughter[1] =
of Rev'd Ralph
Price
1789-1853

Albinia Jane   Wil
1818   182
infant

Figure 43. The immediate family of Elizabeth Faussett, daughter of the antiquary.

L ═ Elizabeth, daughter of
Major Thomas Osborne of Hartlip Place
rt, 1687-1766

8 others, all predeceasing

liam Bland ═ Elizabeth   Caroline John   Elizabeth
52-1835   Faussett   1753   1755   1757-
า. 1787   1756-1789   infant   infant

817
═   (1) William Bland   (2) ═   Isabella, daughter of
      1788-1869   1856   Major Charles Irvine
      antiquary who rebuilt   1799-1894
      Hartlip Place and
      excavated Hartlip Roman Villa

liam Osborne Bland
.0-1841

mother), a plain coffin without plates or handles, and that she should be carried in a hearse but without coach or attendants save the person nursing her in her last illness – ah, how intimate last wishes can be! The pall bearers received 5*s*. each and the minister a guinea. Mindful of her grandchildren, each would have 5*s*., as would the servants then in her employ, instead of the customary bequest of gloves. After disposing of other sundry lands, Mary Bland would receive the Hartlip estate, with other lands descended from Elizabeth's father, via her late husband, now going to the Bland grandchildren. It is easy to see now the means by which William Bland had become secure enough to guarantee his future marriage to Elizabeth Faussett.

William Bland (1788-1869)

We may now return to William Bland junior, the budding antiquary and great-grandson of Bryan Faussett. At an early age he began to secure a reputation by writing scientific works, labouring on in the patrimonial seclusion of Hartlip Place. In his spare time he enjoyed drumming, a pleasure that would sustain him into old age. A sudden collapse in health while still a schoolboy led to withdrawal from formal education and the beginning of other more practical things. He made carts and ploughs, quadrant levels, an orrery and an Archimedean screw, and grew trees from seed on his lands. A second failure of health precluded taking a degree at Caius College, after which he studied medicine in Edinburgh before returning home to become an agriculturalist.

In 1813 he drew up plans for the rebuilding of Hartlip Place, the heating system devised by him, and the 138-feet deep tank and well dug with his own hands. Books followed on agriculture and architecture whilst he grew ever more skilled in farm cultivation and improving machinery, leading to his constructing a lock for granaries and stables (the principle ultimately to be taken over by Chubb's for their safes). In 1837 he rebuilt the chancel of St Michael's Hartlip, his responsibility as the owner of Hartlip Place, and in 1841, after negotiating a purchase from a man named Macnamara for £7900, he took down the old Yauger manor house, which stood beside the farm of the same name, and re-erected it as the splendid Queen Down Warren House in a similarly eponymous situation. The work was done extremely quickly, for within five months one Thomas Hales had moved in. The house would be lived in by various later members of the Godfrey-Faussett-Osborne family in the twentieth century.

His principal claim to antiquarian fame is the Roman villa at Dane Field, Hartlip. Its existence had long been known, but it was never properly explored until he supervised the excavation. At the time Charles Roach Smith opined that its considerable size, substantial buttressing, hypocaust heating and two kinds of baths, of admirable construction and splendid preservation, warranted the possibility of its being one of the Roman *mansiones* between Canterbury and Rochester, adding that the artefacts found in it were generally consonant with that of a country villa of the better kind. The villa brought many visitors to Hartlip, no doubt a great curiosity in the area. Bland exhibited the finds to the Kent Archaeological Society and was thanked at its 1858 inaugural meeting for his 'kind and liberal donation of Roman antiquities' to what is now the society's Charles Museum, the assorted fossils going to other larger repositories.

He died suddenly in 1869, helping the antiquary George Payne FSA with a water-gauge. Payne would later proclaim his indebtedness to Bland for his own inspiration in archaeology, having been invited as a boy to Hartlip to see the Roman villa, then just recently explored, and indeed Payne's boyish enthusiasm so impressed Bland that he introduced him to Charles Roach Smith who happened to be at Hartlip at the time. There were many bequests to churches and schools, for although Bland married twice, only one child, William Osborne Bland survived infancy to die at 21, his memorial tablet in Hartlip church describing him as 'amiable in disposition and exemplary in conduct'.

The other salient point of Bland's will concerned the family surname. A year after his death, on 24 June 1870, his first cousin once removed, Henry Godfrey Faussett, the fifth son of Godfrey Faussett (the Lady Margaret Professor of Divinity at Oxford), in deference to the venerable surname of Godfrey, before long to be borne by increasing numbers of younger family members as an additional forename, changed the family surname to the double-barrelled (and, one hopes, potentially less confusing) Godfrey-Faussett. That surname survives to the present in all direct male family descendants excepting those who descend from Henry Godfrey Faussett himself who, by the terms of Bland's will which meant that he would inherit Hartlip Place in 1871, adopted the triple-barrelled surname of Godfrey-Faussett-Osborne, so perpetuating the Osbornes of Hartlip, now associated with that parish for well over 500 years. Bland gave some leeway on the precise form of nomenclature, allowing the Osborne element to be used either alone or in addition to the usual surname 'but so that the name of Osborne shall be the last and principal name', and also stipulating in similar fashion that the Osborne arms should be used either alone or quartered with the other family arms. Modern descendants today pronounce the Faussett element as 'Fossett'.

Thomas Godfrey Faussett (1829-1877)

It remains to say something of one other antiquarian great-grandson of Bryan Faussett, and one who, fittingly, had reflected deeply on the legacy of his great-grandfather. Younger brother to the above Henry Godfrey Faussett, and eighth son of the Lady Margaret Professor of Divinity, Thomas Godfrey Faussett was born 19 September 1829 at Oxford, the first child of his father originating in the city of dreaming spires after a short family residence back at Heppington. He grew up around College Green in Worcester where his father was then a prebendary. He won a scholarship to, and was a fellow of, Corpus Christi, where he secured a good law degree and was called to the bar in 1863. He initially specialised in conveyancing, and then in turns became a junior sophist, a barrister, afterwards proceeding to a magistracy and position at the district probate registry in Canterbury upon his return to the ancestral county. Adding to these duties an auditorship to the Dean and Chapter, he lived latterly in the cathedral precincts, his health fading and overcome by a creeping paralysis (starting in his thumbs) which would allow him never to hold a pen again (except for signing), confine him to his chair, and take him at the age of 47. He was buried in Nackington churchyard in 1877 under an old yew tree of his own choice.

But such a short life did not mean an empty or a lazy one. His venerable grandfather's wide-ranging interests early enthused him to love manuscripts and relics of the past, leading to a fellowship of the Society of Antiquaries at just 30. By 1850 he had completed the family genealogy, working from his great-grandfather Bryan's notes, and then removed himself to Newfoundland for two years to act as resident tutor to the sons of the governor. In 1863 he became honorary secretary of the Kent Archaeological Society for ten years, a post to which he gave his zeal and time, relinquishing it only because of ill-health. A position on its editorial committee and then a vice-presidency would follow. He was a clever Latin versifier and a writer of hymns and epigrams in that language as well as the vernacular, all the while only too keen to emulate his grandfather's tastes for research. Described as an inexorable taskmaster, not so much to others as to himself, 'it came to pass that he often laboured that others might idle … his mental energy overcame every obstacle, so accurate was his memory, and so distinct were his views.'

Ensconced by 1866 in early retirement in his comfortable rooms within the shadow of the cathedral, he surrounded himself with the books and manuscripts of three generations of antiquarian ancestors, and with family portraits, paintings and Anglo-Saxon relics in abundance. In 1870 he alerted the Society of Antiquaries to the fact that the government had purchased a site in Maidstone for the town post office, and the consequent demolition of the pargeted Astley House in the High St.

Increasing illness did not impede industry until relatively late. He contributed often to *Archaeologia Cantiana* and published much else besides on matters as diverse as the great cruciform foundations at Richborough, the laws of treasure-trove, the Gates of Boulogne at Hardres Court, glass at Nettlestead church and a history of Canterbury down to the Domesday survey. His *magnum opus* was a description of his 1867 carefully recorded excavation (on behalf of the Kent Archaeological Society) of the Anglo-Saxon cemetery of Bifrons at Patrixbourne, accompanied by many engravings of the artefacts from the 100 or more graves. Near the end of his life he devoted much time to overseeing the restoration of Adisham church, where he was ultimately commemorated by a stained-glass window and a suitably inscribed (ie, in Latin) brass memorial plate, penned by Archdeacon Denison. He married in his mid-thirties, and 'walked into love through an open window.' His widow Lucy survived him 58 years. Their only child, Edmund Godfrey Faussett, received his first name in honour of the distant collateral ancestor Sir Edmund Berry Godfrey, the famous magistrate, found murdered with a sword run through him, in a ditch on Primrose Hill in 1678.

In the appendix to *Inventorium Sepulchrale* are recorded Thomas Godfrey Faussett's thoughts on its illustrious author and his style.[8] He considered it generally cool, and that it did not often (with a few notable exceptions) reveal the intense enthusiasm which clearly pervaded his great-grandfather's work; the boyish excitement in overseeing the opening of barrows; the keenness in sifting every crumb of earth; the partial success in enthusing (at least some of) his labourers; the bonhomie when they worked well and the anger when they flagged; the rage and exasperation when vases or dishes were accidentally broken; the animating of the men by sometimes seizing a pickaxe himself, thereby setting no mean example when ridden by gout and infirmity. His generally good humour and generous rates of pay were more remembered than the occasional outbreaks of wrath, and his cottagers rejoiced when freedom from the gout gave the signal for another digging for 'the Squire'.

The curse of the gout had plagued Bryan Faussett for a quarter of a century, all the while increasing in frequency and intensity around the whole of his body, and finally settling in the stomach – but who could have guessed at such a thing when enjoying his firm and clear handwriting, the soundness of his arguments and the vigour of his style? Surely he must have known that death was not far away, and thus spared no effort to commit to posterity the precious details of what he had for so long laboured over. His diligence, his eagerness in investigating, collecting, hoarding – the quintessential and peculiar antiquarian traits – his consummate care and skill in classifying and applying what he had discovered, and, perhaps above all, his clear and extended view of the then infant science of archaeology.

Such praise notwithstanding, he regretted how little the family had had to show for all the time, labour and money expended by Bryan Faussett in his lifelong passion, asserting that:

> Everyone of experience in archaeology knows how expensive an amusement it is, especially when carried to the length of engaging single-handed in excavations and collections as extensive as his were; and though we, his descendants, are justly proud of his labours and fame, we may perhaps be forgiven for feeling that there is very little to show for the number of acres spent upon it; and for wishing that he had spared more of that energy and practical wisdom which we trace in his works, to the management and preservation of his hereditary property.

Other family members were probably in agreement if all that remained were the diaries a few really valuable items in the collections, and Heppington in a diminished condition, the former outlying lands of a once-prosperous estate long since sold off to fund their ancestor's impassioned hobby.

Today, we might not concur, for Faussett's excavations remain immensely important in giving us so much information about those mainly 7th-century graves

<hr>

[8] *Inv. Sep.*: 201 ff.

which would otherwise have been obliterated and gone unrecorded. Gilton would have been quarried out, the Kingston barrows progressively eroded and perhaps utterly destroyed by the widening of the A2 at a time when rescue archaeology was of little effect. One might therefore claim Faussett not only as an archaeologist, but as a rescue archaeologist, and a pioneering one at that. His finds in their totality represent an important control sample, and a large one indeed, of what Kentish Anglo-Saxon burials of their period were really like. There have been no comparable excavations of such sites on a similar scale since: now that the barrows are all gone, the time has passed. Faussett spent freely of his patrimony and time in order to bequeath to his heirs archaeological riches of incomparable value.

Biographies

The history of English antiquarianism over half a millennium encompasses a rich and broad sweep of fascinating, colourful and often brilliant scholars. Not all are directly germane to the narrative of this book, but it is hoped that the inclusion of summary lives of a representative selection will add greatly to the reader's general enjoyment and background understanding of the subject. Much fuller details with be found in the *Oxford Dictionary of National Biography*, on which the following are based and used by permission of Oxford University Press.

AGARD, Arthur (1535/6-1615) was one of the members of the Elizabethan Society of Antiquaries, a list from about 1592 in his hand showing a then membership of about 24. As much an archivist as an antiquary, and of Derbyshire origins, he had an energetic and critical mind, well-versed in common law. Greatly concerned with the safe-keeping and good order of documents, he made many copies, abstracts and indexes, and described the enemies of his work as fire, water, rats, mice and, perhaps the most dangerous of all, misplacement by colleagues or searchers. With a small team he constructed an inventory of the contents of the four Westminster treasuries as well as the records of the crown (today's public records). Domesday Book, despite even its Tudor recognition as being priceless, was then regularly kept apart in his own office. Agard realised that the essentially conservative nature of early documents was under threat from the convulsions of Reformation England, especially in religious observance, and that the Middle Ages now needed constant study and interpretation.

ARCHER, Sir Simon (1581-1662) was a Warwickshire man, a magistrate and MP for Tamworth. He collaborated with Dugdale on the *Antiquities of Warwickshire*. His early interests were in his own family history and its manorial holdings, which by 1628 brought him into contact with William Burton, the pivotal figure in a network of Midlands antiquaries. Burton was keen to sponsor a history of Warwickshire to match his own recently published *Description of Leicestershire*, and chose Archer, who in the 1630s set to and gathered information for a general history of the county, but pressure of public duties meant that he finally handed it over to Dugdale.

ASHMOLE, Elias (1617-1692) was an antiquary also much interested in astrology and magic. In the early 1650s he catalogued the famous collections of rarities belonging to the Tradescant family at Lambeth which, on publication in 1656, was the first published catalogue of an English cabinet of curiosities. As he had borne all the expenses himself, the family then donated the collection to him. His interest in heraldry was kindled by meeting Dugdale, whose daughter Elizabeth he married as a widower. In 1658 he catalogued the Bodleian's collection of Roman coins, and in 1660 the King's coins and medals. His interest in the history of the Order of the Garter led to his appointment as Windsor Herald in the same year, and then to the planning of the coronation of Charles II – the most lavish then ever seen. In 1683 he opened the first public museum in Europe to house the Tradescants' and his own curiosities, housed in a purpose-built repository in Oxford; the collections today are mostly the family ones, as his own objects in the Middle Temple were lost in a serious fire in 1679.

ASTLE, Thomas (1735-1803) was a correspondent of Hasted and known, at least by reputation, to Faussett. He was an archivist and assiduous collector of books and manuscripts, and by 1761 was engaged in indexing (and perhaps also writing the valuable introduction to) the Harleian collection at the British Museum which appeared in 1763, the year of his entry to the Society of Antiquaries. That same year the Prime Minister, George Grenville, nominated him, along with Sir Joseph Ayloffe and Dr Ducarel, to report on records in the state paper office, following which a standing commission was set up, paying them £100 each to sort and regularise the materials in that office. In 1766 a Lords committee consulted him about publishing the ancient records of parliament, and the decision was taken to start with printing the rolls. Astle took over in 1770 after a short spell by his father-in-law Philip Morant, but made only slow progress, not even finishing collating the printed sheets with the originals until 1776. Six (unindexed) volumes of the rolls were finally published in 1783, perfectly serviceable by the standards of the time, but far from being a critical edition. He formed outstanding collections of hundreds of charters (42 being pre-conquest), manuscripts and printed books. The manuscripts were sold after his death for £500 to George Grenville, the 1st Marquis of Buckingham, for whom John Soane built a special room at his seat of Stowe House in Buckinghamshire. They were sold again in 1849 for £8000, and yet again in 1879 to the government for £45,000, the Irish items going to the Royal Irish Academy, and the English ones to the British Museum where they remain as the prestigious Stowe collection.

AUBREY, John (1626-1697) was a Wiltshire man who at a young age was inclined to a love of antiquities which led to a fascination with past ways of life and an obsession to record and conserve as much of it as he possibly could. In January 1649 he discovered the megalithic monuments at Avebury, and on Charles II's visit to the West Country in 1663 Aubrey surveyed the site by royal request. The results appeared in *Monumenta Britannica*, a learned discussion of the 'Druid' temples at Stonehenge and Avebury, Roman towns, castles, camps and other military architecture, sepulchral monuments, roads and ditches, coins, urns and much else, all in all an outstanding fieldworker's survey of ancient sites around Britain, many of which have now disappeared or been greatly altered, and making the *Monumenta Britannica* the foundation text of modern archaeology. Aubrey's studies of architectural history were almost unique in their day, and his attempts to delineate the chronology of evolution in building forms would not be surpassed until the early 1800s. More than this, he stands as an important figure in the development of modern historical scholarship by the mass of interspersed comments in the text on the changes over the centuries in prices, weights, dress, customs, beliefs, handwriting and a host of other miscellanea. He spent a decade from 1660 collecting information for an (unpublished) history of Wiltshire, and also gathered material for *The Interpretation of Villare Anglicanum*, the first work devoted entirely to English place names. Many of his achievements went unrecognised by his contemporaries because of his unorthodoxy, and although he took great quantities of notes with accompanying observations and insights, all written in polished prose, he lacked the ability to arrange and edit it into a coherent narrative ready for publication.

BOLTON, Edmund Mary (1574/5-*c*. 1634) was another Catholic (as his middle name suggested) whose religion had a negative effect on his literary career and prosperity, but did not prevent his matriculation in 1589. A Latin versifier, at Cambridge and the Temple he met Selden, Camden, Cotton and other like-minded men. His strengths were English and ancient Roman history, and antiquarianism, especially philology. He participated in the Elizabethan Society of Antiquaries where he was known for his interests in numismatics, genealogy and heraldry. His first full-length work, one of consuming interest to the gentry, was *The Elements of Armories*, dealing with heraldry and coats of arms. Sir Robert Cotton found him work as a kind of research assistant to the tailor turned historian, John Speed. He now conceived a lifelong ambition of writing a new scholarly history of England that went beyond the Elizabethan chroniclers such as John Stow and Speed's own patchwork history and one in which he would stress the writing and not just the reading of history, in particular drawing attention to the need to found new work based on rolls, manuscripts and other materials to be found in the Tower of London and other archives, as well as in the more traditional chronicle sources. He was the chief exponent of the view that the chronicle was an outdated genre; but he did distinguish between the value that mediaeval chroniclers retained as sources and the unsatisfactory character of Elizabethan historians, and, like Francis Bacon, he believed that proper scholarship would produce a perfect history of the kingdom needing no further revision.

BURTON, William (1575-1645) was a pivotal figure in a group of antiquaries operating in the Midlands in the first half of the seventeenth century. Early research into his own family soon gained him a reputation as an authority on all things antiquarian, and he corresponded and exchanged manuscripts widely. His prized possession was Leland's *Itinerary* which he eventually gave to the Bodleian Library. Much delayed because the author deemed it inadequate and in need of further research, his *The Description of Leicestershire* finally appeared in 1622 and was soon declared by Dugdale to be the one work which had sparked his own interest in working on Warwickshire. Although short and sketchy and not important in its own right, it enhanced his reputation and established him as a father-figure to an upcoming generation of local historians, who now acknowledged him as the driving force to produce comparable histories of the other Midland shires. The publication of *Leicestershire* marked a great advance in county history writing: like earlier works it combined observation of local topography and curiosities with an account of the descent and achievements of leading county families; but it set much higher standards of historical scholarship, for as a trained lawyer Burton adopted a sceptical and questioning approach to his source materials, and provided a rudimentary system of referencing. He ranged more widely than before, drawing heavily on the records in the Tower of London as well as deeds and cartularies of the local gentry. The end result still fell some way short of Dugdale's *Warwickshire* in terms of scholarly thoroughness and the completeness of the manorial and family histories, but it was still the most comprehensive county history so far published.

CAMDEN, William (1551-1623), was the pre-eminent antiquary of his time and published his masterpiece *Britannia* in 1586 on his 35th birthday, thereby putting Britain on the map of humanist scholarship. Camden himself travelled widely and thereby developed his own approach to empirical research, as he searched archives and used the original documents that he found. Coupled with this was his skill in marshalling linguistic and philological evidence which, together with artefacts, were his medium for the interpretation of historical and cultural events. His reputation was secure throughout Europe even before *Britannia* was available to the world, so much so that foreign scholars would meet him, and others, including Mercator, would seek his views. The work, of unprecedented originality and authority in its historical description of Britain county by county, was born of a circle of mutual study and collaboration and deep research into original sources, both printed and manuscript. Its runaway success led to a sixth and much-enlarged edition in 1607, and Philemon Holland's English translation three years later. It stood supreme as a cultural icon affecting the national self-image, and although not unique or unheralded, it culminated in and transformed much of the latest work in different historical genres, drawing on traditions that made its achievement not only recognizable but also strikingly new. It documented the ancient pre-Roman British past by drawing on all possible sources, literary and non-literary, including the landscape and physical artefacts, especially numismatics, where he was a pioneer in recognising the existence of coinage in pre-Roman Britain. As an achievement of the highest order, it is to be reckoned as a work of national rather than local history.

COTTON, Sir Robert Bruce (1571-1631) was a politician and the Jacobean antiquary *par excellence*. Born at Conington in Huntingdonshire (where his splendid funerary bust may still be seen), he attended Westminster school where Camden, then headmaster, instilled in him an early interest in scholarly activity. In 1599-1600 he accompanied Camden on a tour of northern England, surveying and collection Roman remains around Hadrian's Wall, much of which went towards the latter's *Britannia*. By now he was already lending to fellow antiquaries books or manuscripts from what would soon be his legendary library of Anglo-Saxon manuscripts, monastic registers, biblical works, genealogies and state papers relating to England's domestic and foreign affairs. Near the end of his life he began to reorganise it, perhaps prompted by the acquisition from Charles I of 12 porrtraits of the Roman emperors from Caesar to Domitian, under whose marble busts the books would be arranged, and are still classified. Such was the library's standing that in about 1602 he was involved in an initiative to place antiquarian research on a more official footing, and so joined in a petition to the crown for a permanent academy housing the Queen's library with his, merged to form a national one. Such a proposal was unfulfilled, possibly because royal ministers saw the growing potential of antiquarian research to cause them political difficulties, especially in a parliament where debate was dominated by the use of precedent to decide issues of the day. Similar fears among those in power perhaps hastened the early demise of the first Society of Antiquaries, the failure of which no doubt encouraged Cotton, who published little under his own name, to look on his own library as an open resource for scholars desirous of undertaking their own research and publishing.

D'EWES, Sir Simonds (1602-1650) was a lifelong researcher. Disparaging of his law degree, he found the records and monuments of antiquity far more inspiring. Sir Robert Cotton befriended him and introduced him to Selden. As a young man he worked in the national archives at the Tower of London, spending his days copying and analysing original sources for English history, with the professed intention of writing a definitive history of Britain, but his depth of knowledge brought an early realisation that the available sources were too extensive for one man to gain a sufficient overview for the task. He forsook the bar and a promising career and installed himself in Islington with his fine library to devote himself to study. In 1632 he fled to Bury St Edmunds to escape a large fine on those who disobeyed the royal injunction to vacate the capital during the vacation. From a young age he kept meticulous notes of all that he had read, written and seen, and began an autobiographical summary in 1637, but none of this led to much being actually published. Half a century after his death his grandson disposed of his extraordinary library of over 500 original rolls and 7800 charters, which now comprise a goodly portion of the Harleian collections at the British Museum. A well-connected man, he was happier as a copyist and a collector than as a writer of originality.

DODSWORTH, Roger (1585-1654) was aided in his early studies at the York Minster archives by his father's position there. He travelled around Yorkshire churches collecting inscriptions and transcribing parish registers, and in the mid-1630s started work on material relating to the history of the monasteries in England. His particular interest was in monastic charters, and by 1638 he had transcribed enough to fill a manuscript volume which he entitled *Monasticon Anglicanum*, at which point Dugdale contacted him with an offer to help with the project. The Siege of York in 1644 saw the loss of most of the writings contained in St Mary's tower, but Dodsworth had fortunately more or less finished copying all the records taken out of the religious houses on the north side of the River Trent at their dissolution. He now realised that his undertaking was too ambitious, and so confined his work to the northern shires of the kingdom. By July 1651 100 sheets had been put to press, but money was a problem as booksellers were not prepared to undertake the publication of a large work on a politically dangerous subject. Sufficient material was at hand to fill two folio volumes, which appeared with both men's names on the title page. Dugdale gave unstintingly of his time and energy to make ready further sections, but although an accurate transcriber he was less skilled in methodising the material and lacking in the fluency necessary for the introductory narrative prose. The work had benefited from the hands of other scholars as well, but was still a magnificent achievement in its astounding documentation and splendid engravings of mediaeval architecture which, but for Dugdale, would never have seen the light of day.

DUGDALE, William (1605-1686) wrote several works of immense and lasting value. In his and Dodsworth's *Monasticon Anglicanum* he gave the history of the various English orders and an account of all the individual monasteries, including the full texts of the surviving foundation and later charters relating to the growth of the monastic system, and all known benefactions of land. For the first time the importance of charters as both a primary source for the writing of mediaeval history and also as a source for understanding the legal practice of earlier centuries and aspects of the feudal system relating to conditions of tenure was established. His *Antiquities of Warwickshire*, published the next year, had taken him 25 years to write, and stood firmly in the tradition of Lambarde's *Perambulation* of a century earlier. It stands as the first of the classical county histories, and at over 800 folio pages dwarfed all its predecessors. Here for the very first time attention was drawn to flint axes, which were attributed to the ancient Britons, ignorant of the working of iron and brass. References are given throughout to the documents (of prodigious variety) on which important statements are based. He was also indebted to Camden's method of following the county's rivers in his progress from one site to the next. The volume is a mass of coats of arms, set alongside copious amounts of family details, with town histories and etymology following in second place. The *History of St Paul's Cathedral* came two years later in 1658, born of Dugdale's witnessing many years of maltreatment and sacrilegious behaviour in the building, and based on a jumbled mass of unsorted charters and rolls stored in Scriveners' Hall. After the Great Fire the book became a lasting memorial to Old St Paul's, and was much enhanced by Hollar's series of engraved plates.

HABINGTON, Thomas (1560-1647) was a godson of Elizabeth I, and a Catholic of Hindlip House near Worcester, where he was buried. For over 40 years he studied the history of Worcestershire and its parishes as far as 1558, culminating in a small folio on the cathedral and a 760-page manuscript on the parishes, both of which have remained as a standard source for the county.

HARRISON, William (1535-1593), an historian and topographer who wrote much on chronology and wrestled with its chaotic record. In 1576 Holinshed commissioned him to write his *The Description of Britain*, three engrossing books on the history and physical and social geography of Britain, initially turned down as Harrison was too busy, but then hurriedly concocted from printed, oral and personal information and published the next year.

HATTON, Sir Christopher (1605-1670) was a politician, and collector of books and manuscripts who patronised Gregory King and William Dugdale and carried on an extensive correspondence on scientific and philosophical matters.

KING, Gregory (1648-1712) was something of a 17th-century polymath, being a skilled linguist, herald, accountant, surveyor and mathematician, in addition to his antiquarian interests. He was a clerk to Dugdale at the College of Arms and, under him, during five years of criss-crossing the northern counties for the visitations, he gained a detailed knowledge of local and family circles. In London he assisted John Ogilby in minor engraving and the mapping of Essex, and then in 1672-3 joined Sir Christopher Wren, John Aubrey and Robert Hooke on a small committee with links to the Royal Society to draw up a questionnaire for eliciting information about Ogilby's proposed *Britannia*. There was further work in map engraving and a survey of the development of Soho, before returning to the College of Arms to become Registrar, and then Lancaster Herald in 1689. He gained fame from his social table entitled *A scheme of the income and expense of the several families of England calculated for the year 1688* in which he estimated patterns of household size and income and expenses per head for 26 social groups from temporal peers to vagrants.

LELAND, John (*c.* 1503-1552) was both a poet and an antiquary. His early interests were in bibliography, especially the collecting and cataloguing of books, but he moved on to topography and local history, inflamed by a patriotic desire to see the places he had read about in ancient histories and chronicles. This took him travelling for about six years on five journeys in the 1540s throughout England, a critical period when the Dissolution of the Monasteries was rapidly destroying much of the most splendid inheritance of the Middle Ages. All the while he kept notebooks, made maps, measured distances and talked to local people in the pursuit of information for his great *Itinerary* which, to some degree, followed behind William Worcester. He also examined books and charters, and compared sources in cases of conflicting evidence. Despite not producing the many works he had envisaged, his extraordinary undertaking nevertheless marks the beginning of English and Welsh topographical studies. He planned systematic works on the names of places and peoples, all arranged by counties (which unit he considered the basic key), and was widely consulted by historians and antiquaries, all of whom acknowledged their debt to him. At his death the *Itinerary*, perhaps because of insanity in his early forties, remained as a mass of scrappy and undigested notes, not being published until 1710, although even in its unpublished state it was the prototype for Camden's county-by-county chorography, and had a huge influence on other scholars of the next generation.

LE NEVE, Peter (1661-1729) was the son of an upholsterer whose business involved heraldic funerals, and so perhaps evinced in the boy an early interest in the subject. He was Rouge Croix Pursuivant at the age of 29, and both Richmond Herald and then Norroy and Ulster King of Arms in 1704. He was one of the original members of an antiquarian society which met at the *Young Devil* tavern in Fleet St for a little less than a year. Amongst his large personal collections relating to Norfolk and Suffolk were the famous and valuable Paston Letters, purchased from William Paston, Second Earl of Yarmouth. He was elected FRS in 1712, President of the refounded antiquarian society in 1717, and President of the Society of Antiquaries 1717-1724. A freemason, like other fellows he was a Unitarian by faith. After his death his collections of heraldic and genealogical books and manuscripts were dispersed in a twelve-day sale in 1731, and included 2000 printed books and 1252 manuscripts, the latter including 584 heraldic ones, 72 pedigree rolls, 22 portfolios of pedigrees and 28 boxes of charters.

LHUYD, Edward (*c.* 1660-1709) was a polymath of breathtaking originality, and Robert Plot's successor at the Ashmolean Museum. He opened a glittering career as a pioneer palaeontologist and in 1699 published a systematic illustrated catalogue of some 2,000 fossils. He had helped with the Welsh entries for the triumphant revision of Camden's *Britannia* which appeared in 1695 before embarking on his own *Archaeologia Britannica*, treating of the history, customs and languages of the early Britons. The first volume set out the vocabularies and grammars of Irish, Welsh, Cornish and Breton and analysed their interrelationships in a work of comparative philology so staggeringly brilliant that at one stroke it placed such studies on a foundation not improved for nearly two centuries. The wanton dispersal or destruction of his papers has left the world of 17th-century archaeology immeasurably the poorer.

ROUS, John (*c.* 1420-1492) came from Warwickshire gentry stock. He was ordained deacon at Worcester in 1445 and was one of the two chantry priests at Guy's Cliffe near Warwick. A dutiful cleric, he was also a scholar and antiquary, and established a library in St Mary's church (his final resting place) in Warwick which Leland saw in about 1540. His research took him on travels to Oxford, St Albans, Winchester, London and North Wales, and his importance lies in the historical works of his later life. Between 1477 and 1485 he produced two rolls (the 'Lancastrian' and 'Yorkist') displaying the history of the Earls of Warwick, with short descriptions of each earl and countess accompanied by pen-and-ink drawings. Around 1480 he began his *Historia Regum Angliae*, a general history of England which was to supply Edward IV with information on the kings and prelates who might be commemorated by statues in St George's Chapel at Windsor. Unfinished in 1486, it was then dedicated to Henry VII, and included, perhaps not surprisingly, hostile references to Richard III and his alleged physical deformity. It was largely based on written sources but still interesting for its references to legends, folklore, recent events and people, including Rous himself. There were also three long passages condemning enclosures, with a valuable list of 58 places in Warwickshire and adjacent counties he thought had been depopulated as a consequence of such procedures. His reputation as an historian wavers because he was frequently inaccurate about dates and other details, and like many others, he mixed up history with legend; yet he still employed a wide range of writers, named his sources, and compared the population figures in the Hundred Rolls of 1279 with the same places in his own time. His reputation as one of the earliest major English antiquaries thus stands.

SANDYS, Charles (1786-1859), was a Canterbury solicitor with a keen interest in archaeology and antiquities. He joined the newly founded Canterbury Archaeological Association in 1844, and wrote a paper on the Dane John Hill in the city for the Gloucester Congress in 1846. He published a critical dissertation of Willis's history of the cathedral, a history of Reculver, published by Charles Roach Smith, and a history of gavelkind and other Kentish customs in *Consuetudines Kanciae* .

SHIRLEY, Sir Thomas (*c.* 1590-1654) was a member of the circle of Midlands antiquaries associated with William Burton, William Dugdale and Thomas Habington. He collaborated with his fellow Catholic Habington on his history of Worcestershire during the 1630s, and in May 1638 joined Sir Edward Dering, Dugdale and Sir Christopher Hatton to form a group calling itself the Students of Antiquity, dedicated to co-operative research in London archives. The researches of the Midlands group led to a scheme for a series of county histories to match Burton's one on Leicestershire of 1622. He then turned his attention to (an unpublished) history of his own family, tracing its achievements from Anglo-Saxon origins down to his brother Henry, which also provided material for the remarkable Shirley roll, a vast illuminated pedigree commissioned in 1632, which depicted the descent with coloured drawings of deeds, armorial glass and funeral monuments.

SPELMAN, Sir Henry (1563/4-1641) was born at King's Lynn, educated at Walsingham grammar school, and then studied law at Lincoln's Inn, but soon turned away from what he saw as future drudgery and applied himself to history and antiquities. He helped to found the first Society of Antiquaries and delivered several papers, some still extant. He was back in Norfolk at Hunstanton from 1590-1612, during which time he wrote his *Aspilogia*, a treatise on coats of armour. He transcribed many deeds and charters relating to Norfolk and Suffolk monasteries, and was involved in lengthy litigation over his purchase of abbey leases from crown lessees, when he 'first discerned the infelicity of meddling with consecrated places'. In the circle of Selden and Cotton, he confronted the problem of the meaning and definition of terms used in the past, especially Anglo-Saxon and Latin terminology, and in 1626 published letters A-L of *Archaeologus*, a glossary of 'obsolete and barbaric words in the ecclesiastical and legal vocabularies'. In his determination to comprehend fully English institutions he laid the groundwork for future methodology and understanding, and in particular he managed to link separate pieces of evidence together in order to explain the development of feudalism, rather than merely accumulate and present a series of unrelated facts. His comparative work on the language and terms of northern Europe led to the 'discovery' that feudalism developed as a consequence of the Norman Conquest, and that English institutions had not existed from time immemorial.

STOW, John (1524/5-1625) was a deeply knowledgeable and prolific manuscript collector (many of which today are in the Harleian collection) and a man of widely ranging interests, including chronicles, charters, ecclesiastical and municipal records, wills, literary works and learned treatises. He owned the manuscript of Lambarde's *Perambulation of Kent* (which greatly influenced his own *A Survey of London*) as well as a narrative describing the murder of Thomas Arden of Faversham in 1551. His indefatigable searching of historical records such as rolls and charters, combined with a precise knowledge of his beloved London, offered something of a new departure in the art of historical enquiry and well justified his being described as 'the first English historian to make systematic use of public records for his own work'. His *Survey*, published in 1598 and bordering in its comprehensiveness on the remit of a modern encyclopaedia, was widely praised and cited as a topographical work of the capital and its suburbs, developed along the lines of Leland, Lambarde and Camden, and drawing on both classical and mediaeval literature and public and civic records. The work travelled through Westminster and each of the capital's wards, cataloguing as it proceeded buildings and churches, lists of mayors and sheriffs, and also the other side of urban life, poverty, urban sprawl, and the decay of ancient monuments. It was written in English, not Latin, and amply revealed, through his eyewitness observations, important insights into the political and cultural life of his time.

STUKELEY, William (1687-1765), the father of British field archaeology and the first explorer to dig into burial mounds for the purpose of providing information on the past, was a Lincolnshire man whose early studies covered medicine, law, botany, natural philosophy and astronomy. He was a founder member of the re-established Society of Antiquaries in 1718 and its first secretary. He had travelled along Hadrian's wall as a young man, and in 1757 brought the news of its destruction by governmental road builders to the attention of his fellow members. His annual perambulations around English counties led to his *Itinerarium Curiosum* of 1724 where in the preface he declared that it was 'an account of places and things from inspection, not compiled from others' labours, or travel's in one's study'. Stukeley will remain forever famous for his two monographs on the stone circles of Stonehenge (1740) and of the nearby Aveley (1743), each the result of diligent fieldwork, whose sketches, notes, drawings and measurements made over 1718-1724 are remarkable for their wealth of detail and new discoveries. At Stonehenge he was the first to discover and name the neighbouring earthwork avenue and *cursus* and to identify the astronomical alignment of the stones, coining the word 'trilithon' to describe their unique structure. He first visited Avebury in 1719, subsequently making important and extensive surveys of the stone circles and avenues (with a theodolite) at a time when they were being destroyed and robbed for building material. John Aubrey had first suggested that the circles had been built by the ancient British priests called the Druids, but it was Stukeley's publications and his correspondence with the Cornishman William Borlase which established in the public imagination the popular association of stone temples with the Druids. In old age Stukeley was a kind and generous man, and one who had always dispensed with earthly riches in favour of rigorous intellectual curiosity and personal piety. His fault was gullibility in a demanding field, an overactive imagination, and ignoring the advice of more cautious friends. That said, his enthusiasm and dedication never forsook him, and were the qualities which took him to the great heights that he achieved.

THOROTON, Robert (1623-1678) practised medicine initially but acknowledged that he was 'unable to keep people alive for any length of time' and so turned to the study of the dead, employing paid research assistants to look into archives, estate papers, church monuments and the like. His *Antiquities of Nottinghamshire* was started in 1667, freely based on Dugdale's work, even down to the title, and of the same high quality. Indeed, he had assisted Dugdale in the visitation of that county in 1662-4. Like many county antiquaries he was little concerned with his own times or even with his own century, but tried to trace the manorial history of every parish back to Domesday. Today in Nottingham Library reside his notes made on the backs of letters from his patients in Derbyshire, Leicesteshire and Nottinghamshire. He counted Dugdale and Archbishop Gilbert Sheldon as personal friends, and dedicated to them in 1677 his first volume of the *Antiquities* with its engravings by Hollar.

TWYSDEN, Sir Roger (1597-1672) was born at Roydon Hall, East Peckham, Kent. Of a deeply scholarly temperament, he was JP for the county by 1636. He suffered much at the hands of the parliamentarians, losing his estates and incurring heavy fines. Owner of a large collection of books and manuscripts, he was widely read in original sources and wrote extensively on liberty and governance, based on deep learning in mediaeval and constitutional records, and also on religious and ecclesiastical history. He published his *Historiae Anglicanae scriptores decem*, a 1600-page edition of ten Latin histories, in 1652. Ever the Latinist, he composed his own Latin memorial inscription at East Peckham.

VINCENT, Augustine (*c*. 1584-1626) as a youth secured a position in charge of records in the Tower of London, probably only as a clerk, but sufficient to gain him a reputation as an antiquary, where his then somewhat unusual but expert knowledge of public records stood him in good stead. He rose through the College of Arms to become Windsor Herald in 1624, having entered originally through the influence of his friend Camden, then Clarenceux. He travelled in several midland counties as well as Shropshire and Surrey and accumulated a significant reference collection of heraldic and other manuscripts, easily the best of a single herald, and many written by himself. He planned works on the baronage, the Knights of the Garter, and a history of Northamptonshire were all stillborn because of his being overwhelmed with notes. Nevertheless, his work was used by William Burton for his work on Leicestershire, by Dugdale, and by Weever for his work on funeral monuments, who particularly appreciated Vincent's help and encouragement, symptomatic of a general tendency to share the fruits of research within antiquarian circles.

WEEVER, John (1575/6-1632) travelled extensively at 'painful expense' for three decades in pursuit of monumental inscriptions, covering, as he claimed, most of England, parts of Scotland, as well as Italy, France and Germany. Around 1620 he befriended the herald Augustine Vincent who gave him access to the heralds' office and an introduction to Sir Robert Cotton and other antiquaries. He published the fruits of his great labours, or at least a portion of them, in 1631 in his 900-page folio edition of *Ancient Funerall Monuments* which included (many now lost) inscriptions from Canterbury, Rochester, London and Norwich. Notebooks in his hand contain an early draft of the work along with much other unpublished material, now at the Society of Antiquaries.

WORCESTER, William of (1415-early 1480s) was a topographer and author originating from Bristol. In his twenties he was secretary and agent to Sir John Fastolf of Caister in Norfolk, but the experience was not a happy one, as he revealed in a letter to John Paston in 1454; however, the employment gave him the status of a gentleman retainer and contact with culturally minded gentlemen. He spent much time winding up Fastolf's affairs after his death, a period involving legal disputes with Paston and other who claimed they had been passed over. Worcester's cultural interests and writings were extensive and executed on an *ad hoc* basis during a busy career. He was interested in chronicles and translations, foreign languages and medical treatises (this last leading to his incorporating a symbol for Saturn into his signature), but most especially English topographical and historical studies which were probably stimulated by the journeys and legal searches he made for Fastolf. His three journeys of 1478-1480 are well documented, and took in Bristol, Cirencester, Glastonbury, London, Norwich, Oxford, St Michael's Mount, Tintern Abbey, Walsingham Priory and Wells, all providing opportunities for making notes on natural history, buildings, religion and biography which would be written up in his *Itineraries*. He also gathered at least 188 folios of notes for a history of the ancient families of East Anglia, and further notes for a history of Bristol, showing detailed topography of buildings and streets with measurements. He stands as a pioneer of English historical scholarship, comparable only with his slightly younger contemporary John Rous.

Bibliography

Manuscript Sources

Ashmolean Museum. Papers of Sir John Evans [JE/D/1/13].

Bodleian Library. MS. Eng. Lett. d. 43.

British Library. MSS Addl. 5520 and 45,663.

Canterbury Cathedral Archives.
Hasted Correspondence 1765-1785 [U11/6/3].
Parish Registers for Kingston [U3/168]; Nackington [U3/108]; Lower Hardres [U3/107];
Petham [U3/84]; Upper Hardres [U3/114]; Waltham [U3/133]; Wye [U3/174].

Godfrey-Faussett Family. Godfrey-Faussett Family Papers.

Kent History and Library Centre.
Archdeaconry Court of Canterbury Will Registers [PRC17].
Consistory Court of Canterbury Will Registers [PRC32].
Osborne, Bland and Faussett Family Deeds [MS U771].
Parish Registers for Dartford [P110]; Hartlip [P175]; Lydd [P237];
    Milstead [P250]; Monks Horton [P194]; Rochester St Nicholas [P306];
    Sellindge [P329]; Sittingbourne [P338]; and Swanscombe [P362].
Sackville of Knole Papers [MS U269].
Title Deeds [MS U36/T1273].
Toke Family Papers [MS U967].

Lambeth Palace Library. Faussett v All Souls Papers [VVI/4/5/16].

Liverpool World Museum.
Faussett Manuscript Diaries I-VI.
I Tremworth Down, Crundale, 1757, 1759.
II Gilton, Ash, 1760, 1762, 1763.
III Kingston, 1767-1771, 1772, 1773.

IV Sibertswold, 1772, 1773.
V Adisham Down, 1773.
VI Chartham, 1730, 1773.
Day Book, October 1748-May 1750 [2002.25.17].
Daily Account Book, January 1752-December 1754 [2002.25.18].
Daily Account Book, January 1755-December 1765 [2002.25.19].
Expenses Book, 1770-1774 [2002.25.20].
Henry Godfrey Faussett jottings book [2002.25.21].
Field Notebook, 1772.

Privately Owned (J. H.).
Faussett Daily Account Book, 1766-1772.
Faussett Daily Account Book, 1773-1777.
Faussett Housekeeping Book, 1771-1785.

Privately Owned (D. W. H.).
Faussett Genealogical and Heraldic Notebook, 1750s-1780s.

Society of Antiquaries of London.
Kentish Antiquities [MS 723].
Kentish Pedigrees [MS 921].
Parochial Collections relating to East Kent [MS 920/1-4].
Torr Collection [MS 737/1-6].

The National Archives.
Chancery Proceedings [C5, 9, 10, 11, 12, 24].
Prerogative Court of Canterbury Administration Acts [PROB6].
Prerogative Court of Canterbury Will Registers [PROB11].

Wellcome Library.
'Heppington Receipts' (Recipe books from the Godfrey-Faussett family of Heppington, Nackington) [MSS 7997-7999].

Principal Printed Sources

Akerman, J. Y.
1847. *An Archaeological Index to Remains of Antiquity of the Celtic, Romano-British and Anglo-Saxon Periods*. London.
1855 *Remains of Pagan Saxondom*. London.

Alcock, Leslie. 1971. *Arthur's Britain: history and archaeology AD 367-634*. London, Allen Lane.

Arnold, C. J. 1988. *An Archaeology of the early Anglo-Saxon Kingdoms*. London, Routledge.

Avent, Richard. 1975. Anglo-Saxon Disc and Composite Brooches. In *British Archaeological Reports, British Series:* II (i-ii). Oxford.

Bann, Stephen. 1990. *The Inventions of History Essays on the Representation of the Past*. Manchester, Manchester University Press.

Barnard, L. W. 1998. *Thomas Secker: An Eighteenth Century Primate*. Lewes, Book Guild.

Berry. 1830. *Pedigrees of the Families in the County of Kent.* -

Black, Shirley Burgoyne. 2001. *A Scholar and a Gentleman: Edward Hasted, the Historian of Kent.* Otford, Longman.

British Museum.
1854. *Reports, Memorials, &c, on the subject of the Faussett Collection of Anglo-Saxon Antiquities.* London;
1923. *A Guide to the Anglo-Saxon and Foreign Teutonic Antiquities in the Department of British and Mediaeval Antiquities.* London.

Brown, G. Baldwin. 1915. *The Arts in Early England: Vol. III - Saxon Art and Industry in the Pagan Period.* London, John Murray.

Carpenter, Edward. 1888 (revised ed.). *Cantuar – The Archbishops in their Office.* Oxford, Mowbray.

Church, Richard William. 1891. *The Oxford Movement: 12 years 1833-1845.* London.

Clark, Peter. 2000. *British Clubs and Societies.* Oxford, Clarendon Press.

Coatsworth, Elizabeth and Fitzgerald, Maria. 2001. Anglo-Saxon Textiles in the Faussett Collection. In *Mediaeval Archaeology* 45. Maney Publishing.

Colomb, George. 1903. *For King and Kent (1648); A Romantic History.* London, W. H. Allen and Co.

Cook, Jill. 2003. The Discovery of British Antiquity. In Sloan, Kim and Burnett, A. (eds.) *Discovering the World in the Eighteenth Century* 178-191. London. British Museum Press.

Councer, Cyril. 1980. *Lost Glass from Kent Churches.* Kent Records XXII. Maidstone.

Cunnington, Robert H. 1975. *From Antiquary to Archaeologist: a biography of William Cunnington, 1754-1810.* Princes Risborough, Shire Publications.

Daniel, Glynn.
1950. *100 years of Archaeology.* London;
1975. *150 years of Archaeology.* London, Duckworth;
1981. *A Short History of Archaeology.* London, Thames and Hudson.

Ditchfield, G. M. and Keith-Lucas, B. (eds.), 1991. *A Kentish Parson: Selections from the Private Papers of the Rev'd Joseph Price, Vicar of Brabourne, 1767-1786.* Kent County Council Arts and Libraries.

Douglas, James. 1793. *Nenia Britannica: or, a Sepulchral History of Great Britain from the Earliest Period to its General Conversion to Christianity.* London.

Duncan, Leland L. (ed.) Finn, Arthur. 1927. *Monumental Inscriptions in the Churchyard and Church of All Saints, Lydd.* Ashford.

Dunkin, A. J. (ed.)
1845. *A Report of the Proceedings of the British Archaeological Association at the First General Meeting held at Canterbury in the month of September1844.* London.
1855. *History of the County of Kent.* London, J. R. Smith.

Elton, G. R. 2002 (2nd ed.). *The Practice of History.* Oxford, Blackwell.

Evans, Joan.
1956. *A History of the Society of Antiquaries.* Oxford, Oxford University Press;
1973. *The Faussett Collection at Liverpool.* In *Antiquity* 47.

Fawcett, Jane (ed.) 1976 (2nd ed.). *The Future of the Past, Attitudes to Conservation 1174-1974.* London, The Victorian Society.

Foster, J. 1891-2 and 1888. *Alumni Oxonienses: the members of the University of Oxford 1500-1714* [and] *1715-1886: their parentage, birthplace, and year of birth, with a record of their degrees being the matriculation register of the university alphabetically arranged, revised and annotated.* Oxford, Parker and Co.

Gardiner, Dorothy. 1934. *Companion into Kent.* London.

Gatty, C. T. 1878. *The Mayer Collection in the Liverpool Museum considered as an Educational Possession.* Liverpool.

Gent, T. G. 1718. *A Panegyrical Poem on the Fair and Celebrated Beauties in and about the City of Canterbury.* Canterbury.

George, William H. 2001. *Edward Jacob (1713-1788) Surgeon & Apothecary, Botanist, Antiquarian, Bibliophile, Fossil Collector & Mayor of Faversham, Kent.* -

Gibson, Margaret and Wright, Susan M. (eds.) 1988. Joseph Mayer of Liverpool 1803-1886. In *Society of Antiquaries Occasional Papers, New Series* XI. Society of Antiquaries of London, National Museums and Galleries on Merseyside.

Glasswell, Samantha. 2002. *The earliest English: living and dying in early Anglo-Saxon England.* Stroud, Tempus.

Godfrey-Faussett, T. G. 1876. *Canterbury till Domesday.* London.

Gough, Richard. 1780. *British Topography* I. London.

Guillim, John. 1724 (6th ed.) *A Display of Heraldry.* London.

Harmsen, T. 2000. *Antiquarianism in the Augustan Age: Thomas Hearne 1678-1735.* Bern, Peter Lang.

Harris, John. 1719. *The History of Kent in Five Parts.* London, D. Midwinter.

Hasted, Edward. 1778-94. *The History and Topographical Survey of the County of Kent.* Canterbury.

Hawkes, Sonia Chadwick. 1990. Bryan Faussett and the Faussett Collection: An Assessment. In Southworth, Edmund (ed.), *Anglo-Saxon Cemeteries: A Reappraisal.* Stroud, Sutton.

Higenbotham, Frank. 1960. *The Diary of the Rev'd Joseph Price (Vicar of Brabourne and Rector of Monks Horton in the County of Kent 1769-1773), transcribed from the shorthand with an index of names and places.* -

Hoare, Richard Colt. 1812-19. *The Ancient History of South Wiltshire.* London, W. Miller.

Hobley, Brian. 1975. Charles Roach Smith 1807-1890: Pioneer Rescue Archaeologist. In *London Archaeologist* 2 (13): 328-333.

Ireland, William Henry. 1828-30 (4 vols.). *England's Topographer. A new and complete history of the County of Kent...* London.

Jacob, Edward. 1774. *History of Faversham*. London.

Jacob, W. M. 2007. *The Clerical Profession in the long Eighteenth Century, 1680-1840.* Oxford, Oxford University Press.

Jessup, Ronald F.
1930. *The Archaeology of Kent*. London, Methuen;
1950. *Anglo-Saxon Jewellery.* London, Faber and Faber;
1964. *The Story of Archaeology in Britain*. London, Michael Joseph;
1975. *Man of Many Talents: An Informal Biography of James Douglas, 1735-1819.* London, Phillimore.

Jessup, Ronald F. and Zarnecki, George. 1954. The Faussett Pavilion. In *Archaeologia Cantiana* LXVI: 1-14.

Johnstone, Paul. 1957. *Buried Treasure*. London, Phoenix House.

Kemble, J. M. 1856. Review of *Inventorium Sepulchrale*. In *The Archaeological Journal* 13.

Kendrick, Thomas.
1939. The Kingston Brooch. In *Archaeologia* XIX: 195-6;
1950. *British Antiquity.* London, Methuen.

Kidd, Dafydd. 1977. Charles Roach Smith and his Museum. In *Collectors and Collections*, British Museum Yearbook 2: 105-135.

Kilburne, Richard. 1659. *A Topographie or Survey of the County of Kent.* London, T. Mabb for H. Atkinson.

Laing, Lloyd and Jennifer.
1969. *Early English Art and Architecture, Archaeology and Society.* Stroud, Alan Sutton;
1970. *Anglo-Saxon England*. London, Routledge and Kegan Paul.

Lambarde, William. 1576. *A Perambulation of Kent.* -

Lancaster, Charles. 2008. *Seeing England, Antiquaries, Travellers & Naturalists.* Stroud, Nonsuch.

Leeds, Edward Thurlow.
1913. *The Archaeology of the Anglo-Saxon Settlements.* Oxford, Clarendon Press;
1936. *Early Anglo-Saxon Art and Archaeology.* Oxford, Clarendon Press.

Lester, G. A. 1976. *The Anglo-Saxons: how they lived and worked.* Newton Abbot, David and Charles.

Levine, Philippa. 1986. *The Amateur and the Professional: Antiquarians, Historians and Archaeologists in Victorian England, 1838-1886.* Cambridge, Cambridge University Press.

Loftie, W. J. 1878. *Memorials of Thomas Godfrey Godfrey-Faussett.* London.

Macaulay, J. S. and Greaves, R. W. (eds.). 1988. *The Autobiography of Thomas Secker, Archbishop of Canterbury.* University of Kansas Publications, Library Series, 49.

Macgregor, Arthur. 1998. Antiquity Inventoried: Museums and 'National Antiquities' in the Mid Nineteenth Century. In Brand, Vanessa (ed.), *The Study of the Past in the Victorian Age*. Oxford Monograph 73: 125-133. Oxford, Oxbow Books.

Marsden, Barry M. 1999. *The Early Barrow Diggers*. Stroud, Tempus.

Meaney, Audrey. 1964. *A Gazetteer of Early Anglo-Saxon Burial Sites*. London, George Allen and Unwin.

Myres, J. N. L. 1986. *The Oxford History of England: Vol. 1B - The English Settlements*, Oxford, Clarendon Press.

Nichols, John.
1815. *Literary Anecdotes of the Eighteenth Century* 9. London, Nichols, Son and Bentley;
1818-22. *Illustrations of the Literary History of the Eighteenth Century*, III-IV. London, Nichols, Son and Bentley.

Nichols, Joseph Gough. 1846-58. *The Topographer and Genealogist*. 1-3. London.

Noble, Mark. 1818. *Lives of the Fellows of the Society of Antiquaries*. London.

Oxford Dictionary of National Biography; from the earliest times to the year 2000. Oxford, 2004.

Oyler, Thomas H. 1894. *Lydd and its Church*. Ashford, The Kentish Express.

Parsons, Philip. 1794. *The monuments and painted glass of upwards of one hundred churches, chiefly in the eastern part of Kent, most of which were examined by the editor in person, and the rest communicated by the resident clergy*. Canterbury.

Payne, G. 1892. *Catalogue of the Kent Archaeological Society's Collections at Maidstone*. Kent Archaeological Society.

Pevsner, Nikolaus
1983. *The Buildings of England: North East and East Kent* (3rd ed.). London, Penguin;
1986. *The Buildings of England: West Kent and the Weald* (2nd ed.), London, Penguin.

Philipott, Thomas. 1659. *Villare Cantianum*. London, William Godbid.

Piggott, Stuart.
1950 (rev. 1985). *William Stukeley; An Eighteenth Century Antiquary*. London, Thames and Hudson;
1989. *Ancient Britons and the Antiquarian Imagination: Ideas from the Renaissance to the Regency*. London, Thames and Hudson.

Pine, L.G.,
1957. *Heraldry and Genealogy*. London, Teach Yourself Books;
1963 (revised ed.). *The Story of Heraldry*. London, Country Life.

Richardson, Andrew. 2005. *The Anglo-Saxon Cemeteries of Kent*. British Archaeological Reports, British Series 391. Oxford.

Robson, John. 1857. The Faussett Museum, as affording materials for history. In *Transactions of the Historic Society of Lancashire and Cheshire* IX. Liverpool.

Royal Academy. 2007. *Making History: Antiquaries in Britain 1707-2007*. London Exhibition Catalogue.

Scott, Robert and Henderson, Peter. 2010. *The King's School Canterbury Register 1750-1859.* Canterbury.

Seymour, Charles. 1782. *A New Topographical, Historical and Commercial Survey of the County of Kent.* Canterbury. T. Smith.

Sidebotham, J. S. 1865. *Memorials of the King's School, Canterbury.* -

Simmons, Jack. 1978. *English County Historians.* Wakefield, E. P. Publishing.

Smith, Charles Roach.
1848-80. *Collectanea Antiqua: etchings and notices of ancient remains* I-VII. London;
1850. *The Antiquities of Richborough, Reculver and Lymne in Kent.* London;
1854. The Faussett Collection of Anglo-Saxon Antiquities. In *Collectanea Antiqua,* III. London;
1856 (ed.) *Inventorium Sepulchrale: an account of some antiquities dug up at Gilton, Kingston, Sibertswold, Barfriston, Beakesbourne, Chartham and Crundale, in the county of Kent, from A.D. 1757 to A.D. 1773, by the Rev. Bryan Faussett of Heppington.* London;
1883-91. *Retrospections, Social and Archaeological* 1-3. London, G. Bell and Sons.

Society of Antiquaries of London.
1798. *A list of the Members of the Society of Antiquaries of London, from their Revival in 1717 to 19 June 1796;*
1951. *Notes on its History and Possessions (first issued on the occasion of the bicentenary of the Society's Royal Charter).*

Squibb, G. D. 1972. *Founders' Kin, Privilege and Pedigree.* Oxford, Clarendon Press.

Stamper, Paul. 1993. Bryan Faussett the Antiquary: a Shropshire Connexion. In *Transactions of the Shropshire Archaeological and Historical Society* 68: 114-5. Shrewsbury.

Sweet, Rosemary.
2001. Antiquaries and Antiquities in Eighteenth-century England. In *Eighteenth-century Studies,* 34, No. 2: 181-206. Johns Hopkins University Press;
2004. *Antiquaries: the Discovery of the Past in Eighteenth-century Britain.* London, Hambledon and London.

Tankard, Elaine. 1959-60. The Kingston Brooch. In *Liverpool Libraries, Museums and Arts Committee Bulletin,* 8: 4-7. Liverpool, Liverpool Corporation.

Twyne, John. 1590. *De rebus Albionicis, Britannicis atque Anglicis commentarium libri duo.* London, Edmund Bollifant.

Venn, J. and J. A. 1922-27 and 1940-54. *Alumni Cantabrigienses: a biographical list of all known students, graduates and holders of office at the University of Cambridge from the earliest times to 1900.* Cambridge, Cambridge University Press.

Victoria County History of the Counties of England.
1908. *Kent,* Vol. 1. London, St Catherine Press;
1968. *Shropshire,* Vol. VIII. London, Constable.

Willetts, Pamela. 2000. *Catalogue of Manuscripts in the Society of Antiquaries of London.* Woodbridge.

Wilson, D. M.

1960. *The Anglo-Saxons*. London, Thames and Hudson;

1976. (ed.) *The Archaeology of Anglo-Saxon England*. Cambridge, Cambridge University Press.

Woolf, Daniel. 2003. *The Social Circulation of the Past: English Historical Culture 1500-1730*. Oxford, Oxford University Press.

Wrench, Frederick. 1845. *A Brief Account of the Parish of Stowting in the County of Kent and the antiquities lately discovered there*. London.

Wright, Thomas,

1845. *The Archaeological Album; or, Museum of National Antiquities*. London, Chapman and Hall;

1854. *A Lecture on the Antiquities of the Anglo-Saxon Cemeteries of the Ages of Paganism, illustrative of the Faussett Collection of Anglo-Saxon Antiquities, now in the possession of Joseph Mayer Esq*. Liverpool, T. Brakell;

1855. On Anglo-Saxon Antiquities, with a particular reference to the Faussett collection. In *Transactions of the Historic Society of Lancashire and Cheshire* VII: 1-39. Liverpool, Printed for the Society.

Further Reading

Brookes, S. and Harrington S. 2010. *The Kingdom and People of Kent A.D. 400-1066; their history and archaeology*. Stroud, Sutton.

Brookes, S., Harrington, S. and Reynolds, A. 2011. Studies in early Anglo-Saxon Art and Archaeology: Papers in honour of Martin G. Welch. In *British Archaeological Reports, British Series* 527. Oxford.

Brugmann, B. 1999. The role of Continental artefact-types in 6th century Kentish chronology. In *Hines et al.*: 37-61.

Cameron, E. and Hamerow, H. 2000. *Anglo-Saxon Studies in Archaeology and History II*. Oxford, Oxford University School of Archaeology.

Dickinson, T., Fern, C. and Richardson, A. 2011. Early Anglo-Saxon Eastry: Archaeological evidence for the beginnings of a district centre in the kingdom of Kent. In *Hamerow*.

Evison, V. I. 1987. Dover: Buckland Anglo-Saxon Cemetery. In *Historic Buildings and Monuments Commission for England Archaeological Report* 3. London, Historic Buildings and Monuments Commission.

Geake, H. 1997. The use of grave goods in Conversion Period England, *c*.600-*c*.850. In *British Archaeological Reports, British Series* 261. Oxford.

Hamerow, H. 2011. *Anglo-Saxon Studies in Archaeology and History* 17. Oxford, Oxford University School of Archaeology.

Hawkes, S. C. 2000. The Anglo-Saxon Cemetery at Bifrons, in the parish of Patrixbourne, East Kent. In *Cameron & Hamerow (eds.)*: 1-94.

Hawkes, S. C. and Grainger, G. 2006. *The Anglo-Saxon Cemetery at Finglesham, Kent* (ed. Brugmann, B.). Oxford, Oxford University School of Archaeology.

Hines, J., Høilund, D., Neilsen, K. and Siegmund, F. 1999. *The Pace of Change. Studies in Early-Mediaeval Chronology.* Cardiff Studies in Archaeology. Oxford.

Kruse, P. 2007. Jutes in Kent? On the Jutish nature of Kent, southern Hampshire and the Isle of Wight. In *Probleme der Küstenforschung im südlichen Nordseegebiet,* Band 31.

Leigh, D.
1980. *Square-headed brooches of sixth-century Kent* Unpublished Ph.D thesis, University College. Cardiff;
1984. The Kentish keystone-garnet disc brooches: Avent's classes 103 reconsidered. In *Anglo-Saxon Studies in Archaeology and History,* 3: 65-76.

Lucy, S. 2000. *The Anglo-Saxon Way of Death: burial rites in early England.* Stroud, Sutton.

McLean, L. and Richardson, A. F. 2010. Early Anglo-Saxon brooches in southern England: the contribution of the Portable Antiquities Scheme. In Worrell, S., Leahy, K., Lewis M. and Naylor, J. (eds.) *A Decade of Discovery: Proceedings of the Portable Antiquities Scheme Conference 2007,* British Archaeological Reports, British Series 520. Oxford.

Parfitt, K. and Anderson, T. 2012. Buckland Anglo-Saxon Cemetery Dover: Excavations 1994. In *The Archaeology of Canterbury,* New Series, Volume VI. Canterbury Archaeological Trust.

Parfitt, K. and Brugmann, B. 1997. The Anglo-Saxon Cemetery on Mill Hill, Deal, Kent. In *Society for Mediaeval Archaeology Monograph Series 14.* London.

Richardson, A. 2011. The Third Way: thoughts on non-Saxon identity south of the Thames 450-600. In *Brookes, Harrington & Reynolds (eds.:)* 72-81.

Walton-Rogers, P. 2007. *Cloth and clothing in early Anglo-Saxon England.* Council for British Archaeology Research Report 145.

Welch. M. 2007. Anglo-Saxon Kent. In Williams, J. H. (ed.) *The Archaeology of Kent to AD 800.* Kent History Project. The Boydell Press and Kent County Council.

General Index